THE
PROMISE
OF
MULTICULTURALISM

THE
PROMISE
OF
MULTICULTURALISM

Education and Autonomy in the 21st Century

A *NEW POLITCAL SCIENCE* READER

GEORGE KATSIAFICAS AND TEODROS KIROS, editors

ROUTLEDGE
New York and London

Published in 1998 by
Routledge
29 West 35th Street
New York, NY 10001

Published in Great Britain in 1998 by
Routledge
11 New Fetter Lane
London EC4P 4EE

The publisher would like to acknowledge permission to reprint the following materials:
On page 148, Figure 1, and on page 152, Figure 2 are reprinted by permission of Land Slides, 33 Richdale Avenue, Cambridge, MA 02140. On page 159, Figure 3 is reprinted by permission of Hashim Sarkis.

Library of Congress Cataloging-in-Publication Data

The promise of multiculturalism : education and autonomy in the 21st century /
    a new political science reader
    edited by George Katsiaficas and Teodros Kiros.
        p.   cm.
Includes bibliographical references and index.
ISBN 0–415–92126–0 (pbk.)
    1. Multicultural education. 2. Multiculturalism. 3. Politics and education. I. Katsiaficas, George N., 1949–   . II. Kiros, Teodros, 1951–   .
    LC1099.P76   1998
    370.117—dc21   98–7406
                                                                CIP

10 9 8 7 6 5 4 3 2 1

Contents

vi

The Promise Of Multiculturalism:
Education And Autonomy In The 21st Century

INTRODUCTION

This book provides a philosophical and pedagogical examination of the concept of multiculturalism as it applies to the contemporary themes of autonomy, identity and education. The contributors draw from philosophy, literature, sociology, history, and political science, blending theoretical articles with empirical works. We all agree that multicultural values are profoundly transformative and humanizing, that they are good for everybody.

We address the promise of multiculturalism in three intricately interwoven ways: personal narratives, pedagogical interpretations, and global or philosophical perspectives. Some of the essays in this anthology appeared in a special issue of *New Political Science,* a volume which our colleagues unfailingly hailed as a masterly text and described with heart-warming adjectives. We were so encouraged by collegial recognition that we decided to revise and expand the issue into a book. While retaining most of the original essays, we have added several that focus on the international arena.

Multiculturalism is increasingly becoming part of everyday life throughout the world. South Africa, an inherently multicultural society, is faced with the challenges of harmonizing the interests of individuals with profound cultural differences and experiences. In Vietnam, ethnic and linguistic groups impose difficult and sometimes competing demands on the government. In Brazil, battles for self-determination continue to be fought on the land and in the trenches of civil society, that fertile ground for the politics of recognition. In the United States, the entire society – but especially school children of all ages, college students, as well as elementary, high school, and university teachers and administrators – are challenged by the demands and expectations of a culturally and linguistically diverse population. Similar facts with minor variations obtain in Ethiopia among the various language groups. The present Ethiopian regime is seeking to establish an egalitarian principle of respecting all languages equally, but the previously dominant Amharas are profoundly unhappy with the new politics of recognition. They miss the old politics of surrender by minority groups. Numerous other examples could be drawn from the Middle East, Asia and Latin America.

To be sure, multiculturalism takes many forms, and the range of definitions is quite striking. In apartheid South Africa, the term was used to describe the separate institutions of Africans and Europeans. In that context, it provided a polite way of referring to educational segregation. In Germany in the mid-1990s, multiculturalism became a slogan for the Green Party and a red flag for the conservative wing of the Christian Democratic Party, parts of which identified themselves as being opposed to the contamination of German culture by the ideology and practice of "foreign" elements. In Yugoslavia and Rwanda, brutal evidence of the failure of societies to live in a multicultural setting can be found. Canada's bilingual status and its recognition of minority groups are all considered part of its official multicultural policy. Our collection of articles illustrates a global understanding of multiculturalism with articles drawing from Vietnam, South Africa, Brazil, Germany and the U.S.

Our contributors do not portray a uniform multi-culturalism. We have assembled a rich and perhaps irr-econcilable collection of views that we hope will portray a debate – one informed and guided by a spirit of intelligent dialogue. The West is no longer a homogeneous world (if indeed it ever was). Multiculturalists are aware that the West is no longer the center of the universe, and consequently they seek multiple centers, new "concrete universals" in place of the abstract ones posed by centuries of Eurocentric progress. In Europe, Canada, and the United Sates, minorities and women are increasingly identifying themselves as authen-tically different, not merely as exotic "others." For them, multiculturalism provides the fundamentals of a new social construction of modalities of identity.

At workplaces, in neighborhoods, at summer vacations, in public places – in short, at all sites where people meet – Caucasians face the need to ask themselves how they should behave toward all those individuals who look different, speak differently and dress differently. Some Caucasians respond by making sincere efforts to open up toward strangers. They smile affectionately. They even try to talk by asking mundane questions. These are the gestures of recognition, the beginnings of encounters, the paths of potential friendships. Others are much too hesitant, too slow, hyper-analytical, suspicious. These types miss an opportunity to meet human beings with whom they might experience something new. A few succeed at making contacts. They exchange phone numbers and take the risk of encountering others. They remove the veils of vulnerability. As a consequence of opening new forms of human contact, they emerge as transformed members of the human species. Others obstinately prefer to remain in their cocoons, inside caves: ignorant, hostile, puerile. It is these types that give racism its infamous name, its corrosive taint, its diseased appearance. These individuals get overcome by prejudice, suffer from irrational and cowardly fear of others. Such individuals atrophy, their lives marred by hate, insecurity, and indifference. They are incapable of directly witnessing the interiors of love, that intimate sphere where differences are reconciled. Even more, they are unable to face difference courageously and respectfully. This is the stuff out of which racism, the arch-enemy of multiculturalism, is made.

At the same moment as we extol the promise of multiculturalism, its desirability is questioned by neo-conservatives. Attacks on the "political correctness" of multiculturalism erupted in the 1980s, as ideologues like Allan Bloom, Dinesh D'Souza, Charles Sykes and Roger Kimball sought to reverse the gains made from the civil rights movement, feminism and the counterculture. They were the point men in a concerted series of attacks in the domain of higher education aimed at the alleged imposition of campus speech codes that, they maintained, stifle free expression. As previously disenfranchised and despised groups sought to reverse the treatment they have suffered, a far-ranging reaction was generated. Critics of "political correctness" attacked tenure and the reworking of core curricula in colleges and universities. As a corporate model has been increasingly assimilated into institutions of higher learning, full-time teaching positions have dried up; low paying part-time hires have become a significant portion of professors; and early retirements have emptied the academy of an intellectual infrastructure vital to the formulation of critical thinking.

In the mainstream media in the 1990s, the reaction against multiculturalism, rather than abating in recognition of an idea whose time has come, has become even more vituperative, taken up by intellectual heavyweights like Arthur Schlesinger, Jr. and legal scholar, Robert H. Bork. In his recent book, Bork registered a vicious attack on multiculturalism under the rubric of his disdainful view of liberalism (not coincidentally, the same tradition that effectively opposed his becoming a supreme court justice). Five years before Bork's book was published, Arthur Schlesinger bemoaned the shattering of the idea that the United States is composed of "one people." He believes that if the current trend toward ethnicity continues, it will lead to "fragmentation, resegregation and tribalization of American life." Schlesinger is quite unprepared to consider the possibilities that differences do not necessarily lead to antagonisms, that multicultural education might actually be a means of dispelling racial stereotypes and dismantling racial antagonisms.

While we share with him the same vocabulary, we come to entirely different conclusions. For us, part of the solution to racism lies precisely in the recognition of differences that exist rather than in an attempt to fit everyone into the same mold. For us, multiculturalism should be seen as a vehicle for the flowering of individual personalities now stifled, while for Schlesinger, it is multiculturalism that stifles the individual. While we are critical of some varieties of Afrocentrism, we welcome its insights about the originality and significance of Africans. (See the essay within by Ali Mazrui.) For Schlesinger, however:

> If some Kleagle of the Ku Klux Klan wanted to devise an educational curriculum for the specific purpose of handicapping and disabling black Americans, he would not be likely to come up with anything more diabolically effective than Afrocentrism.

In opposition to the attacks on "political correctness" and multiculturalism, our collection of views seeks to pose a scholarly and reasoned account of what the promise of multiculturalism might be. As should become clear, proponents of multiculturalism are neither the politically-correct thought police that conservatives fear nor the running dogs of imperialism as claimed by certain Leftists.

In the U.S., our way of life has been objectively multicultural but the subjective recognition of that phenomena has lagged behind, manifest for example in the cry for English to become the nation's official language. Of necessity, society must accommodate its heteronomous constituencies by recognizing all of them. The system's shortcomings in this regard are many, but they are not our focus. Rather, we focus on the promise of multiculturalism – its potential to describe the global emergence of a "species consciousness" for human beings. In some sense, this is precisely the best dimension of the U.S.: its existence as a land comprised of all cultures and all varieties of people. The promise of multiculturalism is greater freedom for all human beings – both for individuals and for groups. But in order to actualize this freedom, human beings themselves need to be educated members of communities that are capable of creating these very conditions. In the last two decades, multicultural courses and values have proliferated within academia. Since we seek to give space to the now fragmented and self-contradictory voices of educators convinced that multiculturalism is the future, education is this anthology's most abiding concern.

Who will educate the educators? The professors and teachers who inculcate visions and possibilities into their students' universe themselves need to interrogate their own values and entrenched habits. These transformational needs are most evident when universities attempt to hire a diverse faculty. This is no easy task in light of the racist legacies of the U.S. Through exposure to a diverse faculty, administrators and teachers themselves are encouraged to interrogate their own racism and sexism. Exposure is always the first step toward understanding the new and the different, toward a multiversal representation of human beings that is visually and ethically therapeutic.

By multiversal, we mean a new way of integrating the passions and intelligences of many traditions and practices that the old Hegelian concrete universal did not imagine, particularly given Hegel's tendency to assume that the world spirit did not unfold outside the European landscape. Multiversality as opposed to universality captures the inherent diversity of the human species and the simultaneous presence of many disparate elements in any single event. Claims to universality all too often presuppose a one-dimensional view of history, as if history unfolded from one corner of the world, namely Europe. The fact of the matter is that the history of the species did not begin in Europe. The bones of our oldest proto-human ancestors were recently located in modern Ethiopia, where they lived millions of years ago. It is from that region that the world spirit originated, a fact that was foreign to Hegel's racist imagination. We can, however, use his perennially brilliant dialectical method to transcend his own time-bound vision. Much has happened since Hegel's death, both good and bad. The world system has expanded. New cultures and previously subjugated traditions have made their presence felt. Former subalterns are redefining their identities via post-colonial discourses. We think that a new language is needed to capture the ongoing contributions of these diverse ways of doing things, seeing things, and framing experiences. Multiversality, we hope, adequately captures the tone of our times.

In a multicultural society, children will learn how to respect, not merely tolerate, others. Tolerance, of course, is a necessary step toward respect. Tolerance and respect, however, are not the same values. We can tolerate others, without ever respecting them. Once we learn how to respect others, we do not have to ever worry about tolerating them. Respect eliminates the need for tolerance. When we genuinely respect others, all that we need to do is understand their values and norms however different they are from our own cherished ones – no easy task! It is in these moments when we encounter others with radically different value systems that educators have to teach respect, when principled contestations, debates and conversations may lead toward transformational and humanizing education. Education for individual autonomy – the goal of a free society – must allow children unconstrained access to all points of view as generously as possible, in order for them to learn how to choose the values that most fulfill them and complete them as total human beings. Generosity is the mark of a civilized society, whereas stinginess is the mark of moral primitivism. Multicultural education ought to inculcate this broader moral vision.

Once multiculturalism is more widely accepted, then the much needed internal critique of traditions and customs will accelerate. Human beings will be appreciated and criticized as human beings without the appendages of race, gender and ethnicity as is presently the habit. The more other cultures are systematically taught and critically evaluated in classrooms, the more young minds will have genuine freedom of choice. Multicultural education, like education toward autonomy, reduces ethnic chauvinism and racial isolation precisely by bringing to consciousness previously unrecognized dynamics. It is no accident that the American Council of Learned Societies calls for a rewriting of the curriculum through the prism of the cultures of the Americas, Asia and Africa. The Council demands as well that the past history of the species be reconstructed comprehensively and truthfully, and that the multicultural past of human history be critically assessed and acknowledged.

From the beginnings of human history, multiculturalism has defined its contours. The ancient world was composed of many races, each of whom made unique contributions to the formation of modern civilization. One of the virtues of multicultural pedagogy is that it seeks to create a cosmopolitan consciousness by including the contributions of non-European cultures in the understanding of the contemporary world. Whereas race and gender are now used divisively, in multicultural societies of the future, gender, ethnicity and race will become nothing more than harmless appearances. Indeed, they will become the beautiful colors of difference. Instead of fearing difference, the promise of multiculturalism challenges us to recognize it and replace its suppression with an open minded and nurturing attitude.

George Katsiaficas and Teodros Kiros
Cambridge, Massachusetts, November, 1997

Martin Bernal
Cornell University

Politically Correct:
Mythologies of Neoconservatism
in the American Academy

Even some of my harshest critics have congratulated me on my timing. What could be more trendy in the late 1980's and early 1990's than to bring out books with the title *Black Athena* concerned with the cultural diversity of ancient Greece and attacking racism and anti-Semitism in scholarship. At one level it must be seen as pure luck. In 1975, when I began my project, there was no possible way of telling that fifteen years later multiculturalism would be a hot issue in the reorganization of education throughout the country, let alone that European Communism would collapse suddenly, leaving the far right with no targets except for the straw man of "Political Correctness."

On the other hand, the likelihood of an intersection between my work and these trends is increased by the facts that the inherent improbability of extreme Eurocentrism meant that it was bound to become salient sooner or later and that I have been concerned with this issue all my life. Coming from a left-wing home, I was brought up to support what my mother called "the underdog" and this concept often coincided with non-Europeans. Throughout my thinking life, my chief intellectual interest has been that of the relations between Europeans and non-Europeans, two incongruous groupings, both of which, in a typically Eurocentric way, I tended to squeeze into one category.

One of the reasons, I began studying China was a vague and naive hope to distinguish between what was European and what was human by studying a culture that was both distant and elaborate. My choice of a thesis topic on the introduction of European Socialism to China and the modifications socialism underwent there, indicated the same concern with cultural differences and similarities.

Throughout my life, I have been deeply opposed to European provincialism and the extraordinary smugness of those, who knowing nothing about Asian, African and American civilizations are sure that they contain nothing that is intellectually or morally significant. At Cambridge in the 1950's, I was enraged by the fact that the Faculty of History's one course on Asia and Africa was called "European Expansion in the World". The History Faculty's refusal to teach modern Chinese history continued well beyond 1973 when I left the university.

One of the reasons that I came to Cornell was to be in a country – the US – and a university where it was not considered "peculiar" to study China. However, at this point I experienced what I now realize was a great stroke of luck. I was invited to live as a faculty guest at Telluride House. Telluride is a strange institution, that is best described as an "intellectual fraternity". There, just as I was reveling in my colleagues and students in East and South East Asian studies, I found myself living among the most narrow minded would-be Europeans I had ever encountered. I approached a young Japanese American student called Frank Fukuyama to talk about his background but he closed down the conversation immediately, making it clear that he was only interested in European culture. I soon discovered that the whole atmosphere of the House was dominated by two men, neither of whom had I ever heard of before – one dead and the other absent – Leo Strauss and Allan Bloom.

Bloom had fled the Cornell Revolution in 1969 to Toronto where I envisaged him as resembling a French émigré sitting in England sending messengers to inspect his intellectual property. I saw myself cast in the role of a Jacobin commissar in temporary control, but with the uneasy feeling that the king could come into his own again. My record of mistaken political predictions is outstanding. As so often, I was wrong on this case too. In 1991, almost 20 years later, when Bloom came to Cornell he was given a party at one of the most reactionary fraternities on campus. He did not visit Telluride, and had he done so, he would have been given a very rough ride.

The Straussian influence on Telluride alerted me to the political significance of ancient Greece. In Cambridge, I had known many classicists, who were generally charming but slightly stuffy liberals. I had always found ancient Greece and Rome fascinating, but these scholars approached the two cultures in such a technical and boring way that I was not very interested. The Straussians were much more intriguing and frightening because they were using their image of Ancient Greece to bolster their extraordinarily right-wing political beliefs. In order, to confront these, I felt it would be helpful to look into their weird views of history. In what, to me, was an incredibly crude way, they accepted the 19th century Romantic German view of history according to which everything that was of value to humanity, democracy, politics, philosophy, science and art etc. had been created by the European Greeks. For them, the 'civilizations' of other continents were irritating and sterile sidelines.

However, initially the aspect of the Straussians' thought that had the greatest impact on my work was not their complete dismissal sof all non-European culture but their belief that the European miracle and hence the rise of world civilization could only take place after the conquests of Alexander the Great and the rise of Christianity. According to them, these processes had joined the geniuses of what they saw to be the only two creative peoples in the world, the Greeks and the Jews – I realized later, that this view had been very common in the 19th century. Apart from its extreme Eurocentrism, there were two points that worried me about this scheme, one was its inequality, clearly the Greeks were seen, in a patriarchal way, as the husband in this marriage. The existence of Socrates and Plato before Alexander, showed that Greeks had been able to function very well before any encounter with Jews. The other point was that Aryan Greeks and the Semitic Jews were seen as polar opposites and that therefore the marriage of the two cultures encompassed the whole range of humanity.

Knowing something about East Asia and Africa, I realized how parochial such a picture was. This general attitude was given specificity because by this time, I had begun to study Hebrew and Israelite history and I realized that in fact, Greeks and Israelites shared many common cultural features. This was completely to be expected as the two peoples had lived around the same end of an inland sea and because the inhabitants of the Aegean and the Levant had had frequent and intimate contacts for thousands of years before Alexander.

The desire to explore these contacts and the central role of the Canaanites and the Phoenicians in the formation of both Israelite and Greek civilizations was one of the chief impulses behind my project. It was not until four years later, in 1979, that I first realized the importance of Egypt in this history and it was not until three years after that, that I saw the actual and historiographical significance of Egypt's situation in Africa.

I must thank Bloom and the other Straussians not merely for initiating my project but for sustaining it over many years. Their glorification of a pure and European Greece was a constant stimulus to me to investigate the massive Asian and African formative elements in its higher culture and to demolish the myth of Greece as the origin of all good things. In short, they made the study of the ancient Mediterranean a matter of pressing political importance. Thus, in many ways, my work began an early reaction to the Crusade against "Political Correctness".

Allan Bloom claimed that he had been inspired to use the phrase, "Political Correctness," when he heard a student order a "politically incorrect beer" i.e. a Coors. It does appear that, the term was originally used by radicals in a self deprecating way. However, its reification as a bogeyman or conspiracy is very much a construct of the Right. That is not to claim that there is nothing there but there is absolutely no doubt that "Political Correctness" is more a mood or atmosphere than an organization or conspiracy.

In some ways, "Political Correctness" represents a retreat from the political sphere. The radicals' concern with culture especially in the universities should be seen as a form of guerrilla warfare in the face of a sustained right-wing surge for which our liberal progressive outlook had given us absolutely no preparation. Direct political resistance seems hopeless, therefore we take the opportunities that are offered. For other radicals, however, retreat is the wrong word because as consistent idealists they have always believed that culture determines society and that it should be the first area to be reformed.

I am not sure where I fit on this scale. It is true that whereas in the early 1970's I was writing directly political articles against the war in Indochina, in the 1980's I was publishing on the history and historiography of the ancient world. What is more, I am pessimistic about much in contemporary politics. On the other hand, I had no sense of withdrawal, as I moved into the new field. My overwhelming sensation was one of exhilaration at the combination of aesthetic and intellectual delight at making sense of incoherent data and political and social satisfaction at establishing new models that overthrew the old historiography, according to which all the greatest human achievements were attributed to European men.

This, of course leads back to cultural diversity. Before I began, what for want of a better title, I call the *Black Athena* project, I was an orthodox believer in cultural diversity, in that I was opposed to European provincialism and thought that no European or North American was truly educated without some study of other cultures. I have not changed my opinion on this. Nevertheless, I have now faced up to the fact, that whatever our feelings about it, European civilization has been hegemonic throughout most of the world for the past few centuries and therefore, requires special attention. In doing this, however, we should be aware of Europe's massive and repeated debts to other continents. I do not merely refer to the central roles of Egypt and Phoenicia in the formation of Ancient Greece, but to such things as the Israelite and Egyptian bases of Christianity, the substantial contributions of Islamic mathematics to Copernicus' astronomy and the central position of Egyptian Hermeticism to the Scientific Revolution of the 17th century. There was also the role played by the Chinese inventions like the compass, printing and gunpowder not merely in technical progress and the destruction of feudalism but in the creation of the paradigm of progress itself that has been so crucial to European intellectual development. Furthermore, the models of a prosperous and ordered society provided by China and Egypt were central to the thinking and policies of the European leaders of the Enlightenment.

I believe that recognition of this historical pattern has at least three major moral and political advantages. In the first place, it highlights the importance of cultural mixture for intellectual and artistic progress and demolishes the curious but persistent notion that isolation and ethnic authenticity are culturally productive. Secondly, it demolishes the White

Supremacist credo – referred to above – that all true civilization has been produced by European men.

Thirdly there is the extraordinary discrepancy between the conventional view of European autogenesis and what actually took place, demonstrates what a powerful affect externalist forces can have on the writing of history. In particular, it demonstrates how racism and its subset anti-Semitism have effected the historiography of European development.

The last point leads us back to the Crusade against "Political Correctness." One of its most ludicrous myths is that before the 1960's, there used to be a pure objective scholarship, which has now been polluted with the introduction of politics by left-wing radicals. Hence the extraordinary title of National Association of Scholars with its implication that they alone possess universality and objectivity. Here it is interesting to note that while critics of *Black Athena* are hostile to many of its archaeological and linguistic conclusions, there has been a general acceptance of its historiographical scheme. It is precisely this aspect of the work that is most damaging to the Crusaders' case because it shows that the basic structure of the disciplines of Classics and European Ancient History has been constructed along lines laid down not by objective facts but by ideologies of what we now consider to be a particularly vicious kind, namely racism and anti-Semitism. This is particularly devastating because these two disciplines are at the heart of the cult of "Western Civilization."

I use the word "cult" deliberately, but in two senses. The Straussians I encountered at Telluride saw themselves as a succession of teachers and with a limited number of students, with whom strong emotional as well as intellectual bonds were established. Only in this intimate way, could the texts of Plato and the European Great Books – they hate and denounce what they see as the leftist term of "canon" – be properly read and explicated. Although the teacher could be stimulated by the student, the process was essentially one of transmission of the thought of a great writer by a great teacher.

Allan Bloom's life was full of paradoxes. He idealized the university as an ivory tower but was directly supported by big business and he championed the traditional social order but lived outside any family. However, the biggest paradox of all was the wild success of his book. True Straussians are deeply suspicious of books. This is because they can be read unsupervised so that readers can get the wrong ideas. Before the personal musings of *The Closing of the American Mind*, Allan Bloom's books were narrow attempts to transmit the thought of Plato, Rousseau and Shakespeare to students, correctly.

Straussians also have a profound belief in the incapacity and inferiority of ordinary women and men. The snobbish Lord Kenneth Clark was open about the problems posed by his success among the vulgar, when his beautiful but viciously Eurocentric television series and book *Western Civilization* became best sellers in the early 1970's. He stated that he had always believed that anything that was popular must be bad and was forced to the feeble explanation that the situation must have changed with mass popular education, though he had the grace to admit that this solution was unsatisfactory. I am sorry to have missed Bloom's handling of this problem.

The second way in which I think that it is useful to see the treatment of "Western Civilization" as a cult comes out in the Neo-Conservatives' desire to establish an education based on "Great Books" because they believe that:

> in them we find unraveled the whole vast complexity of and ceaseless arguments over the meaning of justice and the common good. The understanding of these debates... is the legitimate and essential core of a truly "liberal" education. [1]

Bloom maintained that the university "must maintain the permanent questions (set out in the Great Books) front and center. This it does primarily by preserving – by keeping alive – the works of those who best addressed these questions."[2] "Preserving – by keeping alive" and the desire to marginalise any study or debate that goes beyond this European canon seem to me to represent the attitude of a

[1] Thomas A. Pangle "Entering the Great Debate" *Academic Questions* II. 2 Spring 1989 p.24

[2] Allan Bloom, *The Closing of the American Mind* (New York: Simon and Schuster, 1987) p.252.

priest rather than an intellectual or educator – education in the sense of encouraging students to look and think for themselves.

"Western Civilization" courses themselves tend to turn their subject matter into a series of holy relics to be approached with awe and kept at a distance, rather than to bring about a recognition that like it or not, American students represent Western Civilization in themselves. While it is true that the Oxford degree of 'Greats' covers some of the same ground, courses on Western Civilization are unique to America. They were started under the title "War Issues" or "War Aims" at Columbia during the First World War with the overtly political aim of providing a motivation to fight the Germans that went beyond the Wasp establishment's knee-jerk loyalty to England. The aim was the forging of a great historical chain of democracy from *Athens to America* as the Scottish American educator Alexander Micklejohn entitled his extraordinarily popular text book of the 1930's. Although the project was naturally completely Eurocentric, it was in many ways was a liberal one. As such, it was taken up at the University of Chicago, where it served what from the liberal view point was a useful function of resisting fascist trends in the USA during the 1930's.

After the 2nd World War, however, "Western Civ." was promoted throughout the American education system as propaganda against Communism. The Russians were alternately portrayed as the Asiatic and slavish Persians against the free and European Greeks or as the rigid authoritarian Spartans against democratic and open Athens. The apparent plausibility of these parallels made their use extremely effective. To do this, however, the painters of this image played down the facts that in Athens in the 5th century BC, slaves and women were treated abominably, residents of 'foreign families' were not allowed to take part in politics and that the leisure and comfort provided by these subordinate groups were essential in all senses to the great thoughts of the philosophers. Some of these aspects of Classical Athens truly resembled the situation of America of the 1950's.

American anticommunism at this time may have been massively popular but it was not a democratic movement. It was used to suppress social progress and dissent of all kinds especially the freedom movement among African Americans. "Western Civ." courses had always been had their prescriptive aspects and had never been mere descriptive or explanatory history. In the 1950's, in an atmosphere of witchhunt, they were turned into a quasi-religious worship of "democracy" which was equated with the "American Way of Life." This involved a fundamental Orwellian paradox of teaching democracy and diversity to preserve a fundamentally unequal social system and to impose conformity.

This use of "Western Civilization" in general and the image of the pure white Greeks in particular used in the 1950's was revived in the 1980's, in what was stated to be a desire to return to higher standards, but which I believe to be an attempt to turn the clock back and reverse the political, social and above all, the academic gains made by the poor, women, people of color and homosexuals during the 1960's and 70's. This is the major reason why two years ago the Classicist Dean of Yale, Donald Kagan was able to raise $20,000,000 in a matter of months, to support the teaching of "Western Civilization" at Yale. There is however, another reason why conservative businessmen should so heartily approve of teaching and studying European civilization along "correct" lines. It is that such activities – unlike social studies and modern history – can be restricted to the ivory tower and therefore can add cultural kudos to its patrons while leaving them free to exploit people and ravage the environment.

To return to the Crusaders' argument that they are objective, while the "Politically Correct" have polluted scholarship with subjectivity and politics. At a superficial level, this claim would seem to be based on the fact that earlier European and American scholars used passive constructions of the type 'it has been found that...' or 'the evidence shows...' and did not make their political views explicit. The new scholars, on the other hand, tend to use the first personal pronoun, 'I found that...' and state their social and political standpoints. One reason for the earlier mode was that as white middle or upper class Protestant men – or others who molded their thoughts on them – scholars shared so many ideological assumptions that personal and political statements would have been redundant. Another was a genuine desire for detachment and objectivity.

Now the latter is certainly a desirable goal, however, very few women and men would now claim that they are completely achievable in natural science let alone in the humanities. Clearly scholars have their attachments and personal beliefs and these can influence their science or scholarship. In this case, there would seem to be two alternatives. The first is to be hypocritical and deny all subjectivity. This is not as despicable as it sounds; hypocrisy is after all 'the tribute that vice pays to virtue' and the attempt to appear objective could very well increase actual objectivity. Objectivity, is to use Plato's term, 'a noble lie.'

The second alternative is to try to assess one's personal preferences as they might affect the treatment of the subject matter and set them out so as to alert the reader. The disadvantage of this is that it might relax the scholar's attempt to be objective, but it seems to me that the advantage of taking the reader into the writer's confidence far outweighs this.

The belief that the views of the scholar or scientist may influence her or his conclusions does not mean that the "Politically Correct" reject all objective constraints. There are some extreme relativists but they are very few and far between. Even the pamphlet *Speaking for the Humanities* put out by the American Council of Learned Societies, which has been violently attacked by the Right as denying any objectivity, does in fact constantly make a contrast between "truth" and "political ideology." Its writers hold the uncomfortable but unavoidable position that scholarship is the product of both subjective and objective influences and that there are better and worse hypotheses which can be measured by their closeness to objective truth, as revealed in their predictive value or their descriptive usefulness over time. In short although truth may not be a place, it is a direction.

The position of the National Association of Scholars seems particularly bad on this central issue of objectivity. Its members claim that they are defending a universal scholarship, that was very largely written by white middle or upper class, ostensibly heterosexual Protestant men. They further narrow their base by emphasizing a literary canon, written almost exclusively by European men. At the same time, they maintain that work on or by people of color, women or homosexuals cannot be 'classical' in the sense of universal and eternal and must necessarily be partial and partisan. Thus, they combine their claims of objectivity and universality with an extreme narrowness of viewpoint.

Having attacked the Crusaders against "Political Correctness," I must admit that they have raised an interesting and important though ultimately insoluble issue, that of the contradiction between justice and freedom. Somehow we tend to think that good things or values can be combined. It is very disappointing to find that they often clash. In this case, radical or reformist academics since the 1960's have been appalled at the inequality of opportunity in American society particularly in the area they know, that of the university. How can people of color and women compete effectively if they are constantly being slighted or treated as objects by their white male fellow students and their white male professors. It should be emphasized that it does not take many incidents of race baiting or sexual harassment to demoralize not only the target but others of the same group for a very long time. More often pressures are less crude and the perpetrator is often unaware of or unable to stop what he is doing – the white male students, who laugh or smile when a woman or Black speaks or who dominate class discussion with units of speech far longer than those taken by other groups; the shy professor who finds it difficult to look women in the eye; or the professor who for pedagogical reasons makes the case for the superior intelligence of whites and East Asians one class – in order to refute it the next – but by that time most of the Black students have dropped out of the course. He simply has no inkling of the degree of their sensitivity. Most common of all are simply matters of differences of tone and expectations when dealing with students of a different gender or ethnic background.

The efforts by students and faculty to deal with such problems seem to me to be laudable but there is no doubt that such pressures do restrict the freedom of some Professors and students especially of those who are white and male. These sometimes feel that they are being marginalized and victimized simply because of their race and gender. To some extent, one could say that it is good that we should get a taste of our own medicine; women and non-Europeans have long suffered the same discrimination, which has been backed by a lifetime of experience, whereas for the white male, this kind of pressure is merely a speck on a mountain of privilege. However, I believe that freedom is not a value to be dismissed lightly and has to be balanced carefully against the claims of justice.

I think that we should take as our example here the case where, "Political Correctness" has been tried for 70 years, the Anti-Defamation League of *B'nai B'rith*. It has clearly not succeeded in its ultimate goal the dissolving of anti-Semitism, but it has had considerable achievements. Crusaders against "Political Correctness" were appalled at the case of a student, who for reasons of his deep Christian faith, called homosexuals immoral and was made to apologize to a Gay organization and attend classes on the subject. Would they have protested so vehemently if the same student for the same reasons had called Jews "Christ Killers" and had been punished in an equivalent way. I very much doubt it. Very few of the professors I know would object to the cleaning out of the anti-Semitic passages of the passion play at Oberammergau on grounds of freedom of speech.

There is no doubt that the Holocaust is partly responsible for the especial sensitivity towards Jews, but it is equally clear that the activities of the Anti-Demfamation League have played a part in this shift. People who now object passionately to what they see as the linguistic abominations of "spokesperson" or "she/he" as a third person pronoun forget that they have become quite used to such cumbersome forms as "Judeo-Christian." Those, who find it an assault on their culture to be prevented from calling their sports teams "Redskins" or "Braves" or not being able to fly the stars and bars, have grudgingly accepted the whittling down of Christian Christmas carols and their replacement by secular winter songs such as Jingle Bells, Rudolf the Red Nosed Reindeer and Frosty the Snowman. It is clear that there has been considerable aesthetic loss here. But there is not the slightest doubt in my mind that the price has been worth paying because for the first time after thousands of years, practicing Jews have at last found a country where they can live more or less at ease.

However, the restriction of anti-Semitism can never be and should never be complete. My respect for the principles behind the First Amendment make it impossible to urge that all anti-Semitic writings should be banned. There are times in class, when students should be allowed to express their – or almost always their parents' anti-Semitism – in class so that it can be discussed and if possible dissipated. Some works of art are so central to our culture or are so beautiful that they should not be obliterated just because they contain anti-Semitic strands. *The Merchant of Venice* provides a good example of this. Because of its beauty and because Shakespeare mitigated some aspects of the essentially anti-Semitic plot, I would not want to see this banned. On the other hand, Marlowe's *The Jew of Malta*, though it too contains beautiful lines, is so viciously anti-Semitic that I am opposed to its public performance. It may be a bore, but non-Jews should respect Jewish sensibilities; that is the minimum requirement of a multicultural society.

I see "Political Correctness" as an extension of the principle of anti-defamation to other groups that have been systematically defamed in the United States: women, native-Americans, African-Americans, Asian-Americans, Muslims, homosexuals and many others. All of these should be granted similar courtesies and with similar caveats. The balance between freedom and justice is always hard to strike and it is even more difficult to say who should make decisions about it. However, I firmly believe that this power should not be restricted, as it is today, to those who are least affected by slurs and loss of self esteem.

Kathleen Neal Cleaver
Emory University

Looking Back Through the Heart of Dixie

I was speeding along Interstate 85 some seventy miles away from Montgomery where I was headed for a 9 a.m. meeting at the Alabama Judicial Council. I realized I'd miscalculated how long it would take to drive from Atlanta when my dashboard clock said 8:30. As I jammed my foot on the accelerator, I noticed the flashing blue lights atop the Alabama state trooper's car that was dipping across the grass meridian. I knew he was after me. When the trooper pulled up behind my car, I slowed down and moved over to the shoulder. I breathed more freely when my side mirror showed a brown-skinned hand sticking out of the trooper's blue shirt sleeve.

"Whut's the emergency?" the trooper wearing a Smoky the Bear hat said slowly.

"I'm trying to reach Montgomery by nine," I answered lamely, relaxing as I heard the familiar cadences of his Southern speech.

"Yew can't get theah thaat soon unless yew kin fly," he informed me.

I handed over my driver's license and the rental car receipt, he began writing on his yellow pad of traffic citations. I felt puzzled when he asked for my social security number, but I rattled it off.

Then he asked, "What is your race?"

"That's a racist question," I blurted out, "and it doesn't belong on that form!"

"Well, yuu've got a point theah," he reflected, turning his head. "But the question is heah, and I need to fill it out."

"No, you don't. Just leave it blank. There is no connection between my speeding ticket and my race, that question shouldn't be there."

He countered that there was no connection between my social security number and speeding either. I argued that it might be relevant to weed out fake driver's licenses, but race was not, and I refused to answer what I considered a derogatory question.

Suddenly, my mind flashed back to those times I heard my parents argue about a racial mix-up when we lived in Alabama during the early 1950's. My mother's driver's license identified her as "white," while my father, whose complexion was lighter and hair was straighter, was identified as "negro," – which bothered him to no end. Hearing that question triggered memories of Alabama's pervasive classification by race and its echo from the traffic ticket rekindled deep fury about racist subjugation.

Segregation saturated my Alabama childhood, and fueled those grass roots movements that erupted enthusiastically in the wake of the Supreme Court's 1954 Brown decision. My home town of Tuskegee was only 45 miles away from Montgomery where the Bus Boycott launched the modern Civil Rights Movement, which pulled me into its vortex by the early Sixties. Of all the deaths that defined that Movement, the killing of my childhood friend Sammy Younge continued to haunt me. He was twenty-one when he died – we were the same age. As a radical student at Tuskegee Institute, Sammy's dedication to voter registration and anti-segregation campaigns generated threats against him and his family. Late on the night of January 3, 1966 Sammy was shot following an argument with Old Man Segrest over which bathroom he ought to use at the Standard Oil gas station. He refused to go to the back one, as he was told to do, the one that used to be for blacks, and insisted he would use the one that previously was reserved for white men. Sammy's body was found lying in a pool of blood across the street by the Greyhound Bus Station, a bullet wound in the back of his head. Marvin Segrest, the white gas station attendant, was charged with murder, but he was acquitted by an all-white jury.

Following Segrest's acquittal in December 1966, the Tuskegee students' protest demonstration erupted into a riot. Unable to pull down the Confederate soldier's statute in the town square, students painted its face black, wrote "Black Power" and "Sammy Younge" on the statue's base, and set fire to the square. Fires raged again and again that summer as urban uprisings, frequently provoked by a police killing of a black youth, exploded across the country. I was attending college in New York city when I learned of Sammy's death. Within six months I dropped out of school, joined the Student

NonViolent Coordinating Committee, returned to the South, and followed a path that led me to the Black Panther Party for Self Defense in Oakland, California.

Back in 1966 it would have been unthinkable for me to talk to any Alabama court official about the trial of the man who killed Sammy Younge, and few Alabama officials would have let me interview them about such a racially charged case. But by 1996 I felt drawn back to Alabama to retrace that history which had so deeply affected my life. And I think, when looked at in a broader frame, the ironic circumstances that took me to Hunter Slaton's office in Montgomery pinpoints ways that the past thirty years have changed our society.

I was teaching law at Emory University in Atlanta by 1994 when I was introduced to Judge Dale Segrest at a reception. He was a tall, pleasant, white haired man from Macon County, who came to teach at Emory's two week-long trial techniques program that May. The name Segrest was riveted in my memory to Sammy's death. When I mentioned to the Judge that the only Segrest I knew of was Marvin Segrest, he replied, "He was my uncle."

Dale Segrest invited me to participate in a Continuing Education Program for Alabama judges he was planning to hold at Tuskegee Institute the following year. I agreed, in part, because I wanted to come home to Tuskegee and research Segrest's trial, and in part because the proposed curriculum, which included studying both W.E.B. Du Bois' *Souls of Black Folk* and Booker T. Washington's *Up from Slavery*, intrigued me. That fall at Tuskegee Institute, where my role was lecturing and leading discussions on Du Bois, I planned to track down the trial record. But no transcript existed, I learned, since Segrest's acquittal meant no appeal could be filed. A staff member of the Alabama Judicial Council which sponsored the program arranged for me to talk to Hunter Slaton, who had served as Macon County's Court Clerk back then and had watched Segrest's trial. He had recounted to the staff member how deeply the trial impressed him, and I was assured his memory of it was vivid. But it turned out that we were unable to meet on the only day I had free. That clear January morning when I was driving to Montgomery to interview Mr. Slaton, I knew he would be leaving his office for

Birmingham about eleven. I called him from a gas station in Lafayette, Alabama to let him know I'd been delayed.

"You can't get here by nine unless you're on a rocket," he told me, repeating the truth Smoky the Bear had first laid out.

Race has been dethroned from its ultimate position in Alabama, which used to be a reactionary bastion of states' rights where every license plate wore the legend "Heart of Dixie." Now a monument to civil rights martyrs stands near the Montgomery State Capital where Governor Wallace used to hold sway. Perhaps because race mattered more in the Deep South, its role has been more effectively rearranged than in regions where de facto segregation and institutional racism remained less vigorously shaken. But in those places where blacks voted and sat anywhere on the bus, rigid socioeconomic and psychological barriers isolated them from the mainstream. After I went back to college at Yale, I was conducting research in 1982 for an oral history project about New Haven's black community. An elderly man I interviewed then informed me that he was the city's first black bank teller – hired, to my surprise, in 1962. Regardless of a state's legal regime, no place in America during the Sixties was colorblind: race determined what type of housing, education, employment, social ranking, and treatment before the law everyone received.

Access and opportunities formerly set aside for "whites only" gradually opened to a broader range of citizens due to civil rights legislation. Yet, when I interviewed for a position on Emory Law School's faculty in 1992, all the professors were white. Emory first admitted two black law students in 1966. One was Marvin Arrington, who later became Atlanta City Council president. When I taught both his nephew and his niece at Emory, they entered a law school where the student body was nearly ten per cent black. My faculty colleagues, when I asked them how they perceived the issue of increasing the school's diversity, told me they believed achieving more racial diversity would require them to sacrifice excellence.

The way Emory Law School entered the Nineties seems fairly representative of the way our reluctantly integrated larger society functions. The scale on which we are expected to tally progress has these broad bands: from total exclusion based on race and/or gender, we've moved through a period of token acceptance when one or two blacks' admission by a previously all-white institution was both attacked and hailed as "integration," to the present stigmatized inclusion where race and/or gender translates into an absence of merit. Even though our world looks different, and has, in some instances, improved, this type of change does not represent the transformation our movements fought to bring about thirty years ago. While being stopped on an Alabama highway by a black state trooper feels different – he enforces the same flawed law as a white trooper would. Admittedly, being free to argue about a question of racial identity represents an improvement over being shot for challenging racial segregation. But, as my then nine-year-old daughter observed when Ronald Reagan ran against Jimmy Carter in the 1980 Presidential election, "That's not a good choice."

Thirty years ago we debated large questions of how to enhance equality and opportunity – chiseled down now to a narrow contest between affirmative action and policies trumpeted as "colorblind." Those laws that effaced overt segregation forced a more intricate and coded racism to surface. White supremacists have appropriated the language of the civil rights era to define flying the Confederate flag as reflecting their "cultural heritage." Our Supreme Court grants first amendment protection both to flag burning and cross burning. While Congress cut the budgets for school lunches, family welfare support, food stamps, rent subsidies, and legal services for the poor, it raised military spending and reduced corporate taxation. It is not hard for blacks to recognize that increased enforcement of death penalties, passage of "three strikes and you're out" laws, and the restoration of chain gangs signal a return to racist cruelty in the guise of fighting crime. In this ominous climate, the government that once fought a War on Poverty now wages war against the poor.

But the poor are no discrete, unfortunate segment of the population with viable hope for upward mobility – nor, despite the insinuations of the welfare reform debate, are they all black. Poverty is expanding. Severe declines in real wages and the crushing downward mobility that has decimated middle class family incomes during the past twenty years have paved the road to skyrocketing megaconglomerate profits. Corporate chief executives now earn salaries that zoom obscenely past one hundred times that of the average factory worker, threatened by lay-offs, salary cuts, and "downsizing." A 1993 *Business Week* editorial noted that when 90% of corporate employees' incomes were barely growing, their work loads increasing, and job insecurity becoming constant, the multimillion dollar windfalls of corporate executives were more than unseemly – they were arrogant. They conveyed the false assumption that only the executives were responsible for productivity. This is a disparity, the editorial concluded, that tears the social fabric.[1]

Since the 1970's, new tax policies and growing corporate domination of agriculture, service industries, manufacturing, mass media, and government has coalesced with dramatic power shifts in international politics to change our social reality. These changes have resulted in an upwards redistribution of wealth, concentrating greater and greater assets into the hands of the top one percent of American families.

When I was a child I was sheltered from the stark poverty surrounding me in the Alabama Black Belt because my father was a college professor, which made me eligible to attend a special elementary school reserved for children of staff and faculty at Tuskegee Institute. My values developed within a society where extraordinary displays of disparity in wealth were absent, and a compassionate sense of community inhibited conceit.

The Alabama lens through which I saw the United States colored my early attraction to the Black Panther Party's community empowerment program. The revolutionaries I joined in 1967 repudiated the liberal view that blacks were treated as "second class citizens," and instead asserted that black subjugation – weighted down by centuries of slavery and racial segregation – was a form of domestic colonialism. Clearly recognizing how our history, economic position, and race collided, we did not fight to become "first class citizens," but like Africans, Asians, and Latin Americans ejecting imperialists from their lands, we too sought liberation and self-determination.

---

[1] "Executive Pay: It Doesn't Add Up," *Business Week*, April 26, 1993.

After sharing my then-husband Eldridge Cleaver's exile in Algeria and France, I returned to the United States twenty years ago. That was when I came to understand how deeply my appreciation of the colonial status of blacks – so obscured by the rhetoric of democracy – was shaped by my own experience of Alabama. In defeat at the end of the Civil War, the former headquarters of the Confederacy became a virtual colony of the larger industrializing United States. My Alabama childhood, effectively, was spent in a third world culture. Now I am stunned to recognize during those years that Alabama has grown to resemble the rest of the United States, the nation as a whole has become more like Alabama – more like a Third World country dominated by the demands of massive multinational corporations whose practices generate vast disparities in domestic wealth.

The United States has become the world's poorest rich country, lagging far behind other industrialized states in guaranteeing basic human needs.[2] One out of four children is born into poverty, not because our economy does not generate wealth, but because that wealth has become so tightly concentrated at the top. The gap separating the rich from the poor has grown so wide that over half our population now earns less than the combined incomes of the upper four percent. Even more glaring than disparities in earning, the accumulated wealth of one percent of America's richest families nearly equals that of the bottom 95 per cent, according to economist Holly Sklar.[3] This degree of inequality portrays an oligarchy instead of a democracy. Oligarchy was the political system that dominated Alabama when I was a child, particularly obvious in the Black Belt counties where blacks were the numerical majority. This form of political economy – here as in the Third World – feeds violence, crime, corruption, and social decadence. It undermines the foundation for democracy, nourishes scapegoating against blacks, immigrants, and poor women as the cause of economic distress, and justifies brutal repression.

More and more low wage employees are forced to work at "jobs without futures," while our youngest generation of workers face "futures without jobs." Understanding the

---

[2] Holly Sklar, *Chaos or Community*, (Boston:1995), p. 14.

[3] Ibid., p. 5.

disproportionately harsh impact this development has on inner city youth, whose unemployment rates soar past 50% in deindustrialized cities like Gary, Indiana or Detroit, Michigan, visually conveys the Third World pattern encroaching upon our society. Although those stuck in vulnerable social positions suffer the most, it is clear that concern over social exclusion, lack of opportunity, insufficient employment, and powerlessness is not restricted to black citizens.

Yet the increasingly concentrated corporate ownership of television networks, film studios, and the news media has resulted in shallow glorification of individual freedom and prosperity. When a tight cluster of conglomerates like Westinghouse, General Electric, and Time-Warner dictate what the majority of Americans see, read, hear, and think about, this profoundly inhibits the private citizen from obtaining any information that questions the corporate view of the world. Debate, criticism, and dissent are being squeezed out of the airwaves and news publications. Instead, a narrower and narrower range of opinion, shifting further to the Right every year, combined with blatantly escapist entertainment, has become the standard fare. The ways in which political democracy and economic self-sufficiency have been vitiated are rarely examined, since mass media permits only the meekest challenge to the corporate interests which control it.

In his book *Opposing the System*, legal scholar Charles Reich described our contemporary government as an "invisible system... that has no name. It represents a combination of two kinds of government – public government and private economic government, functioning together." Reich explained that "this combined system has escaped all traditional limits and controls. It has circumvented the Constitution, nullified democracy, and over-ridden the free market. It usurps our powers and dominates our lives. Yet we cannot see it or describe it. It is new to human history."[4]

Reich acknowledged that "the System" has provided numerous benefits, but that its "hidden costs and failures are now being revealed." As it becomes increasingly incapable of including everyone in the prosperity that was its main justification, we can recognize that "dehumanization and

---

[4] Charles A. Reich, *Opposing the System*, (New York: 1995), p. 16-17.

damage to human beings are side effects of the System's operation. As these pathologies have become more acute, the System has resorted to blame and repression rather than reform. It is now producing a slow but overwhelming social and economic catastrophe that threatens to engulf us all."[5]

When my parents attended college, a catastrophe known as the Great Depression engulfed the country. Back then government leaders implemented radical programs to rescue the disintegrating society – creating the New Deal. But since President Ronald Reagan's election in 1980, the New Deal concept that government could serve to enhance the political power of middle class, working, and poor people disenfranchised by economic powers beyond their control has been viciously undermined. According to Princeton Professor Sheldon Wolin, "The combined consequence of the Republican counterrevolution, the collapse of liberalism into centrism and the general onslaught against government, Washington and public officials is nothing less than the discrediting of the fundamental principle of a democratic society: that political power and office are meant to serve the needs of the vast majority."[6]

During the Sixties when millions of Americans joined together to oppose segregation, sexism, and the perpetration of the Vietnam War, we fought to expand the scope of democracy. We challenged those making decisions that radically affected our lives and insisted that our views be heard. Both the successes and the failures of that effort spawned the radical Black Power movement, which brought to the fore the Black Panther Party. The Panthers opposed the violence visited against black communities with self-defense, and resisted the racism we encountered with solidarity. "All Power to the People" was our rallying call. We not only insisted on power for all people, but engaged in numerous political combinations, including a coalition with the predominantly white Peace and Freedom Party, to activate it. In Chicago we pulled together the Puerto Rican Young Lords, the Appalachian whites' Young Patriot Party, the Asian Red Guards, and the gang called the Black P Stone Rangers

---

[5] Ibid., p.18.

[6] Sheldon Wolin, "Democracy and Counterrevolution," *The Nation*, April 22, 1996, p. 23.

into the "Rainbow Coalition." The leader of this effort, Black Panther Deputy Chairman, Fred Hampton, was assassinated in his sleep during an FBI-planned pre-dawn police raid on his apartment in December 1969. Fred Hampton, a charismatic and devoted revolutionary leader, was only twenty-one when he died.

He met a fate similar to other leaders – like Medgar Evers, John F. Kennedy, Martin Luther King, and Robert Kennedy, all struck down by assassins' bullets – whose eloquent commitment to a better world inspired my generation to resist oppression. Assassins not only silenced their eloquence, but also demolished the social implementation of the democratic vision these men expressed. The repressive assaults of that era mounted all the way up to Democratic Party inner circles during the Nixon administration – ultimately exposed during the Watergate scandal. What is important to recognize is how the reality we confront today has been systematically constructed by those who have arrogated extraordinary powers after the political leadership of a more humane and democratic social order was annihilated.

The presence of millions of blacks among the masses of hard working people, the escalating disintegration of the underclass, and the rapid growth of the middle class testifies to the fact that blacks have become neither fully integrated nor liberated. Instead, African-Americans are fragmented – scattered through all levels of society from the Pentagon to the prison yard. The sustained expansion of the African-American middle class over the past thirty years, juxtaposed as it has been with an era of economic decline, must explain something important about both the dynamics and the limitations of social change. That is something particularly relevant to understand at the time that the legal midwife to that change faces unremitting attack from the Right.

More than a century ago, Alexis de Toqueville conveyed his observations about the condition of nineteenth century blacks in his classic study Democracy in America. "[I]n a certain portion of the territory of the United States, " he wrote, "the legal barrier which separated the two races is tending to fall away, but not that which exists in the manners of the country; slavery recedes, but the prejudice to which it has given birth remains stationary... [I]n those parts of the Union in which the negroes are no longer slaves, they have in nowise drawn closer to the whites. On the contrary," de Toqueville concluded, "prejudice appears to be stronger in States which have abolished slavery than in those where it still exists." He recognized that although "the negro is free... he can share neither the rights, nor the pleasures, nor the labour, nor the afflictions, nor the tomb of him whose equal he has been declared to be."[7]

Alexis de Toqueville noted that "the prejudice which repels the negroes seems to increase in proportion as they are emancipated, and inequality is sanctioned by the manners whilst it is effaced from the laws of the country." He thought that the answer to the question why "the Americans have abolished slavery in the North... why they maintain it in the South and why they aggravate its hardships there, [was] easily given. It is not for the good of the negroes," he wrote, "but for that of the whites, that measures are taken to abolish slavery in the United States."[8]

Although the Civil War had not yet erupted when de Toqueville traveled to the United States, the relevance of his insight that black progress was contingent on the benefit it brought to the dominant whites may be enduring. Why did the extraordinary civil rights victories the Civil War provided blacks collapse so quickly? Within thirty years of the Union victory, the revolutionary transformation of the Constitution it engender-ed lay in shambles. The Fourteenth Amendment, enacted in 1868, permitted Congress to pass a series of Civil Rights Acts, but in the wake of a severe economic depression and the withdrawal of federal troops from the "reconstructed" South, the Supreme Court struck them down during the 1880's. Articulating the doctrine of "separate but equal" in its 1896 Plessy decision, the Supreme Court allowed nationwide disregard of the Fourteenth Amendment guarantee of equal protection under the law, and permitted Jim Crow laws to cover the South. The Court never acknowledged that "separate but equal" violated the Constitution until 1954, when a new cycle of modern civil rights legislation resurrected the 19th century civil rights laws.

---

[7] Alexis de Toqueville, *Democracy in America,Volume I,* (New York: 1961), pp. 427-428.

[8] Ibid., p. 429.

But if our culture of racial stratification has sustained the elements that supported de Toqueville's analysis, then the transformations set in motion by new civil rights laws would, in fact, generate more racism – or, at least, racism of a different sort than the prohibited overt practices. Instead of the law serving to increase racial harmony and understanding, we should anticipate a vigorous destruction of what scholars call the "Second Reconstruction," that panoply of Supreme Court decisions, federal and state legislation, and executive orders that buried the old regime of "separate but equal." In a disturbing parallel to the racially charged politics of the 1890's, thirty years after Congress passed the Voting Rights Act, the Supreme Court has upheld several challenges to electoral districts established under its provisions to counteract black disenfranchisement.

In America, "race" generally refers to the presence of genetic or cultural characteristics indicating non-European ancestry, as in the phrase "race" music, or the "race" card. For centuries, distinctions based on race have masked complex mechanisms of social control, blurring and disguising the divisions of wealth, class, and gender. James Baldwin, writing about the 1981 Child Murders case, described "this country, in toto, from Atlanta to Boston, to Texas, to California," not so much as "a vicious racial caldron – many, if not most countries, are that – [but] as a paranoid color wheel."[9] For Baldwin, the inability "to confront ... this most crucial truth concerning our history – American history – " constituted "the Southern madness. But," he concluded, "as someone told me, long ago, the spirit of the South is the spirit of America."[10]

While many black people share Baldwin's indictment, I think we need to admit that the South represents more than one spirit. Everyone knows about its perversely racialized politics, but the South should be identified as well with the powerful spirit of resistance to its dehumanizing terror. The same Alabama that showed the world "Bull" Connor and his police dogs attacking Birmingham demonstrators shaped the extraordinary leadership of Nobel Prize winner Martin Luther King, Jr. The cry of "Freedom Now," and the creation of the

---

[9] James Baldwin, *The Evidence of Things Not Seen,* (New York: 1985), p.7
[10] Ibid.

first Black Panther Party, represent the Southern spirit just as much as George Wallace's defiant insistence on "segregation forever." The liberating spirit of the millions of people who mobilized to undermine the South's racist hierarchies and achieve democracy is a spirit America would do well to recapture − if we can see through the mask of race.

When the nephew of Sammy Younge's killer can invite Sammy Younge's friend to come back to Tuskegee Institute to teach his fellow Alabama judges about the *Souls of Black Folk,* hope glimmers in the heart of Dixie. That hope could ignite the spirit of resistance needed to bring democracy back to the citizens, as the concentration of public power into corporate hands leaves community after community marginalized and impoverished.

K. Anthony Appiah
Harvard University

Preliminary Thoughts on Liberal Education[1]

Liberalism – it may be worth reminding ourselves in these illiberal times – is not a simple faith. Liberals campaign for civil rights at home and human rights abroad and want to protect the welfare state; but we are worried about using the power of government to limit human freedom except to enforce rights and to guarantee basic welfare. We believe in private property and we believe in civic equality; but we also support progressive taxation, which seems to take property unequally from rich and poor. We champion public education and we recognize the importance of religion in people's lives; but we are distressed when the public school seeks to inculcate any particular religion (even our own). We believe in a vigorous private economy and the jobs and wealth it creates; but we are worried by the racial and gender inequalities the market creates, in allocating those jobs and the incomes they bring, and in access to housing, capital and other goods.

It is easy enough to persuade yourself that all this is just a muddle; and Rush Limbaugh and his chums in the Congress and elsewhere would be very happy if you did. But complexity is not always muddle – this is another lesson for our particular times – and I think it is possible to defend every one of the elements I have just listed and to defend the claim that a just and reasonable politics will try to adjudicate these various demands.

The first thing we need to do, however, if we are to defend the whole package, is to be clear about some of the difficulties. I shall try briefly to give a coherent interpretation of modern liberalism; and I shall try to show how the issue of public education poses challenges to liberalism, while also displaying its flexibility and coherence.

• • •

---

[1] I owe a great debt of gratitude to the members of a reading group at Harvard named (after its one-time meeting place) the "Pentimento" group. My thinking on these questions owes particular debts to four members of that group: Lawrence Blum, Martha Minow, David Wilkins, and David Wong. But, as usual, no one but the author should be held responsible for the views I express.

Liberalism starts with views that are both modern and radical. We are all equal and we all have the dignity that was once the privilege of an elite. When John Locke speaks of "dignity" (in, for example, his draft of the constitution of Carolina) he means the title and privileges of hereditary land owners; it is something associated with a particular station in life. For him, dignity is as much something that the ordinary person does not have as something that belongs to "persons of standing": for modern liberalism, in striking contrast, dignity is something that is to be respected in every human being. Dignity is still, then, as it was for Locke, an entitlement to respect. But now everyone shares that entitlement. Dignity is now human dignity: you get it just by showing up. That is what makes liberalism radical.

But liberals also believe that recognizing individual human dignity entails – in language we owe to Kant – respecting every person's autonomy. The distinctive thought of liberal political philosophy is that individual autonomy is at the heart of political morality. That is what makes it modern.

Kant first articulated autonomy as a philosophical principle, and romanticism lived a peculiarly intense version of this vision.[2] But the central notion is the special province neither of philosophers nor of poets: the claim, put simply, is that what the good is for each of us is shaped by choices we ourselves have made.

This general moral conviction has profound consequences for thinking about the state. Simply put, liberalism values political liberty – freedom from government intervention in our lives – because it holds that each person has the right to construct a life of her own. That right is not unlimited; it must be pursued within moral boundaries shaped, among other things, by the rights of others. But it is fundamental; and every limitation of it is, for liberalism, to be conceded only in the face of a powerful argument.

This picture grew up with Protestantism; which is what accounts for the sense that it is a creature of the West (and, more particularly, of Germany – Kant – and England – Locke). For Protestantism taught, as Locke put it in his *Essay Concerning Toleration*, that worship was a "thing wholly between God

---

[2] For better or worse, however, Kant's understanding of autonomy was more universalizing and rationalist than the understanding most people now have of it; it will not be a Kantian view that I sketch here.

and me and of an eternal concernment."[3] This notion that the most consequential questions were to be decided individually by each person, searching in his own heart (so that conformity to outer forms was less crucial than inner conviction) placed what mattered most in human life decisively beyond the reach of the government. Locke's major argument in the Essay is that state regulation of religious belief is wrong because it is impossible, "[T]he way to salvation not being any forced exterior performance, but the voluntary and secret choice of the mind ..."[4] Locke wants religious toleration because the only things the government can regulate – the outward and visible signs – are simply not what matters; like Kant he thought that virtue lies in why you do things not (or not so much) in what you do. This makes him an ancestor of modern liberalism; but our concerns are, I think, somewhat different.

For the modern liberal objection to regulation of religion argues that the choices I make and the understandings I come to in my own search for religious truth are important in part because I chose them in the course of my own search. The modern point is not Locke's – which is that goodness (piety, in this case) is a matter of motive and intention more than behavior; it is that what it is good for me to do depends, in part, on my reflective appropriation of the beliefs and values by which I guide my life. Merely adopting views "in gross," as Locke put it, assuming religious "opinions ... all at once in a bundle,"[5] is not enough.

It is a crucial point that this moral conviction is not only modern but also, on a world scale, decidedly controversial. It is not the view of the Ayatollahs in Teheran or the Party leaders in Beijing; it is not even the view, to come somewhat closer home, of His Holiness and the various eminences of the Vatican. For all of these people hold that what is morally required of people is given in advance, by an eternal order for the Ayatollahs and the Curia, by the truths of Marx for the heirs of Mao Tse Tung. All of these positions recognize that one can have obligations that arise out of choice – they recognize promises as binding; and duties particular to vocation – they recognize that roles bring obligations. But

---

[3] "Essay Concerning Toleration" in *Political Writings of John Locke* ed. David Wootton (New York: NAL/Dutton, 1993) p. 188.

[4] op. cit. p. 189.

[5] op. cit. p. 197.

none of them agrees with the liberal that sometimes the right thing for me to do is right because I have decided that doing it fits with my chosen sense of the meaning of my own life: none of them therefore accepts the political consequence that in forcing me to do what is best for me according to someone else's conception, you may do me not good but harm.

• • •

Notice that far from being relativist or indifferent to moral truth, the claim of autonomy, as made by the liberal, is a universal moral claim: it is something we believe the Pope and the others are wrong about. There is no general answer to the question how one should live one's life: not everyone should be a priest or a poet or a pipe-fitter; there are lives worth living that focus on family, and others that center on work. Liberals are pluralists about human flourishing, holding that there are many ways for human beings to live good lives and many projects worth pursuing.[6]

But sensible anti-liberals are pluralists too. What's distinctive in the liberal vision is that it holds that there may be an internal connection between what is good for you and the choices you have made: in particular, that your good may depend on the identities you have reflectively appropriated and the values embedded within them. Liberals do not deny that there are some values that are essential components of any good life: honesty, loyalty, kindness are virtues, and cruelty, thoughtlessness, unwarranted hatred are vices, no matter what choices you have made. But this essential moral core does not fix everything that matters; nor does it determine how these virtues and vices should weigh against each other in every situation.

Liberalism is a political morality, which flows like all substantial political ideals, from an underlying vision of human life. But, as a political creed, it does not claim to answer every ethical question, every shallow puzzle or deep mystery about how one should live. It stakes out a position about the ethics of relations between the state and the individual, a position that flows from a vision of human life;

---

[6] One reason for this is that what makes sense for me depends, very often, on the choices of others: if everyone ceased to care about film, the movie-making career I have set my heart on is going to cease to make sense.

and that vision proposes that living up to the many values is best when it flows, in two respects, from the "voluntary and secret choices" of your own mind. First, it is best if people do what is right because they recognize that it is right (but this is a point on which the Curia concurs); second, what is best for people depends, in part (but only in part) on what they have chosen. That is why the liberal state has its most distinctive feature: a regime of individual rights, limiting what the state may require of us, even for our own good.

• • •

Liberals are not relativists, then. Nor need we be skeptics. We need not argue that each should be allowed by the state to make her own choices because there is no knowing who is right. I may, as a liberal, regard it as proper for the state to allow you to do what is, in my judgment, plainly wrong, provided that, in doing so, you interfere with no-one's rights and have freely chosen to do it in pursuit of your aims and in the light of your own knowledge, your best understanding.

This is a separate point from the point about the dependence of the good for you on your choices. Sometimes what is good for me – committing myself to the nationalist struggle against imperial domination – is good because I have reflectively appropriated a nationalist identity; and that identity now gives meaning to much of my life. (Perhaps if I had not developed that identification, a life in the struggle would be worthless, a sham.) But the point I am making now is that sometimes the government should let me do what I have decided to do in the light of my own best understanding, even though what I have decided is wrong. Letting people do something does not, for the liberal, reflect agreement with them. Even when someone is wrong, the state has to have a compelling reason to intervene. And if someone asks why, I would say because it is *her* life.

It is sometimes said that liberalism is not perfectionist, in the sense that it does not aim to shape the citizen to a vision of human good. I think this is somewhat misleading. Autonomy is a vision of human good; and the liberal state will aim to help the citizen exercise her autonomy, by, for example, providing information and encouraging rational public deliberation. What a liberal will not do, is use the coercive power of the state against anyone, except to protect the rights of others. The liberal surgeon-general tells you that cigarettes kill and requires tobacco companies not to sell their products to those, like minors, who are not fully capable of autonomous decision. But if an adult person chooses cigarettes, knowing the harm they do, the most the liberal state may do is limit her access to health care for those harms, if the state does not have the resources to provide it.[7]

• • •

Modern American liberalism, as an approach to the realities of politics, goes back to the New Deal, when, to the classical liberalism of rights was added a new set of economic commitments: the Federal government accepted clearly, for the first time, a national responsibility to guarantee a basic minimum level of welfare to every citizen. This undertaking occurred, of course, in response to the Depression: a massive failure on the part of the private economy to deliver the jobs and the income, that were now recognized as a precondition for enjoying the fundamental civil rights − democratic representation, liberty of religion, expression and association, security of property, equality before the law.

This pious simplification of history ignores a great deal. The New Deal welfare state for example, did not spring full-fashioned from the brow of the Roosevelt administration. There were already provisions for the poor and the destitute in colonial Massachusetts; there were federal Civil War pensions for veterans and war-widows; there were hundreds of charitable institutions, supported by churches and by secular philanthropy, often with tax-exemption from the government, aiming to help people in a thousand kinds of trouble. Still, it was clear to everybody that the New Deal took government provision for the worst-off to a new level.

It is natural to see this concern with basic welfare as simply a new addition to the liberal register, not as something

---

[7] There are issues here that are quite complex. My thought is that, if a state cannot afford to provide the most extensive health care provision that is currently technologically possible, then, in rationing access to health care (or in charging for health care beyond what is available free to all), it may take into account whether the sufferers knowingly accepted the risk of the disease for which they are seeking treatment.

growing out of the basic liberal vision. But I think that is wrong. Basic welfare provision flows from the same fundamental concern with dignity. In a world where land has all been parcelled out (so that no one can simply acquire land to work by moving into uncharted territory); a world where money is essential for adequate nutrition and proper shelter; where a job (or so much money you don't need one) is increasingly a condition for minimal social respect; guaranteeing that everybody has access to a place to live, food to eat, and a form of work, is simply making sure that everyone has access to the possibility of a dignified existence. It is increasingly clear, I think, that a guarantee of access to health care should be underwritten by the state as well. And, because everybody is equally entitled to dignity, whatever minimum conditions the state must guarantee, it must guarantee to everyone.

More than this, autonomy requires, as we have seen, that people be able to shape a life for themselves, to make choices among options. And this requires, naturally, that there be such options – real choices to make; and that the person has some sense of the way the world actually is.

Each of these conditions is hugely important. The existence of real options is something that argues for multiculturalism within states and cosmopolitanism across them.[8] And the importance of the truth, entails that the government has a role in propagating knowledge. To do my will, to act freely, I need not only to have goals but a sense of how I can achieve them. You can undermine my autonomy not only by resisting what I will, but also by depriving me of information – truths – that might allow me to achieve what you desire. Respect for autonomy goes with truth-telling, therefore; respect for autonomy entails a concern with knowledge.

There are hard questions here, questions that, as we shall see, matter enormously for the politics of education. Respect for your autonomy means that, where your aims are morally permissible, it is best if you are able to do what you choose. But you choose to do things for reasons, and those reasons are dependent not only on your aims but also on how you believe they can be achieved. Characteristically, in reasoning out what I want to do, I consider what my aims

---

[8] See my "Cosmopolitan Patriotism," *Critical Inquiry* (forthcoming).

are and what means are available to achieve them. Suppose, then, you know what my aims are, and you know that, in pursuing them I am relying on an erroneous belief. Suppose, for example, that I am seeking to abate my fever, and I take the herbs the traditional doctor in my village concocts; and suppose you know that the herbs are mortally toxic and that I can be cured with the erythromycin in your pocket. If you secretly substitute your authentic medicine for my (as you think) bogus "medicine," are you respecting my autonomy – helping me to the health you know I am after – or failing to do so – by ignoring my clear (but, as you think, fatally misguided) desire to take this stuff that the medicine man provided?

The answer, I believe, is that what respect for your autonomy requires is neither of these things; what it requires is that you tell me what you believe is true (thus putting me in a position to realize my fundamental aim by engaging my goals with the way the world really is). You can urge on me the medicine that will cure me, offering me reasons to believe that it will cure me; but if, in the end, I reject your reasons, if I do not trust you, respect for my autonomy requires that you let me take the worthless portion I believe in. Just as respect for autonomy requires me to recognize your reasons for your choices in matters that affect you, so it requires me to address your beliefs with evidence and reasons; I may not manipulate you into believing what is in fact the truth by offering you phony "proofs" and faked "evidence."

Now I hasten to add that respecting my autonomy is not the only thing that is at stake when I am sick and considering what treatments to undertake. There is also the matter of my physical well-being, which is something that I require for most of my projects and which makes more likely the satisfactory achievement of almost all of them. In dealing with me in these circumstances, you may rank my survival over my autonomy, hoping, perhaps, that once the crisis is over, you can persuade me that you have done the right thing. This may be an especially plausible choice if you have a special responsibility for my health – the responsibility, say, of my doctor – or a special concern for my well-being – the concern, say, of my friend or my parent. But even if you make this choice, it should be clear that you have done so against the weight of an important consideration: respect for me, treating me with dignity, surely entails respect for the reflective choices I make, even when they are mistaken.

I have considered this case as if it were one where your choice was an essential private (i.e. non-state) matter. But if your relationship to me were that of an official to a citizen, then, I think, autonomy would have to loom larger. Governments may not force citizens to do what is good for them, once they have explained why it is good for them and offered them the choice. Provided I am capable of exercising autonomy – provided, that is, I am not mentally incapable at the time that I must think the issue through – my government should let me die, if I choose.

Liberals are not libertarians – our aim is to maximize autonomy not to minimize government involvement. Liberals will normally allow you to take whatever chances you like, once you know the risks; but not if the risk is to your autonomy. Thus, they may regulate access to drugs that threaten – through addiction – the autonomy of every user. In becoming an addict you would give up your autonomy; if you did so willingly, you would be making a mistake that the liberal state might attempt to save you from. This would not be a perfectionist policy: it is not a matter of the state's choosing to make you a better person than you would make yourself. Rather, it is the state's guaranteeing that you can continue to make the choices that are the substance of your freedom.

• • •

I have tried to exemplify what respect for the dignity and autonomy of each person means for a liberal politics. But when we turn to education, we are faced with an immediate problem. We are not born as autonomous adults. We are born, in the Bard of Avon's happy phrase, "mewling and puking," incapable of an even moderately independent existence. Liberalism speaks of respecting the self-chosen projects of others, and of allowing them to pursue them in the light of their own knowledge and their values. But we are born neither with projects nor with knowledge. The fundamental idea of a liberal philosophy of education must be that we need to guide each child from hopeless dependency into an autonomous maturity. Preparing someone to be autonomous requires that we give them access both to values (and the capacity to form projects) and to knowledge (and the ability to learn more).

But now there are so many hard questions: Who is the "we" here? And which projects should "we" help the child to grow into? And who is to decide, in cases of controversy, what is knowledge and what false opinion?

Many people will say that the "we" that has primary responsibility for our development into autonomy is our parents. It certainly seems right to see this as one of the duties (and pleasures) of parents. There is every reason to think that a loving family is the best place to grow into an autonomous adult. No government has found a way to do better than parents generally do: prudence suggests that states interfere only when they must.

But, as hardly need saying, my parents can be an obstacle to the development of my autonomy. And when they are, so it seems to me, the state has a duty to intervene.

Just as the New Deal recognized an extensive system of welfare provision as a condition for a dignified adult life in the modern world, so the development of public education reflects the need for a wide range of skills, knowledge and values, as a condition for an autonomous modern life. These essential prerequisites of autonomy – the elements of a basic education – require time and expertise to teach properly; and in a world where most adults must work for a living, parents cannot be expected to provide them on their own. Further, the elements of a basic education are necessary for all who are not severely mentally disabled: every person, every child, therefore is entitled to a guarantee of at least this minimum. This is why, despite the liberal's general hostility to state intervention in what we ordinarily call private life, the very widespread development of state-funded, state-controlled education, with its intrusion into the relations between children and families, is something liberals are bound to welcome.

Many things are done in public schools that not every parent agrees with. This seems to me just right: for these liberal reasons. If parents had the right to determine what their children should learn, it would be indefensible that we require parents to chose between public education and publicly licensed private education. That we do so require is a reflection of the fact that we believe that children have a right to an education that prepares them for autonomy as adults; and we recognize that this is something many parents cannot and some parents will not provide.

• • •

I do not know whether the framework I am suggesting is likely to seem too radical or too conservative. I suspect that it will seem to many too conservative, in this abstract formulation. I should like to end with a consideration of what it might mean in practice; and here, I suspect, many will find it too radical. But I should like to say that it seems to me that in working out how to proceed in educating our children for adulthood, the notion that we should prepare them for a dignified and autonomous maturity is one that ought to gather support from a very wide range of Americans. This basic idea is, as I have suggested, philosophically liberal: but it is not a liberal idea in the sense in which liberal and conservative are now contrasted in our politics. If contemporary conservatives are skeptical because I have spoken so much of rights, I should remind them that respect for autonomy also entails holding people responsible for their acts and that the existence of rights entails forms of constraint as well as kinds of freedom.

• • •

The basic liberal picture lies at the root of democratic thinking: we are each allowed an equal share in shaping the destiny of our nation, subject to the constraint that we acknowledge what flows from the dignity and autonomy of others. This means that the liberal democracy constrains what majorities can do, by the familiar mechanism of a system of legal rights, enforced by a judiciary that is relatively independent of the contemporary majority will. But it also means that the liberal democracy values not mere majoritarianism, but public deliberation, in which each of us is addressed as a reasoning creature, and invited to think through in the light of his or her own projects and understandings the choices facing our politics. The exercise of autonomy as Kant formulated it, was the exercise of reason: I have been developing a picture of autonomy that is not Kant's; but I want it to share this feature of Kant's theory (albeit with a more indulgent understanding of reason).

It follows (unsurprisingly) that liberal democracy is one of the notions that belongs to the core of the liberal conception of political morality, and that teaching it is, therefore, a matter of giving to each child a proper understanding of politics. But we need to give each child not only a grasp of these general notions but an understanding of the particular form through which our political institutions instantiates, in a rough and ready way, these general abstractions; and we need to give her, too, the tools with which to explore the ways in which the current political institutions of our society fail to meet the basic constraints, so that she can, if she chooses, contribute to the citizen's work of improving them.

●●●

The key to a liberal education is the development of an autonomous self. But there is a regular misunderstanding of what this means, one to which liberals themselves have contributed: a concern for autonomy is often wrongly seen as inconsistent with valuing sociality and relationship. This is a mistake that should be immediately rejected. An autonomous self is a human self, and we are, as Aristotle long ago insisted, creatures of the polis, social beings. We are social in many ways and for many reasons. We are social, first, because we are incapable of developing on our own, because we need human nurture, moral and intellectual education, practice with language, if we are to develop into full persons. This is a sociality of mutual dependence. We are social, second, because we humans naturally[9] desire relationship with others: friends, lovers, parents, children, the wider family, colleagues, neighbors. This is sociality as an end. And we are social, third, because many other things we value – literature, and the arts, the whole world of culture; education; money; and, in the modern world, food and housing

_____

[9] I mean it is natural to us only in the sense that a normal human upbringing produces creatures with such desires.

– depend essentially on society for their production. This is instrumental sociality.

To have dignity and autonomy as values is not, therefore, to refuse to acknowledge the dependence of the good for each of us on relationships with others. Indeed our selves are, in Charles Taylor's fine phrase, "dialogically" constituted: beginning in infancy, it is in dialogue with other people's understandings of who I am that I develop a conception of my own identity. Furthermore, my identity is crucially constituted through concepts (and practices) made available to me by religion, society, school and state, and mediated to varying degrees by the family. Dialogue shapes the identity I develop as I grow up: but the very material out of which I form it is provided, in part, by my society, by what Taylor has called its language in "a broad sense."[10] It follows that the self whose autonomous desires liberalism celebrates is not a pre-social thing – not some inner essence independent of the human world into which we have grown – but rather the product of our interaction from our earliest years with others.

As a result, educating children for autonomy requires preparing them for relationship, not just preparing them to respect, as liberalism requires, the autonomy of others.[11]

• • •

Let me exemplify what an education guided by these ideas might be like in the most practical terms, by describing two classroom practices with elementary school children   that would, I think, embody the ideals I have been discussing.[12]

The first practice is this: we establish a rule that no discussion is complete until everyone has spoken. The idea, of course, is that everyone is of equal worth, and is, therefore, equally entitled to express their opinions and receive respectful

---

[10] The broad sense "cover[s] not only the words we speak, but also other modes of expression whereby we define ourselves, including the 'languages' of art, of gesture, of love, and the like." (*Multiculturalism: Examining "The Politics of Recognition". An essay by Charles Taylor*, with commentary by Amy Gutmann (editor), K. Anthony Appiah, Jürgen Habermas, Steven C. Rockefeller, Michael Walzer, Susan Wolf (Princeton, NJ: Princeton University Press, 1994) p. 32.)

[11] See my "Identity, Authenticity, Survival: Multicultural Societies and Social Reproduction" in *Multiculturalism: Examining "he Politics of Recognition"* op. cit. pp. 149-164.

attention. This does not mean that what everyone says is of equal merit: and it is perfectly consistent to ask everyone to play their role in the discussion and, at the same time, to recognize that some contributions move the discussion forward better than others.

In the second practice, the teacher makes a habit of asking children to explain what other children have said. This, too, teaches that a dialogue of equals requires listening as well as speaking.

These practices are ways of communicating equality of respect and the place of discourse and reason in the relations of people who respect one another. I am sure that many teachers do both of these things (and many more just like them) already. And they are important because they introduce children to practices of respect, rather than simply announcing to them principles of respect. A child who has learned spontaneously to attend to what other children say and who expects a discussion of a question to be one that requires everyone's voice is learning about dignity and respect and learning to live with them. Such a child is in a better position to understand what the principles I have been talking about mean, when it becomes appropriate, as she grows older, for us to articulate explicitly what she has already implicitly learned through such classroom practices and at home.

• • •

What I have just said is, I suspect, likely to seem uncontroversial to many. But it already raises problems in our multicultural society. Not every social group in this country believes that children should be encouraged to speak up: some Chinese-American families teach children that the proper behavior for them is attentive silence in the presence of adults – and the teacher is an adult. Children know nothing, after all; or, at least, nothing of importance. They are in class to learn. From the perspective of certain ways of socializing children, the practices I have just described look guaranteed

---

[12] I am conscious of having come to these ideas in conversation with school and college teachers over the last few years, and in reading about education, without being clear as to where exactly they came from. So, either I made them up (which strikes me as unlikely) or I got them from someone, though I have forgotten when and from whom. If the latter is the right hypothesis, I apologize to my source: come forward and I will be happy to acknowledge you.

to produce children who chatter and expect to be listened to; children, in short, who are ill-mannered.[13]

Our liberal principles help us here, too. The raising of children is something in which parents plainly have the central role. I have insisted that the state rightly intervenes to protect the child's growth to autonomy; if the sorts of practices I have described are necessary for that purpose, they may be warranted by that fact. But the parents do not lose their role because the state's experts have a good-faith disagreement with them about what is best for their children. And because they are entitled to the treatment owed to persons with equal dignity, the proper approach, if such procedures are necessary, is to discuss with the parents the ideas they represent and the theories that guide them.

We should go carefully in such encounters. I have already pointed out that the centrality to liberalism of the idea of choices among options (and its correlative, the reflective appropriation of identities) means that we have a strong reason for encouraging the development of many richly socially-embedded forms of identity both within nations – multi-culturalism – and across them – cosmopolitanism. If a social group takes the attentive silence of its children as the proper and necessary preparation for them to have well-mannered adult lives, then, if they are right, that kind of childhood may be a condition for developing the adult identity embodied in that social group. Because we value the maintenance of a variety of such reflectively-appropriated identities, we have a special reason to be careful that we are right in thinking that practices in schools that appear to threaten those identities are either not genuinely threatening, on the one hand, or, on the other, important enough that they warrant the reshaping of the identities they will bring. We need, in particular, to be careful that we are not simply being ethnocentric, when we suppose, in our talkative modern Euro-American way, that children's talk really develops autonomy and respect for autonomy, because it is how we have come to want to treat our children.

I do not think that my attraction to the practices I described is mere ethnocentrism: facility with language and

---

[13] I am especially conscious of the dependence of what I say here on a discussion with the "Pentimento" group.

its use in social life requires lots of practice; children who are talked to and reasoned with do better, on average, at cognitive tasks that are broadly useful in modern life. But Chinese-Americans have not been having a hard time preparing their children to perform well at the cognitive tasks by which our schools measure their success and failure; and it is not an unreasonable hypothesis that the capacity for careful attention and for sustained intellectual work are connected with being able to sit quietly in the presence of adults. I think it is important, therefore, that the practices I have described place value on listening as well as on speaking: and that both of them are consistent with, for example, insisting that children also learn to work quietly together and alone.

• • •

At the other extreme from these very practice-based ideas, are concerns about the content of the curriculum. How should a liberal state decide curricular controversy?

There are two major kinds of problems here. First, there are topics where controversy is about what the truth is. Religious education is the obvious case here; as is moral teaching on questions, like abortion and homosexuality, about which there is substantial (often religiously-based) controversy. To these issues I shall return.

But there are also questions about what weight to place in education on different topics or different approaches. How much American history should children in America know? Within that history, should the focus be on individuals or on social processes; on America's failures or her successes.

Such questions are extremely concrete. We can agree that Frederick Douglass was a slave who brilliantly articulated an ideal of freedom: but we must also accept that that ideal was expressed in terms that made masculinity – and the freedom of men – more central than the freedom of women. Frederick Douglass was by the standards of his day progressive on "the woman question." But by our standards, there is something unacceptably masculinist in the central opposition of his narrative between slavery and manhood – with its emblematic moment in Douglass's physical resistance to the slave-breaker Covey: "You have seen how a man was made a slave," Douglass writes; "you shall see how a slave was made a man." The question is, at what stage (if ever) do we teach the problem with Douglass. The issue is not what the facts are, but which ones to focus on, which ones to play up.

My example here focuses on a figure who is much taught these days within the framework of multicultural education; but this sort of question has been raised much recently in resistance to multicultural education. Lynn Cheney objects to a history curriculum that has too much of Harriet Tubman and not enough of Thomas Jefferson. But she also objects to a curriculum whose discussion of Thomas Jefferson focusses more on his betrayal of liberty – in his persistent failure to emancipate his slaves – than on his place, as the author of the declaration of independence, as liberty's champion. No doubt a focus too lop-sided shades off into simple untruth: but the real debates here are not about what happened but about what narratives we will embed them in; they are about which of the many true stories we will tell.

From the point of view of liberal politics, these questions are relatively easy. We need to prepare children with the truth and the capacity to acquire more of it. Because they cannot absorb the whole truth, in all its complexity, all at once, we must begin with simplified stories; sometimes, even, with what is literally untrue. The obvious model where untruth prepares the way for truth is physics: the easiest way, we think, to prepare children for Einstein and Schrödinger is to teach them Newton and Maxwell first. But Newton and Maxwell did not know about relativity or about the indeterminacy of the fundamental physical laws: and so, their physics, which assumes absolute space and the infinite divisibility of matter is just not true. And the teaching of history is full of cases where we can delve deeper as we grow older into stories we first heard, in simplified versions, in first grade. It is because it is on the way to the truth, or because it is the closest thing to the truth that, at a certain age, they can understand, that these forms of what is, after all, strictly speaking, misinformation, can be seen as aimed at helping children develop towards an autonomy rooted in the best available understanding of the world.

The hard cases, I think – with which I want to deal in closing – are the ones where the controversy is about what the truth *is*.

•••

The greatest contemporary controversies about what truths should be taught arise about claims that are, in one way or another, connected with powerful collective identities. At the moment, for example, there is controversy about what shall be taught about evolution, abortion, contraception and homosexuality; and, if the first amendment did not prohibit the teaching of particular religions in public schools, there would certainly be controversy about that too. It is clear enough that the controversy about evolution flows from the fact that neo-Darwinian accounts of the development of species in general – and of the human species in particular – are at least prima facie inconsistent with the account of human origins proposed in the Old Testament. People do not want their children taught that "we are descended from apes," at least in part because they want their children to be, for example, good Baptists; and being a good Baptist requires, in their view, assent to the biblical account. But it seems to me that the controversies about sex and sexuality also have the intensity they do in part because American religious traditions have well-developed moral ideas about the proper use of sex and the proper form of sexuality; and conformity to these prescriptions is also seen as essential to being, say, a good Catholic. And those, on the other side, who are themselves homosexual and have come to celebrate a gay identity, are particularly outraged if it is proposed that children should be taught that their sexuality makes them morally depraved.

So far as the teaching of morality is concerned, all of us plainly have a reason to want children to be taught what we take to be morally true, whether or not we associate conformity to those norms and assent to those moral claims as central to an identity we share. Kant's stress on universalizability as the key mark of the moral reflects the way that treating an assertion as a moral claim entails believing that everyone should conform to it.[14] We want our fellow citizens to know what is morally required and what is morally forbidden because we want them to do what they should and abstain from doing what they should not do. But it is very noticeable

---

[14] In recent years, Bernard Williams has argued that there are ethical norms, central to the ways in which we construct our lives, that do not belong to the universalizing institution of morality; see Bernard Williams *Ethics and the Limits of Philosophy* (Cambridge: Harvard University Press, 1985). So, if he is right, not every important ethical conviction will share this universalizing logic of moral belief.

that the greatest controversies surrounding what moral ideas should be taught occur when people feel that their own children are being taught things that are inconsistent with claims that are crucial marks of their own collective identities; or when other people's children are taught things that challenge their own identities. I shall call a claim – whether moral or not – that is, in this sort of way, implicated with a certain collective identity, an identity-related claim.

The currency of controversy about the teaching of identity-related claims is not particularly surprising in this age of what Charles Taylor has dubbed the "politics of recognition." The development, which I have already insisted on, of the liberal idea of an identity, has meant that a great deal of politics – especially nationalist and ethnic politics, but also, for example, a lesbian and gay politics that is somewhat modelled on ethno-national politics – turns on the state's acknowledging a person's identity and protecting each person's ability to flourish while publicly expressing that identity. Each of these state acts recognizes an identity, conferring upon it a certain social respect. Martin Luther King day expresses the state's recognition of African-American identity; anti-discrimination law allows people to express their religion, their ethnicity and their sexuality in public without the threat of loss of employment or access to housing or assault. As Taylor insists, there is a widespread conviction (which comes, as he also says from the ethics of authenticity), that, other things being equal, we have the right to be acknowledged publicly as what we already really are. Much debate about what shall be taught in the schools on the teaching of identity-related claims is thus centrally concerned with insisting on the state's recognition of some identities (Christian, say) or its non-recognition of others (lesbian and gay).

Now it will be immediately clear why the notion of raising children to autonomy – with its corollary that we should equip them with the truths they need – does not help much in deciding what should be taught about these particular questions. It does not help because there is substantial social disagreement as to what the truth is; and such disagreements, we can predict, will not be settled by the appointment of commissions of experts to resolve them, in the cases where the claims in dispute are identity-related. In the case of moral claims, this is because most modern people do not recognize the existence of experts, perhaps because moral autonomy requires that each of us makes up her own mind about these questions. In the case of the dispute about evolution, it is claimed by some that they are simply operating by different epistemic standards: the authority of the Bible is not, for them, something that could be over-ridden by other (scientific) sources of evidence.

The constraints of truth do some work, however. Some of the theses of "creation science" (those, in particular, that are not themselves directly biblically derived) might be shown to be false by standards everyone agrees on; and some of the claims made about homosexuality by its enemies – claims about the "recruitment" of children to homosexuality – are completely without serious evidential foundation.

Nevertheless, this does not get us very far. And the question arises, how we can develop, on the sorts of liberal principles I have been articulating, a policy for public education in the cases where the dispute about the facts remains unresolved.

You might think the answer should be to stress the democracy in liberal democracy. Let us have public debate among equals and then vote for what should be taught. This seems to me how we must decide these questions, in one sense. But among the options in that public debate will be one that says that on some topics we may require the state to step back and leave the matter to the parents. It is not the case that the only option is to teach what the majority believes to be true. And I should like to defend that option in cases where identity-related beliefs are in dispute.

● ● ●

We must begin by recognizing that the role parents play in the raising of children gives them rights in respect of the shaping of their children's identities that are a necessary corollary of parental obligations. We do not believe that social reproduction should be carried out as it is in *Brave New World*. We believe that children should be raised primarily in families and that those families should be able to shape their children into the culture, identity and traditions that the adult members of the family take as their own. One liberal reason for believing this is that this is one way to guarantee the rich plurality of identities whose availability, is, as I have said, one of the resources for self-construction.

There are imaginable other ways. If the state took over the raising of children and did not aim to raise them all to a singular identity, it would have to assign children, effectively arbitrarily, to one of a range of identities. Once the state had taken over this role, respect for autonomy would require it to teach only such truths as it could decide on; teaching children falsehoods in order to give them "interesting" identities would be a paradigm of treating them as means (to the maintenance of a rich range of identities) rather than as ends. The resources for self-construction available would depend solely on the imagination and the will of the state and its servants, along with whatever "spontaneous" inventions would occur among the adults in such a society. Skepticism about this alternative, however, is surely in order. The intimacy of family life; the love of children for parents (and other relatives) and parents (and other relatives) for children; the sense of a family identity, family traditions: all these would be lost. More than this, the state would be invested with a quite enormous power in the shaping of the citizenry, a power whose potential for abuse is obvious enough.

But once we have left the raising of children to families, we are bound to acknowledge that parental love includes the desire to shape children into identities one cares about, and to teach them identity-related values, in particular, along with the other ethical truths that the child will need to live her life well. A state that actively undermined parental choices in this regard in the name of the child's future autonomy would be a state constantly at odds with the parents: and that would be unlikely to be good for the children. A compromise is therefore necessary: where identity-related propositions are at stake, parents are permitted to insist that their children not be taught what is contrary to their beliefs; and, in return, the state will be able to insist that the children be told what other citizens believe, in the name of a desire for the sort of mutual knowledge across identities that is a condition for living productively together.

Thus, it seems reasonable to teach children about the range of religious traditions in the communities within which they live (indeed, in the world), without requiring them to assent to any of them, so that, to begin with, at least, they will assent only to the religion they have learned at home. This allows the children the knowledge to make identity choices as they themselves grow to autonomy; but it gives parents a special, primary, place in shaping those choices. Only where a parent's choice seems to compromise the possibility of an autonomous adulthood – as would be the case with a refusal, on religious grounds, to allow one's children to learn to read – must the liberal state step in.

• • •

I have tried to suggest how one might begin to think about some questions in the philosophy of education, guided by the liberal thought that education is a preparation for autonomy. My aim has been to show that this tradition is both powerful enough to help us with this difficult question and rich enough to allow us answers of some complexity. But these are only beginning ideas: and a liberal, who respects his fellow citizens, will offer them into the public debate expecting to learn from others where he is wrong.

Teodros Kiros
Boston University

Autonomy and Identity in History:
A Philosophical Perspective

We are all the same, treat us as equals. We are all different, treat us with respect. We belong to one human species, although we are born to different races, sexes and classes, but we do not know how we should be treated, as equals or unequals. We have not made up our minds yet. Blacks say that they have been subjected to a selective racial affliction, and that they should be treated with special sensitivity. Women complain bitterly that they are doubly disadvantaged, as women and as subjugated members of a class. Poor women assert that rich women betray them once they make it – by joining the ranks of men and become insensitive to the plight of their poor sisters. Black women speak and write vituperatively about their dual suffering as women at the hands of men of all races, and as black women. Some white men shamelessly stress that intelligence and civilization are white; whereas destitution and cultural primitivity are non-white. Afrocentricists claim that civilization began in Africa, and that moral intelligence and compassion are black. These are the claims of our race, sex and class conscious times. It is out of these paradoxical claims that multiculturalism, as a quest for identity, is born.

There are two models of multiculturalism. I call them the *ancient model* of classical philosophy, in which the self is problematized; and the *modern model,* that raises questions of identity. Identity can be imagined in at least two ways, as private and public. Public identity is socially constructed. Private identity is self-constructed. You and I can internalize public identities that are visited upon us by choosing public identities that society seductively presents to us. We do so, relative to the calculation of our best interests, and our willingness to take on public identities, and play the games of power. Private identity, when it is consummated, is a practice of freedom. It seeks to counter the paths of public identity. As a practice of autonomy, private identity cannot be alienated. Private identity cannot be sold to the games of power. It is as sovereign as the freedom that creates it. Private identity, unlike public identity, is that aspect of personality which cannot be compromised, once it is intimately constructed, as a style of existence motivated by a private ethics of living. One can invent a self by way of constructing private identity. It is in this particular way that autonomy and identity can be said to work in concert during the process of cultivating empowering human values. That history has not been supportive of individuals who sought to invent private identity is not a sufficiently powerful argument against trying. As educators,we must encourage our students to construct values and know how to articulate them intelligently and defend them courageously.

• • •

Philosophers have long wondered about what we moderns have called identity, in a subtler and more complex way. For Plato and Aristotle, who one is or who one wishes to be, or, whom one would like to model himself/herself after, are intricate facets of practices. These are practices undertaken by persons who are directly learning the difficult task of fashioning a self, or, constructing an identity. These philosophers addressed the perplexing question of whom one is through the prior question of developing a technique or method of approaching the question itself. Of course, it is the self which really does not know who it is, but wants to know, who is asking. The puzzle is that, this reflective self does not know how to broach, let alone approach, the question of who one is. It simply does not have a method. In the twentieth century, Heidegger,[1] problematized the question of identity, as the problem of Being. For Heidegger, a human being is the one who does not know the meaning of Being.

In *The Republic*,[2] Plato took seeming to be and really being as so difficult to disentangle that they rendered the possibility of knowing oneself, or discovering one's true identity, as unknowable ideals – at least for reflective human

---

[1] Martin Heidegger, *Being and Time* (London; Harper and Row Publishers, 1962).

[2] Harold Bloom, *The Republic Of Plato* (New York; Basic Books. 1968). See Book Two and Three.

beings. Insofar as seeming and being always remain as inseparable parts of personality, one which cannot be penetrated by language, identity will be beyond the purview of language. Plato argued further that, when one wants to know one's identity and one discovers that it is encumbered with thick layers of unknowables, one is entering the labyrinth of the self's universe, the realm of that sphere of being which language is not allowed to visit. For those who dare to visit the prohibited house of Being, lest they confuse being with appearance, or the seeming to be, there is nothing to know, nothing to disclose. That dimension of identity is where the self risks loss and confusion, where appearance is taken for being, and being is reduced to appearance. For those who disagreed with Plato, all there is is appearance, there is no being. For Plato, there is Being, as he argued in Parmenides[3], but it cannot be known by the human thinker. Being is more complex than the human being who seeks to make it transparent. Identity is part of these complexities that attend the nature of being. The unreflective self gets stuck on this shallow plane, which it uses as one of the sources of self-construction, without paying attention to the problematics of reducing being into appearance.

For the ancient thinkers, such as Plato and Aristotle, the self is condemned not to know its ultimate nature, because language, and therefore thought, is underequipped to carry this monumental task. The human thinker's finiteness prevents the carrying out of the task. Philosophy in turn is humbled by the lesson, from which it learns the finiteness of thought and the limits of language. In general terms, this is what modern philosophy learned from the ancient masters' confrontation of the problematics of identity.

• • •

Beginning with Kant, the problematics of identity are approached in a radically new way. For Kant as well as for me, it is only when the self divulges to itself the meaning and scope of the ideal of autonomy, that one's identity may be revealed. Following Kant, and going beyond him, I wish

[3] Plato, *The Collected Dialogues of Plato*. Ed. by Edith Hamilton and Huntington Cairns (Princeton: Bolligen Series LXXI, 1961), pp. 920-956.

to argue that the depth of the self's identity can be limited only by the mastery of its unregulated passions, which obstruct the realization of autonomy. Autonomy is achieved by its successful governance of some of the rude and undisciplined passions. Genuine desire, as opposed to shallow passions, works in harmony with self-generated principles of reason. Who one is, or what the identity of the self is, can be determined by the degree of freedom that the reflective self has attained. A self that is still trapped in the winds of passion, unregulated by self-generated principles of reason, is still unfree. Such a self is still not autonomous. It is a self which does not and cannot know who it is. The autonomous self, at the minimum, knows that autonomy is a property of identity. Indeed, autonomy is the ontological ground of identity. A self that is struggling with the question: Who am I? is challenged to free itself from historically generated properties, such as gender and race, places itself in the transcendent realm of autonomy so as to be able to know who it is, and who it is not. The contingencies of race, class and gender stand in the way of one's potentiality of attaining autonomy, and therefore, a human identity characterized by freedom.

Our capacity to think for ourselves is vitiated by the impositions of false loyalties to group thinking, manifest in some obstructing attachments to races, sexes and families. The public identities which are imposed on us are also mistaken for the private identities we so much desire to construct. Rare are the opportunities given to us to fashion a self, to invent values, which bear the marks of autonomy. Sometimes, individuals are forced to fight the contingencies of history, such as those insulting badges of stereotypes, which impose the reading of a person's identity, a person's self-conception, very much like a text which is already definitively interpreted. The desire of constructing a private identity is an attempt of a great refusal to be read and scripted like a worn out text. Private identity is a heroic effort of countering the dangers of wearing unwanted public identities.

• • •

Education towards autonomy is itself a mode of socialization. In education, as a formative experience, ideas, power and discipline work in a subtle concert. Unless the person who is undergoing the formative process of education is critically aware of the power of ideas, he/she could easily lose the precious freedom of will, and find himself/herself internalizing values that imprison and subjugate one's freedom of thought. You and I might have never made much of the fact that we have a white skin, or black one, hazel eyes, blonde hair, and much else, but we are trained to impute powerful significance to biological facts. These biological facts could be translated into dangerously politicized values, norms, tastes, and interests. As biological facts that mark differences, the facts are not intrinsically dangerous. It is when judgmental meanings are systematically appended to them that the facts become politicized. They become facts that stir the emotions. These stirred emotions in turn produce modes of thinking that cold-bloodedly distinguish cultural symbols. Cultural symbols are further deliberately distorted. The distortions take on a life of power that privileges certain values as intrinsically superior when compared to others. It is ultimately when otherwise intrinsically harmless differences – such as skin color, eye color, etc. – are made symbols of superiority and inferiority, and they become integral aspects of formative education that the danger begins. Innocent differences are changed into deeply divisive tools of language, desire, and truth. A generation of children, adults, educators, and experts grow up by internalizing these differences in the depths of the unconscious. By the time that children become adults, adults become opinion-framers, and both are subjected to the indiscriminate invitation of aging, the years have often dulled the senses and solidified long-held prejudices. At that point, the possibility of autonomous thinking, aided by intelligent values of tradition and custom, becomes exceedingly difficult to achieve.

• • •

Thomas Mann was intelligently aware of the formative power of values, norms, and tastes that shape the growing self, in the course of constructing identity. Mann captured the essence of how children are exposed to values that give them a sense of identity, a sense that either strengthens their character or damages it. The process is observed by the keen eyes of the narrator in "Tonio Kroger." Tonio, like many other "sensitive" human beings, is an enigmatic figure who doubts the merits of his own identity, a doubting that is increased by the judgments of the "other" who looks and behaves very differently from himself. Tonio is both proud and ashamed of his identity. Tonio Kroger's soul is afflicted by duality. He does not seem to have a great respect for his Italian name. Thus, he laments with the "ironic" words: "Yes, it is a silly name – Lord knows I'd rather be called Heinrich or Wilhelm. It's all because I'm named after my mother's brother Antonio. She comes from down there."[4] Tonio may not have wanted to assimilate the other "low" values of Hans, such as the latter's rather embarrassing interest in riding horses, and dislike of thinking and literature. There are more "ironic" passages that communicate the politicized values of judgment. For example:

> Tonio Kroger looked at them both, these two for whom he had in time past suffered love – at Hans and Ingeborg. They were Hans and Ingeborg not so much by virtue of individual traits and similarity of costume as by similarity of race and type. This was the blond, fair-haired breed of the steel blue eyes, which stood to him for the pure, the blithe, the untroubled in life; for a virginal aloofness that was at once both simple and full of pride.[5]

Tonio Kroger's mother was a negative representation of Hans-Tonio's ideal self to which he had undoubtedly become socialized through the disciplinary power of norms that had subtly instructed him in the form of values. Thus, his mother, who came from the nameless "down there," was dark, fiery, passionate, undisciplined, irregular, and careless.[6] Kroger, however, was enormously proud of his "northern" father's ancestry. The name itself, Kroger, his father's name, radiated brilliance, dignity, light, and even beauty. Tonio Kroger himself describes it almost perfectly: "My father, you know,

---

[4] Thomas Mann, "Tonio Kroger," in *Death in Venice and Seven Other Stories* (New York: Vintage Books, 1959), p. 83.

[5] Ibid., p. 128.

[6] Ibid., p. 78 and p. 133.

had the temperament of the north: solid, reflective, puritanically correct, with a tendency to melancholia."[7]

If we grouped together the dominant values and norms by whose presence Tonio is enlivened and given a self-image, here are the values we get. Noble are the blondes with their steel blue eyes. Their bodies disclose sublime beauty. So do their souls, which communicate the presence of a mind that produces the power of reflection grounded upon solidity, puritanical firmness of intent and resolve, and a deep appreciation for the tragic dimension of life. Inferior are the types whose bodies fervently move toward the fleshy, the sensuous, the festive, the sexual, the irregular, the self-determining.

• • •

Education in the abstract, like many ideas in this world, is potentially harmless. Receiving an education and gaining a dist-orted sense of how life should be lived are not necessarily simultaneous. Education, very much like food and shelter, is an intrinsic good. Again, like food and shelter, education benefits the body and the mind. From the very beginning of our appearance on this planet, we humans are subjected to the subtle process of education and this leads education toward hegemonic ideas that imprison self-empowering thought and liberating imagination by disciplining and domesticating our capacity to determine our thoughts and actions. We are rarely trusted to construct our own values and responsibly fashion a style of existence.

Parents as teachers and educators may reflect on ways to consistently and devotedly introduce the young and old to read, think, discuss, converse about, and debate issues, themes, and topics from the human angle of different cultures. In this concrete way, the generations to come may benefit from the groundwork that could be done by the present generation. We human beings have done an extraordinary job of training human beings in the values of calculation, coldness, mistrust, cruelty, and the will to dominate. Our job has been so successful that the young, the middle-aged, as well as the old, have assimilated values that took centuries to establish. These values have become second nature to them.

[7]Ibid., p. 133.

If we so wish, however impossible my proposal may sound, we can (a) through authentically critical education, and (b) through critical even revolutionary activity, succeed in at least establishing a ground work for a radically new ethics and aesthetics. Self-empowerment may after all become a new norm toward which we can move. We can at least start now before it is really too late. I have argued earlier that education is an intrinsically good experience. In the abstract, I further added, education is harmless. It is a neutral power. When education's role is examined within the context of deliberately destructive socialization, and power, however, we clearly see its truly harmful effects on the body and character of the individual, particularly the modern individual who is a consummation of the history of the sediments of the past. An individual, whose conception of himself/herself and all those "others" is seriously based on skin color, color of the eyes, size of the head, or structure of the bones, is a depressing example of the subtle destruction of the creative powers of the self. When we are reduced to inconsequential outside appearances, we do damage to our ultimate sense of ourselves as beings who are capable of deep reasoning power. This is a power which, when fully and whole heartedly exercised, may even show us the severe limitations of making judgments based on appearance, the angle through which evil in the cloak of thoughtlessness, tyranny, arrogance, and dogma may enter the empirical world of everyday life.

An educational experience which does not foster clear thinking or the need to mistrust the claims which outside appearances have on us (as frail, weak, lazy, proud, forgetful, nasty, and selfishly self-interested human beings) is not an authentic education worthy of us. That this severely crippling mode of education has worked and continues to work is not a justification for not criticizing it. We can, however, wage a merciless attack on modern education by criticizing those very effects that we can directly see: the "sick," "illiterate," "selfish," mindless consumers of modern society. These modern individuals are the bearers of a tradition of faulty education. They are concrete living witnesses of the past. The faults can be corrected only if we create schools which encourage individuals to think and act freely through a direct experience of constructing human values which genuinely empower, such as the simple fact that there are many cultures bearing many and not a singular Eurocentric value, and that global cultures have multicultural colors, the complex blend of which is the perennial idea of beauty.

● ● ●

Self-empowerment or the pragmatic conception of power, a construct which I am still in the process of articulating and developing, has several components. Values, norms, and tastes are its integral parts. To say that human beings are self-constructing and self-empowering raises the questions: What and how do individuals construct, and given the construction, how do they become powerful, in the sense that they use values, norms, and tastes to judge, classify, categorize, recognize, and fail to recognize others, particularly those others who are different from them? To illustrate the claim, I used Tonio Kroger's values and norms, and strove to show how values and norms were used as justifications for racial, gender, and cultural claims, and have given us slavery, colonialism, the Holocaust, and the permanently dependent and poor members of the non-Western world. I further claimed that socialization in concert with formal education, plays a central role in producing the modern "educated" individual – the individual as intoxicated and hypnotized by hegemonic ideas.

● ● ●

I now wish to add a new claim. On a formal level, power as domination and power as self-empowerment can both be systematically cultivated by formal education – education toward ideas that intoxicate, hypnotize, and discipline or imprison the mind and body. But, that is not all. Power as domination, in particular, could also be effected through the subtle role of recognition. Multiculturally oriented discourses on identity are calls for recognition. The thinker who provided us with the concept of recognition is Hegel, in *The Phenomenology of Spirit*. I will now provide a brief discussion of the concept of recognition in that text.

In a general sense, we become powerful as well as powerless through the affective ways in which others do and do not recognize what we do, what we wish to do, how we actually do it, and how we wished to do it. That sense of recognition, so crucial for the development of personality or character is selectively extended to human beings. Unfortunately, across the vast and turbulent stretch of empirical history, recognition has been used as one of the most effective tools of power by the dominators against the dominated. It is one of the greatest merits of Hegel that he unfolded the function of recognition in any human interaction within the family, the work place, and society at large. The nature of power as domination as well as the nature of power as self-empowerment can be deeply understood on the level of recognition – the recognition of (a) self as self on the level of self-empowerment, (b) self and others, (c) the recognizer and the recognized. Long before recognition is deployed within the formal institutions of education, where we have rigid roles such as the educator and the educated, dominant ideas and peripheral ideas, it is firmly embedded in human interaction outside of these educational structures.

When we speak a language at all, we are using words to recognize the meanings and non-meanings of what we intend to say. Those with whom we are speaking play a key role in this basic interaction. It is they who may or may not be able to recognize our meaning. It is they as well who decide to extend or not extend recognition to the act of speaking, as we learned from Habermas and the speech act theorists. The capacities, decisions, intentions, motives and goals of those with whom we speak affect the kinds of characters (dominated, susceptible to domination, or self-empowered) we develop.

•••

Speaking then is not a lonely activity. Surely, the self can speak to itself. In fact, one of the deepest forms of speaking does take place in solitude. However, the form of speaking that interests me here is the form that allows human beings to interact with the sincere intention of understanding each other. My sense of understanding here does not aim at a crystal clear, transparent and perfect communication of thoughts and feelings. Rather, understanding, for me, could never result in perfect, transparent understanding. Understanding is always an approximation of transparency and seeking this transparency is a goal. The joy of the quest for understanding lies not in the result, which may never be attained but rather in the sincere struggle for transparent meaning. In the quest for understanding each other, the place of recognition looms large. The various quests for identity are in the end requests of recognition, and multiculturalism provides a forum for the politics of identity, in our modern times.

The phenomenon of recognition, for Hegel, is explicitly present in one particular interactive space of domination, occupied by a bondsman and a master in the feudalistic stages of European history. To begin with, bondage and lordship, on the level of the formative genealogy of concepts, are really nothing more than two linguistic labels. Immediately speaking, they are simply words. These linguistic labels, however, very much like the color concepts – white, blonde, blue-eyed, etc. – become politically mediated and are thus given particular meanings. These meanings are invested with power. The meanings themselves carry relationships of power. Thus bondage connotes a structurally mediated meaning of inferiority, slavishness, being born to be dominated. Lordship, on the other hand, bears the ultimate virtue of nobility. Thus, the feudal landlord bears the name of the all-mighty, all knowing, awesome lord of lords. Lordship is a symbol of the power born to command, authorize, and dominate. It is a symbol of superiority.

The two linguistic labels, however, do not become actual, concrete languages of power until after they are recognized by those human beings whose spatial habitat they so effectively define. Without recognition, in the form of the internalization of linguistic labels, words, therefore relationships, are meaningless. For Hegel, the relationship between the bondsperson and the master are founded on the integral dependence of one upon the other. The bondsman is taught to think and live as if he is inherently dependent upon the master. Inherent dependence, like bondage itself, is recognized by the bondsman as a natural relationship created by the Lord of lords himself. Similarly, inherent independence – the independence that is thought and lived by the master or the lord – is recognized by the feudal lord as well by the bondsman as a natural relationship – authorized by the Lord of Lords. The bondsman and the master both recognize the power of words. Both transform words into ways of life effectively translated into the relationship of a natural will to power, the will to dominate, and be dominated. The dominated takes on the public identity of a bondsman.

In order for the bondsman and the lord to naturally participate in the interactive experience of domination, language must first lay the groundwork, or else the relationship will not work. It works effectively only after language confers definitive meanings to the relationship of two human beings (with inalienable needs and rights of equality) – a relationship of inequality, in which one is to be the dominator and the other the dominated. The inherent dignity of two human beings is violated by language and transformed into a relationship of servitude and mastery. Servitude and mastery are subtly but effectively internalized and recognized by human beings as natural relationships, founded upon the wishes and desires of the Lord himself. The structure of a relationship of inequality is thus treated as if it were natural and unchangeable. A historical relationship is thus translated into a natural relationship that cannot be challenged by the wills, passions, and intelligence of those human beings who cannot endure a relationship of misery and mistreatment in the hands of the beastly bearers of the so-called "civilization."

• • •

The historical relationship of domination, which is systematically rooted in language, is experienced both by the lord and the bondsman as a definite aspect of natural consciousness. Consciousness, Hegel argues, duplicates itself to form a dual consciousness made up of independence symbolized by the lord and dependence symbolized by the bondsman. Consciousness itself requires the duplication. Without the necessary duplication, consciousness cannot exist. In formal language, one can assert that this duplication is an ontological ground of consciousness. Initially, and for a long stretch of human history, the duplication of consciousness is experienced by the bearers of tradition as natural, as an experience that must be endured both by those who enjoy it (e.g., the lord) and those who suffered silently (e.g., the bondsman). For the bondsmen, suffering, endurance, anguish, and sadness are the necessary tests of the lord before he can be considered worthy of eventual redemption are thus recognized by the Lord of Lords.[8]

The Lord experiences his privileged position of nobility, independence, material abundance, arrogance and pride, all of which confer definite material power on his character as intrinsically good. The intrinsic goodness is lived as a gift from God. The lord considers himself as uniquely gifted, deliberately privileged. The lord ultimately considers himself, I wish to add, as born to be happy, chosen to enjoy. The other side of the coin, where we encounter the bondsman, is a position of dirt and dust, anguish and desolation, self-humiliation and deep sadness, self-doubt and severe self-judgment. Some bondsmen tolerated servitude as the Lord's way of testing their capacity to endure. Some of the bondsmen, however, actually considered themselves members of the race of Cain, cursed to perpetually suffer. Other bondsmen were consistently stoical, silent sufferers who never stopped dreaming about the not – yet, as a fantasy made possible through eventual redemption. Clearly, responses to bondage are extremely varied, and Hegel fully recognized the human diversity of responses to servitude. Hegel himself stipulates his own response in the following passage:

> In the master, the bondsman feels self-existence to be something external an objective fact; in fear. Self-existence is present within himself; in fashioning the thing, self-existence comes to be felt explicitly as his own proper being, and he attains the consciousness that he himself exists in its own right and on its own account (an und fur sich). By the fact that the form is objectified, it does not become something other than the consciousness molding

[8] Hegel, *The Phenomenology of Mind* (New York: Harper and Row Publishers, 1967), pp. 128-134.

the thing through work; for just that form is his pure self-existence, which therein becomes truly realized. Thus precisely in labor where there seemed to be merely some outsider's mind and ideas involved, the bondsman becomes aware, through his re-discovery of himself by himself, of having and being a "mind of his own."[9]

• • •

Previously, I argued, recognition played a rather passive role. Language was used to mystify, mask, and render a human relationship which was anchored upon a blind acceptance of the world as an empirical given, a rendering of the lord into a power which cannot be unmasked, or criticized. The lord was ignorantly, and under the guidance of fear and dread reified into an alien will to power beyond and above empirical history. In certain religious corners of the world, the lord was accepted and recognized as the appointee, the great Leviathan sent by God. In the above sense, recognition played a passive role. The natural duplication of consciousness was the last act of recognition as a pacifier, as the force of language that imposed fate and surrender upon the world of the sufferers, such as the bondsmen. A demeaning public identity is imposed upon many individuals by the violence of language, thereby denying the slaves of many ages the precious ideal of constructing private identities, as potentially autonomous human beings.

Eventually though, recognition began to play a rather astonishing role. Recognition has stimulated the bondsman to rediscover his existence. Existence was rediscovered not as an act of God outside history, time and space, but rather as an act of self-construction and self-empowerment – an act that is inspired by the God-given will, passion, and intelligence. This is the hidden message of Hegel's words in the last passage that I quoted, upon which I would like to elaborate further.

Labor and work are the new self-empowering insights that the bondsman discovered to re-affirm the novel awareness of existence as an act of self-determining freedom. The

---

[9] Ibid., p. 239.

bondsman has now re-awakened from his passive existence – the existence of words that domesticated, enslaved, and impoverished him; words that made dependence natural and servitude as a necessary result of dependence. This was a dependence of man upon man, dependence of the powerless upon the whims and wills of the powerful, and the ultimate dependence of the dominated upon the dominators, the vanquished upon the victors. All these relationships that were once solidified and stabilized by language have now been re-opened, destroyed, to be re-constructed anew, through the ongoing struggles of quests for private identities.

• • •

Recognition in its active form produces in order to destroy the permanently harmful, the traditionally effective understanding that the empirical world is an act of God. Tradition, custom, blind obedience to authority are exploded. In their stead, new forms of life are in the process of discovery. The bondsman's newly-found sense of being as a laborer – a worker who, by his sweat, his mixing of physical labor and the direct involvement of his will, intelligence and passion – allows him to see the inner architectonic of the things upon which he works from beginning to end , as a result of which he develops an aesthetic and ethical orientation toward minerals, stones – the external consciousness of humankind. Out of the inter-action with the "things" of the world, the bondsman, in contrast to the lord, emerges as the true master of labor. Through labor, the world is created. Through the aesthetic and ethical appreciation of the things of the world, and the hard labor that is invested, the laborer profoundly understands the ordeal of laboring – an ordeal that was beautifully and sensitively captured by Van Gogh, the painter of the miners' world – a world characterized by dignity, authentic pride, anguish, a deep sense of mission, a yearning for redemption.

The passage from Hegel, which I quoted earlier, upon a repeated reading, strikes me as deeply tragic. It is a pity that human beings learn about each other's indispensable importance not through reflection, care, and compassion but rather through the direct use of violence or the threat to use it. The freedom that those who are free enjoy, for some inexplicable reason, is not regarded (by the free) as crucially important for those who are not free. Thus, the lord, born to freedom, cannot and is not willing to recognize the burning desire of the bondsman, who is born to servitude, and hard labor. The lord mindlessly or perhaps deliberately considers the bondsman to be unfit for freedom, material comfort, and an existence freed from anguish, fear, and perpetual dependence. The stubborn refusal of the lord to recognize the bondsman as a person with needs and rights, which are similar to the lord's, produces a tense condition, which as Hobbes puts it, is the war of all against all, power against power, ego against ego, desire against desire, bestiality against bestiality. In this tense, hateful and explosive condition, there may never arise victors and losers. The only result is timeless death – the death of precious human lives, the death of those human beings who reluctantly participated in the ultimately meaningless project: war, a condition that fulfills the pathological dreams and sick aesthetic desires of war mongers, killers – the rapists of nations and nationalities.

• • •

72

George Katsiaficas
Wentworth Institute of Technology

The Latent Universal Within Identity Politics

Time and again, theorists mistake ideas relevant to specific contexts for universal truths, and recent social movement research is no exception. While movements are increasingly international and even synchronically connected across national borders, analysis of them largely remains within the nationalistic framework of government funding agencies and language-communities. In France, where political action is so state oriented, Alain Touraine insists that social movements be analyzed by their impact on the state.[1] In the United States, where fragmented activism possessing immense resources abounds, analysis of social movements has been based on

---

[1] He continually defines social movements in terms of power. For his own discussion of this and other issues, see Alain Touraine, "Commentary on Dieter Rucht's Critique," in Rucht (editor) *Research on Social Movements* (Campus Verlag, 1991) pp. 385-391.
 Touraine poses a "new central conflict" like the labor movement in the nineteenth century. From detailed studies of the Polish workers' movement, the anti-nuclear movement, student movements, and regional movements in southern France, he arrives at the conclusion that: "we were able to observe...both the growing autonomy of social movements, freeing themselves from the control of political parties and ideologies, and the central role of cultural problems in societies where 'cultural industries' play a rapidly growing role, especially in health, education and mass communication." (p. 388). For him, unlike industrial societies in which workers opposing capitalists was the central conflict, "programmed societies" are sites where social movements centering on knowledge and identity are crucial.
 Seeking to construct a critical scientific sociology, Touraine engaged social movement participants in hundreds of hours of discussions after which his researchers wrote up and presented their views of the "highest" possible meaning of the movement's actions in order to provoke discussion of larger transformative ideas within focused movements. He seeks to infuse social movements with knowledge. But as each of his books make clear, he is informed by social movements -not necessarily the other way around. Touraine's interventionist sociology is the residue of Leninism in academic theory: The educated outsider bringing knowledge to the committed is nothing but a reformulation of Lenin's notion of the party. In another sense as well, Touraine's conception of social movements is traditional Leninism. For him, diversity and fragmentation go hand in hand and permit the ruling elites to employ tactics of divide and conquer, and universality cannot be present within a diverse array; each stage of social development should have one unifying oppositional social movement. See Ron Eyerman, "Social Movements and Social Theory," *Sociology* Vol. 18, No. 1 (1984) pp. 71-82.

the resource mobilization paradigm.[2] In Germany, where the government's response to social movements was to label them as "terrorists," Habermas puts forth the view that societies could resolve their crises if their members addressed each other with respect in an ideal free speech situation.[3] Habermas's analysis is unmistakably German insofar as he seeks to enhance democratic discourse in a society that for most of the twentieth century has marginalized (if not murdered) its radical critics.[4]

    While it is extremely problematic to treat social movements as simply conditioned by the form and circulation of capital and the structures of social relations, my analysis regards movements as partially conditioned by impersonal

[2] By focusing on issues like the availability of resources for movements and the impact of state intervention against and within movements, such analysis moves the study of movements in the direction of natural science. Instrumental factors are assumed to be central, and "actors" are assumed to make utilitarian choices related to participation. In this sense, social movements are considered to be essentially no different than any other form of institutional behavior. Posing atomized individuals as the building block of movements (and society), the issue then becomes whether identities are rationally constructed by abstract individuals or by groups with specific identities in history.
    Despite its great differences from Touraine, resource mobilization theory also privileges traditionally structured political initiatives over ones which do not seek inclusion in the existing system. (See Margit Mayer, "Social Movement Research in the United States: A European Perspective," *International Journal of Politics, Culture and Society* Vol. 4, No. 1 (1991) p. 464.) According to the resource mobilization perspective: "Victories generally begin with policy successes and culminate in distributional goals." (See Craig Jenkins, *The Politics of Insurgency: The Farm Workers Movement in the 1960s* (Columbia University Press, 1985) p. 21.) Their middle-range perspective prohibits their comprehension of the fundamental differences of "post-political" movements,and they end up (like the more astute Habermas) in advocating traditional forms of political engagement.

[3] Habermas fails to see that the entire world cannot live at the standard of living of the integrated middle class, and that the structural imperatives of the system demand intensified poverty alongside wealth. Can societies democratically decide to limit the system's predatory character vis-a-vis private life and the natural environment? Even from within his own set of assumptions, Habermas's search for communicative competence in the rational structures of language and consciousness ignores entirely the intuitive ties between humans, our passions and unconscious impulses. In the work of Marcuse, art and nature constitute dimensions of freedom (that remain unthematized by Habermas).

[4] The German idea of justice is predicated upon the *Rechtsstaat*, a government that respects laws and inspires and fulfills moral obligations. In the U.S., our liberal tradition emphasizes individual liberty with as little government as possible. As Fredric Jameson commented in his book on postmodernism: "...the culture of the *Spiessbürger* and the philistine suggests the possibility that in this particular national situation Habermas may well be right, and the older forms of high modernism may still retain something of the subversive power they have lost elsewhere." *Postmodernism, or the Cultural Logic of Late Capitalism* (Duke University Press, 1991, p. 59).

economic forces and political dynamics. Postmodernists generally sever analysis of social movements from such categories, regarding notions of structure as vestigial modernist relics. For postmodernists, "society" is a construct; we live in multiple and decentered contexts. Using the language of postmodernists, simulacra (mediated semblances of life) are more important than history in determining our actions. Once understood from this perspective, social movements are no longer vehicles for the transformation of the social order as a whole (since that is simply a phantom) but are "new social movements"[5] oriented around specific contested sites and questions of identity (like race, gender and age).

Locked in debate, the more that postmodernists and Marxists contest each other's assumptions and ideas, the less likely they are to elicit what could be mutually beneficial insights offered by those they define as their intellectual opponent. At their extremes, both become mechanical responses, not dialectical ones, to rapid change. As the

[5] A broad range of analysts besides postmodernists has come to employ the term "new social movements" to refer to various types of post-Fordist social movements: feminist, youth, ecology, peace and gay (and in the U.S., Black, Latino, Asian-American and Native American). As identity became key to the self-understanding of participants in new social movements, ascriptive criteria for membership defined the various emergent formations. The term "new social movements" is actually a misnomer since oppositional forces structured along the lines of identity are not new: Women mobilized no later than 1848 and African-Americans since the arrival of the first African slaves in America.

The best single definition of new social movements I have found is contained in Andrei Markovits and Philip Gorski, *The German Left: Red, Green and Beyond* (Oxford University Press, 1993) pp. 10-13. In the first place, they demarcate the difference between old movements, "which concentrated on the expansion of rights" with new ones which "devote their energy to the expansion of 'autonomy.'" In addition they delineate 8 other characteristics of new social movements, such as: eschewing comprehensive theories, valuing the collective good and identity rather than individual interests and class politics, and independence from political parties. German sociologists Karl-Werner Brand and Roland Roth both characterize new social movements as intermediate levels of communication between isolated citizens and political parties.

An early analysis of new social movements was published as a special issue of *Social Research*, Vol. 52, No. 4 (Winter 1985). Jean Cohen noted that new social movements emerged from civil society rather than mass institutions and that their unwillingness to make formal calculations vis-a-vis the state effectively placed them outside the resource-mobilization paradigm.

Finally, Enrique Larana, Hank Johnston and Joseph Gusfield pose eight characteristics of new social movements including a social base that transcends class structure, pluralism of ideas and values, new dimensions of identity, and autonomy from politcal parties. See their edited volume, *New Social Movements: From Ideology to Identity* (Temple University Press, 1994).

adherents of each position become rigid, prospects for clarification of reality dim. Postmodernism is often written off as an academic fad replete with a jargon of discourse inaccessible to all but a select few, and Marxists are dismissed as dinosaurs. While mechanical Marxists fail to appreciate the radical gap between modernity and post-modernity, crippling their capacity to understand the contemporary world, many post-modernists are unable to link their empirical understanding of the decentered autonomy of local contexts to history, leaving them incapable of articulating a transcendental vision for the future.[6]

In the current atmosphere of recrimination and contestation for hegemony, it is difficult to criticize the politics of identity while simultaneously retaining a sense of their radical potential. Many Marxists lament the appearance of identity politics. They see it as shattering the promise of proletarian universalism, but they miss the latent universality present in new social movements. Identity construction can be a form of enacting the freedom to determine one's conditions of existence, to create new categories within which to live. While the many dimensions of this dynamic are fragmentary, a totality of such quests can eventually become a radically new concrete universal – a reworking of the meaning of human being.

Unlike economic categories imposed by production and social relations, these new categories can be autonomously formulated – or, at a minimum, they are vehicles for the autonomy of groups oppressed by existing structures. The logic of the established system is to enforce particularisms as a means of social control. By bringing control and power to minorities and women, identity politics can be a form of self-defense. As Anthony Appiah expresses it:

> And if one is to be Black in a society that is racist then one has to deal constantly with assaults on one's dignity. In this context, insisting on the right to live a dignified life will not be enough. It will not even be enough to require being treated with

---

[6] For a critical reading of postmodernism, see "In Defense of History: Marxism and the Postmodern Agenda", special issue of *Monthly Review* (July/August 1995). Surprisingly, the entire double issue contains only a single paragraph dealing with economic dimensions of contemporary reality, usually MR's specialty.

> equal dignity despite being Black, for that will require a concession that being Black counts naturally or to some degree against one's dignity. And so one will end up asking to be respected *as a Black.* [7]

When Republicans assault affirmative action and abortion rights, they condition responses from minorities and women reinforcing their group's freedom from encroachment of outside interests.

No matter how much they respond to intrusive outsiders, each form of identity politics contains a latent universality. Gender equality is a universal aim, benefitting all of us. The celebration of racial diversity and mutual recognition of our humanity is in all our interests. Unlocking sexual repression and an end to the compulsory channelling of libido into exclusive heterosexuality benefits all. Cleaning up the environment and disarming the world's nation-states is in the interest of all humanity. At their best, autonomous movements (like Italian *Autonomia* or the German *Autonomen*[8]) bring these latent connections to consciousness and accentuate the universal content of single-issue identity politics. The function of revolutionary theory is not to persuade feminists and nationalists to give up their particularisms but to aid the development from within these streams of a new concrete universalism, one produced by immanent critiques – not imposed from the outside. As part of the struggle for the reformulation of the concrete universal, members of autonomous movements must be willing to risk being called racist for challenging the exclusivity of black oppression, sexist for challenging women to confront class reality, anti-Semitic for demanding that Jews do not treat themselves as a chosen people. It is not incumbent upon them to admire fawningly extreme varieties of Afrocentrism, types of feminism that advocate abstinence from heterosexual relations, or uncritical phylosemitism.

---

[7] K. Anthony Appiah, "Identity, Authenticity, Survival: Multicultural Societies and Social Reproduction," in *Multiculturalism* edited by Amy Gutmann (Princeton University Press, 1994) p. 161.

[8] See my forthcoming *The Subversion of Politics: Civil Luddites and the Decolonization of Everyday Life* (Humanities Press, 1997).

The present fragmentation of social movements preconditions a universal identity of human beings as a species – not as nations, genders or races – an end point that can only be achieved by going through, not ignoring or treating as "secondary" categories of oppression imposed upon us by a system based on heteronomous control (externally inflicted). The road from the abstract universal of "modernist" thought (the positing of a proletarian or other form of universality which corresponded to that of white males) to the future formulation of a concrete multicultural universal necessarily passes through identity politics. Unlike the proletariat, no one identity is the vast majority of society, nor is one by itself able to stop the functioning of the system and reconstruct it. Therefore multiple centers of revolutionary thought and action are historical necessities posing the features of a decentered future society in the making. Identity politics begin the process of unlocking the structures of domination, a process which might eventually result in deconstructing ascriptive identities entirely and reformulating ourselves as autonomous human beings essentially free of externally imposed shackles.

Most analysts of new social movements entirely miss this point. One of the distinguishing characteristics of new social movements, at least as the term is commonly used in academic and research circles, is their specialization, their existence as a fragmentary critique of society, often as little more than interest-group politics conducted by non-traditional means. Accordingly, the anti-nuclear power movement, for example, deals exclusively with the issue of nuclear power plants and nuclear waste disposal. Attempts to link that movement with the feminist movement's call for a new technology based not on the domination and destruction of the environment but on a harmonious relationship with Nature are thought to combine two different movements.[9] The Black movement similarly is understood as having little to do with ecology when in fact, in the 1990's in the U.S., it took the lead in green activism.[10]

[9] One source which demonstrates ecofeminism's breadth is Irene Diamond and Gloria Orenstein's *Reweaving the World: The Emergence of Ecofeminism* (Sierra Club Books, 1990).

[10] See Patrick Novotny's discussion of the "Gulf Coast Tenants' Organization and the SouthWest Organizing Project" in *New Political Science* #32 (Summer 1995).

New social movement theory may be accurate in describing the forms that actions take when observed by outsiders, but it fails to comprehend the sources of protests and the ways in which synchronic movements can form an organic whole.[11] Most significantly, its compartmentalization of new social movements theoretically obliterates in advance the possibility of transforming society as a whole, thereby insidiously maintaining the status quo. Within the vast domain of the literature on "new social movements" in the U.S., fragmented pressure groups become real, and the universal reality of revolutionary social movements "untrue." As Margit Mayer describes social movement research in the U.S.:

> Disaggregated and issue-specific movements that refrain from totalizing their demands flourish all over this country, but movements demanding radical societal change have always remained relatively marginal. Such radical or socialist currents were once again even more marginalized by their omission in social movement research. Questions pertaining to their development and dynamic hardly appear in recent American social movement research.[12]

In my view, the current fragmentation of social movements is a transitional phenomenon, a response both to the conservative character of these times and to the historic restructuring of global capitalism. The most salient feature of identity politics, the fragmentation of constituency, arose after the popular movement of the 1960's had disintegrated. As the unifying effects of the revolutionary upsurge subsided and the forces set in motion continued along separate paths, the system's logic of compartmentalization and atomization asserted itself within the opposition. The distance from the

---

[11] The voluminous literature on the theory of new social movements is itself the subject of articles and books. A good attempt to contextualize theory and practice since the 1960s is the last chapter of Barbara Epstein's *Political Protest and Cultural Revolution: Nonviolent Direct Action in the 1970s and 1980s* (University of California Press, 1991). An anthology which contains empirical observations on Germany is Roland Roth and Dieter Rucht (editors), *Neue Soziale Bewegungen in der Bundesrepublik Deutschland* (Bundeszentrale für Politische Bildung, 1987).

[12] Margit Mayer, "Social Movement Research in the United States: A European Perspective," p. 474.

New Left – the myriad of organizations and individuals that converged in 1968 to form what I've called a world historical movement – to identity politics is partially the difference between the existence of a popular movement challenging the world system and the defeat of that upsurge and dispersal of its many components.

In manifestos like the Port Huron statement, the early New Left spoke of universal needs like increasing democracy but framed its discussions abstractly – without any real understanding of racism and sexism. Like Soviet Communists, they were incapable of integrating racism and patriarchy into their analysis of society. When SNCC expelled white activists in 1965, they sang the first stanza in the contemporary chorus of identity politics. Passing through the phase of Black Power – the prototypical formulation of identity politics – a new concrete universal appeared momentarily at the Black Panther Party's Revolutionary Peoples Constitutional Convention.[13]

To Todd Gitlin, identity politics is an unfortunate consequence of this later phase of the New Left. Like other historians whose roots are in the early phase of the movement, he fails to comprehend this history entirely, in part because he dropped out of the movement when it entered its radical phase. For Gitlin and others, identity politics is a term used to establish a hierarchy of importance that prioritizes new social movements over those defined as universalistic. He believes identity politics leads to struggles that are not against the "real enemy." For Gitlin:

> ... the proliferation of identity politics leads to a turning inward, a grim and hermetic bravado which takes the ideological form of paranoid, jargon-clotted postmodernist groupthink, cult celebrations

[13] Many activists from the early New Left, particularly those who subsequently became historians, were uninvolved then, and their histories pay little or no attention to the more than 10,000 participants in that gathering in Philadelphia who experienced the energy of commonality amid difference. The documents from the Revolutionary Peoples' Constitutional Convention reveal that identity politics complete with autonomous female and black groups can indeed formulate universally transcendent visions. These were small first steps, but the library full of debates about the promise of identity politics would be enriched by consulting this instance of historical praxis. See *The Imagination of the New Left: A Global Analysis of 1968* (South End Press, 1987) pp. 203, 265-279.

of victimization, and stylized marginality.[14]

To be sure, identity politics contains its own internal contradictions: Within every form it is both a universalistic promise and a particularistic chauvinism (In his life, Malcolm X contained both within himself). A failure to comprehend the contradictory character of identity politics unites both their advocates and opponents. Identity politics can keep the movement divided against itself (as Gitlin understands) or point to one structure of domination and overlook another. It can also obscure the existence of a common class enemy — the wealthiest families, top managers and their corporations and governments. By itself, identity politics are not sufficient to transform qualitatively problematic political-economic structures. Indeed, not only is it insufficient for the formulation of a revolutionary transcendence of the class-structured multinational corporate world system, they sometimes conceal that very system by seeking to treat as identical a variety of people who occupy very different positions within the system.[15]

In an epoch when capital's velocity and mobility are at unprecedented levels, identity politics reflects the fragmentation of the proletariat's universal subjectivity. To the extent that material conditions affect social consciousness, the dispersal of production, the adaptation of capitalist principles to all the major institutions of society, and the commodification of everyday life condition the fragmentation

---

[14] Todd Gitlin, "Fragmentation of the Idea of the Left," in Craig Calhoun (editor) *Social Theory and the Politics of Identity* (Blackwell, 1994) p. 166.

[15] By constructing the identity "female," for example, to conflate the interests of New York's super-wealthy women and the poorest women of Bombay, enormous differences are obscured, and the world system of stratification unthematized.

In 1991, the United Nations reported that the top one-fifth of the world's population controlled 83% of its total wealth and the bottom one-fifth only 1.4%. The difference between the world's rich and poor had roughly doubled in thirty years. Alongside 202 billionaires, more than one billion people lived in the worst poverty and 400 million were close to starvation. The average per capita income in the South (the Third World) in 1987 was $670 compared to a corresponding figure of $12,000 in the North. See Walter Corson (editor), *The Global Ecology Handbook* (Beacon Press, 1990) p. 44.

Identity politics can be a means of glossing over this crucial schism in the world, a means of turning attention to the needs of those at the top in relation to each other, not in relation to the whole. As observed in my case studies of autonomous women's movements, however, Italian and German feminists recognized that emancipation within the corporate world is not the same as liberation from it. See my forthcoming *The Subversion of Politics*.

of proletarian subjectivity.[16] Under post-Fordist conditions, capital's global nature makes the seizure of national political power increasingly superfluous (as the fates of Cuba, Vietnam and Nicaragua indicate). Immanuel Wallerstein has formulated this notion as the transition from the state to civil society as object of transformation. Even within the world of corporations, the demographic reconstruction of the working class calls for a multicultural analysis. The working class does not consist predominantly of white, European males (since production is increasingly global and everywhere involves women and non-whites). They understand cooperation as global and multicultural, not simply "social" in terms of the immediate community. To the extent they become revolutionary, their international commitment will be to ecology, feminism, racial solidarity and peace, not any nation-state. Seen in this context, identity politics provides the basis for a free society worthy of the name. It is a necessary step in the development of a new universality that recognizes race and gender as significant domains of a broader historical framework. It is necessary to deconstruct these structures of domination in everyday life.

Making the case for the potential universality of identity politics does not mean that I project their categories as eternally valid. Every time I travel to Germany, the fact that racial categories are socially constructed becomes palpably clear to me. I leave the United Sates as a white person, but when I land in Germany, my Mediterranean features mean that I am a "person of color" (most commonly thought to be a Turk). By referring to my experiences in Germany, I point to the larger reality that race and racism are social constructions, not essential dimensions of the human condition. This statement should not be interpreted to mean that race is inconsequential. Rather, recognizing the social dimension of categories of identity is a step in their transformation.

---

[16] Frances Fox Piven's discussion at the American Political Science Association meetings in 1993 was a significant stimulus to this insight.

Antonia Darder & Rodolfo D. Torres
Claremont Graduate School
& California State University, Long Beach

From Race to Racism:
The Politics of "Race" Language in
"Postmodern Education"

There has been a tendency in postmodern and poststructuralist appraisals of the multicultural project and "race relations" to neglect or ignore profound changes in the structural nature and dynamics of US late-capitalism. At a time when an analysis of capitalism is needed more than ever before, many radical writers (as Ellen Meiksins Wood argues) are busy conceptualizing away the very idea of capitalism. Recent structural changes in the US political economy have made the issues of "race" and racism much more complex than ever before. Rather than occupying a central position, these historical and socioeconomic changes serve merely as the backdrop to the contemporary theoretical debates on the meaning of "race" and "representation" in a "postmodern" society. This represents a significant point of contention, given the dramatic changes in US class formations during the last thirty years. These changes include major shifts in perceptions of social location, prevailing attitudes, and contemporary views and representations of racialized populations.

Recent works in cultural studies, multicultural education, and critical pedagogy have brought new theoretical perspectives to the study of racism and education in society. US scholars such as Cornel West, Michael Omi, bell hooks, Henry Giroux, and others have attempted to recast the debate on the nature of "race" and racism in this county and its implications for social change and educational reform. Although it cannot be denied that these provocative works represent a challenge to the mainstream analysis of "race relations" and have made contributions to our understanding of the significance of racism, they have failed to reconceptualize the traditional social science paradigm that relies on the reified category of "race" to interpret racialized social relations. In the final analysis the conceptual framework utilized by these scholars is entrenched in the convèntional sociology of "race relations" language.

Critique of Multicultural Education Discussions

Nowhere has this theoretical shortcoming been more evident than in contemporary discussions of multicultural education which have been fundamentally shaped by parochial notions of "race," identity, ethnicity, and culture. Despite an expressed "transformative" intent, much of the multicultural education literature has only peripherally positioned public education within the larger context of class relations. Conspicuously absent from much of the writings of even critical multicultural education scholars is a substantial critique of the social relations and structures of capitalism and the relationship of educational practices to the changing conditions of the US political economy. The absence of an analysis of the capitalist wage-labor system and class relations with its structural inequalities of income and power is a serious shortcoming.

A lack of imagination in multicultural education discussions is highly evidenced by a discourse that continues to be predominantly anchored in the Black/White dichotomous framework that has for over a century dictated our thinking and scholarship related to social group differences. One of the most severe and limited aspects of the Black/White framework to the future of the anti-racist project is its tendency (albeit unintentionally) to obstruct or camouflage the need to examine the particular historical and contextual dimensions that give rise to differing forms of racism around the globe. Further, this conflation of racialized relations into solely a Black/White paradigm has prevented scholars from engaging more fully with the specificities of particular groups and delving more fully into the arena of comparative ethnic histories of racism and how these are linked to class forms of social oppression.

Although some would be quick to object to our critique of the multicultural literature, we can see the above at work, for example, in the manner in which critical education scholars have focused their studies in Latino communities. Overall, studies with Latino populations have placed an overwhelming emphasis on linguistic questions tied to identity and culture.

This is illustrated by the large body of education literature that focuses on issues of "language-minority" students, while only marginally discussing the impact of racism and class position on identity and cultural formations – as if somehow the problems of Latino students can be resolved through simply the enactment of language policy.

"Race" as a Social Construct

We would be hard-pressed to find a progressive social scientist in this day and age who would ascribe to the use of "race" as a determinant of specific social phenomenon associated with levels of intelligence or personality characteristics. Nevertheless, traditional arguments about "race" dominate academic and popular discourse. What does it mean to attribute analytical status to the idea of "race" and use it as an explanatory concept in educational discussions of theory or practice? The use of "race" as an analytical category means to position it as a central organizing theoretical principle in deconstructing social relations of difference in the world. For this reason, the idea of "race" should not be employed as a analytical category within the social sciences, and it follows from this that the object of study should not be described as "race relations." Hence, we reject the race relations problematic as the locus for analysis of racism. But we do not reject the concept of racism. Rather, we critique the "race relations" problematic in order to retain a concept of racism which is constructed in such a way as to recognize the existence of a plurality of historically specfic racisms, not all of which employ explicitly the idea of "race."

Unfortunately, the continued use of the notion of "race" in education research, whether intentional or not, upholds a definition of "race" as a causal factor. In other words, significance and meaning is attributed to phenotypical features, rather than the relationship of difference to the historically reproduced complex processes of racialization. The disturbing "scientific" assertion that race determines academic performance made by Richard J. Hernstein & Charles Murray in their book *The Bell Curve,* illustrates the theoretical minefield of perpetuating such an analytical category in the social sciences and the potential negative consequences upon

African-American students and other racialized groups. The use of the term "race" serves to hide the truth that it is not "race" which determines academic performance; but rather, that academic performance is determined by an interplay of complex social processes, one of which is premised on the articulation of racism to effect exclusion in the clasroom and beyond.

The habitual practice of framing social relations as "race relations" in discussions of racialized groups and schooling obfuscates the complexity of the problem. Here educational theorists assign certain significance to "racial" characteristics rather than attributing student responses to school conditions and how these are shaped by the structure of society and the economic and political limitations which determine the conditions in which students must achieve. The unfortunate absence of this critique veils the real reasons why students underachieve, perform poorly on standardized tests, are overrepresented in remedial programs, underrepresented in gifted programs and magnet schools, and continue to dropout of high school at alarming rates. As a consequence, educational solutions are often derived from distorted perceptions of the problem.

The politics of busing in the early 1970s provides an excellent example to illustrate this phenomenon of distortion. Social scientists studying "race" relations concluded that proximal contact among Black and White students would decrease the incidence of prejudice and that the education conditions of Black students would improve if they were bused to White (better) schools outside of their neighborhoods. Thirty years later, there are many progressive parents and educators who adamantly condemn the busing solution (a solution based on a discourse of "race") as not only fundamentally destructive to the fabric of Black and Latino communities, but an erroneous social experiment that failed to improve the academic performance of the children in these communities.

Yet, despite the dangerous forms of distortion which arise from the use of "race" as a central analytical category of theory making, critical education scholars seem unable to break with the hegemonic tradition of its use in the social sciences. Efforts to problematize the reified nature of the term "race" and consider its elimination as metaphor in our work, quickly is met with major resistance among even progressive intellectuals of all communities – a resistance that is expressed through anxiety, trepidation, fear, and even anger. Often these responses are associated to fear of delegitmating the historical movements for liberation that have been principally defined in terms of "race" struggles. Such responses demonstrate the tenacious and adhesive quality of socially constructed ideas and how through their historical usage these ideas become common sense notions that resist deconstruction.

Racisms: Breaking Out of the Black/White Dichotomy

The unproblematized "common sense" acceptance of "race" as a legitimate way to frame social relations finds its way into the classroom. Since the school mirrors the ideological and material structure of the society at large, it is an institution that is powerful enough to socialize and condition students' "racial" perceptions of subordinate groups through the hidden racialized dimensions of the curriculum, textbooks, and classroom life. These racialized perceptions are then projected and internalized by both students of subordinate and dominant populations and, in turn, are used to frame or make conclusions about social relationships, including how they define racism and how they perceive and respond to different forms of racialized discourses and events that involve African-American, as well as other subordinate populations.

To address the issues raised above requires a willingness to shift from talking about "race" to talking about racism(s) and the concept of racialization as a historically specfic ideological process. In other words, progressive scholars should not be trying to seek a critical theory of "race," for this can only lead us down a dead end road that will leave us intellectually bankrupt and further disillusioned by our failure to effectively struggle against conditions of racism in this country and abroad. Instead critical scholars should seek to retrieve a global perspective of historically defined racialized relations and acknowledge the plurality of racisms at work. We are not playing semantics, but proposing an alternative analytic framework in identifying the structures and representations of the contours of racialization. To construct a new language for examining the nature of these racisms requires an understanding of how complex relationships of exploitation and resistance, grounded in differences of class, gender, and ethnicity, give rise to a multiplicity of ideological constructions of the racialized other. This knowledge challenges the traditional notion of racism as solely a Black/White dichotomous phenomenon and directs us toward a more accurately constructed, and hence more politically useful, idea of racisms and the relations of power that shape the social conditions racialized groups face in schools and society.

Implications for Culturally Democratic Education

It is impossible to move schools toward culturally democratic forms of education if the impact of racialized relations and the political economy upon subordinate populations is overlooked. One of the best examples of this blindspot is apparent in the manner in which violence is racialized and systematically identified, defined, and addressed in different schools and communities. For example, when one of the authors was living in Boston a few years ago, a professional, White woman was raped and killed in Cambridge. The Boston community was up in arms. In the midst of all this movement, little attention was given to the fact that several homicides and rapes of Black women had occurred during the same month in Roxbury, a low-income African-American community. The racialized and class-based message inherent in the response of the larger community was that women in Cambridge were deemed more important and valuable, while women in Roxbury were considered disposable. The same dynamics are often present in the racialized expectations held by teachers toward students of different communities and their attitudes toward the achievement potential of these students.

In considering a shift from talking about "race" to talking about racisms, what is clear is that we need a new language by which to construct culturally democratic notions of educational theory and practice. This entails the recasting and reinterpretation of education issues in a language with greater specificity, which explicitly reflects anti-racist notions of society. Such a language must unquestionably be linked to global histories of social movements against inequality and injustice. Although we fully recognize that a new language will not necessarily alter the power relations in any given society, it can serve to more accurately articulate how power is maintained through the systematic racialization of subordinate populations. As such, a new language can provide the foundation for developing effective educational policies that are directly linked to emancipatory principles of cultural and economic democracy.

What we are arguing for is a new theoretical language that reflects the existence of a plurality of racisms – a new language from which educational scholars can reconstruct school curriculum and education programs to more accurately reflect and address the different forms of social and material inequities that shape the lives of students from subordinate groups. Most importantly, this calls for a new language that reinforces and supports our common anti-racist struggle for social justice and economic democracy across ethnic communities in the United States and throughout the world. There are many who have proclaimed the death of the socialist project, but we argue that its renaissance is close at hand and will be articulated through a new language that is fueled by the courage and passion to break with those hegemonic traditions on the left that fail to support a democratic vision of life for all people.

Edward Yuen
University of California, Santa Cruz

Social Movements, Identity Politics and the Genealogy of the Term "People of Color"[1]

The increasing prominence of identity politics in movements for social change has elicited a variety of responses from left intellectuals. Some, like former SDS leader Todd Gitlin, view identity politics as fundamentally at odds with the very idea of the left, in both its liberal and Marxist incarnations. For Gitlin, the decline of the commonality politics he knew in the early New Left and the "thickening" of identity politics of the last two decades are inseparable. As he puts it: "things fell apart *because* the center could not hold."[2] With the decline of the universal subject of history (the proletariat) and the obsolescence of the "universal midwife" (the revolutionary), oppositional politics from the 60's on can be seen to be searching for, in Gitlin's terms, a "surrogate universal." After various attempts at composing a new universality (or at least agency) were exhausted, the movement fragmented into the various difference based political formations that are prevalent today. Gitlin sees in this dispersion the end of the central ideas which for him define the left. By abandoning not only the idea of a universal collectivity but also the very language of collectivity, Gitlin feels that the left has conceded its most appealing characteristics to the right, which is making tremendous political headway using the language of universals. Gitlin stops short of saying it, but it is clear that, for him, the "cultural left" and movements of identity politics are not really of the left at all.

It is hard not to read Gitlin's musings and connect it to his own political biography, since it is undeniably true that as an elite white male leader of the early New Left, he personally lost a tremendous amount of power in the break-ups of the late 1960's. What is clear is that, in focusing so

[1] I would like to thank Barbara Epstein, Herman Gray, Donna Haraway, George Katsiaficas and Dana Takagi.

[2] Gitlin, Todd, "The Rise of 'Identity Politics'; an Examination and a Critique". *Dissent,* Spring, 1993.

single-mindedly on the political losses incurred by the breakup of the universal subject, Gitlin pays short shrift to the concerns of those who were on the margins of the vaunted collectivity. Certainly Gitlin does not take seriously the possibility that mandatory universality may itself be a form of oppression (although he can certainly see this when it occurs on the right!). Nevertheless, Gitlin does offer some trenchant observations about the slide to essentialism evident in some identity politics as well as the possible triviality (or lack of ambition) of some of its goals.

These issues are picked up in a much less defensive way by Barbara Epstein, who is far more understanding of the impulse for identity politics but nevertheless bemoans the "collective powerlessness" which afflicts "the left" (an identification which, as she herself points out, barely exists anymore). Epstein is particularly disconcerted by "the intersection of identity politics and moralism,"[3] the creation of an atmosphere of "self-intimidation" in which people are afraid to comment on or name difference outside of their own experience. Epstein attributes this "political correctness" (a term she attempts to separate from its rightist usage), to the humorless and guilt inducing exigencies of narrow identity politics. She likens the current situation to the old left atmosphere of conformity in which "correct lineism" was utilized to keep healthy discussion in check. In the present case, though, the bludgeon is used not to put people in line for a long range goal but to establish immediate moral supremacy. At its worst, radical politics has degenerated into a game of moral one-upmanship with no impact outside of the academy.

For better or worse, critics such as Epstein and Gitlin retain a certain nostalgia for the grand leftist meta-narrative of history and a certain expectation of what "politics" is or should be. Rather than engage in the debate over post-structuralism and the possibility of "politics" I would instead like to examine the ways in which identity politics intersects with the traditional terrain of left politics. It is in this intersection that we may witness the possibilities for new alliances to be formed and the creation not only of new politics

---

[3] Epstein, Barbara, "'Political Correctness' and Collective Powerlessness," *Socialist Review*, 91, 3/4 1991:13.

but of new identities as well. One recent example of an emergent form of political alliance based on complex identities is Queer Nation, which is described by L.A. Kaufman as being a kind of "post-identity politics of sorts."[4] Within the San Francisco chapter of this group, race, class, gender and political values were all included in the construction of a "queer" identity. "Queerness", as Kaufman notes, "was more a posture of opposition than a simple statement about sexuality." Another example was Roots Against War (RAW), a Bay Area group that attempted to organize "people of color" against the 1990-1991 Persian Gulf war.

I would like to take the lead of Kobena Mercer and emulate his tracing of the "radical reconstruction of black subjectivity" in Britain.[5] One thing which emerges is that the various imaginary forms of identification (Benedict Anderson's "imagined communities[6]") are constantly in flux. Mercer argues that the British construction /black/ (which includes people of Asian, African and Caribbean descent), arises not out of a "binary reversal or a closed anti-white sensibility" but rather from "a pluralistic sense of imagined community."[7] Mercer cites the empowering nature of this move: by constructing an identity based on political rather than biological similarities, the /black/ movement in Britain has articulated a radically pluralistic community. In this articulation are the well-springs of a counter-hegemonic bloc.[8] The term "people of color" in the United States shares a genealogy in common with the British /black/ but has, if anything, a longer history. This has not been reflected in the literature, however. Much of the literature on racial formation focuses on the historical origins of Whiteness as a racial category.[9] Another set of literature maps the shifting categories of black, Chicano, Asian-American, Native American and

---

[4] Kaufman, L.A., "Radical Change: The Left Attacks Identity Politics," *Village Voice*, June 30, 1992.

[5] Mercer, Kobena, *Welcome to the Jungle*, p287, Routledge, New York, 1995.

[6] Anderson, Benedict. *Imagined Communities; Reflections on the Origin and Spread of Nationalism.* Verso, London, 1983.

[7] Mercer, p291.

[8] This category appears to be currently in crisis. See: Rushdie: *Cultural Translator or Object of Communal Wrath* by Behrooz Ghamariushdie-Tabrizi; unpublished paper, UC Santa Cruz Sociology, 1991.

[9] See Alexander Saxton, *The Rise and Fall of the White Republic*, Verso, New York, 1990.

other cultural and/or political identities. Taken together, this work is complementary but not complete; it leaves unexamined a unique political formation created in the crossfire of white supremacy and identity politics. By this I am referring to the imagined community of "people of color." This racial project is more than just the "dark other" of the supremacist white subject. It is my argument that there is a history among non-white peoples of an affirmative construction of unified identity and solidarity along the common axis of being "colored," "third world" or "other." While often either ignored or taken for granted, this formation is seldom given its due as a racial project like any of the others.

There are three reasons why I think the category of Third World/People of Color (henceforth TW/POC) is important. First of all, the origins, evolution and implications of the term have not, to my knowledge, been rigorously analyzed and debated in academia. This is in contrast to the serious and scholarly treatment which the terms "Women of Color" and "British /Black/" have generated. One could conclude that the valence of the American term TW/POC is widely viewed as either too obvious or too trivial to remark upon. If the former is the case, then it should be noted that this obviousness is itself remarkable, since the term is potentially counter-hegemonic, as I will later argue. If the latter is true, than the current outbreak of hostilities among "minorities" would not be perceived as the crisis that it is. Clearly, in the mid-1990's, the construction POC is a site of contestation which must be understood and not merely assumed.

A second reason why TW/POC is an important racial project has to do with its potential as a key category of new social movements. As we will see, the categories of TW and POC emerged from the social movements of the 1960's and have continued to be associated with radical democratic and left political projects. The formation TW/POC has served many purposes in progressive political discourse; it has stood in for "the working class" as the agent of historical change; it has served as a "meta-narrative" of otherness to counteract essentialist claims of nationalism; and it has acted as a site upon which progressive people of color can construct their own politics. Moreover, this association of TW/POC with left political projects is no mere historical accident; for reasons to be explored, hegemonic and reactionary political projects tend to find the term ideologically problematic. Like "women of color" and the British "Black," TW/POC is an identity which is potentially charged with counter-hegemonic politics simply by its naming.

Finally, the formation of TW/POC is important because of the space it opens up for people of color to encounter each other without the mediation of the "white gaze." Although the formation of TW/POC is, at face value, a unified binary to "whiteness," the most significant work that it does is to hook up direct communication between the various people who identify with the sign. It is often remarked upon in groups of people of color (and women of color as well) how refreshing it is to be away from the white (male) gaze, if only temporarily. Without the historically embedded asymmetries and hierarchies which haunt the relationships of whites to "others," people of color are sometimes able to engage in the kinds of sharing and appreciation of each others cultures which are so often elusive to mainstream "multicultural" projects. I say "sometimes" because this is clearly not always the case. People of color may have a bitter history amongst themselves as well, and even if much of it was orchestrated by white supremacy,[10] that does not make it any less strongly felt. Even more importantly, people of color have internalized the white gaze just as women have internalized the male gaze. To the extent that people of color identify as TW/POC however, they attempt to combat this "orientalism" and internalized racism whenever possible. For this reason, the TW/POC formation is important as a prefigurative project of embracing difference.

Although there is no space here to discuss it at length, it is clear that from the earliest constructions of "whiteness" there were also constructions of "non-whiteness" and that those who were being constituted as "other" were, at times, cognizant of the nature of their oppression. At various times during this process, there have been instances of "colored" people constructing themselves as a united and oppositional subject. As "whiteness" was being constructed in the sixteenth to nineteenth centuries, other racialized identities were being

---

[10] Examples of this might include the "Buffalo Soldiers" or the mobilization of African-American, Latino and Native-American troops in the Vietnam war.

formed as well. "Negroes" and, to a lesser extent, "Indians" were forced to abandon their "tribal" (itself a colonial category) identities and become a unified people largely defined by their common physical characteristics. The processes by which this move was completed and the extent to which the non-white peoples themselves initiated or constructed such a move are essential amendments to Alexander Saxton's story of "the rise and fall of the White republic." The history of such proto-nationalist movements as Nat Turner's rebellion and the Ghost Dance movement (the latter a pan-Indian movement) are testimony to the mobilizing power of racialized identity projects in this period.

Once the move from tribal affiliation to "Negro" or "Indian" has been made, the identification as a "colored" person open to alliance with other "colored" people seems a small step. Indeed, there is a literature on "Black Indians" and Maroon communities which indicates that such an alliance did take place at many times throughout the Western hemisphere.[11] Seen in this light, then, the explosion of Third World solidarity in the 1960's was but a continuation of a pattern of alliance stretching back at least to the early 19th century.

The key element in the "racing" of non-white peoples lies in the moment when they resign themselves to the decentering of their own subject position and accept a Eurocentric world view, with themselves inhabiting a peripheral position (one of many). Just as European immigrants had to be actively made into "whites" by a variety of cultural and political institutions, so too did people of color have to be made into "coloreds." The varying speeds and methods by which this happened made for a very heterogeneous history of colonial resistance, and helps to explain why a self-conscious "Third World" position did not develop in this period.

By the early to middle 20th century, an important shift in racial ideology was taking place in the United States. Michael Omi and Howard Winant characterize this shift as being from a "biological" paradigm of racial difference, which was predicated on a notion of essential biological inequality, to an "ethnicity" paradigm which defines racial difference in

---

[11] See William Katz, *Black Indians: A Hidden Heritage*, Atheneum, New York,1986.

cultural and social terms.[12] This shift was made necessary, they argue, because the biological paradigm was no longer compatible with the egalitarian ideals and anti-fascism of the corporate liberalism which was becoming hegemonic. While this is undeniably true, it seems to ignore the resistance of colonized and oppressed peoples and the role this struggle played in forcing a paradigm shift. Articulations of unified resistance were becoming increasingly loud, and the vocabulary of racial unity had already been inadvertently laid in place by the colonial masters. Even the Japanese militarists, in their justification of the "Greater East Asia Co-prosperity Sphere," claimed that their intervention was done on behalf of Asians and against Whites.

The superiority of the ethnicity paradigm to the biological paradigm in fragmenting anti-colonial/anti-racist projects is evidenced by the continuance to this day of neo-conservative and neo-liberal theories based on its premises. Ideologically, the ethnicity paradigm was able to undermine the basis of solidarity among people of color; after all, if assimilation was a desirable and attainable goal, politics based on difference could be cast as "divisive." If integration and assimilation, when successful, served to diffuse inter-group solidarity, the consequences for intra-group solidarity would be even more severe.

As Omi and Winant point out, the hegemony of the ethnicity paradigm turned out to be rather short-lived. Nevertheless, it did leave one legacy that is only very recently being challenged: the "invisibility" of whiteness. With the shift away from overt white supremacy to an official ideology of color blindness (what Ruth Frankenberg names "color evasiveness" and "power evasiveness"),[13] whiteness embeds itself discretely in the language of normality. Like a black hole exerting an invisible gravitational pull on its surrounding cosmos, "whiteness," to the extent that it is unmarked, still organizes all other races as "other." It is this legacy that will give "people of color" its salience when it emerges from the struggles of the 1960's.

---

[12] Omi, Michael and Winant, Howard, *Racial Formation in the United States*, Routledge, New York. 1986.

[13] Frankenberg, Ruth, *White Women, Race Matters*, p139, University of Minnesota Press, Minneapolis, 1993.

In the context of the social movements of the 1960's, the identification with the Third World on the part of blacks and other people of color in the United States became widespread. Indeed, this period is surely the high water mark of "Third World" solidarity in the United States. From the Bandung Conference to Malcolm X's last speeches to the politics of the Black Panther Party and sister (or, more likely, brother) organizations like the Young Lords, Brown Berets and Red Guards, Third World people seemed to be actively creating a common site of struggle from which to learn from and assist each other. The Third World Strikes at SF State and UC Berkeley were perhaps the most explicitly united movements of "Third World" alliance, but, ideologically, they were by no means exceptional.[14] During this period, the agenda of many radical nationalists coincided with that of the New Left. Indeed, a case could be made that a paradigm shift within the international left was taking place in which the "Third World" was replacing the proletariat as the agent of revolution. Thus, in this historical moment, the TW/POC formation served as a vehicle not just for expressions of solidarity among people of color but as historical agent upon which expectations of transformation were attached. Although the equation of "Third World" with "Revolution" soon dissipated, some insurgent aura lingered on well into the 1980's. This leftist residue may be one of the reasons why the TW/POC formation has been largely free of co-optation attempts by the right.

In their summation of the various racial projects, Omi and Winant fault some adherents of the internal colonization model for being "romantically fascinated by Third World revolutionary movements whose 'lessons' were largely irrelevant to US conditions."[15] It is recognition of this flaw, I think, that led to the discursive move from "Third World" to "People of Color" in the early 1980's. There are, however, mixed conclusions that can be drawn from this observation. One is that any attempts to draw comparisons between Third World peoples and oppressed minorities in the US were problematic. Another, and perhaps more widely held conclusion, is that there must be a careful balance between solidarity and particularity, with the former not distorting

---

[14] See Munoz, Carlos, *Youth, Identity and Power,* Verso, New York, 1989.

[15] Omi and Winant, p139.

the latter as was sometimes the case in the 60's. It is this view which most closely informs the term "people of color."

It is worthwhile to note, while discussing the excesses of revolutionary solidarity of the 60's, that the identification with foreign struggles was a two way street. For example, the Black Panther Party was imitated in Jamaica, India (among "untouchables") and in Israel (among Sephardic Jews). The point here is that the movements of the 1960's cannot be looked upon solely from a West-centered point of view. Romantic appropriations of Third World chic have their equally bizarre counterparts in the Third World; in some cases, social forms reminiscent of the New Left may have germinated in remote corners of the world, only to unexpectedly sprout when the opportunity arises.[16]

It is in feminist writings that many of the issues concerning the terms "Third World" and "Women of Color" are most seriously debated. In a report on the 1981 National Women's Studies Association Conference, Chela Sandoval discusses the debate over the terms.[17] While "Third World" was seen by some as highlighting international solidarity, having greater political implications and being "decentered from any point of power in order to be used as the negative pole against which the dominant powers can then define themselves," it was criticized by others for diffusing "the naming of our particular oppressions as Americans." "Women of Color" was advocated for as a title that would point out both the "nature of our oppression and the basis of our political solidarity." It was objected to on the grounds that it had "negative connotations" and that not all women "wear their 'color' in the form or color of their bodies." This debate was not resolved at the conference, although it seems that shortly thereafter "women of color" became the predominant term.

While these debates may be similar to those which accompanied the shift from "Third World" to "people of color", it is significant that they took place in feminist and not in

---

[16] The 1989 student movement in China and the "velvet revolution" in Czechoslovakia both contain elements of this dynamic. George Katsiaficas, in *The Imagination of the New Left*, (South End Press, Boston, 1987) calls it the "eros effect".

[17] Anzaldúa, Gloria, *Making Face, Making Soul, Haciendo Caras*, p62, Spinsters/Aunt Lute, San Francisco, 1990.

"left" circles.[18] Clearly, nationalist projects are much less self-reflexive in examining the multiple levels of identity that any named political category implies. One thing that the introduction of the categories of "Third World women" and "women of color" does is to highlight the gendered construction of "Third World" and "people of color." It is interesting to note that just as the solidarity between the male-led "Third World" revolutionary movements begins to decline the solidarity between "Third World women" appears to expand. Just as the women's movement kept alive the New Left tradition of participatory democracy long after it faded with "the movement," so too did women of color continue the legacy of solidarity and affinity which characterized the "Third World" movements of the '60's and '70's.

Where then does this leave the construction "people of color"? In recent years, the construction "men of color" has emerged in its own right. It is certainly possible that, in the near future, the term "people of color" with its non-gendered, non-sexualized and non-classed subject identity will become as problematic as the unmarked category of whiteness. The construction "people of color" retains a certain discursive familiarity to it in many sectors of American society in the 1990's. But while people of color are linked discursively as though they should be united politically, the latter is not always the case. There are two major sources of tension and instability in the term.

In the first place, the question must be asked as to why a term which encompasses the overwhelming majority of the people in the world and a soon to be majority of the state of California should be seen as demarking difference rather than commonalty. As we have seen, the overwhelming reality of white supremacy is the only reason why "people of color" should have any discursive cachet at all. It is not surprising, then, that "person of color" is a highly contingent and reflexive identity. The designation "person of color" is usually at least *two or more* abstractions removed from a person's primary "racial" community. The categories Latino, Asian-American and Native American already collapse smaller, discrete

---

[18] Note the category trouble here - juxtaposing "left" and "feminist" obliterates their intersections.

communities into larger ones which make sense only in an American context. An identification with "people of color" is always, therefore, a statement of pluralism and political community at a fairly high level of abstraction.

This leads us to the second source of instability of the term which is the reality of difference between actual communities of color. As the proverbial "ocean of masses" which left activists must swim in has slowly evaporated since the 1960's, the construction "people of color" increasingly became a shared experience more on college campuses than in communities of work and habitation. As demography, immigration patterns and employment opportunities changed, the lived experience of racism and exploitation under capitalism began to be articulated in new and complex ways. Inter-ethnic tension between communities of color intensified dramatically during the 1980's and 1990's. The promotion of a racial hierarchy with Asians as a "model-minority," conflicts between African-American shoppers and recently immigrated Arab and Korean shopowners, and clashes between Latino police and Black youth in Miami (or vice versa in Washington D.C.) loomed as inescapable barriers to the construction of a "people of color" identity.

At the same time, the Jackson campaigns of the 1980's, the flourishing of ethnic studies boards and "minority discourse" in the academy, and the recrudescence of a thinly veiled white supremacist discourse on the right gave renewed validity to the "people of color" construction among politically active students and young people. Perhaps even more significantly, the cultural landscape of urban California was becoming increasingly characterized by reciprocal appropriation between communities of color. The emergence of hybrid Asian and Mexican fast food in L.A., the "poaching" of Chinese Kung Fu for break dancing moves, and innumerable cross-cultural fashion statements all attested to some of the positive ways in which communities of color interacted with each other in the absence of a majority white urban presence.

The future of the category "people of color" lies in its capacity to articulate a common positioning as the binary to a crumbling white supremacy while at the same time serving as a site of tense but productive interactions between racialized communities who harbor no a priori affirmative notions of solidarity. Increasingly, too, these racialized communities will come to the formation of "people of color" from vastly different economic and political locations. Nevertheless, as long as white supremacy and racism continue to exist, this racial project will retain its discursive salience and political necessity.

Robin M. Chandler
Northwestern University

Notes from the Briar Patch:
Art at the Cultural Crossroads
The Case of Caravan for International Culture

> "The good road and the road of difficulties were
> made to cross; and where they cross, the place is
> holy." -Black Elk[1]

The American arts community is learning some valuable lessons about retooling for the year 2000 through its maverick past and its insistence on the indispensability of creativity in the cultural life of the American people. The floodlights of arts advocacy expose an international arena in which the arts community has advanced the projects of art education, art history and artist agency in more meaningful ways than we have ever seen. The crossroads at which policy debates, public/private sector support, social control, censorship and power are embattled have become superhighway rotaries where many have pitched their tents. The education of the child as a central focus of these controversial shifts is often lost in the educational and political melee.

I emerged from the studio in the late 1970's, art weapons in hand (studio and education degrees and field experience) and a pilot program was shaped for implementation in Massachusetts schools. This essay is about CARAVAN FOR INTERNATIONAL CULTURE (CIC), an integrated arts-based educational model in cultural studies for the elementary and secondary classroom. As part of a much more wide-sweeping arc of educators, artists, and community-based organizations, CIC was activated by the rhythm of a "new movement" that grew out of fresh thinking about the relationships of the politics of knowledge, human unity and political empowerment and how to bring these realities to the service of children. CIC focused on these in three principle ways.

---

[1] *Black Elk Speaks,* New York: Pocket Books, 1977, p.232.

First, the relationship between public policy, the arts and individual learning has been a fact of American public education since the 1960's with the establishment of the NEA (1965) and subsequent artist-in-schools programs administered through state agencies and state arts councils. In 1980 CIC rode the wave of the artist-in-schools initiatives when it was at its greatest maturation. Second, the need for curriculum development and teacher-training models was an important element of this process. Training in these areas enhanced the studio experience by providing a professional language of assessment, developmental learning style, cognition, methodology, and professional development tutorial, thereby making it possible to engage in frank and honest exchange with front liners – classroom teachers. Third, the global identity of CIC was situated at a crossroads of multiple identities, a point in history when one of the great debates of the Twentieth Century, yet unresolved, would eventually make its way into every facet of human life. Cultural difference, race and gender are the languages of passion at the watershed of the new century. How we learn to interpret, communicate and implement these languages will determine the direction of education in general and arts education.

The Political Two-Step: Two Steps Forward, One Back

The nationalization of the debates on art production, First Amendment rights and the role artists play as recipients of government subsidization has been a hotly contested issue in the last decade following sweeping cuts to the NEA beginning in 1975 and continuing into the year 2000. As NEA director, Jane Alexander has reminded us, our government spends more on military bands than on the arts. Public school children, once the major benefactors of program interventions in the arts in American classrooms, are now less likely to receive broad-based arts training than their predecessors of the 1950's. What do these shifts mean for children? How have the corporate world and public education officials collaborated or contended with political interests, arts lobbies and other partnerships to extend or diminish national debates on arts inclusion? Quantitative and qualitative measures report on the value of the arts and artists in the classroom, yet public policy has shifted away from open debate on American education and the individual learner. It has allied itself with the more lucrative, commercial and titillating aspects of arts production through popular culture venues. Armchair critics of free speech see dollar signs in attaching their energies to despoiling individual artists and their works. Once they realize that the more sensational forms of art production rarely make it into the traditional classroom and that the "traditional classroom" is itself undergoing a conceptual expansion, their time would be better spent independently investigating the hard work of arts organizations, artists and others who remain at their posts in arts education without "fear of fire or hope of paradise."

The strangely encouraging global picture in community-based arts organizing includes many countries (some repressive regimes, some newly democratized, others experimental democracies similar to ours, who despite ideological imperatives, have formulated resilient bonds of multi-racial unity and a dedication to education in the arts). Bonds thus forged translate into technical art skills, cognitive development, teacher-learner exchange and social action which make art accessible to children and youth both in the classroom and in society. Based on fieldwork and data collected in Brazil and South Africa (1988-1994), I discuss arts communities which have carried their initiatives forward in innovative ways, continuing a long history of advocacy, networks of cooperation, national coalitions, and political activism in the face of retrenchment and economic recession. During this period of development in the 1980's, CIC objectives were furthered by contact with many colleagues through INSEA (International Society for Education Through Art), among them J.B. Akolo (Institute of Education, Ahmadu Bello University) of Nigeria and Ana Mae Barbosa, former (recent) President of INSEA and Director of the Museum of Contemporary Art at the University of São Paulo in Brazil.

The capstone of these exchanges produced a CARAVAN which, by the mid-1980's, focused attention on teacher-training as a basic element of the teaching-learning model. Before discussing the CIC professional development component, an understanding of the history of CIC is critical in situating the interface between artist practice and arts education in the 1980's.

The Way We Were

As a masters level graduate student, my fields of concentration were interdisciplinary: art history, art education and curriculum development, and multicultural studies. Shortly after opening a studio in Boston and launching a professional career in the visual arts, I became a consultant to many cultural institutions: the Museum of Fine Arts department of education, the Massachusetts Prison Art Project, the Learning Guild, the Massachusetts Council on the Arts and Humanities, the Artist's Foundation and the Cultural Educational Collaborative. This network of individuals, arts administrators, artists, lobbyists, activists and cultural workers provided a fertile seedbed for collective struggle in advancing agendas in the arts on the local and national scenes. In many ways a symbiotic relation emerged. In one case, as an arts administrator, I placed dance companies, movement specialists, and playwrights in public schools throughput the state. Professional art practice and curriculum development skills familiarized me with the concerns of artists, many of whom were on unfamiliar terrain in the school setting. Many lacked the language with which to speak to teachers about arts-based integration, assessment and evaluation. This was a clear service I could provide. In turn, working across media with performance artists expanded my repertoire of ideas on educational innovation. Travel to the many school sites in the state served to balance the realities of rural versus urban school needs, access to cultural resources, and rising demographic shifts in student/teacher populations.

    In another case, I served on the Merit Aid Panel of the state arts council. During site visits I accumulated versions of the "diplomatic tour" from the MFA and Merrimack Valley Textile Museum, to Provincetown Art Center and others. In each case the "heavy-hitter" institutions who had been monopolizing state-funneled NEA tax dollars for years were now confronting the emergent neighborhood, ethnically-based, and gender-based institutions who were demanding a slice of the pie. My observations of the technical assistance, monitoring and evaluation processes mandated by federal authorities would become critical in shaping the formative structures of CARAVAN. Administrative experience with the "entrepreneurial elites" was akin to a periscope view from the underworld of radical artist practice and it pointed out the potential potholes in cultural studies which, in the late 1970s and early 1980's, was merely a back road and not the well-trafficked expressway it became by the mid-1990's.

Beginning in 1980, I took "the studio" (experience) to the classroom setting up private workshops for students on the Northeastern University campus. This led to a consultancy in the Cambridge Public Schools under a chapter 636 desegregation grant focusing on CIC student workshops and a Commonwealth-In-Service grant for teacher-training. By 1982 CARAVAN had been exposed to 1000 children and teachers in city public schools. Concurrently, a collaborative grant from Salem State College which funded several field visits to Boston cultural and science museums also funded CIC for a seven month residency at the Washington Community School in Lynn, under the visionary leadership of its principal, James Leonard. The residency experience in the classroom, in the school, with teachers, parents and administrators will be discussed further in this essay. Clearly the crossroads of educational innovation, inspired leadership from administration, teacher support and love for students contributed to the success of those programs during this period. Moreover, this was the intense period of rethinking arts education and general education. Grant money was flowing like Victoria Falls. Ideas such as private sector partnerships, performance-based learning, institutional coll-aboration, gifted and talented and special needs initiatives, and cultural diversity were all in full flower. For those committed to children, learning, and the arts, these were arduous but happy times. Cultural anthropologists had shift-ed tracks on us stating that behavior was not genetically but culturally determined and transmitted which led to debates on cultural diffusion and cultural relativism. Social scientists were telling us that normal science no longer wedged itself in a "value-free" intellectual niche and now proudly admitted that all research was "value-laden" and subjective. Political scientists and ecologists were speculating on the notion of a global village (an increasingly despoiled, deforested, polluted and over consumed village at that).

Globalizing and Spiritualizing the Classroom

Sifting through such a reading of globalization, five ideas emerged which formed the conceptual matrix for CARAVAN. The core of CARAVAN theory was the essential spiritual nature and oneness of humanity. Few in academia drew upon spirituality as a pool of constructs about educational and art reform because of its connotations with organized religion and, in some countries, the idea of the separation of church and state. Nevertheless, moving forward with the conceptual matrix of the spiritual nature of reality and its application to curriculum reform in the arts and in schools, CARAVAN identified these five working concepts:

> 1) the need for an inclusionary, "non-political" view of cultural difference;
> 2) the need for interdisciplinary methods and approaches in "the classroom";
> 3) a redefinition of "the classroom", "the teacher", and "the student";
> 4) the centrality of the arts to the process of personal growth and spiritually-based knowledge-acquisition;
> 5) the importance of collaboration, working in groups and consultation

Electing a nation-based curriculum design model, individual units focussed on Ghana, Japan, Haiti, Brazil, Scotland, China, the Iroquois, France, Mexico, Egypt and India. Curriculum units contained facts sheets on each country, handouts on religion, politics, and the arts, maps, and language with a special focus on the worldview of youth and children. Artifacts, costumes, song sheets, games and other items were part of the curriculum package. Individually designed study units customized for each class block enabled the introduction of basic language acquisition (numbers, letters, introductions, etc.), national customs and cultural etiquette, lifestyles, and the central role played by visual and performance art in the history of all cultures. Since many of the children in CARAVAN workshops may not experience transnational travel or exchange, CIC served as a bridge from home to the world. On the other hand, increasing diversification of populations met with schools ill-equipped to service the new demands of the American classroom. For these children, CARAVAN provided validation for individual cultural difference and group respect for many newly-immigrated children of the "Third World."

How were the curriculum units developed? They were developed through the "little-red schoolhouse" strategy, an historical appropriation which places conceptualization, curriculum design, assessment, teaching, training and evaluation of the learning process in the hands of one individual. The working concepts of the CARAVAN philosophy began with a search for an inclusionary and non-political view of cultural difference. Given the exclusionary foundation of public education curriculum, the first working concept demanded an approach of evaluative revisionism applied to existing models in use in public schools. The handbooks on visual arts curriculum objectives for elementary and secondary levels published by various school systems offered a compass point, but I was directing my mission at a broader-based, more interdisciplinary and cross-cultural methodology, one which retained the "artist-as-teacher" at the core of the learning model. While such handbooks proliferate as mandatory operating manuals across disciplines in public schools in Massachusetts and America generally, I was also interested in those curriculum documents implemented in other countries. Nigeria presented a functional model. The *West African Journal of Education*, the Board of Studies in Arts and Crafts (Institute of Education) at Ahmadu Bello University in Zaria and numerous American and British art educators has left a clearly-marked trail of educational interventions in the arts. J.B. Akolo has cited research supporting a Nigerian "artist-as-model" approach in primary art education based upon informal home training in pre-colonial Nigeria.[2] While this model is absent in most mainstream American homes, in the late 1970's it was often present in the homes of Native American, Mexican-American, Chinese-American and other children outside the mainstream. Okolo's text also contained prophetic gems consistent with

[2] J.B. Okolo. *A Handbook for Art Teachers in Post Primary Schools.* Institute of Education, Ahmadu Bello University, Zaria, Nigeria: 117-118.

my own theories about the centrality of culture to the learning curve."While the most important elements in composition are placed at the top in the Western tradition," he stated "they are placed at the centre from where everything else radiates in Yoruba tradition. More attention may be paid to composition as Nigerian works of art are used in our response to art."[3] Akolo's conclusions reinforced my own seminal twin theories. The first concerns the artist as focus partner of an educational triad with student and teacher. The second adopts a notion of cultural subjectivity as a centrifugal force in motivation and self-worth for student learners. In fact, I was later to privilege both of these theories in proposing a multicultural epistemology in artist practice[4] based upon cultural memory and a theory of a *New Movement* in cultural praxis whereby *culture* operates as a center of non-elective self-liberation for a critical mass of global citizens.[5]

In South Africa a "separate but unequal" educational system under apartheid, which conspired to retribalize Black South Africans under the Bantu Education Act (1953), also served to further disenfranchise all South Africans, by excluding Blacks and other people of color from formal art training. A brief history of the evolution of the art-education crossroads at which traditional crafts and modern notions of fine art contend with the self-trained versus formally-trained artist suggests a subversion of creativity which, by inversion (political processes of repression, censorship, exile, forced removal and murder) served up a powerful (though mediated) multi-racial coalition of community-based organizations.[6]

---

[3] ibid, p. 142.

[4] R. M.. Chandler. *Reason and Memory in Artist Performance Practice: Toward a Multicultural Epistemology.* Dissertation, Department of Sociology/Anthropology, Northeastern University, 1992.

[5] R.M. Chandler. "The New Movement of the Center: Theoretical Model for Future Analysis in *Art Worlds.* Ed., Phoebe Farris-Dufrene, *Voices of Color: Art and Society in the Americas,* Humanities Press, 1996. This essay was a revision of a paper presented to the 81st Annual College Art Association conference, panel entitled "Feminism/Gender Studies: Taking Names Seriously," Seattle, February, 1993.

[6] See Gavin Younge, "The Doors of Learning: Art Training and Bantu Education," *Art of the South African Townships.* New York: Rizzoli, 1988, pp. 18-25 for a synopsis of the development of art education, training and social organizing under apartheid. David Koloane, Anitra Nettleton, David B. Coplan (1985), Njabulo Ndebele (1991), Rob Nixon (1994) and many others have discussed various aspects of culture, the arts production and the learning curve associated with the politicization of culture. Judy Seidman's *In Our Own Image* (A Cultural Studies

Since the artists and cultural workers of South Africa remained at the heart of cultural reconstruction, organizational meetings to mediate apartheid were often held outside of the country by the exile community. The Congress of South African Writers (COSAW) held the Zabalaza Festival in 1990 in London to "ensure that young and promising South Africans who have been denied the freedom to travel and who would have had great difficulties in acquiring the experiences and skills offered by the festival within the still extremely restrictive environment of South Africa, formed the core group."[7] The writer Mongane Wally Serote had asserted that "issues of development, the imbalances of apartheid, and the emergence of a flourishing South African cultural expression should be addressed aggressively in that critical transitional period a year before the 1994 elections."[8] Heading for the crossroads of a new consciousness and searching for substantive methods to implement in "the classroom" tools in hand suggested similarities both in CARAVAN and in the community-based arts movements of South Africa.

The Virtual Classroom

In 1981, CARAVAN received a Commonwealth-In-Service Grant for teacher-training at the Webster School in Cambridge, Massachusetts. A theme of "World Games" instructed teachers not only in cross-cultural games as a process for team-building among children of diverse backgrounds, but also offered substantive methods for using gamesmanship to teach other forms of literacy – math, linguistic and cognitive. Gamesmanship was then applied to a class at the Martin Luther King School (also in Cambridge) and the notion of a classroom was extended into what is normally defined as "recess." This represents a small leap across domains.

Textbook for Southern Africa), Gaborone: Foundation For Education with Production, 1990 is a context-centered workbook for synthesizing the material culture, social processes, political history, and enculturation of the arts, a text which, at publication issue, was being implemented in selected southern African schools.

[7] Andries Oliphant, *Culture and Empowerment* (Debates, Workshops, Art and Photography from the Zabalaza festival), Ed., Oliphant, Johannesburg: COSAW, 1993: 15.

[8] ibid, p. 243.

In South Africa, the idea of the "traditional" classroom has been redefined through often unnoticed politics. There are People's Education and People's Parks, an alternative press, moveable theatre, workers' art, and alternative philosophies of education, to name a few. The renegotiation of cultural values is rooted in progressive movements designed to maintain "a strong and vital ethical interest in human affairs ... to look for that area of cultural autonomy and the laws of its dynamism that no oppressor can ever get at."[9] The stories of the issuance of the Bantu Education Act, the SOWETO and Sharpeville Massacres are legendary in world affairs. Black South African children, threatened by educational co-optation and discrimination, marched and burned down their schools in opposition to the South African government's cultural censorship of a system of governance strangely referred to as multiculturalism (separate but unequal). The "traditional" classroom was lost for more than a decade, and the teaching – learning exchange put on new clothes.

Current debate on the production of knowledge, the extent to which our personal, cultural, and national values influence the kinds of information we teach and the way we teach it can be exercises in esoterica until theories are "tested" in the field. The "classroom" in South Africa can take many forms given its history of disenfranchisement and authoritarian state rule. In the arts FUBA (Federated Union of Black Artists) assumed the role of one of many community-based arts organizations at which youth culture was trained in printmaking, painting, graphics production and mural painting. State art schools and academic arts programs were unavailable to many students of color prior to the chartering of predominantly Black, Colored and Indian institutions of higher education. Matriculation at such institutions required rigorous preparatory education, examinations and the social mediation skills necessary to survive in academia. The Mayibuye Center at the University of Western Cape has offered students of color arts training as has the art department at the University of Fort Hare (Alice) for Black South Africans.

Community-based arts organizing remained, however, the sentinel through the anti-apartheid years, cultural

---

[9] Njabulo Ndebele. *Rediscovery of the Ordinary: Essays on South African Literature and Culture.* Johannesburg: COSAW, 1991: 159.

boycotts, and social advocacy. In Brazil, samba schools and community production enclaves for Carnival in the favelas provided training in dance, choreography, music (voice and instrumental), the visual arts, costuming and set design.[10] Other religious and regional festivals served as breeding grounds for artistic development and cultural resistance including the Zumbi Memorial's annual pilgrimage on November 20. During the period of Black nationalism, leading artists, musicians, and playwright-politicians such as Abdias do Nascimento, played a formal role as representatives of the disenfranchised and state repression. The Nascimentos write that "originally the samba schools were meaningful African community cultural organizations, but they have been transformed largely into business enterprises by illicit economic interests controlled by whites who commercialize the samba schools for profit." In both national cases, when the arts community faced disintegration from political repression and state censorship, communities reinvented and reconstituted centers of learning as conditions required.[11] If community theatre was censored for public performance in traditional venues, then it was performed in community centers and churches, and if this was censored, then the private home became a stage. Such stories of hardship and resilience document the insistence of the arts to complete their missions of education, inspiration, information and renewal.

Working in Groups

Between 1981 and 1987, CARAVAN conducted teaching-training workshops for a broad range of teachers from Boston to California. Sites such as the Boston Public Schools, the Central Massachusetts Bi-Lingual Education Committee, the Institute of Contemporary Art (Boston), Bosch Baha'i School (Santa Cruz), Green Acre Baha'i School (Maine), the Wayland Public Schools, the Cambridge Public Schools, the Boston

---

[10] 2 For varied perspectives on Samba, Samba Schools and Carnival see A. Guillermoprieto. *Samba*. New York: Alfred A. Knopf, 1990; Muniz Sodre. *O Terreiro e a Cidade*. Petropolis: Vozes, 1988 and *Samba Dono do Corpo*. Codecri, 1979; Z. Moore. "Reflections on Blacks in Contemporary Brazilian Popular Culture in the 1980's," *Studies in Latin American Popular Culture*, No. 7, 1988.

[11] See Abdias do Nascimento and Elisa Larkin Nascimento. *Africans in Brazil: A Pan-African Perspective*. Trenton: Africa World Press, 1992.

Children's Museum and several others – all were fair game for refining the process of team-building around educational objectives. Many of the human relations exercises for elementary and secondary students which were a mandatory rite of passage for students and teachers, confronted the myths of racial, cultural and ethnic difference which plague the American schoolroom.

The strategy of consultation was a critical path whereby contending passions and non-self-critical interests could become a liberating force for a reconciliation and decision-making far beyond tolerance. Consultation is a kind of valley of search in which issues are presented and a group must balance its communal will with compassion and resolution. I can remember a teacher-training session in central Massachusetts during which an exercise – *Why Do Words Hurt?*[12] – produced tears in the lone Spanish teacher in a class of 30 people. Histories of exclusion erupted in which the teacher lamented the ways in which her attempts to diversify the teaching staff in her district on behalf of the increasingly diversifying student population had fallen on deaf ears. In her case, it was not so much the racial invectives which offended, but the silences, the neglect, the feeling of being at the crossroads alone and unaided. In 1954, the social psychologist Gordon Allport's classic study on prejudice, *The Nature of Prejudice*, was published in the midst of the Cold War. His conclusions resulted from investigations and case studies across variables such as race/ethnicity, religion, nationality and other identities. Identity formation is a critical aspect of personality development in youth and children as Allport's baseline studies uncovered, and he pointed to the importance of symbols as "anchorage points around which the idea of world-loyalty may develop."[13] The transmission of values in the home is evident to many, but few have adequately assessed the transmission of values from teacher to student. Yet "while the national orbit is the largest circle of loyalty that most children learn," states Allport "there is no

[12] This exercise was featured on a popular New York City television program in the 1980's entitled *Vegetable Soup*. Further texts on intercultural training include "Multicultural Education: A Cross Cultural Training Approach," Margaret D. Pusch, Ed. Chicago: Intercultural Press, 1979, and more recent work by James Banks on multicultural education, curriculum development and advocacy.

[13] Gordon Allport, *The Nature of Prejudice*, Reading, MA: Addison-Wesley, 1982:44.

necessity for the process to stop there... When (such) a sense of reciprocity is firmly established, the way is prepared for the integrated conception of larger and larger units of mankind."[14] The author concludes that "until he learns this attitude of reciprocity, he is unlikely to accept other countries as lying within the orbit of his loyalty." Later, in remarks on the those aesthetic, social and religious values which are more decisive than the formation of tolerance, he concludes that "the development of mature and democratic personalities is largely a matter of building inner security."[15]

In the three national contexts mentioned, each maintains constitutional statements regarding racial difference. The United States, particularly since the era of Civil Rights, asserts an ideological position of cultural pluralism. It is not surprising that the American multicultural education movement was initiated in the 1960's, owing a debt of legal, social, and moral advocacy and unity to that era. While there had been organizing, lobbying, and legal battles regarding housing, social welfare, poverty and unemployment, we chose as a nation to wage the battles of school desegregation – the education of the young – as the last bastion of racial conservatism. By satellite, the film footage of police dogs, beatings, lynchings, assassinations, and children escorted by federal troops, made a statement to the world that Americans would no longer permit the evil of racial hatred and bigotry to be passed on to its children. The platform was set and since that time, systems innovation and education reform have run the distance with policies and practices which enhance multi-culturalism and make us believe in the inevitability of world peace. Current efforts to dismantle affirmative action are merely a signal that more of us must revisit the crossroads, where the place is holy, to ensure that America's children and education remain more valuable to us in policy and in practice than military defense.

Brazil's attachment to the myth of racial democracy defies the racial and class stratification of its schools and the drop-out rates. The "New" South Africa, having forced its demons from the closet, negotiates a reconstruction of race-based policies under a concept of "non-racialism" which will require fail-safe

---

[14] ibid, p. 46.

[15] ibid, p. 441.

constitutional laws for public education and which will be a challenge to implement for a majority population disenfranchised for half-a-century. We are all, as world citizens, new to this business of equity and unity. We learn from one another.

The anecdotal history of CARAVAN supports individual action as well as, community-organizing and the "concentric loyalties" of which Allport spoke at mid-century. My experiences with teachers, students, administrators, parents as well as the ones I could not reach are formative in my understanding of what it means to be an educator. I had first seen the traditional art classroom as an undergraduate student doing a comparative observation practicum at Boston English High School and Amherst regional High School. After moving on to higher education, I am a witness to the victories and defeats which students and educators encounter at the crossroads. I notice it has now become a superhighway on which the materialist instinct threatens that more sacred and holy mission of setting our best aside first, not last, for children and youth.

Constructing and inventing is most vital at the place Black Elk suggests is a sacred site. Far from the derogatory reference to interdisciplinary studies and methods as cut and paste curriculum development, the task of working out the framework and educational substance of many disciplines results from years of experimentation. Defending this fort is a matter of spiritual commitment and social responsibility. One waits in a kind of sweat lodge for the spirits to inspire, the mind to withstand the assault of thieves, beggars and self-doubt, and the flesh to wait for everybody else to come around to your (alternative) way of thinking.

Theresa Perry
Wheelock College

Transforming the Academy:
Problematizing our Successes[1]

Scenario #1

In February 1996, as the result of the third faculty search over a three year period, from a pool of four finalists, all of whom were people of color, the Social Work faculty made the offer of Assistant Professor of Social Work to an African American woman, an individual who had more than twenty years of senior level experience in social service and advocacy agencies in the northeast.

That the pool now included African American and Puerto Rican candidates resulted from the intervention of academic administrators – the Dean and the Vice-President for Academic Affairs – who at the conclusion of the two previous searches, would not allow the hiring process to more forward because the applicant and finalist pools didn't reflect the availability of people of color in the region.

It is important to note that over thirty percent of the students enrolled in the Social Work program are African American and Latinos, primarily because of an articulation agreement with Roxbury Community College, and a Child Welfare grant secured by a Social Work faculty member who has been Director of the Social Work program at Wheelock College for the last fifteen years.

Scenario #2

Within a space of one week, as I met with graduating seniors who were seeking letters of recommendation, I became painfully aware of how two of these students, who are white, had decided to construct their pursuit of a multicultural context for living and working. Both students were explicit and genuine in their desire to live and work in a diverse environment. They each expressed no interest in working in towns like Lexington or Belmont. Neither did they have any

---

[1] This is a revised version of a talk given to the American Education Research Association meeting on April 7, 1996.

interest in working or living in Boston. Instead, they had chosen what they perceived as "the safe places" to live and work in a multicultural context: Quincy, Somerville, Revere – interesting places with significant concentrations of new immigrants – Southeast Asians, Brazilians, Dominicans, Haitians. I thought it was more than happenstance that they had chosen to avoid Boston, the place with significant concentrations (to use John Ogbu's terminology) of castelike minorities.[2]

Scenario #3

It was not yet dark, it was what we call in Birmingham, Alabama "dusk dark." As I entered the lobby that led to the administration building, I reached for the door, only to discover that it was locked. As I attempted to pull open the door, a white student, with whom I had met individually on at least three occasions, approached the door. When she saw me, she went into a still pause. I think she must have stood there for about ten seconds. And then, she reluctantly proceeded towards the door and opened it for me. After thanking her, I just couldn't resist saying, "For a moment, I thought you were not going to open the door for me." She looked sheepish and embarrassed and said, "At first I didn't recognize you." I thought to myself, "for a moment, I had become the dreaded 'other'."

These three scenarios and many others capture the dilemmas and complexities, the problems and possibilities, associated with my ten-year attempt to facilitate the transformation of Wheelock College into a multiracial, multicultural democracy. While these are examples of some of the dilemmas embedded in our story and of the problems and possibilities of my leadership, the scenarios raise important philosophical questions: Under what conditions is it possible to transform an historically white institution into

[2] John Ogbu distinguishes between immigrant and castelike minorities, arguing that immigrant minorities come to this country more or less voluntarily, that they believe in the folk theory of achievement - that hard work pays off; that they compare their status in this country not with the mainstream population, but with their peers back home; and in the context of this comparison, their life here appears good. Castelike minorities, on the other hand, were brought to this country through conquest or force. Having lived here over generations, they understand that hard work does not always pay off. Occupying a castelike position in this society, they compare their position here to those in the dominant society, and in the context of this comparison, their situation does not look so good.

one that is multiracial and multicultural? What are the constraints on democratic practice in an undemocratic society? What kind of leadership is necessary for this kind of transformation to occur? What are the conditions that make the transformation sustainable?

Make no mistake, there have been transformations. When I arrived at Wheelock College[3] ten years ago, there were three African American students and two nontenured Asian American faculty members. I was the only Black person on campus, except for two men who worked in maintenance. A review of the course catalog for the 1985-1986 academic year confirms what I remember. There were no courses in the Arts and Sciences that focused on the experiences of African Americans, Latinos, Asian Americans, Native Americans. Nor were there course descriptions indicating that the study of these groups was included either as an "add on," or influenced a reconceptualization of the subject matter, e.g., American History. In the Arts and Sciences, two courses had as their focus "women"; in the Professional Studies department, there were two courses with content that focused on racial and ethnic diversity.

Today, by some accounts, Wheelock is a different world. Our full-time faculty has twenty-five percent people of color. Career planning and placement, student development, library services, field placement, admissions – all-white departments when I came to Wheelock College, can now all boast of having administrators of color in their departments, either as Deans, directors, and/or assistant and associate directors. Thirty-five percent of the College's senior administrators are people of color, including but not limited to, the following: the Dean of the Graduate School; the Vice-President for Student Development; the Associate Dean of Students; the Associate Vice-President for Academic Resources; and the Undergraduate Dean and Dean of the Faculty.

Ten years ago, less than twenty-five percent of our students were in urban field placements connected to their

[3] Wheelock College is a 109-year-old four year institution with the expressed mission to educate students at the undergraduate and graduate levels to work to improve the lives of children and families. In order to accomplish this, Wheelock College offers four multidiscipinary liberal arts and sciences majors, and professional preparation programs in the fields of social work, child life, and education.

professional preparation. Today, approximately eighty percent of undergraduates are in urban placements.

Of the ten Cynthia Longfellow Teaching Awards given to junior faculty members over the last ten years, five have been awarded to people of color: three to Asian American women, one to a Latina, and one to an African American woman.

In the Arts and Sciences, many courses now focus on the experiences of people of color; others foreground race; and still others allow the experiences of the historically oppressed to critically inform their conceptualization. These courses include, but are not limited to, the following: Native American Literature, Afro-Caribbean Literature; African American Literature, African American Women Writers, Introduction to Asian American Studies, Introduction to Latino Studies, Latin American and Caribbean Music, African Drama, American History, Sociology of Women, Advanced Studies in the Novel, Feminist Theories, Psychological Theories and Women's Lives.

Two of our rituals, convocation and graduation, routinely have themes that foreground issues of economic justice and cultural diversity. Two examples of convocation themes, one from last year and another from several years ago, are: "A Tough Mind and a Tender Heart," taken from that famous sermon of Dr. Martin Luther King, Jr., and "Living Our Lives in a Richly Textured and Diverse Society."

While these changes are surely the result of the activity of many individuals, they have been informed – driven – by the way I conceived of my role as Dean, and the way I chose to exercise leadership in that role.

Having rarely as an adult practiced what Evelyn Brooks Higginbothan has termed "the politics of respectability," it would have been difficult, if not impossible, to conceive of my role as Dean primarily as that of "administrator" or "manager." In the midst of the Civil Rights Movement, I had made a point of unlearning "correctness" and "hyper correctness." In other words, I was constitutionally not suited to construe my role as that of the super-administrator, the efficient manager. Coming out of the Civil Rights Movement, it was however, easy to superimpose my vision of social order onto the project of being a Dean.

In my role as Dean, the question that I would ask, over and over again, to large and small groups of faculty and administrators, and to the President of the College, "Can we educate our students so that they can work effectively with all of the nation's children?" Nobody was willing, in this historically progressive institution, to say that we couldn't, so the query was quickly transformed into, *"How* can we educate our students so that they can work effectively with all of the nation's children?" While I kept this query at the forefront of lots of people's minds, I constantly offered answers.

Yes, we can educate our students to work effectively with all of the nation's children, if we create a context where students, as a matter of course, interact with people of color as equals and in positions of power. Yes we can, if we practice a pedagogy that engages the head and heart, if our pedagogy is transformative. Yes we can, if we can teach our students about the history, culture, and traditions of Latinos, African Americans, Puerto Ricans, etc. Yes we can, if our students can, in their placements come to understand that the children come from communities and families with rich histories, cultures, and traditions, communities and families with many, many assets. Yes we can, if our faculty includes individuals from different social locations, who as equals can create curriculum and design learning experiences for our students. Yes we can, if we create field placements in the city. Yes, if we can interrogate our own racism. This last year was too often barely audible and repeated with less frequency than the others.

The question I asked, "Can we educate our students to work with all of the nation's children?" spoke directly to the College's mission. It challenged our ability to enact that mission. And since most of the faculty were deeply committed to the mission of the College, the query itself was very motivating, a call to action. It would be interesting to speculate about what would have happened if the College did not have a mission that was so linked to teacher preparation, to praxis, or if a significant number of faculty and administrators, in the professional studies and liberal arts departments, were not deeply committed to the mission.

Although there are possibilities associated with how I functioned as Dean, there were – and continue to be – problems. I continually used the metaphor and reality of our redefining ourselves as a multiracial, multicultural democracy to define what we could become. I often queried, "what if we projected ourselves into the future, into our notion of what this College would be like if the society were not stratified along race, class, and gender lines? Who would we then want to be part of our community? What narratives would we want to pass on to our children? Who would occupy positions of power, and how would we want that power to be exercised?" This metaphoric, utopian language, while motivating and challenging, was imprecise. I now believe that language itself promoted a pluralist brand of multiculturalism that downplayed issues of power, conflict, and social justice. In other words, the project was framed in a way that didn't explicitly and constantly connect "the cultural policies of identity and difference to a social politics of justice and equality." The project was underconceptualized. I did not ask, in the words of Nancy Fraser, "what differences make a difference?" Thus, it should have come as no surprise that the only Latinos our faculty could muster the consensus to hire were individuals from white, class-privileged immigrant backgrounds: individuals from Venezuela, Spain, Cuba. It should come as no surprise that none of the individuals hired as full-time faculty are deeply connected to the Latino community in metropolitan Boston, none are Puerto Rican or Chicano.

Furthermore, it was incorrect to suggest that we were creating a democracy, or even operating in a fully democratic manner. Neither one nor competing definitions of democracy were put on the table, talked about, or debated. Were we talking about representational democracy, decision making by consensus, self-rule, radical democracy, liberal democracy or Jeffersonian democracy?

If the truth be told, neither representational democracy nor decision making by consensus, had in the past resulted in our faculty deciding to hire faculty of color. (A national study referred to in *Black Issues in Higher Education* suggests that this is the case nationwide; that in point of fact, it is the activity of senior-level administrators, rather than faculty leadership, that has been critical to diversifying both faculty and students at historically white colleges.) As a matter of fact, I am ashamed to say that with the first person of color to whom we offered a faculty position at the beginning of my tenure as Undergraduate Dean, the academic administrators – the Vice-President for Academic Affairs, the Chairs of the Arts and Sciences and Professional Studies departments – did so by overruling the decision of the faculty. The faculty member that we hired would later become quite loved by the faculty and because of her excellence as a teacher, be awarded the teaching award.

As noted earlier, had we not intervened in the Social Work search, the all-white finalist pools for the two successive searches would have resulted in the hiring of another white person. While our intervention served to constrain the terrain in which the Social Work faculty would conduct the search for a new faculty member, it was the Social Work faculty themselves – their deep sense of program mission, their ability to work collaboratively, their shared micro perspective and personal ethic – that allowed us to end up, in the third search, with a diverse, extraordinarily talented pool of finalists. It was the faculty themselves who reached out to their colleagues, encouraged individuals to become candidates, and acknowledged and respected the talents and accomplishments of the candidates.

I don't want to leave you with the impression that we intervened in all or most faculty hiring decisions. Our interventions were strategic. They occurred when we thought these interventions were critical to the work of the College, or pivotal in the advancement of the overall vision. We intervened in the first hire to get the ball rolling, to make the point that the sky would not fall in if a person of color were hired, an individual who had the same degree, from the same school as that of two members of the search committee. And yet this individual was not considered fully qualified.

We argued intensely with the Social Work faculty that the preparation of students for effective work in the child welfare system, in community-based and advocacy organizations, required a diverse faculty. Intellectually, everyone agreed. Emotionally, it was difficult to bypass individuals whom the Social Work faculty considered to be "super qualified" for candidates of color. And thus, while we would not allow the searches to proceed for two years in a row because of an all-white pool, we were not members of the search committees. We didn't review candidates, nor did we participate in the decision-making in the final search. The real question is, "What are the constraints of democratic practice in an undemocratic, stratified society?" "How long can you treat people as objects, and expect them to emerge as subjects?"

In most of the liberal arts and science searches, we have chosen not to intervene, particularly if we couldn't make a compelling case for a different decision, or if we felt that the case would not be viewed as compelling by the area faculty. And thus, at the close of the 20th century, all of our full-time Humanities faculty are white, at a time when some of the most interesting intellectual work in the fields of literature and history is being done by African Americans, Puerto Ricans, and Chicana scholars.

Most of the faculty of color currently employed at the College were sought out by me and/or by other academic administrators. Often, we would invite an individual to candidate for a full-time position. In other instances, we would pass on to faculty in charge of part-time hiring the names of people of color who were interested in part-time teaching. A significant number of faculty of color initially came to the College as part-time faculty, and over time, became half- and full-time faculty. The faculty's current attempt to limit how many years a person can remain full-time and not be in a tenure-track position, as well as their concern with specifying the process by which an individual moves from part-time to full-time, will severely limit our maneuverability in the future. However, this faculty activity gets to the heart of the matter. How much can you constrain self-rule, and not bastardize the whole notion of democracy? Does the practice of self-rule, decision-making by consensus, necessarily promote democracy, social justice, and social equality?

Finally, as suggested earlier, we have not kept at the fore of our conversations about what the College should become, the issue of race and racism. For two years, we have hired a consulting firm to help us interrogate our racism. This project was not very successful. For the last two years, our required first-year students' seminar focused explicitly on race and class identity development, a focus that, in my estimation, made students and faculty uncomfortable. For the Class of 2000, the First Year Seminar focuses on their changing identities: personal identity, gendered identity, community identity, as well as race and class identity. I could be wrong, but I would speculate that in most of the seminars, race and class identity, while still a part of the course, will not be foregrounded.

Herein is an instance where I have decided not to intervene. I decided to let it go, and let the seminar become what the faculty would make of it. At some point, the people, the faculty, have to decide. They have to decide to assume a substantial and central role in sustaining, developing, or reversing the changes that have occurred. It is my hope that through faculty leadership, the politics of identity and difference will be connected to a social politics of justice and equality. This is the next stage.

Joyce Hope Scott
Massachusetts Maritime College

Teaching and Learning the Harlem Renaissance: Reflections on a Faculty Model for Multicultural Reform

> Janie starched and ironed her face and came set in the funeral behind her veil ... the funeral was going on outside. All things concerning death and burial were said and done. Finish. End. Nevermore. Darkness. Deep hole. Dissolution. Eternity. Weeping and wailing outside. Inside the expensive black folds were resurrection and life. She did not reach for anything, nor did the things of death reach inside to disturb her calm. She sent her face to Joe's funeral, and herself went rollicking with the springtime across the world.
> *Their Eyes Were Watching God* p. 137.

Images of twoness and inside/outside evoked by Zora Neale Hurston in her 1937 novel, *Their Eyes Were Watching God*, seem to capture in fictive representation what W.E. B. DuBois suggested in *Souls of Black Folk* as the dilemma facing the Black intellectual on the eve of the Harlem Renaissance, which took place in the early 1920's. The "color line," which DuBois identified as the problem of the 20th century, truly becomes the site of negotiation for artistic space for the African-American writer at this point in American literary history. Seeking to add their voices to the multi-faceted narrative of the American experience, literary artists of the Harlem Renaissance found themselves engaged in a discursive improvisation not unlike the model created by jazz, its musical corollary which is polyrhythmic and multi-instrumental.

Though many of the most well-known artists of the period came out of the Harlem experience, the cultural phenomenon, which was taking place in a number of key cities across the United States in the early 1920's, is probably more accurately characterized by the term, "New Negro Renaissance." "New" reflects the spirit of many Black artists of this time and sums up the transformation that was going on as a result of the migration of Blacks from the South to the urban North and its ghettoes and the proletarianization of rural southern Black farmers. "New Negro," as well, described a wide range of new subjective and ideological developments. A more visible middle class, more critical of the accommodationism of the "old guard" Negro, formed the background against which the flowering of cultural national- ism and artistic and intellectual expression emerged.

Wheelock College's seminar on the Harlem Renaissance in the summer of 1995 was the third and final session of an NEH-funded faculty development project on "moments of renaissance." Having begun the project in the summer of 1994, with a seminar on the Italian Renaissance, which we had approached from the perspective of history, we had learned that historians' narratives are generally concerned with reconstructing socio-political causation. The fact that there were a number of historians among the faculty participants helped to create dialogue and valuable exchanges from the two discursive domains of literature and history. Those, like I, who came from a background in literature and literary criticism, discussed the number of ways that different "readings" of the event might produce meaning and how meanings might shift, depending on the perspective which the critic brings to the task.

Professor Henry Louis Gates, Jr., one of our guest scholars for the Harlem Renaissance seminar, placed the New Negro Renaissance within the historical struggle of the African- American to self-define and rename "himself," and our early focus on James Weldon Johnson, one of the key architects among the Harlem literati, suggested a reframing of the event as an enterprise to create a "marketable" Black persona and cultural product for white consumption; that is to say, one way to see the event was as an experiment in art as cultural capital.

That being the case, then, what would be the "text" of race? In what language would the "new" (public) Negro speak? And, how would he be represented? Johnson had advocated for a linguistic form larger than dialect, which he saw as having two designations: Pathos or humor. Yet, he hoped that the language appropriated in the final analysis would keep the "flavor" of Black dialect. Such a demand, in fact, invited a twoness or double face. What Johnson proposed here propelled our ensuing discussions of issues of self-designation. As self-naming, un-naming, and re-naming is a recurring trope in African-American narratives from Frederick Douglass and Sojourner Truth to Malcolm X, it made sense for me to see the designation "New Negro" as a communal, rather than a private, name-giving to the Black public self.

• • •

Booker T. Washington's classic narrative, *Up From Slavery*, we are told that he took a second and third name as a declaration of independence and achievement of manhood after leaving his master/father's plantation in the South. The New England writers, Emerson and Thoreau for example, were interested in "declaring" their literary independence, thus sparking the impetus for what has come to be called the New England Renaissance in the literary tradition of the United States. In the same way, identity and legitimation were recurring themes for writers and other artists of the Italian Renaissance, and seminar participants saw them as equal forces driving the creative outpourings of Harlemites as well.

In my role as a lead facilitator for the Harlem Renaissance seminars at Wheelock, I became acutely aware of my own "twoness," of Janie's inside/outside construction of self as it applied to me – inside the cultural experience as an African-American woman yet outside at that moment as teacher, colleague, and cultural interpreter. By profession and training, I am a scholar of American literature, with a particular specialty in the literature of the Harlem Renaissance. Thus, I was playing the role of "teacher" in my capacity as facilitator. Yet, the audience, this time, was not made up of my students, but rather, my colleagues, people with whom I worked. This being the case, I was conscious of an ongoing psychic positioning in which I was involved. There was "I" in relation to my peers, participating with them in lecture/dialogue. There was also "I" in relation to the cultural products of my tradition, my heritage, and, armed with the tools of literary criticism, this "I" was invited to revisit the event from within this compilation of selves.

I remembered that shapers of public opinion in our society have a tendency, historically, to "select out" and "confer" legitimacy on African-American personal achievement and cultural production which serve the purposes of the status quo. In this light, then, I was careful to point out to my colleagues our need to understand the period under study, this renaissance, as a phenomenon which was occurring in a number of places at the same time.

•••

A reframing of the texts and times of the Harlem Renaissance became especially crucial for the group when we began to discuss the women writers. For my presentation on women such as Nella Larsen, Jessie Fauset, and Zora Neale Hurston, I considered the fact that this movement, like most movements of cultural nationalism, sought to create a new racialized patriarchal text. The "New Negro," of which James Weldon Johnson and Alain Locke had spoken, was clearly a male referent; thus, it was important to consider the aims of the framers of the renaissance as that of shaping a racial discourse designed to wear a masculine face.

For me, then, in reconsidering the role of women in the renaissance, was the question of not only what the text of race would be or in what language it would be articulated but rather also, and equally important at this time, was who should speak? Who would be "vested" with the authority to determine the textual reconstruction of Black America at that crucial moment of geo-graphical, economic, political, and cultural transformation? A question for us as teachers and learners, then, was: How do women writers of the Harlem Renaissance achieve narrative freedom within the proscribed text and context of the movement? My approach to engaging this question was to focus on Zora Neale Hurston as artist and personality, for it seems to me that her "point d'entre" underscores the problem of text-context, speaking-story-telling, and self-naming at issue for Black writers in general at this time, and for women in particular. I began by calling the group's attention to Hurston's two novels: *Jonah's Gourd Vine* and *Their Eyes Were Watching God.*

In choosing to focus on these two texts, my interest was to point out how they can become rich sources for teaching and learning about literature of the period, the struggle of the Black female writer, and the role of storytelling and language in the African-American tradition. I argued that what these two texts represent, on one level, is an interrogation of the New Negro idea of public text, that is, the "text of the race" and where it is to be found. For Hurston, this authority lay, clearly, in the southern Black folk tradition and its multiple linguistic forms.

• • •

I began with *Jonah's Gourd,* Hurston's first novel, because the textual and contextual struggle in which she and other Black women writers seemed to be engaged presents itself metaphorically in this text in a confrontation between Ned Crittendon and his wife Amy over her mulatto son, John, the protagonist. The conflict escalates as Amy bites back at Ned, word for word, as he threatens to beat the boy, whom he perceives as being too arrogant. Finally, fed up with her acid tongue, he says to her: "Don't you change so many words wid me, 'oman! Ah'll knock yuh dead ez Hector. Shet yo' mouf!" Her reply is: "Ah change jes ez many words ez Ah durn please! Ahm three times seben and uh button. Ah knows whut's de matter wid you. Youse mad cause Beasely done took dem two bales uh cotton us made las' yeah" (17). Key here is the pun on "change, " which for Ned means that Amy is "exchanging" words, thus trying to insist that there be a "dialogue" between them, but Amy's: "Ah change jes ez many words ez Ah durn please!" introduces the possibility of storytelling and myth-making, which is at the heart of the conflicts in her novels, as well as of the conflict between Zora as literary artist and her new Negro renaissance male contemporaries.

Through appropriating the context and the text (the language and vernacular tradition) of the southern Black man and woman, Hurston offers an exchange which poses other possibilities for constructions of the "New Negro," one which does not necessitate the rejection of tradition and culture of the Black South. To further investigate this perspective, I offered a reading of *Their Eyes Were Watching God* as the story of a woman who learns to be a storyteller and all that that implies within the fictive context of the novel. With this text, Hurston privileges an older understanding of literature, in that it acknowledges an alternative authority – that of the mythic tradition of Africans and African-Americans. In this tradition, one sees storytelling redefined as multiple narration.

At this point, it was necessary to talk about the narrative structure as it operates in *Their Eyes:* we, the readers, experience the protagonist, Janie's, story as an "overheard conversation" between her and her friend, Phoebe. We see, also, the communal or village voice, that which introduces us to the story in the beginning by pointing out the different ways that men and women experience the world, men watching it (their dreams) go by like ships passing on the horizon, women seizing it, turning it into what they want as the "dream becomes the reality."

Then, there is also the third level of narrative, that offered by the "porch-sitters" whose "lyin sessions" function to comment on the story that Janie is telling through the appropriation of black folk tales, myths, proverbs, and legends laden with deep meaning and critical insight.

Having grown up sixty miles North of Eatonville, Florida, the site of Hurston's novels and the place where she, herself, grew up, I recognized the specifying, signifying, calling-out, and deadly playing of the dozens in which Jody and Janie engaged and which ushered in his narrative exit as a result of Janie's linguistic conjure. I had witnessed similar word magic in action many times as a child, sitting at my mother's knee as she, my grandmothers and my aunts "wrote and read" texts of man's follies and God's might, of neighbors and friends, blacks and whites. These "picture-talkers," like Zora's porch-sitters, wielded words as an artist does his/her brush, drawing and coloring the contours of their lives according to their creative visions. This ability, it seems to me, is that uniqueness of the Black experience offered by the southern vernacular tradition which Hurston did not want lost in the New Negro's quest to re-designate and reconstruct the speaking voice of the African-American people.

The drawing of the character, Jody, Janie's second husband, is what I used to illustrate this contention. Jody's rhymes of love to Janie soon begin to turn into actions and rhetoric of power and possession. He makes Janie a "mule of the world" by forcing her to carry his stifling notions of what behavior is appropriate for her, based on her class and sex. As he is fond of saying, "Somebody's got to do the thinking for women and children, chickens and cows," all objects that men possess. In this way, Jody goes from"man with a big vision" to a man with a big voice. He would be a "big ruler" (p.49), but as Lige, Sam, and the other porch-sitters point through the metaphor of Pharaoh and the big ole beast, the tyrannical voice of rulership is not a story that can last. The narrator also calls Joe, "the little ruler of the crossroads," but the people know that the only ruler of the crossroads is the trickster god, Esu Elegbara (Legba or Papa LaBas), whose very existence testifies to the temporal nature of all material reality.

● ● ●

The real "born orator" is Janie, as the townspeople point out to Jody, despite his attempts to belittle her intelligence by forcing her to do work which she hates clerking in his store while holding herself aloof from the common folk and their rich storytelling sessions.

Hurston's distrust of tyrannical master text(s) and their origins in repressive racists and sexist discourses is foregrounded throughout the text in what can be seen as an interplay between Jody's "I God" capitalist definitions and Janie's silences where she learns the "inside/outside" postures necessary to maintain her psychic and spiritual wholeness in the face of Jody's rhetorical attacks on her personhood. This failure to take her voice, her story, her "self" into consideration and the damage it has caused is given narrative space in the death-bed scene when Janie reminds Jody: "... You ain't the Jody ah run off down de road wid ... Ah run off tuh keep house wid you in uh wonderful way. But you wasn't satisfied wid me de way Ah was. Naw! Mah own mind had tuh be squeezed and crowded out tuh make room for yours in me."(133)

The group discussed Hurston's crucial role as a writer of this period who transformed the novel form by infusing it with the double-voice characteristic of Black vernacular speech. Here was another opportunity to foreground issues for teaching in multiracial classrooms where African-American youngsters may bring their inherited vernacular tradition – especially through use of language – to the learning experience. Hurston's novels capture the metaphoric nature of southern black speech with its rich use of invective, rhythm, cadence and resonance. Dr. Johnnetta B. Cole points out in her article "Culture: Negro, Black, and Nigger" (*The Black Scholar,* June 1970) that African-American culture has three dimensions: (a) those elements it shares with Euro-American America; (b) those elements it shares with all oppressed peoples; and (c) those elements peculiar to the African-American condition in the USA. Hurston's novel gives narrative space to these three dimensions.

Linguist Geneva Smitherman writes about what she calls the two verbal styles of African-American speech: the sacred style, which she locates as having come from the rural South, and the secular style, a product of the urban North ("White English in Blackface, or Who Do I B?"). Hurston sought to authenticate this "sacred" tradition, it seems, by formulating a way to "endow stigma with authority."

The folklore and rich vernacular tradition that she loved and refused to reject resonates from her novels and invited us to engage these questions: What does it mean to construct a public self for a marginalized, oppressed people as were the Harlem Renaissance writers of the 1920s and 30s? And, how does the Black female writer, in particular, achieve agency as an authentic voice in that construction of public self?

At the end of this seminar on the Harlem Renaissance, I was forced to re-examine my role as teacher/learner/colleague in this experience. The questions put to us during the session on the New England Renaissance by Dr. Stanley Cavell seemed quite appropriate at this point: What is my authority as a teacher? What do I bring to the dialogue? And, where is real textual authority located? For me also was this confrontation with my "selves" who continue to shift as I slip in and out of my role as teacher, learner, and inheritor/keeper of a multifaced, multivoiced cultural tradition.

132

Ngo Vinh Long
University of Maine

Ethnic Pluralism, Multiculturalism, and Development in Vietnam

The aim of this paper is to show that the particular nature of ethnic diversity and economic development in a country like Vietnam can define its efforts at promoting multiculturalism and that, vice versa, the nature of the progress at multiculturalism may have definite bearings on the overall political and economic integration and development of the nation. To this end, we will first begin with a brief discussion of the nature of ethnic pluralism in Vietnam. Next, we will review some of the efforts at promoting multiculturalism since the 1940's. And finally we will examine the impact that *doi moi* ("renovation," or free-market economic reforms as known in the West) has had both on the ethnic issue and on multiculturalism in the last ten years as well as the implications that they may have for the future of development in Vietnam. Hopefully, some lessons could then be drawn by peoples in similar situations elsewhere.

Ethnically, Vietnam has always been a pluralistic society. As a nation it was originally known as *Bach Viet* (Hundred Viets). The word *bach* (hundred) when combined with other words usually means "multitude" or "all-inclusive." Many myths and legends have also served to reinforce the country's awareness of its ethnic and cultural diversity. One creation myth of the nation – with slightly different versions circulated among some ethnic groups – talks of the one hundred children born to Lac Long Vuong ("Lac Dragon Lord") and Au Co. The Dragon Lord, son of *Kinh* Duong Vuong (Canals and Sea Lord), had come from the sea to drive away northern invaders and to teach people in the Red River delta area in present-day northern Vietnam to cultivate rice and wear clothes. Au Co, a princess of the mountains, had been a wife (or, depending on the particular versions of the myth, sister or daughter) of an invading northern general whom the Dragon Lord had chased away.

One day Au Co said that she prefered to go to the highlands and live there for the remainder of her life because the climate there would be more suitable for her. The Dragon Lord, however, told her that he wanted to stay close to his natural elements in the lowlands and coastal areas. Hence, they decided to part and split the children equally among themselves, promising that they, their children, and their children's children would come to each other's aid whenever and wherever needed. Fifty of the children went with Au Co to the mountains and became the ancestors of the highland minorities; the other fifty remained in the lowlands and coastal areas with Lac Long Vuong and became the ancestors of the Viet (or Yueh in mandarin Chinese), a term used in China long before its first unification to indicate collectively all the peoples living south of the Yangtze river.

The term Viet Nam ("Viet of the South", *Yueh Nan* in mandarin Chinese as opposed to Nan Yueh which had been the name of a state that occupied most of southern China before Han time) came into being only after 1803 as a result of negotiations between the Nguyen court in Hue and the Ch'ing court in Peking to indicate the territory under the control of the Nguyen. It was not until the late 1920's, however, that the term Vietnamese was first used to refer to the inhabitants of this territory. In time, the term came to be used more restrictively – mostly by outsiders – to indicate the lowland majority who were ethnically mixed but who, through a long process of acculturation and integration, had learned to speak a common language (Vietnamese).

The ethnic minorities living in the midland and highland areas, however, traditionally referred to the lowland population collectively as the *kinh* ("capitol city" people). This was perhaps because historically they were the only group that was ever under the effective direct control of the kings and his courts. *Kinh* also means canals and irrigation ditches; and it has also been speculated that the name was given to the wet rice cultivators of the lowland partly because of their skills in controlling water. Whatever the case, the term *kinh* has been used officially by the Democratic Republic of Vietnam (DRV) since 1945 to differentiate the lowland majority from other ethnic minorities since each ethnic group has its own names and since members of these groups have all been considered citizens of the state of Vietnam.

When the DRV was first established, there were perhaps as many as 70 different ethnic groups in Vietnam. Linguistically, these groups belonged to two overall families – the Sino-Tibetan and the Austro-Asiatic families – which were further divided into scores of groupings. Often members of one linguistic grouping could not understand the languages used by peoples belonging to another grouping. The various ethnic groups had distinct ways of life and economic practices. Some had been deep rice cultivators for hundreds and thousands of years. Others practiced slash-and-burn farming. And many were still semi-nomadic, living off nature through hunting, gathering, and fishing.

In spite of the differences, historically there had always been a high degree of social and economic interchanges between the various ethnic groups as well as close collaboration in the common fights against foreign aggressors. Hence, even though the French colonialists intentionally pitched the various ethnic groups against each other and used the *kinh* majority to repress and oppress the other ethnic groups after the Nguyen court had surrendered all of Vietnam in 1884 to the French, most ethnic groups collaborated with each other in the continuing anti-colonial struggles.[1]

As soon as the Indochinese Communist Party was established in 1930, one of the main goals stated in its platform was: "To achieve the unity of all nationalities [*dan toc*, or ethnic comm-unities] on the basis of equality and mutual assistance with a view to winning together independence, freedom and happi-ness."[2] To this end, an anti-illiteracy and adult education campaign was carried out in all areas where the revolutionaries operated. In the 1930's, about 95 percent

---

[1] For a summary of these struggles and the oppression of ethnic minorities under the French, see: Viet Chung, "National Minorities and Nationality Policy in the DRV" in *Vietnamese Studies*, No. 15-1968, pp. 4-23 [hereafter "National Minorities...DRV]. *Vietnamese Studies* was an imprint of the Foreign Languages Publishing House in the Democratic Republic of Vietnam.

[2] "National Minorities...DRV," p. 11. The Vietnamese language makes a distinction between *sac toc* ("color lineage," or race) and *dan toc* ("people lineage," or ethnic groups). Since each ethnic group has its own identity in terms of language, culture and areas of habitation and is referred to as *dan toc Kinh, dan toc Thai, dan toc Nung* and so on, the term *dan toc* embodies the idea of an autonomous ethnic community in the same way that the American Indians referred to their tribal units as "nations." Hence, the official Vietnamese translation of the term *dan toc* into western languages as "nationalities" and the term for ethnic minorities (*dan toc it nguoi*) as "national minorities".

of the entire population in Vietnam was illiterate; and in the highlands the rate of illiteracy was close to 100 percent. In the 1939-1940 school year, which was the year with the highest school attendance during the entire French colonial period, there were only 15,000 minority students in all schools in Vietnam. There was only one junior high school, located in Lang Son province, for all the mountainous provinces in the north. But almost all of the 130 students attending this school either came from *kinh* (Vietnamese majority) background or from privileged classes of the more important minorities such as the *Tay, Nung, Muong,* and *Thai*.[3]

With the founding of the DRV, efforts at promoting multiculturalism were stepped up. Many people from the urban and lowland areas went to the highlands to conduct literacy and adult education courses as volunteers. In 1946, eighty teachers from 24 ethnic minorities who had been given special multicultural training were sent to the highlands as the core group for spreading literacy and for conducting the adult education campaign there.[4] In addition, the 1946 Constitution guaranteed equal rights for all ethnic groups irrespective of their "sex, social condition, social class, and religious belief" and specifically promised that "the national minorities will also received assistance in all fields so as to attain the general levels [reached by all in the nation] within a short time."[5]

After the departure of the French colonialists and the return of peace to the northern half of the country in 1954 the DRV, under the slogan of "unity in diversity," tried to promote the welfare of the ethnic minorities through multicultural education and the establishment of autonomous regions. In 1955, the Tay Bac (Northwest) Autonomous Region that included the three provinces of Son La, Lai Chau, and Nghia Lo and over half a million inhabitants belonging to 25 ethnic minorities was establish-ed. In 1956, the Viet Bac (Northern Viet) Autonomous Region came into being. It was composed of the six northeastern provinces of Lang Son, Cao Bang, Ha Giang, Tuyen Quang, Bac Can and Thai Nguyen and had a

---

[3] Nhat Hung, "Education in the Service of the National Minorities," *Vietnamese Studies,* No. 15, pp. 110-112 [hereafter "Education...Minorities."]

[4] "Education...Minorities," p. 112.

[5] "National Minorities...DRV," p. 15.

total population of over 1.5 million peoples from 14 different ethnic groups. Almost all key positions in state and party organs in these autonomous regions were held by local people; and from 70 to 80 percent of all the executive positions in some provinces were occupied by members of the various ethnic minorities. The minorities not only managed their own affairs but also took an active role in state and party leadership at the central levels. Sixty four of the 455 deputies to the National Assembly of the DRV were said to have come from the various highland minorities.[6] Percentage-wise they seemed to have been adequately represented since, according to the 1960 census, there were 2,363,000 peoples belonging to the 37 ethnic minorities out of a total population of 15.9 million in the northern half of Vietnam.[7]

The rights and autonomy of the minorities were established in Article 3 of the revised 1960 Constitution as follows:

>The Democratic Republic of Vietnam is a unified multinational State.
>
>All the nationalities living on Vietnamese territory are equal in rights and duties. The State is to maintain and develop solidarity among them. All acts of discrimination against, or oppression of, any nation-ality and all actions which undermine the unity of the nationalities are strictly forbidden.
>
>All nationalities have the right to preserve or reform their own customs and habits, to use their spoken and written languages, and to develop their own national cultures.
>
>Autonomous zones may be established in areas where people of national minorities live in compact communities. Such autonomous zones are integral and inalienable parts of the Democratic Republic of Vietnam.
>
>The State will strive to help the national minorities attain the general economic and cultural

---

[6] Ibid., pp. 16-19.

[7] See the two appendixes on pp. 221-225 of *Vietnamese Studies*, No. 15, for a breakdown of the various ethnic groups by numbers and percentages and where they were living in the DRV in 1960.

level within the shortest time possible...[8]

According to the author of the article on minorities cited above, besides a whole array of achievements in the social and economic fields for and by the minorities from 1954 on,

> Illiteracy had been wiped out by 1961. General education schools, complementary education classes for adults, and vocational schools make up a dense network. All school-age children go to school. The languages of the minorities have been given the place of honor. The more important minority groups, 85% of the total minority population, now have their own scripts. Cadres have been trained at an accelerated tempo and will soon cover all the needs of the national and ethnic minorities.[9]

In the northern highlands, there was at least one teachers' school in every district to train teachers for primary schools and one teachers' college in every province to train teachers for secondary classes. In the 1966-1967 school year there were about 6,000 teachers and 255,000 students from ethnic minority backgrounds at the various general education levels in the DRV.[10]

However, the ravages of continual warfare since the mid-1960's – first against the United States, then against China, and finally against Pol Pot in Cambodia – had pushed back many of the gains for all ethnic groups in the north by the late 1980's and had also compounded problems for others in the south who had suffered years of neglect and repression under the various Saigon regimes. By 1986, budget deficits and other economic woes forced the government to begin to cut back on subsidies to the minorities and the poor as it embarked on its economic reform program *(doi moi.)* By 1989, the year that Vietnam withdrew all its troops from Cambodia and thus ended its war economy footing, virtually all consumer subsidies were eliminated and budgets for

---

[8] Cited in ibid., p. 16.

[9] Ibid., pp. 20-21.

[10] "Education...Minorities," pp. 118-119.

education and health care were also drastically reduced. All these had a pronounced impact on education for the whole society; and multiculturalism took the back seat to economic priorities.

The impact was uneven, however, and depended largely on whether the particular ethnic group was living in the northern or southern half of the country, whether it was scattering in remote areas or concentrating in urban communities, and whether it was engaging largely in agricultural work or mainly in commercial and industrial activities. Those who scattered in remote areas had the lowest literacy rates partly because they were hard to reach by educators and partly because they were much poorer and hence could not contribute to teachers' salaries to get them to come. Those who were living mainly in urban centers and engaging principally in commercial and industrial activities, such as the *Hoa* (Chinese), had the highest literacy rates both in their own ethnic languages and in Vietnamese. The 1989 population census has produced 454 large pages of detailed statistics on the educational situation of the 54 ethnic groups living in Vietnam, with breakdowns by age groups and by provinces and towns.[11] Below we will cite a few examples of the literacy rates among some ethnic groups to give the reader a rough idea of the deteriorating situation.

In 1989 Vietnam had a total of 54.3 million people five years of age and above, of whom 45.3 million were literate – 22.3 million of them males and 23 million females – and 9 million were illiterate. The *kinh* **(Viet)** majority had 47.3 million in this age group, of whom 41.2 million were literate – 20.1 million males and 21.1 females – and 6.1 million were illiterate. The *Tay* minority – who lived chiefly in the northern provinces of Cao Bang, Lang Son, Ha Giang, Tuyen Quang, Bac Thai, Lao Cai, Quang Ninh, Yen Bai, Ha Bac, and Son La and in the southern provinces of Lam Dong and Dak Lak as a result of migration since 1975 – had 976,000 people in the same age group. Among them 811,000 were literate – 411,000 males and 400,000 females – and 165,000 illiterate. The *Muong* – who lived mainly in the northern provinces of Ha Tay, Hoa Binh, Thanh Hoa, Vinh Phu, Son La, Yen Bai, and Ninh

---

[11] "Vietnam Population Census, 1989: Complete Census Results, Volume II," Central Census Steering Committee, Hanoi, 1991.

Binh – had 746,000 people in the same age group, of whom 609,000 were literate – 304,000 males and 305,000 females – and 137,000 illiterate. The *H'mong* **(Meo)** – who lived in chiefly in the northern provinces of Ha Giang, Tuyen Quang, Lao Cai, Yen Bai, Lai Chau, Son La, Cao Bang, and Lang Son – had 438,000 people in the age group, of whom only 44,000 were literate – 38,200 males and only 5,800 females – and 393,000 illiterate. The *Gia Rai* – who lived chiefly in the Central Highland provinces of of Gia Lai, Kon Tum and Dac Lac – had 198,000 people in the age group, of whom 40,000 were literate – 28,000 males and 12,000 females – and 158,000 illiterate. The *Ba Na* – who lived chiefly in Gia Lai, Kontum, Binh Dinh, and Phu Yen – had 111,000 people in the age group, of whom 21,800 were literate – 14,900 males and 6,900 females – and 89,200 illiterate. The *M'nong* – who lived principally in Dak Lak, Lam Dong and southwestern province of Song Be – had 54,300 people in the same age group, of whom 21,000 were literate – 12,700 males and 8,300 females – and 33,300 illiterate. And the *Khmer* (Cambodians) – who lived mainly in the Mekong delta and in Ho Chi Minh City – had 750,000 people in the age group, of whom 385,000 were literate – 210,000 males and 175,000 females – and 365,000 illiterate. In general, about one-half to three-fourths of the smaller ethnic groups scattered in remote areas of the country were illiterate.[12]

Nonetheless the Vietnamese government seems to be proud of the accomplishments that have been made so far by the ethnic minorities. The September 9, 1996 issue of the official party daily, *Nhan Dan* (People), pointed out that by 1989 more than 90,000 cadres from ethnic minority backgrounds were working in scientific, technical, literary and cultural fields; and that by 1993 more than 9,000 political cadres from ethnic minority backgrounds were occupying key positions from the district to the Politburo levels. It also stated that in addition to the efforts at expanding the general education network of schools in the last five years for the minorities, the government has also established 198 boarding high schools where 36,000 students of ethnic minorities from remote communities had come to stay and study. Every year 2000

[12] Ibid., pp. 256-259.

graduates from these boarding schools are chosen to attend various universities. In addition, the government has established 3 preparatory schools – located in Viet Tri, Nha Trang, and Ho Chi Minh City – that were reserved exclusively for minority students as well as a high school that teaches the Pali language and culture, located in Soc Trang province in the Mekong delta, to people from the Khmer ethnic background.

It is true that the government has increased its investment in education slightly in the last few years. From 1991 to 1995 the budget for education as a percentage of the state budget was 9.3%, 7.9%, 5.4%, 8.4% and about 10% respectively. But by 1995 illiteracy rate was still at least 20 percent in the rural areas on the average and over 50 percent in the highlands. Only about two percent of the highland population and 20 percent of the lowland inhabitants had high school education.[13]

What is most surprising, however, is that statistics from recent surveys show that the Mekong delta provinces have the highest rates of illiteracy in the country. About 2.8 million people above the age of ten cannot read and write; and twenty three percent of all the women in the region are illiterate. The dropout rates of primary school students are also high: 8 to 13 percent, depending on the particular province, as compared to the average national rate of 6.58 percent. The main reason has been because of the increased differentiation and hence poverty in the area. Twenty two percent of the population, or more than 3.4 million people, in the Mekong delta – the biggest rice producing area in the country – are said to be undernourished and to have an average income of only about 40,000 dong (US$4) a month. Another reason for the high illiteracy rates is the serious shortage of teachers since salaries for teachers in the Mekong delta are lower than the national average. The starting salary of a primary school teacher and the regular pay of an instructor

---

[13] For details on education see: Anh Vu, "Education Developing with Economy," *Vietnam Economic News,* No. 9, March 1-7, 1996, p. 29; Thu Hanh, "Slow Investment in Educational Services," *Vietnam Courier,* June 9-15, 1996, p. 1; and Duong Ba Phuong, "Gop Them Y Kien ve Cong Nghiep Hoa Nong Thong Trong Giai Doan Hien Nay" (Additional Suggestions on Rural Industrialization in the Present Period), *Tap Chi Cong San* (Communist Review), No. 16, November 1995, pp. 32-35. Communist Review is the official theoretical organ of the Vietnamese Communist Party published bi-weekly in Hanoi.

at a teachers' training school is about US$14 and $20 respectively a month in the region.[14]

Increased differentiation and poverty, which in turn produc-ed problems for education and multiculturalism, have come about partly as a result of the market-oriented reforms during the last decade. A Hanoi English-language weekly has this to say in a recent article:

> According to most observers, the 10-year shift to the market mechanism combined with rapid economic development has meant the country has faced fiercer social problems... The latest Government statistics show a deeper polarization with a small portion of the population is getting richer and a large proportion is getting poorer.
>
> According to Vietnam's Ministry of Labor, War Invalids and Social Affairs, the country now has some three million households regarded as being below the poverty line, accounting for 20.3 percent of the total number of households. The statistics show nearly 600,000 families are starving and 2.3 million are living in poverty.
>
> A household is classified as poor when the average monthly per capita income is less than VND 50,000 (US$4.50) in the countryside and less than VND 70,000 (US$6.30) in the cities...
>
> Some 80 percent of Vietnam's population lives in rural areas and some sociologists say that during the last few years under the market economy an alarming phenomenon has emerged of farmers losing their land.
>
> Around seven percent of eleven million farmer households have either very little or no cultivable land. In 1992, only 12 percent of farmer households in the suburban areas of Ho Chi Minh City lost land; but the corresponding percentage in 1995 climbed to roughly 34 percent.

---

[14] Tran Dong Bang, "Illiteracy Plagues Mekong River Delta," *Vietnam Investment Review*, September 9-15, 1996, p. 32. This is a weekly published by the Ministry of Planning and Investment in cooperation with Vietnam Investment Review Ltd.

The same situation is now prevailing in other provinces, mostly in the southern Mekong river delta...[15]

Strangely enough, in a recent economic forum held by the International Monetary Fund (IMF), IMF officials and experts from the World Bank and other American institutions singled out Vietnam as the most successful country in transition into a "free market economy." One expert attributed Vietnam's recent impressive GDP growth – at an average rate of 8.2 percent during the 1991-1995 period – to the fact that the focal point of its "development strategy is the export-oriented industrialization that its Southeast Asian neighbors have successfully pursued." And David Dollar of the World Bank said that exports, which had grown 25 percent annually over the previous seven years, were "really the key to why the Vietnamese economy was able to grow during transition."[16]

In reality, however, this export-oriented development strategy has turned Vietnam into a flea market instead of a free market. Much of the GDP growth has come from wanton stripping of Vietnam's resources for export without much concern for environmental and social consequences. About 40 million tons of crude oil has been extracted by one joint venture alone, for example. And it is expected to extract 47 million tons more in the next five years.[17] Oil spills have destroyed farm land and marine life. Deforestation has been so indiscriminate that the World Wide Fund for Nature says Vietnam's forest cover is just 19 percent today and that, at current reduction rates, the natural primary forests will disappear within 20 years.[18]

Much of the deforestation, according to Dr. Y Ngong Niek Dam who is chairman of the "Council of Nationalities" (Hoi Dong Dan Toc) at the National Assembly, has been caused

[15] Nguyen Tri Dung, "Economic Growth Must Not Ignore Social Impact," Vietnam Investment Review, September 2-8, 1996, p. 2.

[16] IMF Survey, a publication of the International Monetary Fund, July 1, 1996. The conference was held on May 29, 1996 and the quotations are on p. 215 and p. 216 respectively.

[17] Tan Duc, "Vietsovpetro Se Khai Thac 47 Trieu Tan Dau Tho" (Vietsovpretro Will Extract 47 Million Tons of Crude Oil), Thoi Bao Kinh Te Saigon (Saigon Economic Times), July 18-24, 1996, p. 25.

[18] John Chalmers, "Vietnam Pays Lip Service to Environment," Reuters, May 29, 1996.

by ethnic minorities living in the highlands. He said that serious differ-entiation brought about by the market economy had made many ethnic minorities desperately poor and hence they have had to resort to cutting down the forests to make a living. He added that tens of thousands of members of various ethnic minorities from the northern highlands have also migrated to the central highlands and that this migration have also resulted in land wars, increased deforestation, and ethnic conflicts. But Dr. Dam, who himself is from an ethnic minority and who had become deputy director of the Department of Ethnic Minorities *(Nha Dan Toc Thieu So)* as early as September 1946, is optimistic that if all the policies and programs of the party and government regarding ethnic minorities were to be carried out as intended then not only would the economic and cultural conditions of the minorities in the highlands be greatly improved but "the 54 brotherly ethnic groups in the Vietnamese national community would live in harmony with each other like 54 solid pillars holding up the beautiful and comfortable common house of Vietnam..."[19]

At the Eighth Congress of the Vietnamese Communist Party which was convened in Hanoi from June 28 to July 1, 1996, both the party political platform and the "1996-2000 Five-Years Economic and Social Plan" reserved whole sections to describing the priorities and plans for the "socio-economic development of the highlands and of regions inhabited by ethnic minorities."[20] The goal, as stated in Section 10 of the Five-Year Plan, was "to mobilize the resources of the entire nation to create faster economic and social progress, to stabilize living conditions, and to improve the natural as well as the social environments" of the minorities. And economically the goal is to raise GDP growth rates in areas inhabited by minorities at least to the national average level and even higher so that their GDP per capita would be doubled by the year 2000. Great details for development in every economic and social sector for the different regions are listed.[21]

---

[19] Interview published in the September 9, 1996 issue of *Nhan Dan*, p. 3.

[20] For details and full transcript of both documents see *Nhan Dan*, June 30 and July 1, 1996.

[21] *Nhan Dan*, June 30, 1996, p. 6.

On September 13, 1996, Prime Minister Vo Van Kiet also signed Decree 656/TTG, a master plan which includes eight specific "solutions" for developing the Central Highlands – composed of the provinces of Kontum, Gia Lai, Dak Lak and Lam Dong – socially and economically during the 1996-2000 period as well as until the year 2010. The central government will invest between US$7.3 and US$8.6 billion in this region from now until the year 2010, with about US$1.1 billion during the current Five-Years Plan period. Average annual GDP growth rate will be increased by 10 to 11 percent from now until the year 2000 so that GPD per capita will be increased from the present average of about US$186 to about $260. The region is said to be the home of some 37 ethnic minorities. But since the labor force is mostly untrained, the government will focus its efforts on education and on giving them the appropriate skills needed for the tasks ahead. Basically, priority will be given to the development of agriculture and forestry as well as processing industries for products such as timber, cotton, cashew, coffee, rubber, and tea.[22]

Whether the Vietnamese Communist Party and the government will be able to realize their goals for the ethnic minorities as a whole, however, still depends on many factors. Economically, for example, it must be willing to depart from the current export-oriented industrialization strategy and channel some resources to the highlands as well as to other areas. Currently 65 percent of all state capital is invested in eleven biggest state conglomerates alone – out of a total of 6,000 state enterprises – which are located in or around large metropolitan areas such as Ho Chi Minh City, Hanoi, and Haiphong.[23] Most of the US$19 billion foreign investment pledges by 1995 have also been in industrial and commercial projects in the urban areas.[24] As a result, in 1995 the average income was US$695 and $912 in Hanoi and Ho Chi Minh City respectively in comparison to the national per capita

---

[22] "Tam Giai Phap Phat Trien Kinh Te-Xa Hoi Tay Nguyen" (Eight Solutions for the Development of the Central Highlands Socially and Economically), *Nhan Dan*, September 18, 1996, p. 1; Nguyen Tri Dung, "Standards Predicted to Rise in the Central Highlands," *Vietnam Investment Review*, September 16-22, 1996, p. 2.

[23] *Thoi Bao Kinh Te Saigon*, May 23-29, 1996, pp. 9-10.

[24] *Vietnam Courier*, January 28-February 3, 1996, pp. 1-2; *Vietnam Economic News*, February 2-8, 1996, pp, 5-6.

average of about $220. From 1996 to 2000 GDP in both Hanoi and Ho Chi Minh City is slated to grow by an average of 15% annually while national GDP is expected to increase by 9-10% a year, and that of the rural sector by the mere 4%.[25]

In order to realize the above goals, however, the government will have to attract an additional US$42 billion in investments during the 1996-2000 period. In an article that gives a detailed listing of investments made by 54 countries, Minister of Planning and Investment Do Quoc Sam has stated that he expects fifty percent of this amount to come from increased mobilization of foreign capital. Even if this could be done, it is clear from the statistics given by Mr. Sam that the Vietnamese economy will soon be dominated by foreign concerns since about 40% of capital formation in Vietnam in 1995 was already generated by foreign enterprises. This percentage is several times higher than that of Hong Kong and about the same as Singapore, which is the most commercialized country in Asia. More interestingly, close to 40% of all foreign investments have come from Chinese-speaking countries such as Taiwan, Hong Kong, and Singapore.[26] This connection has aided the ethnic Chinese living in Vietnam tremendously in their commercial and industrial activities and has, consequently, raised concerns among other ethnic groups. The Vietnamese government has also inadvertently helped enter-prises with access to foreign capital through a tight monetary policy along the IMF lines which has made the Vietnamese *dong* many times more expensive than most foreign currencies. By 1995, many domestic enterprises that did not have access to foreign capital had already collapsed or were on the verge of bankruptcy.[27]

---

[25] *Vietnam Economic News,* January 5-11, 1996, p. 6 and February 9-22, 1996, pp. 18-19 and 40-42.

[26] *Thoi Bao Kinh Te Saigon,* July 18-24, 1996, pp. 15-16. For an analysis of capital formation in Vietnam and to dominating roles of foreign enterprises, also see *Thoi Bao Kinh Te Saigon,* May 23-29, pp. 9-10.

[27] For detailed treatments of these issues see *Thoi Bao Kinh Te Saigon,* November 9-15, 1995. In fact, the ethnic Chinese community in Ho Chi Minh City has again begun to dominate economic activities in this city as they used to under the French and the Americans through business practices that have raised quite a few eyebrows from other ethnic groups. But this is an issue that is too complicated to go into here.

In conclusion, success or failure of policies on ethnic equality and of programs on multiculturalism depends not only on cultural sensitivity and political sincerity but also on the overall directions of social and economic development of a country. A market-oriented development strategy, with its focus on fast GDP growth through exports and industrialization, may end up leaving many people behind – among them members of the most vulnerable ethnic and social groups.

Hashim Sarkis
Harvard University

Space for Recognition: On the Design of Public Space in a Multicultural Society[1]

Introduction: The Space of Representation

What shape should a public space assume in a pluralist society when the nature of 'public' is a source of contention?

Ask a Boston-based architect, *as The Boston Sunday Globe* did on September 25, 1994 (figure 1) in response to a call for ideas to renovate the Boston City Hall Plaza, and you'll hear that architects should aim at "providing places and experiences that bind people together for a society that is more diverse."[2] Another citizen, Hubie Jones, a community activist in Boston, said that "the litmus test of whether the right uplifting atmosphere has been achieved will be the day he can walk through the Plaza and not have his mind occupied by the image of Ted Landsmark, a black youth, who was speared with an American flag by a white teenager on the plaza in 1976 during a protest of court-ordered busing."[3] For the plaza to become more inclusive, memories of exclusion and oppression will have to be erased. As illustrated by the competition entries, conventional attributes of 'publicness', such as general accessibility, common use, and management by the public sector, no longer make a space public, nor does the dignified architecture of a public building, like City Hall or the Federal Center which were meant to evoke inclusiveness and equality. Public space has to respond to citizens who are turning more toward individual and group identities, than to their citizenship, in order to claim recognition. Only by ostensibly including the activities and symbols exclusive to certain disempowered groups could the new design of the

---

[1] I wish to thank George Katsiaficas and Teodros Kiros for building this expanded platform and making room for an architect to formulate arguments about identity and multiculturalism. I am also grateful for their editorial comments and those of Conrad Schmidt.

[2] Sandy Coleman, "Wanted: Ideas for City Hall," in *The Boston Sunday Globe,* September 25, 1994, pp. 1 and 6.

[3] Coleman.

Figure 1: Aerial View of downtown Boston with Government Center
in the foreground.

Plaza help them erase memories of their exclusion. In the
present architectural scene, public space will have to move
people like the Vietnam Memorial and graft, as it were, the
names of all the participants in every collective act.

The responses to the *Boston Globe* queries do not apply
to the case of Boston alone, nor are they meant to illustrate
how a lay audience interprets architecture symbolically.
Today, even architects have come to readily accept a predominantly symbolic interpretation of pluralism in architecture.
While it would seem that such a response, and the resultant
public spaces, adequately address the politics of recognition,
I want to join a growing band of skeptics in regard to this
symbolic, iconographic, attitude towards recognition.

In other disciplines and professions, the politics of recognition are prompting a re-examination of frameworks of
thought and institutions that have long claimed to advance

the ideals of liberalism but that have, too often, turned out repressive and exclusive.[4] In design, we continue to think new social problems through old mechanical responses, responses which, at best, perpetuate inadequacy. For example: Eliminating the kitchen in a house leads to emancipating the woman of the house; adding color to the white classical architecture acknowledges the influence of other cultures that use color on contemporary culture; or stylistic eclecticism is more inclusive than rigor.

The present tendency to fragment the public 'by design' should be considered suspect for two main reasons: [5]

First, the 'public' has become fragmented and the fragments hold no relational identity to each other. The political content of the public sphere – for example, raising issues of contention among groups in public or engaging in questioning one group's identity – has been removed from public spaces. In order to radicalize the pluralist conception of contemporary society, that is, in order to acknowledge that conceptions of what is right, what is good, and what is of value, will remain in contention, "pluralism," as Chantal Mouffe insists, "must also be distinguished from the postmodern conception of the fragmentation of the social."[6] Extending from politics, current pluralist aesthetics exaggerate this problem even further and play "right into the ideology of the 'free market'."[7] In the arts, historical revivals of all sorts, each dense with its own social associations, have developed an immunity from criticism because of direct, and usually insular, associations with particular social, ethnic, or cultural groups. But if aesthetics no longer serve to constitute

[4] The Critical Legal Studies movement is a case in point.

[5] The coincidence between the request for ideas for changing the plaza and a change toward this development approach raises suspicions but not because it has blurred over the distinction between private and public. When it comes to the production of public spaces, the public/private distinction has always been tentative, and the success and failure of public spaces has, for the most part, depended not on the extent of public sponsorship but on the balance between the power of private and communitarian interest groups on the one hand and society-wide accountability systems, such as the state, on the other. It has also depended on whether the plaza is used heavily or not and whether it encourages intermixing among different groups or not- and that is way before recognition became an important concern.

[6] See Chantal Mouffe, *The Return of the Political*, Verso, London, 1993, p. 6.

[7] Hal Foster, "Against Pluralism," in *Recodings, Art, Spectacle, Cultural Politics*, Bay Press, Seattle, Washington, 1985, p.15.

identity, and if each group already possesses its own aesthetics, then an architectural practice cannot engage in the "politics of recognition" beyond affirmation. If one of the main political questions in the United States today revolves around questions of identity, then, in politics, as well as in architecture, we need to look at how identity is spatially constituted. We are incapable of complete identification without space or aesthetics. Is it possible, for instance, to address racial issues in the United States, without dealing with spatial segregation or without attacking Western forms of expression such as architecture for their exclusiveness?

Second, the aesthetic visions described above are removed from the procedural issues involved in design: who pays for what, what functions are included, which groups are consulted, empowered (or disempowered) in the process? Unfortunately, and when subjected to such scrutiny, pluralist architecture would turn out to match the private developers' need for marketing flexibility more than it would support the concerns of disempowered groups. In the specific case of the Boston City Hall competition, it also coincides with the increasing patronage by private enterprises of public activities and spaces. Many private enterprises are laying claims to enhancing, protecting, and using public spaces. In today's processes of decision-making about public space, political models of representation such as consensus building, voting, or negotiation are used. Instead of developing frameworks that pertain better to their craft, architects mostly refuse to engage in such laborious tasks and confine their role to aesthetics. However, one of the main projects of the politics of recognition is to develop political frameworks that could include experiences from all forms of life, architecture included.

In brief, an aesthetic practice such as architecture has yet to engage the politics of recognition more effectively. Architectural solutions do not solve social problems, I hurry to say, but architects should align themselves with progressive solutions to social problems and search for pertinent forms through which they could enable these solutions (not simply justify them). And if the social problems revolve around the issue of recognition, then a further dimension of the architects' engagement should lie in elucidating questions of identification through form.

There are aspects of knowledge and life that are peculiar to architecture, and they should be recognized. They could help expand and enrich the process through which other forms of difference are recognized. These are the larger ambitions which this paper broaches but which I do not claim to fully develop here. In the following two sections, I will propose two alternatives for responding more effectively to the questions of recognition in architecture. These two alternatives draw from recent experiences in the United States and try to recover attributes which could be pertinent to the present.

Alternative I: The Space of Iconoclasm

Ironically, the first alternative draws from the experience of designing Boston City Hall Plaza itself, from the period between 1958 and 1961, when Kevin Lynch, then professor of urban planning at MIT, served as consultant to the Plaza's planners. Lynch applied the research on Boston's urban layout from his canonical book, *The Image of the City*.[8] In this book, Lynch had argued that there was a strong need to make the image of the city more intelligible to its citizens if they were to feel at home and to move about without the fear of getting lost. Instead of searching the discipline of architecture for means to achieve intelligibility through urban design, he went out to the citizens, and through an interviewing process, identified which areas of the city were easy to move about in and which were disorienting. With the help of interviewees representing different ethnic, social, and geographically located groups, Lynch identified five common components by which they anchored their movement in the city: *districts, edges, paths, nodes,* and *landmarks*.

When asked specifically about the area of Scollay Square, the area earmarked for demolition and designated to become Government Center, Bostonians said they felt disoriented there, and reluctant to enter and intermix. In its place, Government Center was to become a clear point of reference in the daily commutes of the citizens as well as a mutual destination for all groups. In his preliminary design proposal,

[8] Kevin Lynch, *The Image of the City*, MIT Press, Cambridge, Massachusetts, 1960.

Lynch strongly demarcated the edges of the contiguous (but socially and ethnically distinct) districts that surrounded it. The West End, a run-down area of recent immigrants was separated from the main open space by the federal building which acted as a strong edge. The North End, the Italian district, was to be bounded by a linear motel building. Even transient citizens were to be included. Beacon Hill, the hub of the old Boston, was separated from the plaza by a long curved office building. All these edges were urban in scale, and as drawn by Lynch, minimal in articulation. They delineated the plaza and created an open, *neutral* space in the middle of which was placed the landmark, City Hall. To further emphasize the connection between the plaza and the city at large, Lynch dipped the ground toward the north exposing the ocean. The Plaza was also made visible to the commuters on the new elevated highway. From the Plaza, a Bostonian, no matter to what neighborhood he or she belonged, could now feel connected to the city as a whole (figure 2).

Figure 2: Boston City Hall and City Hall Plaza.

If these design moves are interpreted symbolically, Government Center would come out to be a highly segregationist environment: The edges strongly demarcate ethnic and class districts. The introduction of the highway is celebrated visually whereas the social displacement it causes is ignored.[9] I believe, however, that the ambitions of Lynch's idea are by far more progressive. For Lynch, as well as for the behavioral psychologists who inspired his search for legibility, a clear physical environment helped make the organism more tolerant.[10] The clearer the image of the city, the more citizens were able to understand their placement with respect to other citizens and, therefore, to tolerate others and intermix around the public institutions that brought them together, irrespective of class, race, or political affinity.[11] It is important to recall that an image's clarity, or "legibility," was extracted from the citizens' "collective memory" (a phrase Lynch borrowed from Maurice Halbwachs who also stressed a place's importance in constructing its inhabitants' identity).[12] Instead of mimicking the social differences, the space was meant to use them as markers for people to come together on neutral turf. Public space, to Lynch, is at once neutral and simultaneous.

We do not have to accept behaviorist determinism in order to appreciate how such a distinction between legibility and iconography could enrich the pluralist project in architecture today. What seems more important, is how this model seeks first to determine a common ground, to look for a means of engaging all citizens alike in the design of the

[9] Indeed, some critics of the Government Center Plaza associate Lynch's work with the elitists and segregationist plutocracy of the fifties. Others locate Lynch within the urban and political culture at the time reading in his tone fifties optimism or, as it may be, looking at his work as an acceptance, as an aestheticization of the large scale urban interventions of urban renewal. For this interpretation of Lynch, see Manfredo Tafuri and Francesco Dal Co, *Modern Architecture*, Harry Abrams, Inc. Publishers, NY, 1976.

[10] See, for example, Edward Tolman's "Of Cognitive Maps in Rats and Men," in *Psychological Review*, 55, 1948, pp. 189-208.

[11] Lynch also played an active role in transforming the procedural conditions of urban planning in favor of an advocacy approach. The aesthetic practice that follows, and which dissociates the form of the urban space from its content, stands far off from the emotive practices of recognition that pervade the contemporary design scene. The radical potential of this practice was left unexplored even by Lynch.

[12] See Maurice Halbwachs, *The Collective Memory*, Harper and Row Books, New York, 1980, p. 157.

collective space. Only after having secured public accessibility (both mental and physical) does one turn to a discussion of style or meaning. At the level where each architect proposes a particular style or language for a particular building, the discussion could very well then turn to meaning and its production, to representation. This alternative therefore involves *defining a moment before iconography which makes representation, or the plurality thereof, more effective.* This distinction between legibility and iconography, between the behavioral dimension of the image and the symbolism embedded in it, does not necessitate dissonance between the two. The cool, modern style of City Hall and its surroundings, was indeed intended to elevate the institutions of City Hall Plaza above racial tensions and ethnic difference. As such, a modernist, almost, iconoclastic style, such as the one Lynch proposed in his drawings, could be seen as consistent with this restraint.[13] Another corresponding iconography may very well be the pluralist aesthetic being advocated today for the Plaza. Neither option is needed to justify the search for legibility which is conducted through other means.

The first alternative then entails searching for the underlying commonalties among different groups and for attributes of the constitution of their members, as *individuals,* that are spatial. In order to participate in public life, one has to leave his group identity in his 'district,' behind the 'edge,' and enter as an individual among individuals. Moreover, this alternative suspends a direct engagement with the styles and symbols of each group and prefers to develop a simultaneous common grounds among their individual members. Historically speaking, the potential of this alternative was not fully fleshed out. Lynch is partly to blame for not exploring it himself. The radical potential of his idea would be eclipsed by the search for consistency between form and content which persisted even in his own work. Whether in premonition of postmodernisms to come, or because he underestimated the power of signs, Lynch downplayed iconography's power. Furthermore, the progressive ambitions of

[13] What supports this interpretation is Lynch's refusal to engage in the symbolic value of signs even when he and several other colleagues embarked on studying signage in the city. Many of the city signs upheld segregation, separated the citizens and created areas of exclusion in their territory rather than areas of tolerance.

City Hall Plaza would soon after be eclipsed by the social displacement and racial tensions spurred by urban renewal projects in the fifties and sixties (like the Boston Government Center).

Understandably, with the rise of the advocacy movement in the sixties and the growing awareness of the social ills linked to urban renewal, Lynch's model was shelved under 'regressive formal discourses about public space'. However, the progressive social agenda of the previous decade would be picked up and, in certain aspects, taken to the hilt by planners and architects aligned with the New Left. Most experimental among those were architects operating out of universities and in parallel with the student movement, the inspiration behind the second alternative I will discuss.

Alternative II: The Space of the Voice

Popular memory often confuses the student movement of the sixties with anti-war action, the Civil Rights uprisings, and other counter-culture movements. Indeed, the Students for Democratic Society (SDS) of the early sixties did eventually join forces with a national and, even, worldwide network of student and grassroots movements that called for upholding universal ideals about equality and freedom, and then, shortly before their eclipse, protested militantly against the oppressive power of the modern state.[14] Recent revisionist studies of the New Left have emphasized the unprecedented challenges it presented to the institutions and frameworks that were thought to uphold democratic ideals, taking them to task for what they failed to deliver.

These challenges were to take place in a new form of public space. All scales of public interaction, taking place at every moment in daily life, were seen by the New Left to contribute to this total transformation. Every street-corner, coffee shop, and living room could be witness to a public debate which touches on fundamental political issues. 'Publicness' was now erupting in spaces previously sealed in privacy. Such mobilizational strategies, the revisionist historians add, did not suddenly emerge out of direct grassroots

---

[14] See George Katsiaficas, *The Imagination of the New Left*, South End Press, Boston, 1987.

mobilization nor out of civil rights activism alone. They were preceded by yearnings so apparent in the fifties for an unrestrained individualism, and more significantly, foreshadowed by the civic republicanism of the thirties. Both reform movements were inspired in large part by John Dewey. It is in Dewey's conception of public space and public action that we can locate one of the central dilemmas faced by the architects associated with the New Left. In their own right, they set out to solve this dilemma both procedurally and aesthetically.

In *The Public and its Problems*, his most pronounced political theory, Dewey called for unrestrained, accelerated communication and local, face-to-face interaction – at the scale of the neighborhood and local community – as the initial steps towards a society-wide, participatory democracy.[15] At the very end of the book, he introduces a curious distinction between the eye and the ear.

The connections of the ear with vital and out-going thought and emotion are immensely closer and more varied than those of the eye. Vision is a spectator; hearing is a participator. Publication is partial and the public which results is partially informed and formed until the meanings it purveys pass from mouth to mouth. There is no limit to the liberal expansion and confirmation of limited personal intellectual endowment which may proceed from the flow of social intelligence when that circulates by word of mouth from one to another in the communications of the local community. That and that only gives reality to public opinion.[16]

By adopting Dewey's radical democracy, the SDS founders were advocating incremental change towards more

---

[15] See Andrew Jamison and Ron Eyerman, *Seeds of the Sixties*, University of California Press, Berkeley, 1994. See also James Miller, *Democracy is in the Streets: From Port Huron to the Siege of Chicago*, Simon and Schuster, New York, 1987. Many of the drafters of the 1962 Port Huron Statement, the manifesto of the Students for Democratic Society, had been members of the Student League for Industrialized Democracy. As the campus arm of LID, a leftover of the socialist party, and over which Dewey himself presided briefly, SLID was chartered with the aim of "education for strengthening democratic principles and practices in every aspect of our common life." James Miller tells us that the main influences on the Port Huron Statement, Al Haber, Tom Hayden, and C.W. Mills were all greatly influenced by John Dewey's dictum about the individual's ability to transform the stable world around.

[16] John Dewey, *The Public and its Problems*, Swallow Press, Ohio University Press, Athens, 1927, pp. 218-219.

effective institutional reform. They were also to face a dilemma about participatory democracy's inability to directly affect large scale politics. Whether in the small community and direct communication model prescribed in *The Public and its Problems* – a model which could not account for the more complex urban and industrial America – or in his emphasis on indirect reform through education and intellectual inquiry, Dewey failed to provide a practical model as to how these changes would affect reform at the institutional level.[17] The New Left would confront this problem head on.

How then to go from informal dialogue, which takes place in everyday encounters in public space, to large scale reform? As SDS would soon find out, introducing democracy in the streets, applying it to every aspect of life, in every space, would not lead naturally, and without interim coordination, to reforming the institutions of the political framework. Architects associated with the New Left would face two coordination problems, 1) between their designs of discreet public spaces and the transformation of the public realm at large and 2) between the participation of user groups in the design of their buildings on the one hand and with the transformation of the way business is conducted in architecture and the way the discipline thinks of buildings on the other. Some architects would resort to an organic iconography that enforced a natural link between the organs of local communities and the organism of human society.

An example to this regard is the master plan produced by the Berkeley architect, Christopher Alexander, for the University of Oregon at Eugene. Alexander's "Oregon Experiment," as he called it, proposed that the University should involve its different communities of students and staff in thinking about the physical environment and, even further, in designing their own institutional buildings themselves. Any change in the built environment should be incremental, organic, and locally generated (figure 3, *next page*). When confronted with questions about how a master plan would emerge from such incremental change, and how state funding and infrastructure would be supplied incrementally, Alexander fell back on a muddled organic discourse. Beautiful

---

[17] See Roberto Mangabeira Unger, *Social Theory, Its Situation and its Task,* Cambridge University Press, Cambridge, England, 1987, p. 219.

environments – like pre-industrial towns which were built in small increments over long periods of time – were always beautiful, he argued. If we could replicate this organic process, we could both recapture the beauty and perform the normative link between the local and the total. Given how impossible it was to plan the physical facilities of a 30,000 student university and its budget in tidbits, Alexander's position could survive only in the aesthetics of the buildings. The buildings reflected an organicism that brought people's domestic image to their institutions. As such, the music school would acquire porches and fireplaces, and the dome of the welding room would look like a child-built structure in a suburban backyard.

The significance of the University of Oregon example is that, unlike the disengaged attitude among most architects today, Alexander fully immersed himself in the procedures of building in order to be able to push discreet spaces to the foreground. For the purposes of this paper, Alexander's project could be summed up in two dilemmas: On the one hand, he heightened the voice of his publics but dimmed their vision. For example, he would enlarge the spaces in the university where students and staff were likely to casually meet and talk, like stairs, hallways, and water fountains, yet he would also subdue the institutional iconography of the architecture, avoiding symmetry and tall, massive buildings. On the other hand, Alexander suggested that an aesthetic practice which brought about organic forms could help solve the problem of coordination between local action and more comprehensive change. He found *a constitutive role* for aesthetics. Regrettably, proposing that an aesthetic solution could solve a procedural problem, he and other New Left sympathizers were in effect professing their own failure.

Poltical vs. Spatial: Conceptions of Public Space

Each of the above two alternatives displays a different understanding of where public life occurs in a pluralist society, who the participants are, the patrons, and which institutions embrace it. Moreover, they differ in defining the role of architects and their buildings and spaces in affecting public life.

Figure 3: "Domestic Gazebo" added to the Education Department at the Universityof Oregon following Alexander's recommendations.

These two models of public space need not be fully justified by the political projects the architects were advocating at the time. Inversely, they need not rigorously represent predetermined political ideas. As illustrated in Oregon, they may in fact be internally contradictory if explained using a political model. However, if one seeks some level of consistency between form and content, these historically specific architectural conceptions of public space, could be aligned with certain contemporary models of the public sphere.

In contemporary discussions around normative political theory, about what constitutes politics, the public, and the rights of citizens, the framework through which major political concerns are debated has been figuratively referred to as 'public space'. The importance of this concept lies in the way it extends the imagination of normative theories from basic principles of justice to their actual application in the public realm. Thus, in political theory, 'public space' refers to the format and context in which issues of significance to the public are contested and discussed.[18]

Political theorists use the term 'space' metaphorically, but the notion public space does afford some literal implications: Since society needs not only be just but also appear just, the spatial manifestation of this appearance becomes significant. The discussion of public space can extend into a discussion about actual physical spaces particularly when these spaces coincide with the context and frameworks of public debate and when they act as physical vessels for public activity. There is a further temptation, which I will not resist, to extend the distinctions among physical models of public space to bear on political models. Indeed, the association of the words 'public' and 'space' does encourage those disciplines that claim some knowledge of physical space to address the theme of public space through their own disciplinary terms and indeed attempt to transform it.[19]

---

[18] The discussion of public space, which finds its first articulations in Hannah Arendt's work , has been revived in several disciplines, most notably by political theorists in the Habermasian tradition. For these theorists, such as Seyla Benhabib, the notion of public sphere as presented by Habermas in *The Structural Transformation of the Public Sphere* is further elaborated as the social context and procedural framework in which power relations regarding central political concerns are discussed and debated through different procedures of dialogue.

[19] Geographers like David Harvey and Ed Soja, art critics like Rosalyn Deutsche, urban sociologists like Richard Sennett, and architects like George Baird, to name a few, have been addressing the questions and problems of politics and the public as they emerge in their respective spatial terms.

It is clear that Kevin Lynch advocates John Rawls' justice as fairness that gives equal access to a basic scheme of rights and liberties to all individuals (including right of access).[20] Importantly, he also cites Rawls' distinction between the operation of a just system and the expression of justice. Rawls distinguishes between the practice of justice and the need to make justice visible to the citizens. Lynch understood the significance of this subtle distinction in Rawls' theory: "The rules of distribution must *seem* just," he repeats after Rawls, "since justice lies in the mind."[21] Since we are "light years away from a just world," it is very difficult to construct a just world without a cognitive map that renders the presence of justice legible to a diversity of citizens.[22] The imageability of justice is separate from, but necessary for, the sound exercise of justice. Imageability, for both Lynch and Rawls, is the means through which the images of society and justice, respectively, are conveyed to a pluralist society.

The visual accessibility of a space, a quality Lynch refers to as its imageability, has a very different function than representation. Imageability, like justice, is a means for achieving equality. In parallel, it is a means by which a complex system of spaces is arranged and presented to a diversity of citizens who can then move about on equal terms.

The problem both Lynch and Rawls face is that these qualities may not be accessible, that they have to undergo a process through which they are made manifest to all citizens. Representing justice to citizens is distinct from practicing it. Whether it is the same elements that acquire a symbolic order and come across as the image of justice or whether it is a second order of formal symbols and signs, it is not clear in Rawls. Nor does it seem right to determine once and for all.[23] For Lynch, this is a second order discussion which renders

---

[20] John Rawls, *A Theory of Justice*, The Belknap Press of Harvard University Press, Cambridge, Massachusetts, 1971. The book was circulated in manuscript form during the sixties. It was written with the struggles for social and racial equality and recognition in mind. See also Kevin Lynch, *A Theory of Good City Form*, MIT Press, Cambridge, Massachusetts, 1981, p.227.

[21] Ibid., p. 227.

[22] Ibid.

[23] I am here embracing Richard Rorty's defense of Rawls' political conception of justice and extending it to the realm of aesthetics. See Richard Rorty, "The Priority of Democracy to Philosophy," in *Objectivity, Relativism, and Truth*, Cambridge University Press, Cambridge, 1991, pp. 193-194.

the public spaces of the city and its buildings represent the conviviality or tolerance of its groups. It would be possible then to imagine an extension of this distinction in political liberalism that elaborates on the different tools with which justice is exercised and represented.[24]

In associating Lynch's project with a Rawlsian conception of public space, I have to contend with some important criticism of the latter. I have in mind, for one, Seyla Benhabib's who differentiates between the liberal model and what she calls a deliberative model of public space.[25] The differences between these two models reach down to such fundamental issues as the nature of pluralism and the interpretation of the practical consequences of the application of public reason. Each model also seeks articulation in different public spheres. Benhabib yearns for a public discourse that is not structured, that does not mark the speaker but rather constitutes her: a café or a living room. Rawls and Lynch, on the other hand, prefer a more formal and restrained space: the floor of the parliament or, better yet, the civic plaza located between ethnically different neighborhoods. The implicated community of the café may be smaller than that of the plaza. However, the networks of cafés together, or cafés and other forms of communication (newspapers, markets, television) may generate a debate that acquires the scale of society-wide public space. Benhabib, true to the Habermasian tradition, elaborates extensively on procedures of linking local informal debate to large-scale action. It is not difficult to see how the second alternative, the Oregon example, could be linked with

---

[24] One could further connect Lynch's project with that of political liberalism through the concept of public reason. Public reason, for Rawls, extends the political conception of justice in political liberalism into the public realm. Through its exercise of public reason, a democratic society can address its own good by deciding on its plans, priorities, and on the execution of these plans. It is the fact of pluralism that makes public reason so essential for the extension and application of the political conception of justice. After all, one of the aims of political liberalism is to bring forward into the public, to make visible, as it were, the ways in which fundamental political questions are addressed. For Rawls, it is necessary for the notion of public reason to succeed as a platform to discuss "constitutional essentials" before its extension to other political and social debates could be imagined. Perhaps physical space could be included among these "other" debates or among a third tier of applications of the principles of justice.

[25] See Seyla Benhabib, "Models of Public Space," in *Situating the Self: Gender, Community and Postmodernism in Contemporary Ethics*, Routledge, New York, 1992, and "Toward a Deliberative Model of Democratic Legitimacy," in Democracy and Difference, Princeton University Press, Princeton, New Jersey, 1996.

the deliberative model. What could be inferred from both is the possibility of complementing political means with aesthetic (or other) means.

Aesthetic Challenges to the Politics of Recognition

What then is the link between the physical models of public space and the political models, and how do the aesthetic questions raised in the first half of this paper illuminate the political questions in the latter? Two rash retorts, which architects, unfortunately, often use are that 1) they do not, because architecture is an autonomous discipline that does not have any links to social problems or to political theory; and 2) physical models simply follow the larger, more important political models and represent them. If anything, I hope that this paper has succeeded in illustrating the fallacy of these responses and the importance of complicating the relation between the physical and the political.

In the first alternative, the link between the physical and the social occurs at two levels, a "behavioral" and an aesthetic. Different social groups converge at the first level. Their differences would then be expressed aesthetically using architecture's power to convey meaning to citizens. Examining Lynch's example in retrospect, we could, and should, imagine alternative models: for instance, situations where differences are manifest in behavior. That is, the space could encourage different groups to behave differently, and perhaps a common iconography would make difference more behaviorally manifest. The possible alternatives could be further multiplied if we introduce the political models of public space. Lynch's double-tiered model displays remarkable consistency with a liberal conception of public space, even when it precedes it chronologically. This consistency is contingent upon the context in which Lynch operated.

Through an organic aesthetic, Alexander aimed to address a fundamental problem in the New Left's conception of public space using aesthetic means. An organic aesthetic was believed to offer small groups and communities the hope that their local and specific struggles would eventually be linked to a larger struggle. Alexander went to the extent of turning this provisional solution into an transcendental, "timeless way of building" which pervades all organic, beautiful environments. This second alternative may have failed to effect any real change, and ultimately its altruistic overtones may have further contributed to a reaction, within the profession, against any form of social engagement. The failure was not as important as the potential it foresaw for aesthetic practices in the political arena. Furthermore, and in line with Benhabib's deliberative model, the procedural project undertaken by New Left architects also showed that discussions around physical space help reveal, the political content of professional, private discourses. By proposing different methods of public participation to fit the different problems and groups implicated, they also helped citizens lay claim to the built environment, an important aspect of their lives which, for long, remained wrapped in professional discourse. Moreover, unlike both Rawls' liberal model and Lynch, and unlike the deliberative model, they rejected the possibility of entering the public realm on individual grounds. It is group identity that should be expressed in the public realm no matter how discreet.

We should not seek to recreate these historical experiences as much as to open up the range of options they promote even further, and we could immensely benefit from the wealth of past experiments that could still be of relevance. We cannot wholly dismiss past experiences for partial problems they have failed to solve. We need to build on them in order to produce more carefully worked out alternatives. Working with historical examples raises another issue: The physical environment survives the political ideas that will it. Given this, many architects have concluded that they should detach themselves from any 'worldly' concerns and focus on the transcendental attributes of form. (Paradoxically, and because of the alternative worlds it imagines, the physical environment could also become a source of empowerment by being disengaged.) Neither this option, for all its seductiveness, nor the cases discussed above, for all their simple instrumentality, could be fully accepted anymore.

In order to effect change, to be engaged, architecture has to remain partly disengaged. And in seeking to work out which aspects of form should express their context and which aspects should resist it and transform it, we would be multiplying possibilities beyond simplistic symbolism. We should be encouraged by the proliferation of possible links, and combinations thereof, between the physical experiments and the constituencies they address. This is one of the main ambitions of the politics of recognition, to encourage diversity by making choice ever more real.

166

Teodros Kiros[1]
Boston University

The Colors of Multiculturalism:
An Interview with Henry Louis Gates

Kiros: If, as Andrew Hacker, has written, in *Two Nations:* "America is inherently a white country in character, in structure and in culture..." how is the multicultural vision of reordering the world going to be realized, at least for our generation?

Gates: I don't think that America's essentially a white culture. I think America is essentially a middle class culture. One of my critiques of Hacker's work is that there are two nations: one, rich or comfortable; one, poor. I think that Americans are caught in a binary logic, because of slavery, because of the enslavement of African human beings. This does not reflect the reality, and I think consequently our rhetoric analyzing our social problems and our rhetoric analyzing proposing solutions to those social problems reflects a world that no longer exists. The world's not as simple as black and white in America. The world is middle class and no class; middle class, working class and lower class – however you might want to put it. Let me give you an example. Since the day Dr. King was killed, the black middle class has quadrupled, doubling in the 1980's alone. Yet simultaneously and paradoxically, fully one-third of the black community is worse off today than it was the day Dr. King was killed. You cannot say that I'm a victim of racism, as a Harvard professor, in the same way that someone who lives in the inner city in Roxbury is a victim of racism. Hence the metaphor of two nations, which of course come from Disraeli, only works if you think economically rather than ethnically. Furthermore, the Bureau of Population says that by about 2020 America will be brown

---

[1] This interview was held at the Afro-American Studies department at Harvard University on August 6, 1996. I would like to thank my friend and intellectual companion, George Katsiaficas, for co-editing the interview as well as disussing the formulation of questions.

in the majority, or at least mulatto in the majority, meaning there'll be more non-white people than white people. I don't think that really addresses your question, however, but it is an interesting fact.

The only time power concedes, Frederick Douglas said, and I'm paraphrasing, power concedes only in the face of power. One of the brilliant things about capitalism, and I think this is especially true for American capitalism, is that it appears to be infinitely adaptable. I think that for the same reason that apartheid fell so relatively easily in South Africa, America has embraced multiculturalism and will continue to do so, not really in the superficial ways it enacts it now, but in much more profound ways. By that I mean, DeClerk and company in South Africa decided to let Mandela out of prison and to go to one person, one vote, because it was profitable for them to do that. They would rather make profit than anything, even sit down with these jigaboos that they'd been talking about like monkeys, comparing them with monkeys and apes for a century. Anything, anything. I'm telling you, anything. And that's remarkable to me. Principles – shoo! – out the window. They say: Well, they were niggers yesterday, maybe they're still niggers today, or brother niggers. I think the same is true in America. For example, if black people voted to their full potential, we would have an enormous amount of power that we don't now have. If we had economic organization where we pooled our resources, we would have an enormous amount of power. There's nothing inherently racist about any system; there are historically racist systems. And America's been historically racist. Inherently, it's neutral. Inherently, capitalism is neutral. It wouldn't care who were the superordinates, who were the subordinates. It just functions, it flows. Just because something has been historically sexist or historically racist, I don't mean to say that's not important. I don't mean to say that that doesn't have pressure and weight. Of course it does. But you can counteract that by effectively engaging in the wielding of power. Look at World War II: The most evil civilization in modern times was the Germans, followed closely by the Japanese. History erased these just like that. Why? Corporate capital. The same could happen with black America. Now I'm sure my friend Cornel West finds me hopelessly romantic in this issue, and maybe I am. But it's what I actually believe. And I see my position as advocating the use and mastery of the master's tools to renovate the master's house, to reconfigure the master's house, rather than – in contradistinction to – Audre Lord who wrote famously that you cannot use the master's tools to dismantle the master's house. My response is, What other tools are there, you know? There's a hammer, there's a saw, the nails, you know? I mean, what are you going to use – a screw driver? Are you going to reinvent new tools? You know? What are they going to be called, the Zubeede?, the Whoopastan? I mean, Nigger, please! These are the only tools we have. Now multiculturalism for me stems from the belief that, first of all, beauty and excellence come in all diverse shapes and sizes. I firmly believe in that aesthetically. But secondly, I believe that the integration of the canon – integration of the curriculum, integration of aesthetic judgement, making it more cosmopolitan – is a prelude and a necessary part of larger structural changes. I mean, I find it morally reprehensible that all these homeless people live out in Harvard Square. And then multiply that by a million. And that's the situation in America. 45% of all black children live at or beneath the poverty line. One in three black males between the ages of 20 and 29 are in the care of the prison system. It's unacceptable to me. To me, though, you have to fight against those reprehensible statistics on various levels, and multiculturalism is my way. And I think we've been successful, and I think we'll continue to be successful as well.

Kiros: And how do you understand multiculturalism? How do you assess it conceptually?

Gates: First of all, as Cornel West has pointed out, multiculturalism is a word, the language of bureaucrats. For me, it's just something that we're straddled with, strapped with. But I also am talking about integrating, let's say my field, the study of literature, so that the canon refers to the best, most sophisticated, most accomplished works of literary art from around the world, not just something that happens to fall in the arc of the Greco-Roman and Judeo-Christian traditions. Whenever I use "tradition," it's (in a scarecrow quotes)and quotation marks, because traditions are fictions, I mean they're "made" in the literal sense of the word "fiction." And they're arbitrary. For too long, we thought that there was this great tradition of excellence and beauty, and then there was all this stuff all these people of color did. To me, it is decentering our notion of beauty and truth and excellence. I still believe in beauty and truth and excellence; I just think they're represented in different cultures from around the world. And I'm certainly an anti-relativist, as I've written. I think that the best you can do is to say, and this is my perspective, I could be wrong, I'm of my time and of my place, but this is what I believe, and I'm going to say it – call it the way I see it. You have to make a judgement. You have to say the stuff is more sophisticated than "Mamma" or "Waiting to Exhale," and you have to know the difference, otherwise, you shouldn't be in my profession.

Kiros: How did Multiculturalism shape the emergence of your seminal work *The Signifying Monkey*? This difficult book has admirers all over the world and yet they find it virtually impossible to summarize in everyday language.

Gates: *[laughter]* Well, it's my tenure book, *The Signifying Monkey*. It's not meant to be summarized in everyday language. It's meant to be understood by a tenure committee. *[laughter]* But my motivation was not multicultural, my motivation was black nationalist. I mean, if you asked me what my politics were, I would say "I'm a nationalist." I mean I love black cultures. I wrap myself in them. I study them. I chose to make my living this way. I love writing about black people, and whether they're from Ethiopia or from Harlem. But I've wanted to show the gods of theory that we had a tradition of theorizing, too. And I wanted to find it in the black vernacular, in the most vulgar, nasty language, and force them to deal with it. I wanted to use their theories as analogies, and say: Look, what we do in the black tradition is analogous to Jacques Derrida's theory of deconstruction or whatever and, you know, people at Yale hated it. When I came up for promotion to tenure and they voted, they split right down the middle. They promoted me to an associate professorship without tenure. My tenure vote was something like ten to nine. And so I left. I mean, they didn't fire me; I could have stayed there and written another book. But it's a polite way of firing somebody. And so I left and went to Cornell. I became a full professor at the age of 33, so I'm not exactly crying, but I'm just saying not everyone agrees to your assertion that *Signifying Monkey* was some subtle work. They thought it was crazy and full of shit. Many people did, and some probably still do. I happen to like it myself. I wanted to theorize from within the tradition. I wanted to theorize on the grounds of the African-American vernacular, which is the purest and least assimilated of all the grounds, though even the phrase "signifying monkey" reflects the pun, the visual pun in French, between "monkey" and "sign." So it is highly likely that the actual ritual was formulated after World War I by ex-GI's. And that we could see – someone was very clever, because there is that pun between S-I-G-N-E and S-I-N-G-E. So it's great.

But I'm very – you know, there are a lot of things I would do differently, now, 13 years later. I wrote the first draft in 1983 or so. I write in a much more accessible way now and to a much more accessible audience. I'm more secure. I mean, I have tenure. There's nothing wrong with jargon, per se. If you talk to your mother that way, there's something wrong with you. But pipe fitters talk to each other in jargon. Electricians talk to each other in jargon. Dentists do. My brother's an oral surgeon, and when he's talking to some of his friends, I say, "What did you say?" And he explains " You have a tooth ache." *[laughter]* I had no idea. Jargon is shorthand for those who are fluent in the jargon. But I tend, now, to find these changing fads in critical theory boring, not very interesting. I write the way I write. If people like it, great; if they don't like it, too bad.

Kiros: In *Loose Canons*, a different kind of book, you seemed to be uncomfortable in relating Marxist theory and all its transformations to the idea of Black Studies. Can you explain?

Gates: Am I anti-Marxist? Is that what you're asking?

Kiros: I'm just wondering *[laughter]* You seem to be uncomfortable with Marxist theory.

Gates: To me, Marxism – I mean, what are we – are we going to be the last Marxists in the world, but only Marxist – I mean even Russians aren't Marxist. Marxism exists in the academy. It is a useful tool for reading, for analyzing, and one of my most important professors at the University of Cambridge was Raymond Williams. One of my closest friends is Stuart Hall. They're both Marxists, I would guess. If you start talking Marxism, about who's a Marxist and who's not, you know, it's a can of worms. They're both on the left, socialists – and I find aspects of Marxist critical analysis enormously enlightening, understanding the society's economic relationships and how they impinge upon a text or are reflected in a text absolutely great. Frederick Jameson's a genius. So is Terry Eagleton. You know, these are some of the truly great critics of our time. So as a mode of critical analysis, Marxism is absolutely essential. As a philosophy or theory for ordering human society? Forget it. It's not going to happen. It's not going to happen in Ethiopia. It's not going to happen in Nigeria. It's not going to happen in the United States. It's just not going to happen. I think it was an interesting idea, but it doesn't make sense to me. But, that said, I think we need a more humane form of capitalism. I think – I heard Hugh Price, the head of the National Urban League say, recently, that capitalism was in danger of de-civilizing itself, and I think when you look at the new welfare bill, you see it. I mean, we need a socialized form of capitalism. We need a mixed economy. We need entitlement programs. You need that. You can't enslave people for 100 years, 200 years and expect them to be playing on a level playing field. Structurally, in a capitalist system, there is a certain percentage of people who are unemployed. That's the way it is. Somebody's got to take care of those people, and that's got to be us. I mean, I don't want to live in a pure laissez faire economy. I don't think that it exists at all. And I think it's quite dangerous what the Republicans are doing, and indeed what Bill Clinton, in the process of Republicanizing himself, is doing or sanctioning.

Kiros: Is there a relationship in your mind between concerns with multiculturalism and the construction of canons, or are these two separate themes?

Gates: No my concern about canons began because I heard Professor John Hollander, a distinguished poet and my colleague in the English Department at Yale say in a meeting that only the Western tradition could have a canon, which I thought was one of the silliest things I ever heard in my life. He probably doesn't even remember and would probably deny saying it, but I heard him. I mean it seems like the Dark Ages, now. But that was the kind of idea I was fighting against in this great English Department: that there was a canon, and it was Western and white and male, primarily, and everything else was just, I don't know what. Less than that. And what I wanted to show was that a canon was to tradition like marrow is to the bone. A canon is just what each generation, or even an individual professor, finds to be the hallmarks of the tradition. Well, in order to defend my own tradition, I had to make a case generally rather than specifically. It's the only way to go for that kind of thing. And I also realized that I couldn't lose, because we were talking about the whole world. We were talking about China and India and Africa. And we're talking about the whole world's traditions. And so I used them, and I put the black American tradition with them in my arguments about the nature of canon reformation and influence. And actually, it wasn't very hard to poke holes in notions of both tradition and the canon. I mean, the idea that you would just exclude all the rest of the world's literature almost a priori was ridiculous! I mean, that was not going to survive close scrutiny. So I didn't want to relocate the African-American tradition outside of America textually. But I wanted to locate my aesthetic argument, my philosophical basis for claiming the existence of separate canons, different canons, different traditions in the broadest possible way. It was the only way to do it.

Kiros: Just a slight continuation of that question. What kind of canons are multicultural children of the future going to produce, or even more radically, what forms of others are they going to be? If you so like, we can talk about your own children, as you did so beautifully in *Colored People*.

Gates: I have no idea. I mean, it's a wonderful question, but

I would need a crystal ball. I think that they will be more comfortable with themselves, put simply, as world citizens. That's what I hope: that the kind of narrowness of vision and concern of so many people in my generation – I'm 45 – and generations older than I in this country that that narrowness of horizon will not be a disease that afflicts my children's generation. With the globalization of culture, I would hope that that's true. People still have a Euro-centric, American-i-centric perspective, of course, but at least they'll be familiar with, the range of cultures around the world which is better than Americans of times past have been. I'm not a very good prognosticator.

Kiros: As you know, Professor Gates, there's so much talk about the politics of identity these days, and most of it is quite incomprehensible to me. I always thought that identity is the only dimension of the self that is beyond politics, that which occupies, as it were, an intimate space in which others should not be allowed. What is your analysis of this phenomenon?

Gates: Oh, but there are different kinds of identity. I mean, if you're talking about Teodros, the sweet, loving man that his wife fell in love with, that's one thing. But if you're talking about the identity that's created as soon as you announce that you are Ethiopian, that is an identity that is visited upon you in the minds of other people beyond your control. If they think they know what you are – I mean, if I walk into a jewelry store, let's say, then I'm treated like another African-American male, more likely than not. That doesn't have anything to do with my individual identity. Barbara Johnson, my colleague here in the English Department, defined the stereotype as "an already read text." And that means, when they see you, they have read you. They know you. They know who you are, and it's a stereotype. That's what a stereotype is – it's a brilliant definition of stereotype. That is a form of public identity that is absolutely 180 degrees contrary to the wonderful definition of identity that you gave, which is one definition of identity; but there are many definitions. And that is the one that we're dealing with, the one shaped through social construction.

Now just because an identity is shaped through social construction doesn't mean that it's not real. The pen I'm holding in my hand is socially constructed, but it has ink in it, and I just wrote a sentence. The Ethiopian food I ate last night at The Red Sea was socially constructed, and it tasted damn good. *[laughter]* Just like your Mamma's food. But it means that they have pressure and weight, too, and that you have no choice over them. You have no choice over these identities; they just come with you. They're part and parcel of your being, and you have to react against them, or you have to fight them, you have to argue with them. But you're always doing battle with them. It's like women. You know, if women are cheated and stereotyped and seen and envisioned in a certain way in this society, they have to fight against that. They have to disprove it, whether they do it subtly, whether they do it boldly, whether they do it vulgarly or whether they do it elegantly – they're still fighting and railing against those kinds of stereotypes, those kinds of confines that would seek to "read you" in advance. And I think each of us in disempowered situations has to be aware of that and do our best to fight back. The process is true of everybody. It's true of Wall Street bankers, but they happen to have a lot of positive reinforcement going with them, in terms of that image, that stereotype. The question becomes more urgent when the connotations are negative.

Kiros: Many of our readers consider you to be one of the most important public intellectuals of our times. Do you see yourself within a tradition or creating a tradition as a public intellectual?

Gates: Well, to me, there's a contradiction in terms between being an intellectual and being a public intellectual. Being a scholar and being an intellectual are two different things. Being a scholar means, you bury yourself away in archives, and the real world may or may not impinge upon your work and your consciousness. To be an intellectual means to be in the arena, so I think that it's a pleonasm. But I also, in terms of me, I like to write. And I like to write in very accessible ways, and I like to write in ways, though less and less, that are less accessible. And in part because of my job as the

Director of the premiere African-American research institution in the world, in my opinion, and of the best Afro-American Studies Department in the world, I'm thrust into public debates in ways that I'm not trained for. My Ph.D. is in English literature. My Ph.D. prepared me to read Phillis Wheatley's poems closely, not to talk about race and class. I engage in public debate and public discourse about issues effecting African-Americans, specifically, and the broader society in general. But I always do so as a generalist, as just a reasonably well-educated, reasonably well-read, eclectic, thinking person, I would hope. That's one reason why it was incumbent upon this department to recruit people like William Julius Wilson. We just made an offer to Larry Bobo – people who actually do public policy, because we want them to be we want the institute to be actively engaged in those issues. For myself – I have my heroes; I wouldn't be so immodest as to put myself on their level: James Baldwin, the great Du Bois, Paul Robeson, Frederick Douglas, Fanny Lou Hamer, Zora Neale Hurston, Toni Morrison. These people mean a lot to me, and I would be honored if history remembers me in their company, but only history will decide.

Kiros: In *Loose Canons* once again, you seem to be quite upset with those who are hostile to the liberal tradition. I'm wondering why?

Gates: Well, I don't think that it's good to throw the baby out with the bath. I think that – one of the things about the great Western tradition, What are we going to do? Throw Plato out? You going to throw Shakespeare out? I mean, it's ridiculous. They're geniuses. They're brilliant people. And the idea that you would demonize a whole tradition is utterly, utterly ridiculous. Or to say that – to quote Du Bois, "I sit with Shakespeare, and he winces not" is somehow problematic! Of course it's not problematic. I want Western people to be able to sit with Soyinka and wince not. Just like I want to feel comfortable with the canonical writers of the Western tradition. I mean literature is about virtual reality anyway. Literature as Said said is about time and space travel. It's about imagining yourself across gender, across ethnicity. You know, you could even identify with an animal, through folktales and Brer Rabbit. And I'm sure in Ethiopia, there are those tales. You don't have to be a rabbit to *[laughter]* to identify with Brer Rabbit. The whole principle of literature is that it's all transference. You're free. You can range. You can be whoever you want to be. And I happen to like that. I mean, it's one of the reasons that I'm a professor of literature to this day.

Kiros: To what extent are you sympathetic with those who continue to talk about "otherness." Who are these others that they talk about? Who is "the other?"

Gates: Well, I think we got so stuck on the concept of "the other" that I knew people who would write to their mother, and they'd put the "M" in parenthesis. *[laughter]* You talk about Euro-centric. I mean, if you define "us" as the subject and everyone else as the object, "us" as the self and everyone else as "the other," I mean, how much more Euro-centric can you get? I think that a lot of subtlety has to be brought to the concept of self and other, which so often is not, at least, in the work of theorists of English and American literature.

Kiros: And finally, my last question and a very academic one, but it must be asked. The celebrated Bulgarian theorist, Todorov, has observed "The constant interaction of cultures results in the formation of hybrid, crossbred, creolized cultures at every level: from bilingual writers, through cosmopolitan metropolises, to multicultural states." How in a human context, do you make sense of this passage?

Gates: Hybridity?

Kiros: Yes.

Gates: That's what it is! I mean, if you're black American, the idea of hybridity and creolization which Todorov and all these people are just discovering is part and parcel of your every day historical experience. The African-American culture is a hybrid, but so is American culture. It's just that America's been in denial about that hybridity, that cross-pollination, that creolization for centuries. My understanding of multiculturalism depends on bringing these subterranean cultures – that which has been buried, that which has been denied, that which has been repressed – to the surface and redefining our common public culture, because our common public culture has always been hybrid. It's just that our official public culture was this fantasy of white Anglo-Saxon Greco-Roman this and that, you know, with no spooks allowed. And what I want is for all that to change. And it is changing. It sounds superficial to say that it's changed in terms of restaurants and food, or in the Benetton's motto of a little color representing the whole world, but those things, as superficial as they might seem, are part and parcel, or can be part and parcel, of a larger phenomenon. Certainly the average white American is much more comfortable with persons and cultures of color than she or he was when I was growing up. Just take the ease and the facility with which foreign names are spoken by announcers in the Olympics, for example. They used to butcher their names. They would just say them in the most mispronounced way possible, just, I think, as a statement about otherness and foreignness. And now, even on that level, again small, again superficial – but even those things are beginning to reflect a more cosmopolitan consciousness of the cultures of color. And that's all to the good. That process will only increase, particularly as the number of people of color increases, which they will do, again, to end where we began, until the year 2020 when people of color will be in the majority.

Kiros: Thank you very much.

Gates: Thank you.

Ali A. Mazrui
State University of New York at Binghamton

Afrocentricity Versus Multiculturalism?: A Dialectic In Search Of A Synthesis[1]

Afrocentricity and multiculturalism have become hot concepts in the last decade or so. Among those who have pursued the Afrocentric perspective, Maulana Karenga and Molefi Kete Asante stand out.[2] Multiculturalism, by its very nature, has had more proponents, especially in the academic arena.[3]

There are those who regard Afrocentricity as an aspect of multiculturalism, and there are those who regard them as parallel themes, separate but equal. It is conceivable to regard them as in fact antithetical paradigms, paradigms which pull in different ways. In this essay, I hope to put before you those different levels for your consideration.

Let us first identify elements important to the definition of the Afrocentric perspective. What are the elements which go towards the Afrocentric perspective?

First, Africa as subject rather than object. Related to it is Africa as active rather than passive. Third, Africa as cause rather than as effect. Fourth, Africa as center rather than periphery. And then Africa as maker of history rather than an incident in history.

[1] Revised and updated version of a lecture delivered at the University of California, Los Angeles, under the sponsorship of the James S. Coleman Center for African Studies, May 5, 1993. An earlier version of this lecture was delivered at the University of Wisconsin, Madison, in June 1992.

[2] Works by Asante include *Malcolm X as Cultural Hero: and Other Afrocentric Essays* (Trenton, NJ: Africa World Press, 1993); *Kemet, Afrocentricity, and Knowledge* (Trenton, NJ: Africa World Press, 1992, 1990); *Afrocentricity* (Trenton, NJ: Africa World Press, 1988); and *Afrocentricity: The Theory of Social Change* (Buffalo, NY: Amulefi Pub. Co., 1980). Works by Karenga include *The African American Holiday of Kwanzaa: A Celebration of Family, Community, and Culture* (Los Angeles, CA: University of Sankore Press, 1988) and *Introduction to Black Studies* (Inglewood, CA: Kawaida Publications, 1982)

[3] On multiculturalism, consult the following recent compilations: Lawrence Foster and Patricia Herzog, eds. *Defending Diversity: Contemporary Philosophical Perspectives on Pluralism and Multiculturalism* (Amherst, MA: University of Massachusetts Press, 1994) and David T. Goldberg, *Multiculturalism: A Critical Reader* (Boston: Blackwell Publishers, 1994). The New York State Library has a bibliographical guide called *Multiculturalism Bibliography; Selected Sources from the Collection of the New York State Library* (Albany, NY: SUNY, State Education Dept., 1994).

But what is the Africa we talk about in Afrocentricity? Sometimes the term used is Africana, meaning the Black world as a whole.[4] I often prefer the term Global Africa as the sum total of the following: continental Africa; the diaspora of enslavement, which was created by the dispersal caused by the horrors of enslavement; and the diaspora of colonialism, the dispersal caused by the destabilization and long-term consequences and disruptions of the colonial era.

It is possible to regard Jesse Jackson as part of the diaspora of enslavement and Ali Mazrui and his children as part of the diaspora of colonialism. Jamaicans in Britain are both part of the consequences of enslavement and part of the consequences of colonization. Global Africa becomes the sum total of that massive African presence on a world scale.

Defining Afrocentricity and Multiculturalism

Yet Afrocentricity goes beyond that. It is not enough simply to look at global Africa from a global perspective; Afrocentricity looks at the world from an African perspective. Afrocentricity is the study of the human condition from an African perspective. We shall return to that theme.

What are the defining elements in the multicultural perspective? A basic assumption is the parity of esteem of all cultures. It is almost as if there was a founding father, a kind of multicultural Jefferson, who has pronounced that all cultures are created equal and are endowed with certain inalienable rights, among them cultural life, cultural liberty, and the pursuit of cultural happiness.

Of course, not all cultures are factually equal, any more than all human beings are factually equal, but they are morally equal just as all human beings are morally equal. Moral equality cannot be equated with factual equality because people are not equal if they are tested against a yardstick of empiricism. Similarly, cultures are not equal if they are tested against the yardstick of pragmatism. However, just as one starts from the moral position that all people are created equal, then the issue of whether this person is more intelligent than that one, this man is taller than that, this woman is

---

[4] For instance, see Clenora Hudson-Weems, *Africana Womanism: Reclaiming Ourselves* (Troy, MI: Bedford Publishers, 1993).

more clever than that – all that ceases to be relevant. At some moral level all people become equal. Similarly, the multicultural perspective assumes that all cultures deserve parity of esteem. They are morally equal regardless of whether they are empirically equal. They contribute to each other, and a synthesis emerges of "cultural holism."[5]

In 1990-91 I served on the New York Syllabus Review Committee of the State of New York for High Schools. We spent about a year determining whether what children in the high schools of New York were exposed to was excessively Eurocentric. The majority of us on the committee concluded after our deliberations that education in the state of New York was excessively Eurocentric. Our Syllabus Review report was called *One Nation, Many Peoples: A Declaration of Cultural Interdependence*, published of course by the State of New York's Education Department.[6] It was as if the whole system assumed that the pyramids were built by the Pharaohs instead of by the Egyptian people or the Egyptian peasants. This pyramid called the United States of America was not built just by the founding fathers, the pharaohs. It was also built by a lot of women, black people, other minorities within the system, a lot of workers and peasants, a variety of people who have little recognition in the history books of the United States. The pyramid was not built just by Anglo-Americans. It was also built by varieties of nationalities, who have had scant salute in the annals of this particular society. There is then, the pyramid called human civilization which, was not built by European pharaohs only, but included a lot of other people in its construction.

Our Syllabus Review report was inevitably controversial. No less controversial was my appendix to the report, which was called "Multiculturalism and Comparative Holocaust."[7] American children needed to learn that genocide did not begin with the Nazis, but was perpetrated in the Americas

[5] Consult, for example, Betty Jean Craige, *Laying the Ladder Down: The Emergence of Cultural Holism* (Amherst, MA: University of Massachusetts Press, 1992).

[6] See *One Nation, Many Peoples: A Declaration of Cultural Interdependence* (The Report of the New York State Social Studies Review and Development Committee (Albany, NY: New York State Education Dept, 1991).

[7] Ali A. Mazrui, "Multiculturalism and Comparative Holocaust: Educational and Moral Implications," in *One Nation, Many Peoples*, pp. 41-44.

by white men against Native Americans.[8] Enslavement of Africans was also an experience of Holocaust proportions.

But what are the analytical differences between Afrocentricity and multiculturalism – apart from these elements which I have mentioned? Firstly, multiculturalism is a pluralistic method, seeking to represent diverse cultures – Latino (including Chicano of course), Asian, African, Native American, women. Therefore multiculturalism is pluralistic in that sense.[9] Afrocentricity is a dialectical method, seeking to negate the negation in an almost Hegelian sense, seeking to negate the negative portrayal of the most distorted history in the world, that of the African people.

While multiculturalism is a quest for diversity, Afrocentricity is an antithesis. It is an antithesis to the thesis of Eurocentrism. The antithesis is searching for a synthesis.[10] The thesis ultimately was white history, the antithesis was Africana history. Is there a synthesis? The thesis is Eurocentrism, the antithesis is Afrocentricity – is the synthesis multiculturalism?

Multiculturalism is also a rainbow coalition representing the colors of different global realities. Afrocentricity is a quest for a reconciliation of opposites, confronting Eurocentrism with its ultimate other – Africanity. It is confronting white focus with its ultimate Other – black focus. Politically, multiculturalism is a quest for the solidarity of the oppressed. It unites Blacks, Latinos, Native Americans, women and other oppressed peoples. Politically, Afrocentricity is a declaration of racial independence as it seeks to promote global Africana and self-reliance.

Urgent questions arise for those of us who are in Africana studies or who are ourselves Africans, in that global sense.

---

[8] See, for instance, David E. Stannard, *American Holocaust: Columbus and the Conquest of the New World* (New York: Cambridge University Press, 1992).

[9] On the "multiculturalism/pluralism" issue in the United States, consult, for example, John Higham, "Multiculturalism and Universalism: A History and Critique," *The American Quarterly* 45 (June 1993): 195-226; Mary Lefkowitz, "Multiculturalism, Uniculturalism, or Anticulturalism," *Partisan Review* 60 (Fall 1993); 590-6; and John D. Buenker and Lorman A. Ratner, eds. *Multiculturalism in the United States: A Comparative Guide to Acculturation and Ethnicity* (New York: Greenwood Press, 1992).

[10] For some, it is a synthesis; see Ayele Bekerie, "The Four Corners of a Circle: Afrocentricity as a Model of Synthesis," *Journal of Black Studies* 25 (December 1994): 131-149.

Should we be inspired by Afrocentricity or should we respond to a quest for multiculturalism? Afrocentricity is predicated on the uniqueness of the African peoples. Multiculturalism is predicated on the universal cultural interdependence of all people. Afrocentricity emphasizes the impact of the African people on world civilization. Multiculturalism sees world civilization as a pooling of the cultural resources of many peoples. What Negritude is to the Black poet, Afrocentricity is to the Black scholar. They are a celebration of Africanity. Multiculturalism, on the other hand, is a chorus of diverse legacies. By definition, Afrocentricity is unipolar – a world centered in Africa. Multiculturalism is multipolar; a universe of many centers. The question persists – where should I belong, where should Edmond Keller belong, where should Maulana Karenga belong, where should all those of us who are in Africana studies belong?

A Cost Benefit Analysis

There is a case to be made for Africana Studies to go in either direction, either to commit itself to unrelenting Afrocentricity, or to dedicate itself to uncompromising multiculturalism.

First, the case for Afrocentricity. Africana studies has been neglected for so long that only a thoroughgoing Afrocentric approach stands a chance of narrowing the gap. This is part of the reason why we should go the Afrocentric way, those of us who are in Africana studies. This field has been neglected for so long that only an Afrocentric crusade stands a chance of producing results.[11]

Secondly, there is so much prejudice against people of African descent that only an Afrocentric approach could change their image before the world. We are confronted with a massive wall of prejudice, and therefore a thoroughgoing Afrocentric approach becomes part of the necessary wherewithal for confronting that wall.

Thirdly, African contributions to world civilization have been so underestimated or even denied, that only an

---

[11] Of course, the seeds for this have to be sown among young minds in college; consult, for example, Jerome H. Schiele, "Afrocentricity: Implications for Higher Education," *Journal of Black Studies* 25 (December 1994): 150-69.

Afrocentric crusade can hope to restore the balance.[12]

Fourthly, the African peoples may indeed be the Chosen People of history; a people of the day before yesterday and a people of the day after tomorrow. Afrocentrism is a paradigm shift which looks at human affairs as a response to the African condition. Afrocentricity becomes a perspective which moves Africa and people of African ancestry to the center stage of world history.

And there are two types of Afrocentricity. Gloriana Afrocentricity emphasizes the great and proud accomplishments of people of African ancestry – Africa at its most complex, Africa on a grand scale. This would include the castle builders, those who built the walls of Zimbabwe, or the castles of Gondar, or the sunken churches of Lalibela, and indeed, some would argue, those who built the pyramids of Egypt.[13] This is Gloriana Afrocentricity.

There is also Proletariana Afrocentricity. This emphasizes the sweat of Africa's brow, the captured African as a co-builder of modern civilization. This emphasizes the enslaved as creator and innovator. There is a volume of work documenting the role of slave labor in helping to build the Industrial Revolution in the Western world. Slave labor, for better or for worse, helped to fuel the capitalist transformation in the northern hemisphere.[14]

A corollary factor in the development of the industrialized modern world was colonialism and the colonized peoples, both as victims and as builders. The resources of Africa including the minerals of Africa, extracted from beneath our feet, have been used for factories which have transformed the nature of the 20th century. Without those resources this

---

[12] An exception is renowned scholar Martin Bernal's *Black Athena*; see Martin Bernal, *Black Athena: The Afroasiatic Roots of Classical Civilization* 2 vols. (London & New Brunswick, NJ: Free Association Books & Rutgers University Press, 1987-).

[13] Some examples include Ivan Van Sertima, ed., *Egypt: Child of Africa* (New Brunswick, NJ: Transaction Publishers, 1994) and Asa G. Hilliard, "The Meaning of KMT (Ancient Egyptian) History for Contemporary African American Experience," *Phylon* 49 (Spring/Summer 1992): 12-22.

[14] See, for example, Eric Williams, *Capitalism and Slavery* (London: Andre Deutsch, 1987, 1944); Elizabeth Fox-Genovese and Eugene D. Genovese, *Fruits of Merchant Capital: Slavery and Bourgeois Property in the Rise and Expansion of Capitalism* (New York: Oxford University Press, 1983); and Joseph E. Inikori, "Slavery and the Development of Industrial Capitalism in England," *Journal of Interdisciplinary History* 17 (Spring 1987): 771-93.

century would have been vastly different.[15]

Proletariana Afrocentricity is a story of victim as Creator. In a way, even Negritude is a kind of Proletariana Afrocentricity, at least when it indulges in romantic primitivism, as Aime Cesaire did. "Hooray for those who never invented anything. Hooray for those who never explored anything. My Negritude is no tower and no cathedral. It delves into the deep red flesh of the soil."[16]

The primitivist version of Negritude celebrates Africa's simplicity rather than Africa's complexity. It salutes the African cattle herder not the African castle builder. To that extent it is part of Afrocentricity Proletariana.

As for the case for multiculturalism – the argument would go this way. The problem is not merely the demeaning of African culture. It is the threatening hegemonic power of Western culture, particularly European culture. Western cultural hegemony – or Eurocentrism – in the world cannot be challenged by Africana Studies alone. Eurocentrism has a long history, deep roots, and powerful allies all over the global system to be threatened seriously by Africana studies.[17] It must be tackled by an alliance of all other cultures threatened by Western hegemony – sometimes even by an alliance which includes dissident elements within Western culture itself.

The present world culture is Eurocentric but the next world culture is unlikely to be Afrocentric, even if that was desirable. The best solution is therefore a more culturally balanced world civilization. That is the burden of the next

[15] Consult, for example, Alan K. Smith, *Creating a World Economy: Merchant Capital, Colonialism, and World Trade, 1400-1825* (Boulder: Westview, 1991); Heinz Dietrich, "Five Centuries of the New World Order," *Latin American Perspectives* (Summer 1992): 48-52; J. M. Blaut, "Colonialism and the Rise of Capitalism," *Science and Society* 53 (Fall 1989): 260-96; and comments by Samir Amin in Vol. 54 (Spring 1990): 67-72 and Albert Prago, Vol 55 (Winter 1991): 469-70 in the same journal.

[16] This is a summary version of the lines, quoted in Ali A. Mazrui, et al, "The Development of Modern Literature since 1935," in Ali A. Mazrui, ed. *UNESCO General History of Africa, Vol. VIII: Africa Since 1935* (Paris, London, Berkeley: UNESCO, Heinemann, and University of California Press), p. 556. Those lines were from S. W. Allen's translation of J. P. Sartre, "Introduction to African Poetry," in *Black Orpheus* (Paris: Presence Africaine): 41-43.

[17] For a social history analysis, consult Samir Amin, *Eurocentrism* (New York: Monthly Review Press, 1989); for a literary view, see Vasilis Lambropoulos, *The Rise of Eurocentrism: Anatomy of Interpretation* (Princeton: Princeton University Press, 1993).

generation, to attempt to enlist the participation of other civilizations, not to provide an alternative hegemony, but to provide a new balance. Africana Studies should do joint projects with groups like Latin American Studies, Middle Eastern Studies, or studies of other parts of the Third World.

Part of the mission is to reduce the global Eurocentric presence in scholarship, in research, and in education. The problem is not simply that African culture has been demeaned. African culture will continue to be demeaned as long as Western culture is hegemonic and triumphant in the very citadels of Africa – for Western culture has deep roots.[18]

Only an alliance with other groups can even approximate a dent on this ever expansionist European giant, and its extensions. If Africana is to go multicultural, it must internally go comparative. African studies should include the study of global Africa. Even within Africana Studies we need to broaden out.

The history of Africa does not end on Africa's shores. In fact, African children in African schools in continental Africa are wrongly taught that "African history" is assumed to be the history of that piece of land which is bounded by those particular oceans. And yet one must ask "When did those Africans exported as slaves cease to be part of African history – when they left Cape Coast in Ghana? when they were midway across the Atlantic? when they got the Western Hemisphere? in the first hundred years? in the first two hundred years? – what was the African cutoff point of those captives? When did they cease to be African? When did they walk out of African history?"

Those are questions which children in Africa itself ought to be encouraged to ask themselves. But this is not yet happening. On the contrary, current researchers are under-playing the slave trade in Africa itself. They are underplaying some of the links which could constitute the bridge with the externalized Black world. This shrinkage of the African consciousness needs to be arrested as a matter of urgency.

---

[18] See, for instance, George K. Kieh, "The Roots of Western Influence in Africa: An Analysis of the Conditioning Process," *The Social Science Journal* 29, 1 (1992): 7-19, for one account of the how Western ways and patterns are imprinted among Africans.

The World Is Africa Writ Large

To return to Afrocentricity as a perspective on world studies. Afrocentricity is not just a method of looking at the history of Africa, but it is a method of looking at the history of the world. Afrocentricity moves the African experience to the middle stage. There is first the concern with the evolutionary genesis, the origins of our species. Because on present evidence our human species begins in the African continent, the entire human race becomes a massive global African diaspora.[19] Every human being becomes a descendant of Africa. It is in that evolutionary sense, that the rest of the world is a massive African diaspora.

Then there is the cultural genesis. If from present evidence our species began in Africa, then our basic institutions also began in Africa – human language, human family. Some of you who saw my television series probably remember my startling statement "WE invented the family." By that I precisely meant that if the species began in Africa, then Africans must have begun the kinship institutions which crystallized into the human family.

When I was filming the TV series "The Africans," I wanted to do something about the First Supper. We went around looking for evidence of the First Supper. We were concerned not with the religious doctrine of Christianity of the Last Supper, but with the origins of socialized meals. When was the first time the satisfaction of a biological need was converted into a social routine called a meal? When did human beings begin to socialize on the basis of the satisfaction of biological needs?

We went to Tanzania to places where some of the earliest remains of our species were discovered. We were not looking for the remains of the first meal, but we did find places which did look like some of the earliest "dining tables." We took pictures and I did address the camera about these ideas,

---

[19] There is some controversy over whether humans first emerged "out-of-Africa" only or were co-terminus with other areas such as Asia; for one view, leaning to the former, see Leslie C. Aiello, "The Fossil Evidence For Modern Human Origins in Africa: A Revised View," *American Anthropologist* 95, 1 (March 1993): 73-96; contrary arguments can be found in Alan R. Templeton, "The 'Eve' Hypothesis: A Genetic Critique and Reanalysis," *American Anthropologist* 95, 1 (March 1993): 51-57.

about African origins of some of these institutions. Television being what it is, the pictures were not strong enough for the story I wanted to tell. So in the end those particular pictures were part of the casualties in the film editing room. The story was too big for the pictures we managed to acquire. On the line was the issue of the First Supper, when human beings began to move from mere biological satisfactions to socialized institutions within our continent. On the line were the cultural origins of many of our other institutions, in the African continent. Here then is the cultural genesis arising out of the evolutionary genesis.

Third, there is the civilizational genesis, which is not exactly the same as the cultural genesis. Civilizationally, much of Africana studies has focused especially on the role of ancient Egypt as a grand civilization which shaped not only other parts of Africa, but had a considerable impact on civilizations in the rest of the Mediterranean.

Most recently discussion has emphasized Egypt's impact on ancient Greece. Martin Bernal's book, *Black Athena*, has generated a new examination of that debate.[20] Bernal's approach to the subject is telling us that these distortions were not made by ancient Greeks. It was not the Greeks who did not acknowledge their debt to ancient Egyptians. It has been modern Europeans who have changed classical history. This massive macroplagiarism of lifting a whole civilization without footnotes was done not by the ancients but in the 18th and 19th centuries with revisionist European historians of the classics.

Bernal's thesis is that modern Europeans, entering a new era of racism and anti-Semitism, could not make themselves bear the thought that what they regarded as the pristine origins of their civilization should have had much to do with either Africans or such Semitic peoples as the Phoenicians. Modern Europeans therefore promptly understressed, if not "obliterated", Egypt's contribution to Athens.[21]

[20] See Bernal, *Black Athena*.

[21] For some of the more notable reviews of Bernal's work, see, for example, Leonard Lesko's review of volume 2 in *The Journal of Interdisciplinary History* 24 (Winter 1994): 518-21; Bruce G. Trigger, *Current Anthropology* 33 (February, 1992): 121-3; John Coleman, *Archaelogy* 45 (September/October 1992): 48-52; David Gress, "The Case Against Martin Bernal," *The New Criterion* 8 (December 1989): 36-43; G. W. Bowersock, *The Journal of Interdisciplinary History* 19 (Winter 1989): 490-1; and Martha Malamud, *Criticism* 31 (Summer 1989): 317-322.

Martin Bernal is not of course a Pan-African Black nationalist. He is a white Irish Jew, a very different phenomenon from Edmond Keller, Maulana Karenga and Ali Mazrui, who have their own Pan-African ax to grind. Bernal has since issued the second volume of Black Athena, a very detailed work with a lot of linguistic as well as archival evidence. Bernal was previously a fellow at a Cambridge College in England, and he is currently based at Cornell University. His work has certainly strengthened Africa's civilizational genesis.

Fourth, there is the geographical centrality of Africa. It is almost as if the Almighty in His infinite wisdom had cut Africa into in two equal parts. Africa is certainly the only continent that is thus cut almost in half by the equator. Africa is also the only continent that is traversed by both the tropic of Cancer and the tropic of Capricorn. In many ways, therefore, Africa is also the most tropical of all continents by its centrality. The geographical centrality of Africa is therefore clear.

It is true that Europeans played games with the size of Africa, in its representation on the map, but there were certain things even European map-makers could not tamper with. Once they started drawing lines called latitudes, and identified the equator, there was nothing they could do but reveal Africa as geographically the most central of all continents.

Fifth, there is the monotheistic genesis, the debate as to whether monotheism began in Africa. There is disagreement among Africana scholars whether the Pharaoh Akhenaten was in fact the first thoroughgoing monotheist in history or not. His reign was from 1350-1334 B. C.[22] There is the related debate as to whether the Semites, who helped universalize monotheism, were originally African or not, because their distribution has since been on both sides of what is now the Red Sea. After all the Red Sea itself was created by one massive earthquake which also created the Rift Valley. Indeed, was Moses an African? Was he an Egyptian? If he was indeed an Egyptian, did that therefore make him an African? All this is part of the monotheistic debate concerning the origins of Africa in that regard. It is in this sense that Afrocentricity has

[22] On this king, consult Peter A. Clayton, *Chronicle of the Pharaohs* (London: Thames and Hudson, 1994): 120-126; for a book-length treatment, see Donald B. Redford, *Akhenaten: The Heretic King* (Princeton: Princeton University Press, 1984).

to be considered in many fundamental ways as a perspective on world history. The forces of world history often have their origins in Africa.

Great debates of Africa's global impact include the questions: was ancient Egypt of the Pharaohs an African civilization? Was it a black civilization? Cheik Anta Diop of Senegal led the way, long before Martin Bernal.[23] In fact Martin Bernal's first volume refers to Cheik Anta Diop only on one page.[24] And yet this Senegalese man had been working on that theme for several decades before Martin Bernal. Ancient Egypt's Africanity is therefore one of the great Afrocentric themes.

There has also been the debate about the Columbus Phenomenon. This has had two areas. One is the chronological debate, as to whether Christopher Columbus was really the first to cross the Atlantic. Had there been in fact others who did it before? And did those others include Africans? There are those huge discoveries in Mexico, of sculptured faces that bear so-called Negroid features. The stone heads weigh tons. Nobody disputes that they are about 2,000 years old. They are pre-Christ, let alone pre-Columbus. There is no scientific disagreement about their age. The question is: why do they look so African? People are arguing about the likeliest explanation as to why they look so African, but the most straightforward explanation would be that they look African because Mexico had been exposed to Africans before Christ, when those facial features were carved out.[25]

There is also the moral debate about Columbus distinct from the chronological debate. Was Christopher Columbus a noble man who brought civilization and allowed for the development of a "savage" society where the "natives" had not exploited their resources ruthlessly? Or was Christopher Columbus the ultimate Black Man's Burden? Did he really inaugurate an era which devastated much of the African world,

[23] See, for example, Cheik Anta Diop, *The African Origin Of Civilization: Myth or Reality* (New York: L. Hill, 1974).

[24] See Bernal, Black Athena, p. 436.

[25] Some works in this genre include Ivan Van Sertima, ed., *African Presence in Early America* (New Brunswick, NJ: Transaction Publishers, 1992); Patrick Huyge, *Columbus Was Last* (New York: Hyperion, 1992); and R. A. Jairazbhoy, *Ancient Egyptian Survivals in the Pacific* (London: Karnak, 1990).

quite apart from the more devastating impact on Native Americans? Indeed, in some ways the Native American tragedy is also more irreversible. Civilizations were destroyed and genocide perpetrated.[26] For native Americans and the Black world, calamity came after Columbus!

Africa between Cause and Effect

Let us now return to contemporary Africa, and be sure we are looking at it from an African perspective – Africa as cause, rather than as effect. The same events in the 20th century can be seen as cause or effect, depending upon the perspective. One of my favorite examples is looking at France and Algeria. A Eurocentric point of view would see the story mainly in the following terms. The French first claimed Algeria as part of France in 1832, and kept the North African country under its control until 1962. When Charles de Gaulle was returned to power in 1958, he was soon convinced that it was an anachronistic crusade to try and keep Algeria as part of France. And then De Gaulle, the grand master of strategy, succeeded in handing over power to the Algerians in 1962. That version of the story recurs, I am sure, in many history books. De Gaulle is the hero of reconciliation. The version is taught to many Africans, and certainly to many Africans in Francophone Africa. It is Eurocentric, in its emphasis on De Gaulle as the causal factor.[27]

The real story is that Algerians fought for their freedom, and by doing so, changed not only their history, but the history of France. France was re-orientated fundamentally. Nor was the price paid by Algeria in this trans-Mediterranean equation negligible. The total number of lives lost in all Africa's anti-colonial wars were about three million. A third of those were Algerians, killed between 1954 and 1962. Algeria was the costliest single anti-colonialist war in Africa's history. The French were utterly ruthless in wanting to keep Algeria

---

[26] Consult Stannard, American Holocaust.

[27] For one version of the De Gaulle-Algeria interaction, see Michael Kettle, *De Gaulle and Algeria, 1940-1960* (London: Quartet, 1993); and for a journalistic account, consult C. L. Sulzberger, *The Test: De Gaulle and Algeria* (London: R. Hart-Davis, 1962).

French.[28] As Algerians fought for their freedom and shook the foundations of the Fourth Republic of France, they did so much more fundamentally than the Vietnam War shook the foundations of the American system. After all, the Vietnam War shook the foundations of American politics, but not those of the American constitution.

The Algerian War undermined the foundations of the French constitutional order itself. The French Fourth Republic finally quivered as it approached collapse. Indeed the French people hovered over a civil war. I was a student across the English Channel in England at the time. We were following the events hour by hour, and trying to understand what was going on "across the border." Some British newspapers were carrying editorials in French for the first time in their history, appealing to the French people, to step back from the abyss. It turned out that only one man could save them, they thought. Charles de Gaulle came to the rescue. But who had created the situation where the old system was failing? It was Algerians fighting for their freedom. Charles de Gaulle insisted on a new fifth Republic for France. "The Republic is dead; long live the Republic."[29]

France became a little more stable under the Fifth Republic. The European Community had a more effective leader in France, and it also consolidated its leadership in important areas of Europe. France under de Gaulle created its own nuclear program, called "force de frappe." France opted out of the NATO military command while retaining political links with the North Atlantic Treaty Organization. France gave formal independence to Algeria in 1962 after giving formal independence to the bulk of its empire in 1960.[30] And all these events happened because Algerians were fighting for their freedom, in the deserts, and streets of Algeria, and releasing historic forces far from home.

---

[28] Algeria was extremely important to the French; consult, for example, Tony Smith, *The French Stake in Algeria, 1954-1962* (Ithaca, NY: Cornell University Press, 1978); an account of the savage war may be found in John E. Talbott, *The War Without a Name: France in Algeria, 1954-1962* (New York: Knopf, 1980).

[29] The transition from the French Fourth Republic to the Fifth Republic--and details on the latter's institutions, laws, and personalities--is well-covered in Philip M. Williams and Martin Harrison, De Gaulle's Republic (London: Longman, 1960).

[30] On French foreign policy in the European-American theater, see A. W. DePorte, "The Fifth Republic in Europe," in William G. Andrews and Stanley Hoffman, eds., *The Impact of the Fifth Republic on France* (Albany, NY: SUNY Press, 1981), pp. 247-60.

While a Eurocentric point of view would glorify the role of de Gaulle in handing over independence, an Afrocentric view would say "The history of France was changed by Africans fighting for their freedom, and not the other way around."

Then there is the history of Portugal too, and its own anti-colonial wars. Did Portugal just hand over independence to its colonies in the 1970s? We know how stubborn and lethargic Portugal had been for centuries. Portugal had resisted the Renaissance, it had ignored the Enlightenment in Europe, it had defied the Reformation, it had turned its back on the American and French revolutions, it had let the Industrial Revolution bypass it. And then the same Portugal which had been so resistant to every progressive movement in the history of Europe, the same Portugal at last felt the pressure of Africans fighting for their freedom – in Guinea Bissau, in Angola, in Mozambique.[31] The same Portugal that had stood up against major historical forces in its own historical continent in Europe suddenly could no longer sustain its lethargy much longer.

In April, 1974, the whole superstructure of lethargy, fascism and conservatism collapsed. It was not a case of the Portuguese graciously handing over freedom to Angolans and the Mozambicans. It was a case of Mozambicans, Angolans and Guineans pushing Portugal into the 20th century. They were helping to democratize Portugal precisely by forcing it to decolonize, compelling it towards new arenas of self-transformation. To be sure, there was internal opposition to the Salazar regime; but the external pressures were probably as important.[32]

An Afrocentric approach to modern history therefore requires that we pause and say, "That's an African event." Be sure you do not overlook the impact of Africa upon Europe, while you are busy being mesmerized by the influence of Europe upon Africa.

---

[31] For an account of the Portuguese in Africa, see, for instance, M. D. D. Newitt, *Portugal in Africa: the Last Hundred Years* (London: Hurst, 1981); and, for a bibliographic guide, see Susan J. Gowan, *Portuguese-Speaking Africa: A Select Bibliography* (Braamfontein, South Africa: South African Institute of International Affairs, 1982).

[32] On internal resistance to the Salazar regime, consult, for instance, David L. Raby, *Fascism and Resistance in Portugal: Communists, Liberals and Military Dissidents in the Opposition to Salazar, 1941-1974* (Manchester, UK and New York: Manchester University Press and St. Martin's Press, 1988).

In any case so much of knowledge has already been captured by the Eurocentric perspective. Europe named the world. It named the Atlantic and Pacific Oceans. Nigeria is on the same longitude time as Britain. Nobody talks about Maiduguri Mean Time. We are guided by Greenwich Mean Time. Europe timed the world.

Europe named the continents as well as the oceans. Europe chose its own name "Europe," and then chose the Americas, Australia, Antarctica, and even Asia and Africa. The name "Africa", originating from North Africa as a name for a sub-region, was applied to Africa as a whole by European map-makers and cartographers. Although the name "Africa" and the name "Asia" were not themselves of European origins, their application to their respective continents as we know them today was part of European cultural supremacy.

Then Europe proceeded to name the universe – Mars, Venus, Saturn, Pluto – and named the tropics Cancer and Capricorn. And Europe positioned the world, as we have viewed it. We look at the map and Europe is at the top while Africa is below it. We do not know which observer in the cosmos decided that the world looked that way, placing Africa below Europe. There is no cosmological necessity for that way of looking at the world. It could have been the other way around, with Africa positioned above.

Such geographical perspectives are unlikely to change in the foreseeable future. We are unlikely to change the names of the planets, or the names of the oceans and continents, indeed even the name of Africa. Some names of African countries have changed but not many. If the name was outrageously colonial (like the two Rhodesias), we have changed them. But Nigeria, probably named by Lady Lugard if the legend is correct, is unlikely to change its name. Kenya was named after one of its mountains, but the pronunciation was modified by English people. We modified the pronunciation. So the British used to pronounce it KEENYA. After independence we have exercised our self-determination, and changed the pronunciation to KENYA.

On balance this is a world which was designed and shaped in most of its boundaries, many of its names, many of its directions, by outsiders. The naming of the universe has similarly been Eurocentric. In the face of this massive

Western hegemony it becomes important for us to ask ourselves "Can we fight Eurocentrism simply with Afrocentricity? Or should we join up with others?" Indeed, should we join up even with some Europeans, since not all Europeans are Eurocentric. In the United States the danger is narrower – it is Anglocentrism, rather than Eurocentrism. Let us enlist even Italian-Americans against Anglocentrism.

Conclusion

Asia might be the mother of all existing world religions that have spread across the nations. Europe may be the mother of all existing world secular ideologies. Africa is the mother of the human species itself. Can those three continents find ways of linking up? The most successful Semitic religion is Christianity, because it has spread out the most. The most successful Semitic language is Arabic, because it has spread out the most. The most successful Semitic people are the Jews, because per head of population they have performed better than any other single group in recent history. The most ancient Semitic home may be Africa. Are there ways of linking up between Semitic civilizations and African civilizations? Can multiculturalism absorb Afrocentricity? Can Afro-centricity absorb multiculturalism?

I have been groping in that direction in relation to Africa, with my concept of Africa's Triple Heritage, which is an effort to link up multiculturalism with Afrocentricity, a marriage of perspectives. It takes more than one culture to create an Africa of today. It takes more than one civilization to give meaning to human reality.

> Every woman has two cultures
> Her own and her neighbour's.
> Every man has two races
> His own and the human race.
> Winds of the world give answer
> They are whimpering to and fro'
> And who should know of Africa
> Who only Africa know?

W.L. van der Merwe
University of Stellenbosch

African Philosophy And The Contextualisation Of Philosophy In A Multicultural Society

Introduction[1]

In this contribution I want to relate African Philosophy to the need for a self-reflective contextualisation of philosophy in multicultural societies. Being a South African, I am obviously writing from and of such a need with regard to the practise of philosophy in my own country. But few – I hope! – would disagree that such a need and the encounter with multiculturalism it entails is not peculiar to South Africa but a major present and future challenge to philosophy in many other, increasingly multicultural societies. The South African experience may be exemplary of the issues at stake in other multicultural societies where the cultural particularity of the type(s) of philosophy taught and practised is increasingly challenged. As elsewhere in the West, the practise and teaching of philosophy in South Africa is characterised by a rich diversity of approaches, representative of the whole range of well-established traditions and recent developments within what is generally referred to as "Western Philosophy." In many cases South African philosophers also applied these approaches in their analyses of problems and critiques of practises peculiar to or at least prevalent in the South African context similar to the way in which, for example continental approaches are applied elsewhere in other cultural contexts. This may be one way of understanding the contextualisation

[1] An earlier, more extended and differently focused version of this article was presented as a paper "The Contextuality of Philosophy: From African Philosophy to Multiculturalism" at the Second Pan-African Symposium on the *Problematics of an African Philosophy*, Addis Ababa. Another version was published as the leading article in a special issue on multiculturalism, entitled "Identity, Difference and Community," of *the South African Journal of Philosophy* (16/3, 1997:73-78). The financial assistance of the Centre for Science Development (Human Sciences Research Council, South Africa) towards this research, as well as a Senior Research Fellowship of the Catholic University of Leuven (Belgium) is hereby acknowledged. Opinions expressed and conclusions arrived at are those of the author and are not necessarily to be attributed to the Centre for Science Development.

of philosophy. The need for contextualisation that I am referring to means something different and far more challenging though. It is not only about reflection and application, but about appropriation and interpretation. For example: although the presence of other non-European cultures is one of the prevalent features of the South African context it had little impact, at least until recently, on the ways in which philosophy was taught and practised. Little attempt has been made over the years to engage in constructive dialogue with forms of African thought and wisdom or to participate in and assess the relevance of African Philosophy.[2] In other multicultural societies a similar absence of any real impact of other minority cultures may indicate the same need for a self-reflective contextualisation.

In substantiating this claim and exploring some of its implications, I will first give an assessment of the significance of the development of and debate about African Philosophy. The intention is certainly not to proclaim that a self-reflective contextualisation of philosophy in a multicultural context like South Africa amounts to doing only African Philosophy, neither to elevate African Philosophy to a position of privilege or superiority. Rather, the debate about African Philosophy is discussed in order to show how a proper engagement with it, neglected in the past, could have contributed to a self-reflective contextualisation of philosophy in a multicultural society like ours, but also – as a second step – to show that the quest for a distinctive *African* Philosophy is surpassed by the multicultural contexts of present-day societies in Africa and elsewhere. Subsequently the meaning of multiculturalism will be explained before I will venture, in conclusion, some preliminary remarks on the philosophical appropriation of multiculturalism.

Contextualisation and African Philosophy

It may be common knowledge today that a intensifying and increasingly complicated debate has developed over the last fifty years amongst African philosophers, their European counterparts and anthropologists with a special interest in

[2] Notable exceptions are Rauche, G.A. (1992) *Selected Philosophical Papers* in Louw, T.J.G (ed) (Fort Hare University Press, Alice) and Shutte, A. (1993) *Philosophy for Africa* (UCT Press, Cape Town).

indigenous African cultures, "systems of thought" and oral traditions of wisdom, with regard to the question of the "identity" and even the possibility of an "*African* Philosophy."[3] Taking stock of the historical development and all the issues at stake in this debate – the only way to trace the "différance," the differences and deferral of the meaning(s) of African Philosophy – cannot be done extensively here, but the following observations may suffice.

The controversiality of the notion of an "African *Philosophy*" from an European as well as an African perspective is not surprising or unwarranted, given the presumed historical origin of the concept, activity and discipline of "Philosophy" in Ancient Greece and its crucial foundational function in the (intellectual) histories and cultures of Europe.[4] This integral link between "Philosophy" and Europe was reinforced during the Enlightenment, the development of the "new sciences" since the eighteenth century and the European belief in – what Stephen Toulmin aptly named a "Cosmopolis"[5] – an all encompassing vision of a society as rationally ordered as the Newtonian view of nature in terms of which human

---

[3] There are many introductions to and surveys of the historical development of and current positions in this debate, but Wright, R.W. (ed) (1984) (3rd ed.). *African Philosophy. An introduction* (University Press of America, Maryland) and Floistadt, G. (ed) (1987) *Contemporary Philosophy: A New Survey* Vol.5: African Philosophy (Marthinus Nijhoff, Dordrecht) can be taken as authoritative. Wright also provides an extensive bibliography, as does Neugebaur in Nagl-Docekal, H. & Wimmer, F.M. (1992) *Postkoloniales Philosophieren: Afrika* (mit einer Bibliographie zusammengestelt vor Christian Neugebauer), (R. Oldenbourg Verlag, Wien/München). My own knowledge and interpretation of this debate relies to a considerable extent on the recent critical exposition by Masolo, D.A. (1994) *African Philosophy in Search of Identity* (Indiana University Press, Bloomington).

[4] Locating the historical origin of philosophy in Ancient Greece is of course contested by some African philosophers and scholars. See for example the reconstruction of the crucial role of Africa in the genesis of civilization in: Diop, C.A. (1974) *The African Origin of Civilization. Myth or Reality* ed. and transl. Cook, M. (Lawrence Hill and Company, Westport, Connecticut); followed on and strengthened by Olela, H. (1980) *An Introduction to the History of Philosophy: From Ancient Africa to Ancient Greece* (Select Publishing Company, Atlanta) and Olela, H. (1984) "The African Foundations of Greek Philosophy," in Wright, R.A. (ed.) *African Philosophy: An Introduction* (University Press of America, Lanham, Maryland); and culminating in Martin Bernal's (1987) controversial *Black Athena: The Afroasiatic Roots of Classical Civilization*: Vol. 1: *The fabrication of Ancient Greece, 1785-1985* and Vol. 2 (1990)*The Archeological and Documentary Evidence* (Rutgers University Press, New Brunswick, New Jersey). See also for references on the controversy, criticisms and defenses, footnote 8 in Blok, Josine H. (1996) "Proof and Persuasion in Black Athena: The Case of K.O. Müller," *Journal of the History of Ideas* 57(4): 705-724.

[5] Toulmin, S. (1990) *Cosmopolis: The hidden Agenda of Modernity* (The University of Chicago Press, Chicago).

nature and society could and should be understood and structured according to exact rational categories. This vision and its philosophical legitimation accompanied the colonising of other parts of the world, like Africa, in the wake of the supposed superiority and universality of European modernity. Accordingly, the question from the outset in the debate about African Philosophy was whether the description of "Philosophy" as such, is not irrevocably Eurocentric and imperialistic. Thus, whilst seeking to establish its own identity – at least initially – the debate itself contributed towards the exposure of some of the universalist claims of Western Philosophy as masquerading forms of Eurocentric particularism.

Three developments in the recent history of Western discourses on Africa and the African responses to it need to be mentioned in this regard. Firstly, the ethnographical studies published since the late forties, which attempted to articulate the implied worldviews, moral values and conceptual systems embedded in the cultural codes and customs of indigenous African peoples. The debate about their viability which took a decisive turn during the sixties with the publication of Peter Winch's article "Understanding a Primitive Society" is not primarily important with regard to the identity of African Philosophy.[6] It's importance may instead be located in the shift it brought about towards the questioning of the formerly uncritically assumed neutrality of the conceptual schemes and categories of anthropology and philosophy, and thus the questioning of the claims of "objectivity" and "universality" of (Western) rationality and the methodologies of the sciences.[7]

Secondly, the contributions of African intellectuals who went abroad for a professional training in Continental philosophical trends, but returned to Africa and began to articulate in various ways, by the application and adaptation of these trends within the context of African experience, what one could call Philosophies *for* Africa, for example Panafricanism, Black Consciousness, African Socialism and the conceptualisation of "negritude" (and its different inter-

[6] Winch, P. (1964) "Understanding a Primitive Society," *American Philosophical Quarterley*, No 1, 1964:.307-324. Reprinted in Wilson, B.R. (1970) (ed.), *Rationality*, (Harper & Row, New York).

[7] Masolo (1994:124-146) see footnote 3.

pretations) in the writings of Cesaire, Senghor and Fanon.[8] In a dialectical way their existential and social analyses utilised the conceptual schemes and integral ideas of Continental philosophies for a critique on the universalistic claims and supposed superiority of Western philosophy, science and culture.

Thirdly, following mainly on the political liberation and decolonization of Africa, the contributions of European trained African philosophers like Crahay[9] and more recently Mudimbe[10] – inspired mainly by structuralist and poststructuralist approaches – who began to analyse the strategies and discursive power/knowledge formations in terms of which "Africa" was marginalised as the inferior "Other" of European culture in the philosophical and scientific discourse(s) of modernity. This approach made it possible to deconstruct certain ethnophilosophical accounts of African thought in as far as they are merely constructs of Western power /knowledge discursive practises and opened the possibility of an authentic reappropriation of African traditions of wisdom in an African discourse on and of philosophy. The important work done presently on the documentation of African sagacity and the recording and further development of "Sage Philosophy" serves as primary example in this regard.

Consequently, what one encounters in scanning through the major developments within the debate about African Philosophy is a rich tapestry of diverse and disparate forms and modes of philosophising and indeed a variety of philosophies often engaged in critique of one another. Discerning some pattern in the tapestry, may be useful – as for example in the late Odera Oruka's distinction between four varieties of African Philosophy: ethnophilosophy, professional philosophy with little or no reference to ethnographic data, Africa's modern political and ideological thought which focuses on the production of a postcolonial discourse,

---

[8] Clifford, J. (1988: 177)*The Predicament of Culture: Twenthieth Century Ethnography, Literature and Art* (Harvard University Press, Cambridge, Massachusetts).

[9] Crahay, F. (1965) "Le Décollage conceptuel: conditions d'une philosophie bantoue" in *Diogène*, No. 52.

[10] Mudimbe, V.Y. (1988) *The Invention of Africa* (Indiana University Press, Bloomington) and (1994)*The Idea of Africa* (Indiana University Press, Bloomington).

and African philosophic sagacity.[11] But the fact remains that there simply is not *an* African Philosophy, reducible to a singular identity, a normative method, or a shared set of premises. And still there is African Philosophy – but then only in the Wittgensteinian sense of referring to a range of family resemblances pertaining to all the articulations of philosophy of and for Africa. The whole historical and polemical discourse about the identity of African Philosophy is thus in itself exemplary of the heterogeneous traditions of philosophical reflection and the conversation referred to by the common name of African Philosophy.

The significance of African Philosophy should thus not be sought in a distinct identity on par with, parallel to or as an alternative to a supposed distinct identity of "Western Philosophy." As postmodern critiques from within "Western Philosophy" have shown philosophy may have been primarily associated with the histories and cultures of Europe until the twentieth century, but is in fact also a family name for various and extremely divergent attempts to come to grips with the demands of life in specific historic and cultural circumstances. From this perspective "Philosophy" is not an all-encompassing, unified, universal, meta-narrative of the ultimate meaning of human existence in spite of the pretensions to the contrary in the writings of some classical, medieval or especially modernist European philosophers. In many respects African Philosophy pictures synchronically what has been the case diachronically through the history of so-called "Western Philosophy."

To my mind this is the prime significance of African Philosophy. It exemplifies in a paradigmatic way the historical and cultural contingency, the contextual particularity, of philosophy – the reciprocity between reflection and the pre-reflective conditions of thinking which constitute our "Lebenswelt" or the "forms of life" of our everyday existence.[12]

---

[11] For an excellent critical appraisal of this conceptual schematisation of Odera Oruka, see Deacon, M. (1996) *African Philosophy: From Drums and Masks to Rationality?* (MA-dissertation, RAU).

[12] For a comparison of the Husserlian notion of the "Lebenswelt" and the Wittgensteinian notion of "forms of life" and a discussion of the dialectic of reflection (language) and the prereflective conditions of thinking (experience) Van der Merwe, W.L. (1993) "Wittgenstein and Husserl on the Constitution of Meaning," *Schriftenreihe der Wittgenstein-Gesellschaft* Band 20/2 (herausgegeben von Klaus Puhl), (Verlag Hölder-Pichler-Tempsky, Wien).

This reciprocity, due to which any claim to universality in philosophy can only be the universalisation of a particularity, belongs to the forgetfulness of Western metaphysics. Perhaps the same forgetfulness accounts for the neglect of South African philosophy under apartheid to appropriate the cultural diversity in its immediate social context, because exactly in this neglect it reflected the divisions within that societal context. In African Philosophy the silence of this forgetfulness has been broken in the conscious attempt to make this reciprocity explicit in the inevitable diversity of discourses particular to the cultural, historical and social conditions of Africa. This was done by seeking to articulate and reappropriate the conceptions of meaning and value embedded in the cultural practices and languages within the immediate contexts of African societies, by forging conceptual tools more appropriate to the interpretation, critique and transformation of Africa's own cultures, and by utilizing various discourses of Western philosophy and traditions of indigenous thought as vehicles for the theoretical articulation of the "identities" of African peoples or to contest alienating "identities" imposed upon them.

In this way African Philosophy succeeded in making philosophy a heterogeneous family of philosophical discourses particular to Africa, and in doing so set an example of how a self-reflective contextualisation of philosophy may look like, what it may be able to achieve and where it may meet its limitations. Such a self-reflective contextualisation – only in a much more complicated way – is what is called for in the challenge of multiculturalism, i.e. in the need to come to terms with the sociocultural diversity or multiculturality of contemporary societies.

The Meaning Of Multiculturalism

What multiculturalism refers to, or should refer to, is in itself a source of dispute in philosophy and the human sciences.[13]

---

[13] Goldberg, D. Th. (ed) (1994) *Multiculturalism. A Critical Reader* (Basil Blackwell, Oxford) provides an extensive bibliography of literature on multi-culturalism and a useful selection of articles for the purpose of an introduction to the issues. For a proper introduction to the current philosophical reflection, see Gutman, A. (ed.) (1994) *Multiculturalism* (2nd rev. ed.), (Princeton University Press, Princeton) with contributions by major philosophers like Charles Taylor, Jürgen Habermas, Michael Walzer and K. Anthony Appiah.

In political philosophy it may mean the claim that a political society should recognise the equal standing of all stable and viable communities belonging to it[14] with all the difficult questions pertaining to the granting of culture-specific rights and the protection of minorities.[15] With regard to education and science it may mean the demand to revise methodologies and syllabuses in order to make them more representative of the cultural goods, histories, achievements and values of other than Western cultures with all the questions pertaining to the epistemic status of scientific practises and canonisation.[16] However, when used in a more general normative sense multiculturalism may express quite diverse ideals and imperatives. On the one hand it may refer to the advocation of a fusion of different cultures into one syncretistic, cosmopolitan world-culture through intercultural under-standing and cross-cultural assimilation. On the other hand it may refer to the advocation of an appreciation for cultural differences and the positive affirmation of diversity as a necessary condition of human existence as such.[17]

To avoid being sidetracked by this dispute, I will use multiculturalism in a fairly neutral, encompassing and descriptive sense to refer to the presence of distinct cultural differences within a society and to emphasise that such differences are not trivial, but real and should be recognised as such. Multiculturalism in this sense refers to the paradoxical nature of the present, globalising late-modern or "postmodern" culture. On the one hand there can be no doubt that the cultural "forms of life" of modernity which developed out of the European Enlightenment – for example democracy, market economy, science and technology – have expanded and will continue to expand globally. The result of this globalisation of modernity is the transformation and equalisation of the everyday existence – the "Lebenswelt" – of all peoples of all

[14] Raz, J. (1994) *Ethics in the Public Domain* (Oxford University Press, Oxford).

[15] Kymlicka, W. (1995) *Multicultural Citizenship* (Clarendon Press, Oxford).

[16] Bak, H. (ed.) (1993) *Multiculturalism and the Canon of American Culture* (VU University Press, Amsterdam).

[17] The opposites referred to here is in the first case approaches, mainly inspired by Habermas, such as "communicative ethics" or "deliberative democracy" and in the second case approaches inspired by French philosophers like Derrida and Lyotard.

cultures.[18] But, perhaps contrary to what might have been expected, this globalisation of modernity is accompanied by a heightened awareness of and attachment to particular cultures and culture-specific values. The process of globalisation is not a process of cultural homogenisation, but of increasing fragmentation and pluralisation. [19]

This paradoxical coincidence of the de facto realisation of a modern world culture and a simultaneous diversification of culture may seem enigmatic but is fully explainable in terms of the logic of modernity. Modernity developed out of the Enlightenment on the basis of ideas and values which were understood to be universal. For example: the freedom of the individual to act autonomously and the authority of reason over traditional sources of meaning and morality like cultural conventions, religion or collective history. The historical evolution of democracy, the articulation of basic human rights, the development of science and technology and the concomitant technologisation of the human lifeworld and the expansion of capitalist economy, can be traced back at least to these two ideas: the primacy of the autonomous individual above the particular cultural community, and the primacy of a supposedly "universal" human reason above culture-specific codes and beliefs. The logic of modernity thus presupposed a detachment of or emancipation from a particular cultural community or collectively shared horizon of significance. For this reason modernity could expand transculturally and develop into a global world culture. But for this very same reason – and this is the resolution of the paradox – it cannot provide people with an attachment to those specific meanings and values for which they are dependent on cultural forms of life.

Thus as a global world culture modernity does not eradicate cultural differences, but creates an existential

---

[18] This is forcefully and convincingly argued by Dupré, L. (1993) *Passage to Modernity. An Essay in the Hermeneutics of nature and Culture* (Yale University Press, New Haven/London). who concludes: "Its innovative power made modernity, which began as a local Western phenomenon, a universal project capable of forcing its theoretical and practical principles on all but the most isolated civilizations." (p.249). However, although this is true, it is not correct to state – as Dupré does – that 'modern' has become the predicate of a *unified* world culture. Modernity or "modern culture" is accompanied by an increasing awareness of and attachment to cultural differences.

[19] Welsch, W. (1987) *Unsere postmoderne Moderne* (VCH Verlagsgesellschaft, Weinheim).

vacuum which can only be covered by a falling back onto specific forms of collective identity and cultural attachment. The expansion of the cultural "forms of life" of modernity is therefore not a process of transcultural unification, but the global extension of the conditions which make it possible to affirm cultural differences and claim public recognition for and protection of culture-specific values. Accordingly, the revival on a worldwide scale of ethnicity, nationalisms and other forms of cultural particularism, or the emergence of new ones, should not be understood as the last convulsions of almost bygone premodern attitudes and tendencies, nor as short-lived counter-reactions to the globalisation of modernity. It is simply the vital supplement of modernity, the inevitable shadows of the universalised values of the Enlightenment.

This ironic logic of modernity in terms of which it realises a radical pluralisation of society and culture in the same movement in which it achieves global expansion, is also what "postmodernity" as a description of the distinctive cultural conditions of our present existence refers to.[20] The distinctive differences of the past between the cultural contexts within which Western Philosophy as opposed to African Philosophy were practised may fade with the inevitable modernisation of African societies and the globalisation of modernity. But the commonality of sharing increasingly the same postmodern societal context is not the sharing of a homogeneous culture but a common encounter with multiculturalism as a universal feature of postmodern societies.

What the impact on philosophy of this encounter with multiculturalism will be and to what extent philosophy may be able to contribute towards the self-understanding and well-being of multicultural societies are complex and wide-ranging questions. It is beyond the scope of this contribution – and beyond my competence – to explore them in a satisfactory way. Nevertheless it is extremely important to put these questions on the agenda for collective reflection and philosophical debate and I hope the following preliminary remarks will serve this purpose.

---

[20] Welsch (1987:53-85).

The Appropriation Of Multiculturalism

Many contributions to the growing discourse on multiculturalism amount to reflections about sociocultural diversity as if it is but another problem to be solved, a problem towards which neutral ground can be assumed. However, this is not what a proper philosophical encounter with multiculturalism demands. It should be clear from the preceding explanation that multiculturalism does not confront us with a problem to be solved through reflection, but rather with a postmodern condition of thinking which has to be appropriated in our reflection. It demands a philosophical reflection from within the criss-crossing of and breaches between the various particular histories, traditions and modes of thinking intermingled in the multicultural context of present-day societies. Such a self-reflective multicultural contextualisation of philosophy entails, to my mind, at least the following.

Firstly, the realisation that there is no neutral ground, no "view from nowhere" in philosophy with regard to cultural differences, because of the cultural contingency of every philosophical viewpoint, and the histories and traditions of philosophy – Western or African – as such. This realisation impels one to enter into dialogue with the traditions of wisdom and thinking of other cultures – not so much in the hope that one will reach a transcultural, metaphilosophical consensus, but as a way of acknowledging the particularity of one's own viewpoint and discovering the cultural contingency of one's own philosophical presuppositions and allegiances.[21]

Secondly, the realisation that the particularity and cultural contingency of one's own viewpoint, indeed one's identity as a person and a philosopher, is itself heterogeneous and much more "multicultural" than one would have thought. To quote Amy Gutman[22]: "Not only societies, but people are multicultural." – meaning not "cosmopolitan" in the sense of

---

[21] I appreciate the theoretical justification of and the pioneering intercultural philosophical writings of Kimmerle, H. (1991) *Philosophie in Afrika – Afrikanische Philosophie,* (Qumran in Campus Verlag, Frankfurt) and (1995) *Mazungumzo. Dialogen tussen Afrikaanse en Westerse filosofieën* (Boom, Amsterdam/Meppel) as an examplary model in this regard.

[22] Gutman, A. (1993:183) "The Challenge of Multiculturalism in Political Ethics," *Philosophy and Public Affairs* 22(3), 171-206.

sharing a similar mixture of cultures, but that one's identity is a continuous reweaving of various patterns of the cultures one is exposed to. Thus, there needn't be a contradiction between acknowledging the cultural contingency of one's own philosophical viewpoint and the self-reflective appropriation of multiculturalism as a condition of thinking. It is simply the flipside of the coin. Every philosophical viewpoint is already inscribed or embedded in the multiculturality of our existence. With this I do not only mean the empirical fact that our existence is increasingly marked by a daily encounter with cultural differences. Rather, as I have argued, that the experience of cultural diversity has become the postmodern condition of philosophical reflection. But it can be so either with an awareness of the fact or without. Having an awareness of the fact, is to take multiculturalism as a starting point; thinking from within it not only in a first mode of reflection as is always the case, but also in a second mode of self-reflectivity.

Thirdly, the realisation that the understanding of multiculturalism in terms of different cultures co-existing as it were alongside one another in one society is a misconstrual of the matter at stake; "a bewitchment of our intelligence" by the noun "culture" – to paraphrase Wittgenstein.[23] It presupposes that cultures are monolithic, transparent and neatly demarcated wholes, whilst this is not the case. Obviously, it cannot be denied that there are different, distinctive cultures. But to conceptualise multiculturalism or the distinctive sociocultural diversity of present-day societies in this way, forces one into acceptance of an essensialistic, substantive and static understanding of culture and cultural diversity.

This is where the demands of multiculturalism eclipse various forms of cultural relativism, ethnocentrism and universalism which all presuppose such an essentialistic understanding of culture.[24] The minimalist claim common to cultural relativism and sophisticated forms of ethnocentrism, namely that there is no culture-transcendent Archimedean point from where different cultures can be studied, understood and judged; or in Rorty's words no "skyhook with which to

---

[23] Wittgenstein, L. (1988: 109) *Philosophical Investigations* 3rd rev. ed. transl. by G.E.M. Anscombe (Basil Blackwell, Oxford).

[24] For a short overview of some forms of cultural relativism, ethnocentrism and universalism, see Procee (1991:11-63)

escape from the ethnocentrism produced by acculturation,"[25] need not presuppose such an understanding of culture. But cultural relativism normally involves more substantial claims which do presuppose such an understanding of culture, for example the claim that different cultures are incommensurable or that cross-cultural understanding and translation is not possible or that different cultures are of equal value.

Not only are such claims conceptually and empiricially false, they are also politically dangerous – as we experienced under apartheid. It should not be forgotten that the cultural-anthropological justification or rationalisation that was given for apartheid, at least initially, was that different cultures are incommensurable, that the integrity of each culture should be respected and its survival safeguarded, and that the only way to do so in a multicultural society is by political and geographical separation, i.e. by creating a homeland for each ethnically defined cultural group. To a large extent apartheid became a "self-fulfilling prophecy" in this regard. The social engineering program of separation and the very real way in which it isolated communities from one another effected misunderstanding, bigotry and animosity. But even in spite of this massive and violent institutionalization of separation, cross-cultural assimilation still took place.

Universalist approaches to cultural diversity however also presuppose an essentialistic conception of culture, for example by postulating some universal cultural constants, a single core of "human culture," present in all the different cultures, or only manifested differently in different cultures, or still to be discovered and realized through the merging or forging of different cultures into one. Such a universal "human culture" is of course an abstraction without real content, or a regulative idea which only appeals to those who share a particular, culture-specific teleological understanding of history.

Fourthly, as the decisive albeit simplified conclusion, the realization that multiculturalism should rather be understood or approached not as the problem of "different cultures" co-existing alongside one another, but rather as the condition of "cultural differences," running across various

[25] Rorty, R. (1991:2) *Objectivity, Relativism, and Truth* (Cambridge University Press, Cambridge).

cultures and being inherent in any distinct culture, because of the cultural heterogeneity of present-day societies. Such cultural differences can be as real between members of the same culture as between members of different cultures.[26]

The relevance of this viewpoint with regard to most mullet-ethnic societies is that the congruence of "ethnicity" and "culture" needn't be considered on the one hand negatively as an evil to be extinguished where and whenever possible. But neither should it be understood on the other hand as a convergence which corresponds to some essential, homogenous identity. Although ethnic culture cannot be negated as a real social and cultural phenomenon, it should not be absolutised theoretically. More and more people participate in and encounter more than one of the various, distinguishable diverse ethnic and sociocultural forms of life prevalent in their society. Intercultural communication and cross-cultural assimilation are possible and do take place in their daily lives in spite of the embeddedness of their existence in different ethnic and sociocultural forms of life. Part of this intermingling of cultures is the reality of cultural differences with regard to certain beliefs, values and practises. And in cases of conflict, no culture-transcendent set of criteria can be applied to judge the conflicting positions or legitimate the objective validity of any one position.

Certainly this impels philosophers, educators and intellectuals in general, to engage in intercultural dialogue, and on a more theoretical level to explore the possibilities of intercultural philosophy. Through such a dialogue and discourse it may be possible to develop what Charles Taylor calls "a language of perspicuous contrast," a public discourse through which the divergent communities could develop a mutual understanding of their cultural differences and commonalities.[27] In and through this process, it might become evident that certain aspects of the other's culture are inadequate and/or that aspects of the one's own are – in which case the understanding of the other may lead to a

---

[26] Caws, Peter, (1994:375) "Identity: Cultural, Transcultural, and Multicultural," in Goldberg, D.Th. (ed), *Multiculturalism. A Critical Reader* (Basil Blackwell, Oxford).

[27] See also the exposition of the importance of Taylor's proposal by Van Niekerk, A.A. (1993) "Relativism versus Ethnocentrism," *South African Journal of Philosophy* 12(2), 31-37.

transformation of one's own.[28] Without doubt one of the implications of multiculturalism for philosophers, educators and intellectuals in general is to be or become such transversal cross-cultural interpreters of the divergent experiences, values and practises in their societies.[29]

But this view also accounts for the reality that there will always be misunderstandings and conflicts that cannot be resolved through dialogue and deliberation, i.e. for the realisation that a "merging of horizons" is not always possible or desirable in the case of certain cultural differences people attach too. However promising and of vital importance the exploration of intercultural philosophy may be, the same will hold true for it. In such extreme cases – whether of philosophical dissensus or societal conflict – one reaches those cultural differences which refer to what people value ultimately, as for example in differences of religious belief. Such differences concern what people belief to be of ultimate significance, "the good." And as Wittgenstein (1988b observed: "You cannot lead people to what is good, you can only lead them to some place or other. The good is outside the space of facts."[30] People's beliefs about the good, are not beliefs that people hold, but rather beliefs that have them in their hold. Consequently, there will always be a point, both in our intercultural philosophical endeavours and in our societal life where we will stumble upon the incommensurable – not because of a supposed mutual exclusion of our cultures or the impossibility of intercultural communication and understanding, but because our culturally embedded values defy even our own understanding, justification and explanation.

[28] See Taylor, C. (1985:125)*Philosophical Papers* Vol.2 (Philosophy and the Human Sciences), (Cambridge University Press, Cambridge). To expect though as Taylor does that this will be "a language in which we could formulate their way of life and ours as *alternative possibilities* in relation to some *human constants* at work in both (my italics)" is again to hope for a teleological resolution of all cultural differences. As in the case of other similar proposals with regard to the resolution of conflict caused by multiculturalism, for example Habermasian models of deliberative or communicative ethics, such a hope is based on an overestimation of rationality and an underestimition of the extent to which some cultural differences are not of such a nature that people can be persuaded to exchange them or leave them behind. Why defending this position is not an endorsement of relativism, see the excellent study by Rescher, N. (1995) *Pluralism: Against the Demand for Consensus*, (Clarendon Press, Oxford).

[29] Bauman, Z. (1987) *Legislators and Interpreters* (Polity Press, Cambridge).

[30] Wittgenstein, L. (1988b:§3e) *Culture and Value* repr. and transl. by Peter Winch, (Basil Blackwell, Oxford).

At this point even an intercultural philosophy encounters its limitations and the only way to minimize potential conflict will be the political negotiation of a modus vivendus. But the continuous negotiation of a modus vivendus in our societal life will not be possible if people are told that their cultures are incommensurable; only if they are reminded of their finitude in their attachment to culturally contingent values. And in this regard a self-reflective contextualised philosophy can play an important role in multicultural societies.

Douglas Kellner
University of California Los Angeles

Multiple Literacies and Critical Pedagogy in a Multicultural Society[1]

We are in the midst of one of the most dramatic technological revolutions in history that is changing everything from the ways that we work, to the ways that we communicate with each other, to how we spend our leisure time. The technological revolution centers on information technology, is often interpreted as the beginnings of a knowledge society, and therefore ascribes education a central role in every aspect of life. This Great Transformation poses tremendous challenges to education to rethink its basic tenets, to deploy the new technologies in creative and productive ways, and to restructure schooling in the light of the metamorphosis we are now undergoing.

At the same time that we are undergoing technological revolution, important demographic and socio-political changes are occurring in the United States and throughout the world. Emigration patterns have brought an explosion of new peoples into the U.S. in recent decades and the country is now more racially and ethnically diverse, more multicultural, than ever before. This creates the challenge of providing people from diverse races, classes, and backgrounds with the tools to enable them to succeed and participate in an ever more complex world. Critical pedagogy considers how education can strengthen democracy, create a more egalitarian and just society, and deploy education in a process of progressive social change.

In this paper, I argue that we need multiple literacies for our multicultural society, that we need to develop new literacies to meet the challenge of the new technologies, and that literacy of diverse sorts – including an even more funda-mental importance for print literacy – is of crucial importance

[1] An earlier and different version of this study appeared in *Educational Theory* and I am grateful to its editor Nicholas Burbules for discussion that helped develop my ideas, and am also grateful to George Katsiaficas and Teodros Kiros for discussions of this version which helped with clarification of my position.

in restructuring education for a high tech society. My argument is that education today needs to foster a variety of new types of multiple literacies to empower students and to make education relevant to the demands of the present and future. My assumption is that new technologies are altering every aspect of our society and we need to understand and make use of them both to understand and transform our world.

I first discuss how critical pedagogy can promote multicultural education and sensitivity to cultural difference, and then focus on the importance of developing media literacy to critically engage the wealth of media materials that currently immerse us. Media literacy involves teaching the skills that will empower citizens and students to become sensitive to the politics of representations of race, ethnicity, gender, sexuality, class, and other cultural differences in order to promote critical thinking and enhance democratization. Next, I discuss the need to cultivate a wide range of types of multiple literacies to deal with the exigencies of the cultural and technological revolution that we are currently involved in, ranging from computer literacy to multimedia literacy to new forms of cultural literacy. Such concerns are part of a critical pedagogy which summons educators, students, and citizens to rethink established curricula and teaching strategies to meet the challenge of empowering individuals to democratically participate in our increasing multicultural and technological society.

The Question of Multiculturalism

It is ever more apparent that we live in a multicultural society and the term multiculturalism has become a buzz-word for our time, used in multiple contexts in a plethora of ways. It is indeed a highly contested term with diverse social groupings and political forces either appropriating it for their own agendas or virulently contesting it to preserve established modes of culture, schooling, and society. The term means quite different things in different contexts and is thus overloaded with diverse and sometimes conflicting meanings articulating different political agendas and discourses. In Canada, for instance, multiculturalism is the official government policy of a state with liberal emigration policies, diverse races, and is thus a legitimating ideology, serving much as melting pots ideologies functioned in the United States in an earlier era. In South Africa, the term initially was used to support segregation between Africans and Europeans, but is now also official government policy that functions more progressively as an attempt to get different racial groups to put aside the virulent hatred and racism of an earlier period.

In the United States, the term is contested between conservatives who would vilify it as a threat to traditional canons of education and as a cover for liberal reform of education and society and those who would defend it. On the whole, in post-60s U.S. society, "multiculturalism" signifies a mode of affirming otherness and difference, and the importance of attending to marginalized, minority, and oppositional groups and individuals who had previously been excluded from the cultural dialogue. In the educational context, this meant practically proposals for curriculum changes, involving new canons, the inclusion of excluded voices and cultures, and sometimes new programs like African-American, or Mexican-American, studies. Multiculturalism elicited new cultural wars as conservatives defended Western culture, with its canons of great (mostly) European males against the multicultural offensive. In opposition to multiculturalism, conservatives thus (re)affirmed monoculturalism leading to intense battles over education and culture wars that are still raging.

Yet there are a variety of discourses of multiculturalism in the U.S. today, including liberal versions for whom multiculturalism serves as did previous ideologies of tolerance and humanism to cover over differences and inequalities, as opposed to more radical versions who would use the concept to restructure education and society, exactly as conservatives fear. But here too there are tensions between nationalist groups and advocates of identity politics who use it to advance their own particular agenda, as opposed to those who support a politics of alliance and solidarity and call for fundamental social restructuring. Appiah calls the version of multi-culturalism which calls for separatism and which loudly trumpets the superiority of one's specific culture as "illiberal multiculturalism".[2]

---

[2] Appiah, K. Anthony (1997:30ff) "The Multiculturalist Misunderstanding," *The New York Review of Books,* October 9, 1997: 30-36.

Likewise, there are those who would use the term as a cover for liberal notions of tolerance and humanism, contrasted to those who want to reconstruct our conceptions of human beings, such as Katsiaficas and Kiros (in this volume) who propose multiculturalism as a "concrete universal" which resists Western ethnocentrism and sees humanity as constructed through differences and hybridities which makes possible new modes of identity and solidarities.

To distinguish more progressive brands of multiculturalism from more liberal versions and the conservative attempt to vilify it, a variety of forms of multiculturalism have appeared. While a large number of people adopted the term "critical multiculturalism" to distinguish a socially critical version from an socially affirmative liberal version, Giroux proposes the term "insurgent multiculturalism" to denote the efforts of oppositional and previously excluded groups contesting their exclusion and marginalization and McLaren proposes "revolutionary multiculturalism" for projects of radical social transformation.[3] In our forthcoming book, *The Postmodern Adventure*, Steven Best and I propose the concept of "critical, progressive, and postmodern multiculturalism" to signify that we need a multiculturalism that transcends the liberal pluralism of many varieties and assimilates the moments of activism and oppositionalism involved in the concepts proposed by Giroux and McLaren.[4]

There are thus diverse strands of multiculturalism ranging from liberal and centrist versions which replicate melting pot ideologies that celebrate the existing society as egalitarian and open to all, to more critical versions which affirm the value of diversity and the need for oppressed groups to struggle against institutionalized forms of hierarchy and domination. This "insurgent" or "revolutionary" multiculturalism responds to '60s activism and demands for acceptance of otherness and difference combined with appreciation of marginal, minority, or different ideas, people, and practices. It articulates the '60s belief that individuals of

[3] McLaren, Peter (1996) *Revolutionary Multiculturalism* (London and New York: Routledge).

[4] Giroux, Henry and Peter McLaren (eds) (1994)*Between Borders. Pedagogy and the Politics of Cultural Studies.*(New York: Routledge); McLaren, Peter (1995)*Critical Pedagogy and Predatory Culture* (London and New York: Routledge) and McLaren (1996) *Revolutionary Multiculturalism.* (London and New York: Routledge).

diverse races and styles could live together in peace and harmony and that tolerance, cooperation, and community were positive values upon which a more democratic and egalitarian social order could be founded. Insurgent multiculturalism is often advocated by precisely those individuals who have been excluded from modern culture and society because of their gender, race, or class positions. The critical moment involves constantly reflecting on one's presuppositions, criticizing conventional and conservative forms, and deploying multiculturalism to serve as a lever for radical social and cultural transformation.

A progressive postmodern multiculturalism requires acceptance of difference and appreciating otherness, which in turn demands that one come to understand other groups' experience, culture, and history. This entails the active education of each person in the history and culture of others, a goal that has been pursued in some Universities in recent years through advancing a program of multicultural education which contains a critique of Western civilization courses and the "Great Books" program. Although standard Western civilization courses are valuable in teaching literacy skills and offering an introduction into important figures and texts, they often reinforce elitist values and ignorance of non-white and non-Western cultures. Critical postmodern multicultural-ism therefore wants to expand the curricula, to include voices, perspectives, and groups excluded from the main-stream and canons of "Western civilization." Thus, whereas traditional modern curricula focused and centered on the West and dominant white male authors, a postmodern multiculturalist curricula is less ethnocentric, more decentered, and open to voices and cultures excluded from the modern canon. Yet it should be strongly emphasized that, with few exceptions, the attempts to create a new "canon" have been those of supplementing not replacing the standard works of Plato, Shakespeare, or Bah. I personally know no professors or students who want to jettison Western culture in the manner of Mao's Red Guard armies of destruction, though this is the impression generated by conservative critics of multicultural education.

A critical postmodern multiculturalism also involves grasping the contradictory nature of a multicultural reality where our identities are overdetermined and multiple. An identity politics often suppresses differences within their group, for instance, ignoring gender, class, or race distinctions in favor of a fixed, essentialist, and unitary simple identity – black, white, Christian or whatever. A critical multiculturalism, by contrast, recognizes that we all have multiple identities that should be affirmed and celebrated. Rather then reducing identity to one fetishized term (be it gender, race, sexual preference, or whatever) we should recognize that each of us is defined by a multiplicity of differentiations and should see ourselves as complex and overdetermined in our identities. This involves accepting and affirming hybridity as well, a condition that is quickly becoming something of a norm, rather than the exception.[5] Becoming a unique individual in today's world thus requires developing complex identities that affirms multiple determinations of our being, that generates development of a many-sided identity.

Education has traditionally been involved in the process of self-constitution and thus in the construction of identities. A self-constituting individual is able to select and evaluate ideas, values, forms of behavior, cultural forms, institutions, and social practices in a critical and discriminatory mode, to make them her or his own, and to engage in a process of self-discovery and self-development. Education, then, provides the tools, the abilities, and the knowledge to create a self-constituting individual capable of thinking and making choices for oneself and capable of getting along with other people, respecting and appreciating differences, and able to reach consensus on common goods, to settle arguments and resolve differences amiably, or to accept and live with differences that cannot be resolved. The twofold challenge of education in a democratic and multicultural society is thus to produce self-constituting and democratic social selves.[6]

---

[5] Recent studies have indicated that there are rapidly growing categories of individuals who do not fit into standard racial or ethnic categories because of their hybrid backgrounds - a situation that will only become more salient in the years to come. See the *New York Times,* July 6, 1996: A1 on the dramatic rise of multiracial families and the problems this is creating for census forms; on the struggle for identity of the growing number of multiracial Americans, see the *New York Times,* (July 20, 1996: A1). Hybridity, of course, is a defining feature of the culture, experience, and identity of immigrants who have settled in societies other than their homeland over the past centuries.

[6] For parallel and complementary perspectives to education for autonomy and self-constitution, see Kiros in this volume.

Accordingly, in the next sections, I will address what is involved in multicultural education and what sorts of literacy are necessary to produce a healthy, diverse, and vibrant multicultural society, as well as democratic and self-governing and empowered selves. I will argue first that media literacy is necessary to produce individuals capable of developing critical consciousness and self-empowerment in a media culture and, then, that new forms of what I call multiliteracies are necessary to create active subjects able to engage and deploy the new technologies in a creative, democratic, and empowering fashion.

Media Literacy, Multiculturalism, and the Challenges of Contemporary Education

A number of educators and theorists recognize the ubiquity of media culture in contemporary society, the growing trends toward multicultural education, and the need for media literacy that addresses the issue of multicultural difference.[7] There is expanding recognition that media representations help construct our images and understanding of the world and that education must meet the dual challenges of teaching media literacy in a multicultural society and sensitizing students and publics to the inequities and injustices of a society based on gender, race, and class inequalities and discrimination. Recent critical studies see the role of mainstream media in exacerbating these inequalities and the ways that media education and the production of alternative media can promote a healthy multiculturalism of diversity and more

---

[7] Carson, Diane and Friedman, Lester (1995) *Shared Differences. Multicultural Media & Practical Pedagogy* (Urbana and Chicago: University of Illinois Press). contains studies dealing with the use of media to deal with multicultural education. Examples of teaching media literacy which I draw on include Masterman, Len (1989 [1985]) *Teaching the Media* (London and New York: Routledge); Schwoch, James, Mimi White, and Susan Reilly (1992)*Media Knowledge* (Albany: State University of New York Press); Fleming, Dan (1993)*Media Teaching* (Oxford: Basil Blackwell); Giroux, Henry (1994)*Disturbing Pleasures* (New York: Routledge). and (1996)*Fugitive Cultures: Race, Violence, and Youth* (New York: Routledge); Sholle, David and Stan Denski (1994)*Media Education and the (Re)Production of Culture* (Westport, Conn.: Bergin & Garvey); McLaren, Peter, Rhonda Hammer, David Sholle and Susan Reilly, (1995) *Rethinking Media Literacy. A Critical Pedagogy of Representation* (New York: Peter Lang); McLaren, Peter (1995) *Critical Pedagogy and Predatory Culture* (London and New York: Routledge); and Kellner (1995) *Media Culture* (London and New York: Routledge). See also the work of Barry Duncan and the Canadian Association for Media Literacy at http://www.nald.ca/province/que/litcent/media.htm

robust democracy. They thus confront some of the most serious difficulties and problems that face us as educators and citizens as we move toward the twenty-first century.

Multicultural education is in part a response to deal creatively with growing diversity, which facilitates "strategies for sharing, understanding, and enjoying" our proliferating cultural multiplicities and differences.[8] A variety of educators have thus been urging developing pedagogic practices that will promote multicultural understanding, that will empower students, and that will strengthen education. Since cultural differences are constructed at the level of meaning and significance through the mediation of media and cultural representations, students and citizens must become aware of the ways that culture constructs a system of social differences, with hierarchies, exclusions, defamations, and sometimes legitimation of the dominant social groups' power and domination. A critical multicultural education will thus make teachers and students sensitive to the politics of representation, to how media audiences' images of race, gender, sexuality, and cultural differences are in part generated by cultural representations, how negative stereotyping presents harmful cultural images, and the need for a diversity of representations to capture the cultural wealth of contemporary America.

But the media can also be used to teach positively multicultural understanding and education. Through cultivating the skills of media literacy, teachers can discover how to use media to promote multicultural education and to use this material to teach media literacy as well. If multicultural education is to promote genuine diversity and expand the curriculum, it is important both for groups excluded from mainstream education to learn about their own heritage and for dominant groups to explore the experiences and voices of minority and excluded groups. Moreover, as Friedman stresses, while it is important and useful to study cultures and voices excluded from traditional canons, dead white European male authors may have as much of importance to teach all students as excluded representatives of minority groups whom multiculturalists want, often with good reason,

[8] Carsons (1995:x) in Carson, Diane, and Lester D. Friedman (1995) *Shared Differences. Multicultural Media & Practical Pedagogy* (Urbana and Chicago: University of Illinois Press).

to include in the curriculum.[9] Thus, Friedman convincingly argues that: "Western culture, despite its myriad faults, remains a crucial influence on American political, intellectual and social thought and, as such, should play an important role in classrooms".[10]

In reality, few advocates of multicultural education call for jettisoning the traditional canon and altogether replacing the classics with new multicultural fare. Genuine multicultural education requires expanding, not contracting, the curricula, broadening and enriching it, not impoverishing it. It also involves, as Friedman stresses, including white ethnic groups in the multicultural spectrum and searching out those common values and ideals that cut across racial and cultural boundaries. Thus, multicultural education can both help us understand our history and culture, and can move toward producing a more diverse and inclusive democratic society.

Moreover, media culture constructs models of multi-cultural difference, privileging some groups, while denigrating others. Grasping the construction of difference and hierarchy in media texts requires learning how they are constructed, how they communicate and metacommunicate, and how they influence their audiences. Textual and semiotic analysis of media artifacts helps to reveal their codes and conventions, their values and ideologies, and thus their meanings and messages.[11] In particular, a critical cultural studies should analyze representations of class, gender, race, ethnicity, sexual preference, and other identity markers in the texts of media culture, as well as attending to national, regional, and other cultural differences, how they are articulated in cultural representations, and how these differences among audiences create different readings and receptions of cultural texts.

The argument for developing media literacy as part of standard educational training is that the media themselves are a form of cultural pedagogy and thus must be countered by a critical media pedagogy that dissects how media communicate and effect their audiences and how students

[9] Carsons & Friedman (1995).

[10] Carsons & Friedman (1995:3).

[11] Kellner, Douglas (1995) *Media Culture* (London and New York: Routledge) and (1995) "Cultural Studies, Multiculturalism, and Media Culture," in Dines, Gail, and Jean Humez (1995), editors, *Gender, Race, and Class in Media* (Thousand Oaks, Ca. and London: Sage) pp. 5-17.

and citizens can gain skills to critically analyze the media. A large number of books on media literacy over the past decade start from the premise of the ubiquity of media culture in contemporary society and produce a more general argument for critical media literacy as a response to media bombardment. "Media literacy" involves knowledge of how media work, how they construct meanings, how they serve as a form of cultural pedagogy, and how they function in everyday life. A media literate person is skillful in analyzing media codes and conventions, able to criticize media stereotypes, values, and ideologies, and thus literate in reading media critically. Media literacy thus empowers people to use media intelligently, to discriminate and evaluate media content, to critically dissect media forms, and to investigate media effects and uses.

A critical media literacy is necessary since media culture strongly influences our view of the world, imparting knowledge of geography, of technology and the environment, of political and social events, of how the economy works, of what is currently going on in our society and the world at large. Media entertainment is also a form of cultural pedagogy, teaching dominant values, ways of thought and behavior, style and fashion, and providing resources for constituting individual identities.[12] The media are both crucial sources of knowledge and information, and sources of entertainment and leisure activity. They are our story tellers and entertainers, and are especially influential since we are often not aware that media narratives and spectacles themselves are a form of education, imparting cultural knowledge, values, and shaping how we see and live our social worlds.

Consequently, media literacy is an important part of multicultural education since many people's conceptions of gender, sexuality, race, ethnicity, and class are constituted in part by the media which are often important in determining how people view social groups and reality, conceive of gender roles of masculinity and femininity, and distinguish between good and bad, right and wrong, attitudes and behavior. Since the media also provide role models, conceptions of proper and improper conduct, and provide crucial cultural and political information, they are an important form of pedagogy

[12] Kellner, Douglas (1995) *Media Culture* (London and New York: Routledge).

and socialization. A media literate person is thus able to read, understand, evaluate, discriminate and criticize media materials, and ultimately, produce media artifacts, in order to use media as means of expression and communication.[13]

Sometimes "the media" are lumped into one homogeneous category, but it is important to discern that there are many media of communication and forms of cultural pedagogy, ranging from print media such as books, newspapers, and magazines to film, radio, television, popular music, photography, advertising, and many other multimedia cultural forms, including video games, computer culture, CD-Roms, and the like. Media literacy thus requires traditional print literacy skills as well as visual literacy, aural literacy, and the ability to analyze narratives, spectacles, and a wide range of cultural forms. Media literacy involves reading images critically, interpreting sounds, and seeing how media texts produce meaning in a multiplicity of ways.[14] Since media are a central part of our cultural experience from childhood to the grave, training in media literacy should begin early in life and continue into adulthood, as new technologies are constantly creating new media and new genres, technical innovations, aesthetic forms, and conventions are constantly emerging.

It is the challenge of education and educators to devise strategies to teach media literacy while using media materials to contribute to advancing multicultural education. For, against McLuhan[15] who claims that the younger generation are naturally media literate, I would argue that developing critical media literacy requires cultivating explicit strategies of cultural pedagogy and models of media education. Media literacy involves making unconscious and prereflective

---

[13] See Hammer (1995) in McLaren, Hammer, Sholle & Reilly (eds) who indicates how student video projects can empower students to learn the conventions and techniques of media production and use the media to advance their own aims. Whereas film production involves heavy capital investment, expensive technology, and thus restricts access, video production is more accessible to students, easier to use, and enables a broad spectrum of students to actually produce media texts, providing alternative modes of expression and communication. Video technology thus provides access to a large number of voices excluded from cultural production and expression, materializing the multicultural dream of democratic culture as a dialogue of a rainbow of voices, visions, ideas, and experiences.

[14] Kellner , Douglas (1989), "Reading Images Critically: Toward a Postmodern Pedagogy," *Journal of Education*, Vol. 170, Nr. 3: 31-52 and (1995)*Media Culture* (London and New York: Routledge).

[15] McLuhan, Marshall (1964) *Understanding Media: The Extensions of Man* (New York: Signet Books).

understanding conscious and reflective, drawing on people's learned abilities to interact with media. All people in a media culture such as ours are media literate, they are able to read and interpret the multitude of cultural forms with which they daily interact, but their media literacy is often unconscious and unreflective, requiring the cultivation of cognitive skills of analysis, interpretation, and critique. Moreover, as many students and teachers of media literacy have discovered, most individuals who cultivate media literacy competencies actually reach new levels of media enjoyment due to their abilities to apply critical skills to reading media which discloses new dimensions, connections, and meanings.

Yet within educational circles, there is a debate over what constitutes the field of media pedagogy, with different agendas and programs. A traditionalist "protectionist" approach would attempt to "inoculate" young people against the effects of media addiction and manipulation by cultivating a taste for book literacy, high culture, and the values of truth, beauty, and justice, and by denigrating all forms of media and computer culture. Neil Postman in his books *Amusing Ourselves to Death* and *Technopolis* exemplifies this approach.[16] A "media literacy" movement, by contrast, attempts to teach students to read, analyze, and decode media texts, in a fashion parallel to the cultivation of print literacy. Media arts education in turn teaches students to appreciate the aesthetic qualities of media and to use various media technologies as tools of self-expression and creation. Critical media literacy, as I would advocate it, builds on these approaches, analyzing media culture as products of social production and struggle, and teaching students to be critical of media representations and discourses, but also stressing the importance of learning to use the media as modes of self-expression and social activism.

Critical media literacy not only teaches students to learn from media, to resist media manipulation, and to empower themselves vis-à-vis the media, but it is concerned with developing skills that will empower citizens and that will make them more motivated and competent participants in social life. Critical media literacy is thus tied to the project of radical democracy and concerned to develop skills that will

---

[16] Postman, Neil (1985) *Amusing Ourselves to Death* (New York: Viking-Penquin) and (1992) *Technopolis: The Surrender of Culture to Technology* (New York: Random House).

enhance democratization and participation. Critical media literacy takes a comprehensive approach that would teach critical skills and how to use media as instruments of social change. The technologies of communication are becoming more and more accessible to young people and average citizens, and they should be used to promote education, democratic self-expression, and social progress. Thus, technologies that could help produce the end of participatory democracy, by transforming politics into media spectacles and the battle of images, and by turning spectators into cultural zombies, could also be used to help invigorate democratic debate and participation.[17]

Indeed, teaching critical media literacy should be a participatory, collaborative project. Students are often more media savvy, knowledgeable, and immersed in media culture than their teachers and thus can contribute to the educational process through sharing their ideas, perceptions, and insights. On the other hand, critical discussion, debate, and analysis should be encouraged with teachers bringing to bear their critical perspectives on student readings of media material. Since media culture is often part and parcel of students' identity and most powerful cultural experience, teachers must be sensitive in criticizing artifacts and perceptions that students hold dear, yet an atmosphere of critical respect for difference and inquiry into the nature and effects of media culture should be encouraged.

Another complexity in developing critical media pedagogy results from the fact that in a sense it is not a pedagogy in the traditional sense with firmly-established principles, a canon of texts, and tried-and-true teaching procedures. Critical media pedagogy is in its infancy, it is just beginning to produce results, and is thus more open and experimental than established print-oriented pedagogy. Moreover, the material of media culture is so polymorphous, multivalent, and polysemic, that it requires sensitivity to different readings, interpretations, perceptions of the complex images, scenes, narratives, meanings, and messages of media culture which in its own ways is as complex and challenging to critically decipher as book culture.

---

[17] Kellner , Douglas (1995) *Media Culture* (London and New York: Routledge) and (1995) "Intellectuals and New Technologies," *Media, Culture, and Society*, Vol. 17: 201-217.

I have, in fact, so far downplayed hostility toward media education and the media themselves. Educational traditionalists conceive of literacy in more limited print-media paradigms and, as I suggested above, often adopt a "protectionist" approach when they address the issue of the media at all, warning students against corruption, or urging that they limit media use to "educational" materials. Yet many teachers at all levels from kindergarten to the University have discovered that media material, judiciously used, can be valuable in a variety of instructional tasks, helping to make complex subject matter accessible and engaging. Obviously, media cannot substitute for print material and classroom teaching, and should be seen as a supplement to traditional materials rather than a magic panacea for the failures of traditional education. Moreover, as I argue in the next section, traditional print literacy and competencies are more important than ever in our new high-tech societies.

It is also highly instructive, I would argue, to teach students at all levels to critically engage popular media materials, including the most familiar film, television, music, and other forms of media culture. Yet, here one needs, however, to avoid an uncritical media populism, of the sort that is emerging within certain sectors of British and North American cultural studies. In a review of *Rethinking Media Literacy*,[18] for instance, Jon Lewis attacked what he saw as the overly critical postures of the contributors to this volume, arguing: "If the point of a critical media literacy is to meet students halfway – to begin to take seriously what they take seriously, to read what they read, to watch what they watch – teachers *must* learn to love pop culture".[19] Note the authoritarian injunction that "teachers *must* learn to love popular culture" (italics are Lewis'), followed by an attack on more critical approaches to media literacy.

Teaching critical media literacy, however, involves occupation of a site above the dichotomy of fandom and censor. One can teach how media culture provides significant statements or insights about the social world, positive visions

---

[18] McLaren, Peter, Rhonda Hammer, David Sholle and Susan Reilly, (1995) *Rethinking Media Literacy. A Critical Pedagogy of Representation* (New York: Peter Lang).

[19] Lewis, Jon (1996) "Practice What You Preach," *Afterimage* (Summer 1996): 25-26.

of gender, race, and class, or complex aesthetic structures and practices, thus putting a positive spin on how it can provide significant contributions to education. Yet one should also indicate how media culture can promote sexism, racism, ethnocentrism, homophobia, and other forms of prejudice, as well as misinformation, problematic ideologies, and questionable values. A more dialectical approach to media literacy engages students' interests and concerns, and should, as I suggested above, involve a collaborative approach between teachers and students since students are deeply absorbed in media culture and may know more about some of its artifacts and domains than their teachers. Consequently, they should be encouraged to speak, discuss, and intervene in the teaching/learning process. This is not to say that media literacy training should romanticize student views, however; that may be superficial, mistaken, uniformed, and full of various problematical biases. Yet exercises in media literacy can often productively involve intense student participation in a mutual learning process where both teachers and students together learn media literacy skills and competencies.

It is also probably a mistake to attempt to institute a top-down program of media literacy imposed from above on teachers, with fixed texts, curricula, and prescribed materials. Diverse teachers and students will have very different interests and concerns, and will naturally emphasize different subject matter and choose examples relevant to their own and their student interests. Courses in critical media literacy should thus be flexible enough to enable teachers and students to constitute their own curricula to engage material and topics of current concern, and to address their own interests. Moreover, and, crucially, educators should discern that we are in the midst of one of the most intense technological revolutions in history and must learn to adapt new computer technologies to education, as I suggest in the following section, and this requires the development of new multiple literacies.

New Technologies, Multiple Literacies, and Postmodern Pedagogy: The New Frontier

The studies on multicultural education and critical media literacy that I have examined neglect to interrogate computer culture and the ways that the Internet and new computer technologies and cultural forms are dramatically transforming the circulation of information, images, and various modes of culture. And so in this concluding section that is looking toward education in the next century, I want to argue that students should learn new forms of computer literacy that involve both how to use computer culture to do research and gather information, as well as to perceive it as a cultural terrain which contains texts, spectacles, games, and new interactive multimedia. Moreover, computer culture is a discursive and political location in which they can intervene, engaging in discussion groups and collaborative research projects, creating their web sites, and producing new multimedia for cultural dissemination. Computer culture enables individuals to actively participate in the production of culture, ranging from discussion of public issues to creation of their own cultural forms. However, to take part in this culture requires not only accelerated forms of traditional modes of print literacy which are often restricted to the growing elite of students who are privileged to attend adequate and superior public and private schools, but new forms of literacy as well, thus posing significant challenges to education.

It is indeed a salient fact of the present age that computer culture is proliferating and so we have to begin teaching computer literacy from an early age on. Computer literacy, however, itself needs to be theorized. Often the term is synonymous with technical ability to use computers, to master existing programs, and maybe engage in some programming oneself. I want, however, to suggest expanding the conception of computer literacy from using computer programs and hardware to developing, in addition, more sophisticated abilities in traditional reading and writing, as well as the capability to critically dissect cultural forms taught as part of critical media literacy and new forms of multiple literacy. Thus, on this conception, genuine computer literacy involves not just technical knowledge and skills, but refined reading, writing, and communicating ability that involves heightened capacities for critically analyzing, interpreting, and processing print, image, sound, and multimedia material. Computer literacy involves intensified abilities to read, to scan texts and information, to put together in meaningful patterns mosaics of information, to construct meanings and significance, to contextualize and evaluate, and to discuss and articulate one's own views.

Thus, in my expanded conception, computer literacy involves technical abilities concerning developing basic typing skills, using computer programs, accessing information, and using computer technologies for a variety of purposes ranging from verbal communication to artistic expression. There are ever more implosions between media and computer culture as audio and video material becomes part of the Internet, as CD-Rom and multimedia develop, and as new technologies become part and parcel of the home, school, and workplace. Therefore, the skills of decoding images, sounds, and spectacle learned in critical media literacy training can also be valuable as part of computer literacy as well. Furthermore, print literacy takes on increasing importance in computer world as one needs to critically scrutinize and scroll tremendous amounts of information, putting new emphasis on developing reading and writing abilities. Indeed, Internet discussion groups, chat rooms, email, and various forums require writing skills in which a new emphasis on the importance of clarity and precision is emerging as communications proliferate. In this context of information saturation, it becomes an ethical imperative not to contribute to cultural and information overload, and to concisely communicate one's thoughts and feelings.

In a certain sense, computers are becoming the technological equivalent of Hegel's Absolute Idea, able to absorb everything into its form and medium. Computers are now not only repositories of text and print-based data, but also contain a wealth of images, multimedia sights and sounds, and interactive environments that, like the media, are themselves a form of education that require a critical pedagogy of electronic, digitized, culture and communication. From this conception, computer literacy is something like a Hegelian synthesis of print and visual literacy, technical skills, and media literacies, brought together at a new and higher stage. While Postman and others produce a simplistic Manichean dichotomy between print and visual literacy, we need to learn to think dialectically, to read text and image, to decipher sight and sound, and to develop forms of computer literacy adequate to meet the exigencies of an increasingly high tech society.

Thus, a postmodern pedagogy requires developing critical forms of print, media, and computer literacy, all of crucial importance in the new technoculture of the present and fast-approaching future.[20] Whereas modern pedagogy tended to be specialized, fragmented, and differentiated, and was focused on print culture, a postmodern pedagogy involves developing multiple literacies and critically analyzing, dissecting, and engaging a multiplicity of cultural forms, some of which are the products of new technologies and require developing new literacies to engage the new cultural forms and media. In fact, contemporary culture is marked by a proliferation of cultural machines which generate a panoply of print, sound, environmental, and diverse aesthetic artifacts within which we wander, trying to make our way through this forest of symbols. This requires development of new multimedia literacy that is able to scan, interact with, traverse, and organize new multimedia educational environments.[21] Multimedia literacy involves not just reading, but interacting: clicking to move from one field to another if one is involved in a hypertext environment such as one finds on web sites or CD-Roms; capturing, saving, and downloading material relevant to one's own projects; and perhaps responding

[20] For my take on postmodern theory, see Kellner, Douglas (1989) (ed) *Postmodernism/Jameson/ Critique* (Washington, D.C. Maisonneuve Press) and (1989); Best, Steven, and Kellner, Douglas (1991) *Postmodern Theory: Critical Interrogations* (London and New York: MacMillan and Guilford Press) and (1997)*The Postmodern Turn* (New York: Guilford Press) and(forthcoming)*The Postmodern Adventure* (New York: Guilford Press); and my website:
http://ccwf.cc.utexas.edu/~kellner/pm/pm.html
For an earlier sketch of postmodern pedagogy, see Kellner (1989), "Reading Images Critically: Toward a Postmodern Pedagogy,"*Journal of Education*, Vol. 170, Nr. 3: 31-52.

[21] For other recent conceptions of multimedia literacy, see the discussions of literacies needed for reading hypertext in Burbules, Nicholas C. and Callister, Thomas (1996) "Knowledge at the Crossroads: Some Alternative Futures of Hypertext Learning Environments," *Educational Theory* (Winter); the concept of multiliteracy in Cazden, C., Cope, B., Fairclough, N., Gee, J., Kalantzis, M., Kress, G., Luke, A., Luke, C., Michaels, S. & Nakata, M. (1996) "A Pedagogy of Multiliteracies: Designing Social Futures," *Harvard Educational Review* and Luke, Carmen (1997) *Technological Literacy. National Languages & Literacy Institute* (Adult Literacy Network); and an expansion of the concept of hyperreading in Burbules, Nicholas C. (forthcoming) "Rhetorics of the Web: Hyperreading and Critical Literacy in Page to Screen," in *Taking Literacy Into the Electronic Era* Ilana Snyder (ed) (New South Wales: Allen and Unwin).

verbally or adding one's own material if it is a site that invites this kind of participation.

In addition to the linear cognitive skills needed for traditional reading of print material, multimedia literacy requires the ability to read hypertexts that are often multidimensional requiring the connecting of images, graphics, texts, and sometimes audio-video material. It also involves making connections between the complex and multilayered cyberworld and its connection with the real world. Moreover, as Carmine Luke reminds us: "Since all meaning is situated relationally – that is, connected and cross-referenced to other media and genres, and to related meanings in other cultural contexts – a critical literacy relies on broad-based notions of intertextuality".[22]

Thus, one must learn to read multimedia forms that are themselves overlapping and interrelated, switching from text to graphics to video to audio, decoding in turn sight, sound, and text. In a global information environment, this also may involve switching from sites from one country to another requiring contextual understanding and literacy that is able to read and interact with people and sites from different cultures. As Carmen Luke puts it: "[N]ew [forms of] virtual communication are emerging, which require an intertextual understanding of how meanings shift across media, genres, and cultural frames of reference. Whether one 'visits' the Louvre on-line, joins an international newsgroup of parents of Downs Syndrome children, or visits the www site of an agricultural college in Kenya, cross-cultural understanding and 'netiquette' is increasingly crucial for participating effectively in global communications".[23]

In addition, multimedia literacy should be contextual, it requires thematizing the background and power relations of cultural forms (i.e. including analysis of the political economy of the media and technology, of how corporate organizations control production and dissemination, and how oppositional and alternative media and uses are possible),[24] as well as the context and power relations of the specific media use in

[22] Luke, Carmen (1997:10) *Technological Literacy* (National Languages & Literacy Institute. Adult Literacy Network).

[23] Luke, Carmen (1997:10) *Technological Literacy*.

[24] See Kellner , Douglas (1995) *Media Culture* (London and New York: Routledge).

question (i.e. the differences between television watching in the classroom, at home with one's family, with one's friends or alone; or the differences between computer use for research, data organization, email, or playing games, etc.). Multimedia literacy also envisages new modes of collaborative work on research projects or web sites, new forms of student/teacher participation and interaction, and new pedagogical uses for the new technologies which may often appear exotic in the present, but which will become increasingly commonplace in the future and will force a rethinking of education.

And so we need to begin learning how to read and deploy these new multimedia environments and interact with these fascinating and seductive cultural forms whose massive impact on our lives we have only begun to understand. Surely, education should attend to the new multimedia culture and teach how to read and interact with new computer and multimedia environment as part of new forms of multiple literacy. Such an effort would be part of a new critical pedagogy that attempts to critically empower individuals so that they can analyze and criticize the emerging technoculture, as well as participate in its cultural forums and sites.

In addition to the critical media literacy, print literacy, computer literacy, and multimedia literacy discussed above, multiple literacies involve cultural literacy, social literacy, and ecoliteracy. Since a multicultural society is the context of education in the contemporary moment, new forms of social interaction and cultural awareness are needed that appreciate differences, multiplicity, and diversity. Therefore, expanded social and cultural literacy is needed that appreciates the cultural heritage, histories, and contributions of a diversity of groups. Thus, whereas one can agree with E.D. Hirsch that we need to be literate in our shared cultural heritage, we also need to become culturally literate in cultures that have been hitherto invisible, as Henry Louis Gates and his colleagues have been arguing in their proposals for a multicultural education.[25]

Social literacy should also be taught throughout the educational systems, ranging from focus on how to relate and get along with a variety of individuals, how to negotiate

---

[25] Hirsch, E.D. (1987) *Cultural Literacy* (New York: Random House) and Gates, Henry (1996) *Loose Canons*.

differences, how to resolve conflicts, and how to communicate and socially interact in a diversity of situations. Social literacy also involves ethical training in values and norms, delineating proper and improper individual and social values. It also requires knowledge of the contemporary societies and thus overlaps with social and natural science training. Indeed, given the tremendous role of science and technology in the contemporary world, given the threats to the environment, and need to preserve and enhance the natural as well as social and cultural worlds, it is scandalous how illiterate the entire society is concerning science, nature, and even our own bodies. An ecoliteracy should thus appropriately teach competency in interpreting and interacting with our natural environment, ranging from our own body to natural habitats like forests and deserts.

The challenge for education today is thus to promote multiple literacies to empower students and citizens to use the new technologies to enhance their lives and to create a better culture and society based on respect for multicultural difference and aiming at fuller democratic participation of individuals and groups largely excluded from wealth and power in the previous modern society. A positive postmodernity would thus involve creation of a more egalitarian and democratic society in which more individuals and groups were empowered to participate. The great danger facing us, of course, is that the new technologies will increase the current inequalities based on class, gender, and racial divisions. So far, the privileged groups have had more direct and immediate access to the new technologies. It is therefore a challenge of education today to provide access to the new technologies and to the literacies needed for competence in order to overcome some of the divisions and inequalities that have plagued contemporary societies during the entire modern age.

Yet, there is also the danger that youth will become totally immersed in a new world of high-tech experience and lose its social connectedness and ability to interpersonally communicate and relate concretely to other people. Statistics suggest that more and more sectors of youth are able to access cyberspace and that college students with Internet accounts are spending as much as four hours a day in the new realm of technological experience.[26] The media, however, has been generating a moral panic concerning allegedly growing dangers in cyberspace with lurid stories of young boys and girls lured into dangerous sex or running away from home, endless accounts of how pornography on the Internet is proliferating, and the publicizing of calls for increasing control, censorship, and surveillance of communication – usually by politicians who are computer illiterate. The solution, however, is not to ban access to new technologies, but to teach students and citizens how to use these technologies so that they can be employed for productive and creative rather than problematical ends.

To be sure, there are dangers in cyberspace as well as elsewhere, but the threats to adolescents are significantly higher through the danger of family violence and abuse than seduction by strangers on the Internet. And while there is a flourishing trade in pornography on the Internet, this material has become increasingly available in a variety of venues from the local video shop to the newspaper stand, so it seems unfair to demonize the Internet. Thus, attempts at Internet censorship are part of the attack on youth which would circumscribe their rights to obtain entertainment and information, and create their own subcultures.[27] Consequently, devices like the V-chip that would exclude sex and violence on television, or block computer access to objectionable material, is more an expression of adult hysteria and moral panic than genuine dangers to youth which certainly exist, but much more strikingly in the real world than in the sphere of hyperreality.

Throughout this century, there has been a demonization of new media and forms of media culture, ranging from comic books to film to popular music to television and now to the

---

[26] *Wired* magazine is a good source for statistics and data concerning growing computer and internet use among all sectors of youth and documents the vicissitudes of cyberculture. The main story in the business press during the mid-1990s is the consolidation of the information and entertainment industries, so the daily newspapers are also full of copious material on adventures in cyberspace which may be the locus of the next stage of the postmodern adventure See Best and Kellner*The Postmodern Adventure* (New York: Guilford Press).

[27] On the attack on youth in contemporary society and culture, see: Giroux (1996) *Fugitive Cultures: Race, Violence, and Youth* (New York: Routledge) and (1997) *Channel Surfing: Race Talk and the Destruction of Today's Youth* (New York: St. Martin's Press); also, Manes, Mike A. (1996) *The Scapegoat Generation. America's War on Adolescents* (Monre ME: Common Courage Press).

Internet. As Jenkins[28] argues, this demonization is supported by an assumption of the innocence of childhood, that children are merely passive receptacles, easily seduced by cultural images, and in need of protection from nefarious and harmful cultural content. But as Jenkins contends,[29] the myth of "childhood innocence" strips children of active agency, of being capable of any thoughts of their own, of having the ability to decode and process media materials themselves. Of course, children need media education, they need to be involved in an active learning process concerning their culture, but censorship and vilification of media does not help young people become active critics and participants in their culture.

Accordingly, Jon Katz[30] has argued for children's "cyber-rights," arguing that our youth's access to Internet cyberculture and media culture in general is necessary for their participation in the larger culture and their own education and development. Mastery of the culture can be the difference between economic success and hardship, and the Internet in particular allows participation in many dimensions of social and cultural life as well as the cultivation of technical skills that can help children in later life.

Therefore, it is necessary to divest ourselves of myths of childhood innocence and the passivity of children's media consumption, positing instead the possibility of active and creative use of media material in which media education is seen as part of youth's self-development and constitution. Accordingly, Henry Jenkins proposes "a new kind of radical media education based on the assumption that children are active participants within popular culture rather than passive victims. We need to help our children become more critically reflective about the media they use and the popular culture they embrace, yet we can only achieve this by recognizing and respecting their existing investments, skills, and knowledge as media users. In the end, our goals must be not to protect our children but to empower them".[31]

---

[28] Jenkins, Henry (1997) "Empowering Children in the Digital Age: Towards a Radical Media Pedagogy," *Radical Teacher*, 50: 30-35.

[29] Jenkins (1997:30f).

[30] Katz, Jon (1996) "The Rights of Kids in the Digital Age," *Wired*, July 1996: 120ff.

[31] Jenkins (1997:31).

Thus, rather than demonizing and rejecting out of hand new technologies, we should see how they can be used constructively for positive ends. Indeed, in studying the kaleidoscopic array of discourses which characterize the new technologies, I am rather bemused by the extent to whether they expose either a technophilic discourse which presents new technologies as our salvation, that will solve all our problems, or they embody a technophobic discourse that sees technology as our damnation, demonizing it as the major source of all our problems.[32] It appears that similarly one-sided and contrasting discourses greeted the introduction of other new technologies this century, often hysterically. To some extent, this was historically the case with film, radio, TV, and now computers. Film, for instance, was celebrated by early theorists as providing new documentary depiction of reality, even redemption of reality, a new art form, new modes of mass education and entertainment – as well as demonized for promoting sexual promiscuity, juvenile delinquency and crime, violence, and copious other forms of immorality and evils. Its demonization led in the United States to a Production Code that rigorously regulated the content of Hollywood film from 1934 until the 1950s and 1960s – no open mouthed kissing was permitted, crime could not pay, drug use or attacks on religion could not be portrayed, and a censorship office rigorously surveyed all films to make sure that no subversive or illicit content emerged.[33]

Similar extreme hopes and fears were projected onto radio, television, and now computers. It appears whenever there are new technologies, people project all sorts of fantasies, fears, hopes, and dreams onto them, and I believe that this is now happening with computers and new multimedia technologies. It is indeed striking that if one looks at the literature on new technologies – and especially computers – it is either highly celebratory and technophilic, or sharply derogatory and technophobic. A critical theory of technology, however, and critical pedagogy, should avoid either demonizing or deifying the new technologies and should

---

[32] Kellner, Douglas (forthcoming) "New Technologies, TechnoCities, and the Prospects for Democratization," in John Dowling (ed) *New Technologies and TechnoCities* (London: Sage Books).

[33] Kellner, Douglas (1997) "Hollywood and Society: Critical Perspectives," in John Hill (ed) *Oxford Encyclopaedia of Film* (Oxford: Oxford University Press).

instead develop pedagogies that will help us use the technologies to enhance education and life, and to criticize the limitations and false promises made on behalf of new technologies.

Certainly there is no doubt that the cyberspace of computer worlds contains as much banality and stupidity as real life and one can waste much time in useless activity. But compared to the bleak and violent urban worlds portrayed in rap music and youth films like *Kids* (1995), the technological worlds are havens of information, entertainment, interaction, and connection where youth can gain valuable skills, knowledge, and power necessary to survive the postmodern adventure. Youth can create new, more multiple and flexible selves in cyberspace as well as new subcultures and communities. Indeed, it is exciting to cruise the Internet and to discover how many interesting web sites that young people and others have established, often containing valuable educational material. There is, of course, the danger that corporate and commercial interests will come to colonize the Internet, but it is likely that there will continue to be spaces where individuals can empower themselves and create their own communities and identities. A main challenge for youth (and others) is to learn to use the Internet for positive cultural and political projects, rather than just entertainment and passive consumption.

Reflecting on the growing social importance of computers and new technologies makes it clear that it is of essential importance for youth today to gain various kinds of literacy to empower themselves for the emerging new cybersociety (this is true of teachers and adults as well). To survive in a postmodern world, individuals of all ages need to gain skills of media and computer literacy to enable ourselves to negotiate the overload of media images and spectacles; we all need to learn technological skills to use the new media and computer technologies to subsist in the new high-tech economy and to form our own cultures and communities; and youth especially need street smarts and survival skills to cope with the drugs, violence, and uncertainty in today's predatory culture,[34] as well as new forms of multiple literacy.

[34] McLaren, Peter (1995) *Critical Pedagogy and Predatory Culture* (London and New York: Routledge).

It is therefore extremely important for the future of democracy to make sure that youth of all classes, races, genders, and regions gain access to new technology, receiving training in media and computer literacy skills in order to provide the opportunities to enter the high-tech job market and society of the future, and to prevent an exacerbation of class, gender, and race inequalities. And while multiple forms of new literacies will be necessary, traditional print literacy skills are all the more important in a cyberage of word-processing, information gathering, and Internet communication. Moreover, what I am calling multiple literacy involves training in philosophy, ethics, value thinking, and the humanities which I would argue is necessary now more then ever. In fact, how the Internet and new technologies will be used depends on the overall education of youth and the skills and interests they bring to the new technologies which can be used to access educational and valuable cultural material, or pornography and the banal wares of cybershopping malls.

Thus, the concept of multiple literacy and the postmodern pedagogy that I envisage would argue that it is not a question of either/or, e.g. either print literacy or multimedia literacy, either the classical curriculum or a new curriculum, but it is rather a question of both/and that preserves the best from classical education, that enhances emphasis on print literacy, but that also develops new literacies to engage the new technologies. Obviously, cyberlife is just one dimension of experience and one still needs to learn to interact in a "real world" of school, jobs, relationships, politics, and other people. Youth – indeed all of us! – needs to learn to interact in many dimensions of social reality and to gain a multiplicity of forms of literacy and skills that will enable us to create identities, relationships, and communities that will nurture and develop our full spectrum of potentialities and satisfy a wide array of needs. Our lives are more multidimensional than ever and part of the postmodern adventure is learning to live in a variety of social spaces and to adapt to intense change and transformation. Education too must meet these challenges and both utilize new technologies to promote education and to devise strategies in which new technologies can be deployed to create a more democratic and egalitarian multicultural society.

Contributors

K. Anthony Appiah is Professor of Afro-American Studies and Philosophy at Harvard University. His many books include *Assertion and Conditionals, For Truth in Semantics, Necessary Questions,* and *In My Father's House.* Appiah's scholarly interests range from African and African-American intellectual history and literary studies, ethics, and philosophy of mind and language; he has also taught regularly on philosophical problems in the study of African traditional religions. He has been Chairman of the Joint Committee of African Studies of the Social Science Research Council and the American Council of Learned Societies and President of the Society for African Philosophy in North America. He is an editor of *Transition* magazine.

Martin Bernal is Professor of Government Studies at Cornell University. He was formerly a Fellow of King's College, Cambridge. Among his numerous books is the widely discussed, *Black Athena,* one of the most celebrated works of our time.

Robin Chandler is a professional artist, writer and sociologist on the faculty of Northeastern University. She is currently a Fulbright fellow in South Africa. She teaches in the fields of cultural studies and the arts. The author has been an exhibiting artist, lecturer, consultant, and resident artist in the United States, Brazil and South Africa through various grants including the NEA. She is the director of the Peace Doors Project.

Kathleen Neal Cleaver, an assistant professor of law at Emory University, is currently a scholar in residence at the Schomburg Center for Research in Black Culture at the New York Public Library. After devoting many years to the Black liberation movement, during which time she worked in the national office of the Student Nonviolent Coordinating Committee and became the first woman on the Central Committee of the Black Panther Party (1968-1971), she received a J.D. from Yale Law School in 1989. She was a Bunting Fellow in 1994, and is now on leave from Emory to complete her memoir, *Memories of Love and War,* which will be published next year by Random House.

Antonia Darder is Associate Professor of Cultural Studies in the Center for Educational Studies at Claremont Graduate School in California. She is the author of *Culture and Power in the Classroom:*

A Critical Foundation for Bicultural Education (Bergin and Garvey, 1991).

Henry Louis Gates is Professor of English and the Humanities and Chairman of Afro-American Studies at Harvard University. He is the author of *Colored People, The Signifying Monkey,* and *Loose Cannons.* He has edited several books and is a frequent contributor to the *New Yorker* as well as the *New York Times.* He is widely recognized as a literary theorist and critic.

George Katsiaficas is Professor of Humanities and Social Sciences at Wentworth Institute of Technology and Managing Editor of *New Political Science.* Among his books are *The Imagination of the New Left: A Global Analysis of 1968* and *The Subversion of Politics: European Autonomous Social Movements and the Decolonization of Everyday Life.*

Doug Kellner holds the George F. Kneller Philosophy of Education Chair at UCLA. Among his numerous books are *The Postmodern Turn* (with Steve Best), *Television and the Crisis of Democracy,* and *The Persian Gulf TV War.* He is currently working on a book entitled *The Postmodern Adventure* and editing the papers of Herbert Marcuse.

Teodros Kiros teaches philosophy at Suffolk University, political philosophy at Boston University, and is an Associate of Afro-American Studies at Harvard University. He is the author of *Toward The Construction of A Theory of Political Action* and *Moral Philosophy and Development.* He is currently an editor of *New Political Science* and is currently finishing a book, entitled *Self-Construction and the Formation of Human Values.*

Ngo Vinh Long is Associate Professor of Asian Studies at the University of Maine, teaching courses on China, Japan, South Asia, Southeast Asia, and the United States' relations with various Asian countries. He also serves as a coordinator of several research projects on social and economic issues in Vietnam and an adviser to several international non-governmental organizations (NGOs) such as Oxfam America on policies, programs and projects for Asia. His numerous works include *Before the Revolution: The Vietnamese Peasants Under the French* (1973,1991), *Vietnamese Women in Society and Revolution* (1974), and (co-editor) *Coming to Terms: The United States, Indochina, and the War* (1991). He has had recent studies and articles published in Stanley I. Kutler (ed.), *Encyclopedia of the Vietnam War* (1996); Jason Gilbert and William Head (eds.), *The Tet Offensive* (1996); Nanette J. Davis, *Prostitution: History and Trends* (1994) and *Asia Times* (January & April 1996).

Ali A Mazrui is an internationally known scholar, an author of numerous books and articles. He is particularly known for his highly acclaimed narration of the PBS series "The Africans." He is currently Albert Schweitzer Professor in the Humanities and Director, Institute of Global Cultural Studies at the State University of New York, Binghamton; Albert Luthuli Professor-at-Large, University of Jos, Nigeria; Ibn Khaldun Professor-at-Large, School of Islamic and Social Sciences, Leesburg, Virginia; and Senior Scholar in Africana Studies, Cornell University.

Theresa Perry is Associate Professor of Education and Undergraduate Dean at Wheelock College in Boston. She previously taught in the Philosophy and Theology Department at Xavier University in New Orleans, Louisiana, and in the African-American Studies department at Northeastern University in Boston, Massachusetts. She is currently completing a book on the development of a theoretical perspective on African-American school achievement. She edited *Teaching Malcolm* and *Freedom's Plow*.

Hashim Sarkis is lecturer and design critic at Harvard University Graduate School of Design. He is a founding member and programs director of Plan B, a non-profit organization based in Beirut, Lebanon and in Cambridge, Massachusetts, concerned with the improvement of the urban environment in Lebanon after the war. He is also a practicing architect involved in the reconstruction of Beirut. He is Co-editor of *Open City: Rebuilding Downtown Beirut's Waterfront* (Harvard Graduate School of Design, 1996). Sarkis has taught at MIT, Yale, RISD, and American University of Beirut.

Joyce Hope Scott is an Associate Professor of English at Massachusetts Maritime College and Adjunct Professor of African and African American Literature at Wheelock. She is a former Fulbright Professor to Burkina Faso, West Africa, 1991-1993. Her publications include "Texts and Testimonies," in *Teaching Malcolm*, edited by Theresa Perry, and "Black Folk Ritual in Home to Harlem and Black Thunder" in *Claude McKay: Centennial Studies*. Her current projects include the translation of the first novel to be written by a woman of Burkina Faso and a critical volume on the literature of countries of the African Sahel.

Rodolfo D. Torres is Professor of Comparative Latino Studies and Public Policy at California State University, Long Beach. He is co-author of *Latino Metropolis: Racialized Boundaries and Class Relations in Postindustrial Los Angeles* (forthcoming, University of Minnesota Press). He is a frequent contributor to the Los Angeles Times.

W.L. van der Merwe teaches philosophy at the University of Stellenbosch, South Africa. He holds degrees in philosophy, literature and theology and received his D.Phil. with a comparative interpretation of Husserl's and Wittgenstein's understandings of the relation between language and experience. His first book on philosophical theories of metaphor is widely used at South African universities. Apart from philosophy of language and philosophical hermeneutics, his other interests include philosophy of religion and more recently philosophy of culture and multiculturalism. During 1995-1996 as Senior Research Fellow and Visiting Professor at the Higher Institute of Philosophy of the Catholic University of Leuven (Belgium) he did research on philosophy and sociocultural diversity. Until 1996 he served as secretary of the Philosophical Society of Southern Africa (PSSA), the only professional philosophical society in southern Africa. In 1997 he was guest editor of a special issue of the *South African Journal of Philosophy* on multiculturalism, entitled *Identity, Difference and Community.*

Edward Yuen is a graduate student in the Sociology Department at the University of California, Santa Cruz. He is currently working on a dissertation on race, culture, political economy and the environment.

Acclaim for Matthew Kneale's WHEN WE WERE ROMANS

"If you enjoyed *The Curious Incident of the Dog in the Night Time*, definitely pick up *When We Were Romans*. It will make you thank God for children in a world made absurd by adults."

—*St. Petersburg Times*

"Masterful. . . . Lawrence's voice is irresistible. . . . As Hannah spins an ever more implausible tale about her ex-husband's malicious intentions, readers of all stripes will find themselves turning pages until there aren't any more."

—*The News & Observer* (Raleigh)

"Arresting. . . . There have been plenty of coming-of-age stories that pit a child's innocence against the inexorable force of a parent's insanity, but perhaps none that has captured the tension, confusion and ultimate loss of that innocence any better."

—*BookPage*

"Fresh and moving. . . . Kneale—and Lawrence—allow you to escape not only to another place and circumstance but to another age all together." —*Fiction Writers Review*

"Think of the delicate balancing act involved in creating a child narrator—a nine-year-old, say, with a single mother and a baby sister. The boy has to be cute, of course, and also wise in unexpected ways, fragile, protective, funny, solemn and, well, childlike. Matthew Kneale achieves all that brilliantly in *When We Were Romans*." —*The New York Observer*

"How much Lawrence understands of his family's tribulations is the book's central, poignant mystery; the consummate artistry with which Kneale captures this child's voice, its chief pleasure." —*Entertainment Weekly*

"Kneale deftly captures his nine-year-old narrator Lawrence's awe and angst upon moving from London to Rome." —*Elle*

"With descriptions of Caligula's cruelty or Nero's mania, Kneale weaves Lawrence's story together with the history of Rome, and of the known universe (as Lawrence understands it, of course)." —*The L Magazine*

"A poignant, haunting, and lovely novel."
—*The Guardian* (UK)

"Substantial and engaging. . . . With consummate subtlety and sympathy, Kneale finds metaphorical hinges between the family's unfolding story and Lawrence's two intellectual interests—Roman emperors and astronomy." —*The Times* (UK)

"The strength of Kneale's novel is . . . Lawrence's delicate sensibility. . . . Lawrence's touchingly ingenuous language, his tetchy irritation with his baby sister, and his beleaguered optimism make him a genuinely affecting protagonist."
—*The Independent* (UK)

Matthew Kneale

When We Were Romans

Matthew Kneale was born in London in 1960, the son of two writers. He is the author of numerous prizewinning novels, including the bestselling *English Passengers*, which won the Whitbread Award and was shortlisted for the Booker Prize. He lives with his wife and two children in Rome.

When
We Were
Romans

When We Were Romans

– a novel –

MATTHEW KNEALE

Anchor Canada

Library and Archives of Canada Cataloguing in Publication has been applied for

ISBN: 978-0-385-66778-4

Book design by Gretchen Achilles

Printed and bound in the USA

Published in Canada by Anchor Canada,
a division of Random House of Canada Limited

Visit Random House of Canada Limited's website: www.randomhouse.ca

10 9 8 7 6 5 4 3 2 1

For my father, who taught me so much about how to build a story.

When
We Were
Romans

CHAPTER ONE

One day scientists found something strange out in space. This thing was pulling millions of galaxies towards it, one of them is the Milky Way which is ours, but the scientists couldn't see the thing because it was hidden behind lots of dust. They thought "this thing must be huge to pull all these galaxies towards it, and we are getting pulled towards it really fast, it is at millions of miles per hour, but it could be anything, nobody knows, it is a mystery." They thought "this is strange, this is scary" and then they said "I know, let's call the thing the Great Attractor."

The great Attractor is pulling us right now. I think it is probably a huge black hole, because black holes eat everything, they even eat light so you can't ever see them, they look just like a piece of really dark night. One day I bet there will be a big disaster, we will go nearer and nearer and then suddenly we will get pulled right in. It will be like a big hand gets us so we will vanish, because nothing can get out of a black hole you see, we will be stuck there for ever. It is strange to think that every day, every minute we are all being pulled towards the Great Attractor but hardly anybody knows. People go about their ordinary every day lives, they have toast for breakfast and go to school, they watch their favorite programs on the telly and they never even guess.

We were coming back from the supermarket, we went to a further away one where we never went before so it would be all right, and it was an adventure mum said, we must be really quick, we must be like birds diving down and getting some food and flying away with it in their mouths. It was fun, actually, we got our cart and we almost ran, we just grabbed all the tins and packets and milk and tinfoil etc etc. Then Jemima saw some sweets in a little purple tin and she said "oh I want them, I need them, please mum." Mum said "don't be silly now, Lamikin" which is what she calls Jemima sometimes "anyway those aren't real sweets their cough sweets, their bad for you." But Jemima didn't listen, she never does, and she started crying like a big crybaby, she said "but I need them, I need that purple tin."

She was still saying it when we were coming back in the car and suddenly we were almost home. We went past Mrs Potters house and the droopy trees which look funny like hair and I thought "uhoh" I thought "now there will be trouble" but I didn't say anything of course, because we couldn't ever say anything in front of Jemima, because she was too young to understand. But then there was a surprise, because it was fine after all. Jemima was terrible just like I expected, when mum stopped the car she said "I'm staying here, I want to go back to the supermarket" but mum was ready, she said "if you come with me then I'll give you a nice treat" and it worked. Jemima went quiet and said "all right." Then we were so fast. Mum got Jemima out of her car seat and we all got all the plastic bags out of the trunk, I carried lots, even though they were really heavy, we went to the door, we were almost running, and Mum had her key all ready. That was when I looked round, I didn't really want to but I couldn't help it, I just had to. I looked at the fence and the bushes. But it was all all right, there wasn't anybody at all.

Then we were inside, mum shut the door, she locked it, and I thought "hurrah hurrah" I thought "look at all this food, this will last ages." We put it away in the fridge and the cupboards, and after that I went up to see Hermann. I cleaned his bowls and gave him some new nuts and water. Jemima followed like always so I let her watch, I said "no you can't hold him." Then it was time for robot wars, which is one of my favorite programs, there was a robot called the obliterator and another called the stamper which had a big sort of foot. So we sat on the sofa and I thought "I bet everything will be all right now" I thought "I bet dad will go away back to Scotland and then I can go back to school again, because I'm all better from my flu now" I thought "I wonder if Tania Hodgsons cat had its kittens yet, I wonder if they were all tabbies like their mum?"

Jemima was being annoying like usual. She said "I don't want to watch robot wars, I want to watch the other side." I said "there isn't anything on the other side Jemima you big silly, its just the news" but it didn't work, she said "I want the clicker, I never get the clicker, its my turn." Jemima is terrible with the clicker, she just does it again and again really fast so you can't watch anything, so I said "you can't Jemima, you'll break it like you broke your new pink sunglasses."

That was when mum came in. She said "here's your treat lesonfon" which is what she calls us sometimes, it is "children" in French, she told us once. It was our supper, usually we can't eat it when we watch telly but she said "just this once" and it was hot dogs and oven chips which was a treat too, because mum says we can't have oven chips because their too expensive, their a real waste of money. Usually I would just be pleased by those treats, I would think "oh yes, how delicious" but this time I wasn't actually, which was because I noticed mums face. You see, all that smiling she got from getting the food from the supermarket was just gone away again, it was like it all went down the plug hole, she tried to smile when she said "heres your treat, lesonfon" but it didn't work, I saw it, she just looked all worried and desperate.

I looked at Jemima but she hadn't noticed, she was too busy watching robot wars and trying to eat her chips too quickly, she said "ow too hot" she is such a greedy guts. I thought "what will I do, I must help mum" I thought "but I really want these chips, if I don't stay and eat them then Jemima will steal them secritly, perhaps I should just stay and eat them really fast" but then I thought "no no, I must help mum now." Suddenly I had an idea. I said "Jemima I am going to the loo, you can have the clicker just until I get back" and she was really pleased of course, she said "oh yes" and grabed it right out of my hand. I said "I've counted all my chips really carefully, Jemima, if you eat even just one tiny one

4

then I'll notice and I'll put all your favorite dolls on a high shelf so you'll never get them again."

Mum was sitting in the kitchen. She jumped up a bit when she saw me, she said "Lawrence." I said "whats wrong mum?" and she went really quiet, she said "what dyou mean?" so I said "somethings gone wrong, I can see it in your face." She closed her eyes a bit, she said "oh Lawrence, I don't want to upsit you with all of this" and she sort of squinted her eyes. I thought "she will tell me now" so I said "all of what mum?" and she did a little moan, she said "I don't know what to do, its so awful, we just can't go on like this."

I really hated it when poor mum went sad like that. I thought "what can I do to help her?" but I couldn't think of anything, I tried and tried, I thought "this is bad" until suddenly I had an idea. So I said "why don't we go away for a bit, just until he's gone away, we could go to Uncle Harry's or somewhere." Uncle Harry lives in London, he has a big house. We went there for Christmas but it was just for lunch, we didn't stay because we are too noisy so aunt Clarissa gets a head ache, and mum gets worried Jemima will break Uncle Harries old plates which are stuck on the walls like pictures, they cost lots of money. But mum shook her head, she said "they're away, they've gone skiying." I thought "oh dam" I thought "there must be somewhere we can go" but it was hard actually, because mum doesn't know many people, usually its just us in the cottage. I thought "I'm not going to give up now when everythings going so well, when we got all that food." So I said "what about Grandma and Grandpa in Kew."

Mum shook her head again, she was blinking, she said "he'd just follow us . . ." But then she stopped, she frowned like she was thinking really hard, and she said "unless . . ." This was good, at least she wasn't just saying "no, nothing will work" so I said "unless what?" And then she said it, she said "unless we went somewhere really far away. Somewhere he'd never be able to find us. Somewhere like Rome." Now she sort of squinted like this was better and better and she said "actually we could you know. I've got our passports from that time we almost went to France."

This was different, this was a big surprise. Mum sometimes talked about Rome where she lived years ago before I was born, and how we must all go one day to see the fountains which were so beautifull and eat the food which was so delicious, but I never thought it would happen, especially suddenly like this. Another surprise was that mum didn't look so worreid anymore, in fact she even did a little tiny smile, that was good. I didn't want to stop mums new smile of course, I really wanted it to stay, but I just didn't know, I couldn't help it. So I said "but what about school?" because I had tests at the end of term, you see, and I had my science project too, I was doing SPACE for Mr Simmons, who was my favorite teacher. But Mum didn't mind, that was good too, she didn't go sad after all. She said "we could take all your books so I can teach you for your tests and help with your project. And anyway it wouldn't be for very long, just till we are sure dads gone away. I could ring the school and say you've still got the flu."

I thought "I suppose so, if its just for a short time. I can take my book on Space that I got for Christmas from Uncle Harry and Aunt Clarissa, that will be for my science project." I thought "it'll be a shame if I miss Tania Hodgsons kittens" but then I thought "it will be nice to see the lovely fountains." But then before I could think anything else the door pushed open with a bang and Jemima came in and said "robot wars finished." Probably she guessed we were talking about something without her, she had her spying look so I bet she was listening at the key hole but she couldn't hear anything. You have to watch Jemima because she is everywhere. Mum pretended she wasn't surprised, she pretended she was expecting her to come in suddenly like that, she clapped her hands in the air like she had a special treat and said "Jemima, we've got some big, big news. We're thinking of going away."

I thought "I will help mum" so I said "Yes, isn't it exciting, we are going to Rome, won't that be nice." I don't think Jemima knew anything about rome really, but she made her silly surprised face to pretend she did, then she clapped her hands and shouted "oh yes Rome Rome".

So suddenly it was a real plan now, it was all finished. Mum was so pleased, she was smiling and smiling, that was good, that was wonderfull, because she hardly did that for weeks, not since I got the flu and dad came down from scotland secretly. It was like it was bubbeling out of her and making her eyes go blink blink. I thought "oh hurrah" I thought "this is good" I thought "I hope it doesn't all just go away again."

I went back and ate my hot dogs and Jemima didn't eat lots of my chips after all, she might have got one or two, it was hard to tell. Then mum said there was no point in dillidallying, we must go to Rome right now, we must go tommorrow morning, which meant we had to start packing straight away. She said we had to be very careful, we mustn't take too many things because they wouldn't fit in the car, so she gave me and Jemima three boxes each. Jemima talked to all her dolls and her animals, she said "are you going to be good, no, then you can't come" or "all right then, you can come to Rome" then she threw them into her boxes with some other things all in a rush, and she didn't take any notise when I told her "Jemima you must chose carefully or you'll leave your favorite things behind and then you'll cry," she just got angry and shouted "but I have been careful, I won't cry."

I thought "wow, we are going to Rome, that's amazing." It wasn't easy packing. I wanted to take my computer consel, my football game, my drawing paper and pencils, and also all my Tintin and Asterix books, all my lego, my hot wheels cars and track, my school books and my book on space and of course there was Hermann and his cage, but that was much too much for my three boxes, so I thought "uhoh, this will be hard." I could hear Mum in her bedroom packing, she wasn't keeping watch at all, sometimes she just forgets, so I thought "that's silly, mum" and I went into the sitting room so I could look.

It was a bit frightening actually, because when I started opening the curtain I thought "dads face might be right here on the other side of the window looking right at me." But there was a strange thing too, because d'you know a bit of me sort of hoped he would be there, that was funny. That bit wanted him to look in with his silly smile and his hair that goes up like smoke, it wanted him to say "hey there Larry hower you doing?" But then I squashed that bit, I blew it up, I thought "oh no you don't" and I thought "I don't like you dad, just go away, don't start pretending to be nice." But of course he wasn't there anyway, there wasn't anybody, it was just the window pane, all tall and black. I put my hand on it, it felt cold, and then I went right up close to the glass to look out, but it was really dark, the light just went a little way, it did a bit of the grass, there was some of a bush, and I could hear the wind making the trees move, swish swish swish.

After that I did my boxes. None of them were big enough for my school books and the tintin books together, so I took the biggest one, I cut its corners with scissors and then selotaped them round the books leaving gaps, though I had to put more selotape on the inside so it would not stick and wreck them. I was worried mum would get angry that I made the box bigger but she never did, but of course everything got so busy after that she probably never even noticed.

When I tried to pack my other things I found there wasn't enough room, Hermanns cage took up a whole box by itself, so I had to leave my football game, my Asterixes, and some lego behind, that was a real shame, but I thought "I like Tintin better than asterix anyway." Then I saw there was an empty space in one of Jemimas boxes, she was in bed now, so I put my Lego in there because otherwise that space would just go to waste. After that I cut lots of holes in Hermanns box so he could see out, but then I threw the box away completly, I thought "he doesn't need it, he will just have his cage" so it was late when I finished, but not really late, not dawn this time. I put the boxes downstairs, I put on my pijamas and brushed my teeth, four times each tooth like mum says, then I gave mum her kiss, she was still packing, she was smiling like before, and I went to bed.

When I woke it was just getting light and I could hear mum outside shouting "dam dam" so I knew something had gone wrong. I thought "uhoh, what now?" so I got dressed like a hurricain and ran downstairs without even brushing my teeth and it was cold downstairs because the front door was wide open. Mum was standing by the car, there were some bags already in it and lots more on the ground. She said "dam this car" and her smile was all gone now just like I thought, she looked tired and scared and she said "I just cant get everything in." Then she looked all round and suddenly she shouted "I don't care if your out there."

Though I hadn't even had my breakfast I thought "I will help, I will make her all right again" so I said "don't worry mum, I'm sure they'll all go in" and I helped her try the bags in different ways, but they just wouldn't fit at all, that was a shame. Mum was scratching her arm, it was all red again, and she said "oh god, we'll never get away, dad will come now, I just know he will."

That was when a funny thing happened. When she said this I heard a car coming up the road, so suddenly I got really worrid, I thought "that's him, he went away to a shop or to eat his breakfast and now he's coming back in his car" I thought "I know I will pick up a big stick" but there wasn't one anywhere, that was bad. I thought "uhoh what will I do" but then when I looked up d'you know there wasn't any car after all. The road was just empty, there wasn't even any noise, which was really strange, because I was sure I heard it, it was like a mystery. So I thought "we're safe after all" and suddenly I felt much better, I thought "everything will be all right now." So I took mums hand to stop her scraching and I said "mum, we will just have to leave some things behind" and d'you know she got better too, she said "your right Lawrence, of course you are."

Mum is really clever, she can always help me with my home work, she makes funny jokes, she knows just what everybodies thinking, even strangers shes never met before, but sometimes its like she just gets stuck and doesn't know what to do next, so I have to help her and give her a little push. I was worried she would say I must leave one of my three boxes behind but it was all right, she took one of hers instead. It had the big silver candel stick that we never used, some cups and other metal things, and she said "he can have it all, I don't give a dam" then she put it back into the house. Afterwards she took out two other boxes too, and when we tried again d'you know everything just fitted. I thought "hurrah now we are all right." I noticed she had put Hermann in his cage just beside my seat so I could look at him on the way, that was nice.

Now Mum got her smile back again and so did I, I thought "we will be fine now." We hurried back to the house, I brushed my teeth really quickly and then I made toast while Mum woke up Jemima and got her dressed. We were both in our nicest clothes which mum calls our Sunday Best, because mum said we must look nice for the passports man who would look at our passports when we went through the channell tunnell. Jemima ate her breakfest without making a big fuss which she does sometimes, she says "I want another egg" so that was good, and we washed up all the dishes really fast. But then, just when we were all ready to go suddenley she looked up and said in her wining voice "but I want to take my dolls house."

This was impossible of course, this was really stupid. Mum said "but you can't Jems love, the cars completely full" and I helped Mum, I said "Jemima, I told you yesterday you must think carfully about what you put in your boxes, remember, now stop being a big cry baby." But Jemima just isn't fair, instead of saying "oh yes you are right" she stuck her chin high in the air, thats always a bad sign, and she said "I'm not going without my dolls house, its my very favorite thing" which was just a lie, actually, because I hardly saw her play with it for weeks. Then she ran back into the kitchen and I thought "uhoh this is a disaster, I bet dad will come right now like mum said" and I almost said to Mum "maybe we should just leave her behind" but of course mum would just say "don't be silly."

Jemima is very hard to catch, she is fast and when you think you've got her she goes all squirmy and wriggles away and she bites. We caught her in the kitchen but she bit my hand and screamed right in my ear, so I could hardly hear anything for severel minutes and she got away. When she got away again in the living room, and then in the bathroom too, Mum blinked and scrached her arm and said "all right all right, Jemima, you win, we will take your dam dolls house." Straight away Jemima stopped running off and she came down the stairs quiet as a mouse with a special smile on her face that I hated, it was like she was thinking "ha ha I won again."

Actually Jemimas dolls house isn't very big, its a cottage just like ours, it was about the same size as one of her boxes, so I thought "we will just do a swap" but when we looked in the boot her boxes were stuck right underneath all the other things. Mum's voice went quiet and squeeky and she said "oh for christs sake. Look, I'm really sorry Lawrence but we just haven't got time to unpack everything again. We'll have to take out one of your boxes." I just couldn't believe it, I said "thats not fair." But Mum didn't take any notice, she said "Lawrence, I'm really sorry but I just can't be doing with this, we've got to go right now." After all the things I had done for mum, getting up fast like a hurricain to help her pack the car because she said "dam, dam" and helping her in every way, I just wanted to go far away, this was so unfair, I wanted to say "all right then I'm not coming either." But then something told me I could not do that, it was like a little voice. I thought "this is an emegency, dad might come any moment and mum is desperete" so though I was really really angry I didn't say anything, it was like I put all my anger in a little bag and did a knot.

I took out one of my boxes from the car trunk, it was the one with my hot wheels track and most of my cars and also my computer consel and my games, I took it because it was on the top, I thought "I don't care." Then I walked back in to the house and put it in my room and I got Jemimas dam dolls house, I carried it down and put it in the trunk instead. When I went past Jemima in her car seat I gave her a look and I said "I hope your happy now" but she didn't look sorry or cry or anything, she just kept kicking her feet and singing itsy bitsy spider. So I got into my own seat and I did up my seatbelt with a click. Mum came over and leaned down so her face was near mine and she said "I'm really sorry, Lawrence, I know that wasn't right but its an emergency. I tell you what, I'll get you a treat in Rome, something really special, how about that?" but I didn't say anything, I just sat very still and didn't even look at her, I thought "I don't like you mum."

Then I must have gone to sleep because suddenly I woke up, we were driving, Jemima was crying and mum was saying "but we can't stop, Jems love, we're on the motorway." What happened, you see, was that Jemima was sleeping too and then she peed in her car seat. I didn't say anything to her, because I still wasn't speaking to her, but I looked at Hermann who was going round in his wheel, and I told him "can you smell that nasty smell, Hermann, thats Jemimas pee." Finally we got to a Service Station, mum took off the car seats cover and put it in a plastic bag, she put a towel on instead, and she changed Jemimas tites and dress and said "poor lamikin." That meant Jemima wasn't in her sunday best any more, she was a real miss match, so I said to Hermann "I wonder if the passports man will let Jemima through now or if we will just have to leave her behind?" Then Jemima started crying and mum got cross and said "of course he'll let her through, don't upset your sister like that" which wasn't fair because I didn't actually, I was only talking to Hermann.

Mum got more petrol and got us some chocolate bars and sweets as a treat for the journey, and when I ate mine d'you know suddenly I didn't mind so much any more about the hot wheels track and even the computer consel, I thought "I was getting bored with my computer games, actually." I looked out of the window at the motorway, I watched to see that dad wasn't following us in his yellow car but he wasn't, and then it was like everything was new. I thought, "hurrah, we're going away" I thought "dad hasn't done anything really terreble after all and now we are safe in our car, driving off on an adventure to go all the way to Rome. Hurrah hurrah."

Eventually we got almost to the channel tunnel but then something bad happened. Just after we passed the sign for the tunnel suddenly mum said "oh god, I completely forgot, what about Hermann, he's not allowed." This was because of Rabbies you see, which is a disease they have in France and Europe, you get it when animals bite you, cats or dogs or rabbits, it makes you fome at the mouth and die. I thought "what can we do, this is a disaster, we can't leave him behind?" But then suddenly mum laughed a bit and she said "wait a minute, I've got it wrong, that's only the other way when we come back."

Even then I was still really worried. I said "what d'you mean, mum, we'll have to leave him in rome?" but she said "no no, don't you worry Lawrence love, it'll be fine, we'll get him a pets passport, its really easy nowadays, I heard all about it on the radio." I thought "oh thank goodness" but I was still a bit worrid, I thought "what if mum made a mistake" because she does sometimes, like when we were going to Edinburgh to see Dad and she went on the wrong road so we almost went to Glasgow instead, or when she left her hand bag in the library. Jemima was worried too, because she really likes Hermann, she always wants to change his water and give him his food though I won't let her of course, because she is just a baby, she would do it all wrong. She said "what if there isn't a pets passport" but mum said "don't be silly, lamikin, of course there will be."

We bought our tickets for the channell tunnell and we showed our passports to the passports man, who didn't mind about Jemimas clothes being miss matched, so we didn't have to leave her behind after all. We drove our car right onto a train, that was funny, and I put some coats on Hermanns cage so nobody would see him, just in case mum got it wrong, but I don't think anyone looked. After that we went through the tunnel and it was really quick, I thought it would take hours. At the other end we were in france, mum said I had been there once but it was years ago so I probably didnt remember, and I didn't actually. We stopped for lunch and I had chicken and chips, it was really delicious, and mum said "dyou know when I was in Rome I was almost in a film." I knew about that of course because she already told me lots of times. She met a man who was making a film about a lady who lives on an island in the War, and he wanted mum to be in it. She was going to be another lady who waves from a boat, but she couldn't because she was just about to come back to England with dad, because she met him there in Rome you see, so I said "yes mum, you already told me about that."

Then we drove on the french motorway for ages, we had supper at a Service Station and afterwards I went to sleep and dreamed I went to the cinema and saw mum in the film about the island in the war, we built a big fence to stop anybody getting on to the island and she had her sell phone to warn us if he was coming, so we were really safe. When I woke up it was dark and we were still on the motorway so I looked out of the window at France where everything was different, the houses had different rooves and windows and even the writing on the signs was different, with funny lines on top of the letters. I thought "I should tell mum that I woke up" but then I thought "no I won't, I will just stay awake secretly like this" so I just sat there and I didn't say a word. I looked up at the sky, there were some stars, so I looked at a black space in the middle and I thought "is that you, Great Attractor?" Jemima was off away in dreamland, Mum was driving, Hermann was going round and round in his wheel, and the car was making its engine noise but everything was really quiet. And d'you know it felt so nice, just us, driving in our car in france in the night.

Later I woke up, the car was stopped and mum was shaking me and saying "come on Lawrence, come on, Jemima, we're staying here." It was a hotel, it had big windows like the library, and I was so tired I just wanted to stay in my car seat, Jemima was too, she said "I just want to go home" but we went in in the end. Then it was funny because though I was so tired I couldn't sleep. So I lay in my bed, I listened to mums breatheing, I looked at the curtains, when a car went past light moved at the edges, it was like eyes going from side to side, and I worried about Hermanns pets passport. I thought "what if we get stopped by the passports man and he says "no, you'll have to leave him here in france, you'll have to give him to a pet shop."

Then I woke up again and everything was better. It was just getting light, mum was already in her clothes and she said "come on lesonfon we've got to make an early start." So we all got back in the car, we went on the motorway again until we stopped at a huge Service Station for breakfast, it was crussons. And suddenly I wasn't so worried about Hermann any more, I thought "Mum is really clever, she knows everything, I am sure she is right about the pets passport."

SPACE IS SO BIG. We are in the solar system, which is Earth, Mars, Venus etc etc. The solar system is in a galaxy that's called the Milky Way, which is really huge, it has a hundred and fifty billion stars in it and its a hundred thousand light years across. That means that even if you went at the speed of light, which is impossible actually because no space craft ever can, its too fast, only light can do that, it would still take a hundred thousand years to go across it. Mum says a hundred thousand years ago people were still just cave men.

But our galaxy is tiny really. Scientists say in the universe there are a hundred billion galaxies. So if you were standing on the edge of the Universe looking for our galaxy you'd never even find it, it would just be a speck. Scientists say the universe is spongey, the galaxies are in long strings and flat parts like paper hankercheaves, so it is like a big squashy net. In between the strings and flat bits there are holes, which are called voids, and actually most of the universe is just these holes, which are really enormous. A really big one is called Bootes void, which is two hundred and fifty million light years across. Mum says four hundred million years ago there were just fish and amphibians etc etc dinosaurs hadn't even started yet.

That means that if you thought "I know, I think I will take a lovely trip across Boots void" and you went at the speed of light, which nobody can, you would have to sit in your space craft from when there were just fish and amphibiens to right now, and all the time you'd never see anything because there's hardly anything there, just a few galaxies which would probably be miles away on the other side. All you'd see is maybe an atom every now and then, which would be so tiny that you wouldn't even notice it anyway, so I think it would get very boring. But in the whole universe Bootes Void is just tiny, it is like a little bubble, so you'd hardly ever see it. Its strange but sometimes thinking about the universe makes me feel funny, I want to hold on to something, like the table or a window sill, just so I won't drop up into space forever. Sometimes I don't like it, actually, I want to say "go away solar system, go away galaxies, go away universe, I don't want to know about how you go on forever." I want to say "why don't you just leave me alone."

After our crussons it was cloudy, and though mum played I spy with my little eye and who can see a red car first, Jemima said the towel on her seat felt lumpy, she said "I'm bored, I want to go home." Actually I felt bored too. I tried reading my Tintin but it made me feel car sick, so I asked mum "d'you think dad's gone back to Scotland yet?" Even when I was still saying it, when I was almost at the end, I thought "uhoh, this is a mistake, this is a disaster." I was right too, I could see from mum's face in the little mirror that she was really cross and Jemima was frowning like she was thinking "wait a minite, this is new, whats this?" She said "what d'you mean, where did dad go?" and though I tried to stop it, I said "he just went on one of his work trips, Jemima" it was too late, it was like Jemima guessed something was funny, because sometimes she just knows things even though she is still just a baby, she said "why can't we go home till dad's in Scotland?"

Mum said "don't be silly, lamikin, of course we can go back" but Jemima was frowning like she still wasn't sure, but then mum did a clever thing, she gave a little shreek and said "oh look over there, it's the alps." So we all looked, and up ahead there were mountains, they were white with snow and some were sharp like arrows, they were really lovely, I thought "I never saw anything like this except on television" I thought "we really have gone a long way now." Then I helped mum, I said "look Jemima aren't they amazing" and she said "oh yes they're just like christmas" so it worked, she forgot about what I said about dad.

After that the alps got nearer, it took ages, until there were mountains right beside the motorway, and I could see tiny houses high above us, so it was like they were almost in the sky. Suddenly we went into a tunnel that went on for hours, I think it was as long as the channell tunnel, and when we came out of the other end everything was completely different. It wasn't cloudy any more, the sun was shining, the sky was blue and all the bushes and trees and flowers and houses were lovely colors so it was like we were in a cartoon. All at once mum laughed really loudly and it was like she was singing, she said "hurrah hurrah, we are in Italy." That was funny, for several minutes we drove beside a big lake, I could see trees with long floppy leaves like dinosours might eat them, and we all shouted again and again "hurrah hurrah we are in Italy."

After that the mountains stopped and everything went flat as a board until mum pointed up ahead and said "look over there, it's an amusement park" and I saw there was a big wheel. I thought "it would be nice to go there but mums in a hurry, we will just go past" but I was wrong actually. Mum said "shall we have a go?" Sometimes she is like that, she makes everything fun like you are at a party. So we turned off the motorway, we paid the motor way tole, which you have to do in France and Italy, and we parked the car. Then I got worried, I said "what about Hermann, we can't just leave him" but mum said "don't worry, he'll be fine, Lawrence, we'll lock it." I wasn't sure, I thought "mum is really clever" and I watched to make sure she remembered to lock the car, the little stick things all went down, so I thought "I hope he's all right."

First we went on the big wheel and when I looked down I could see the car park but all the cars looked the same, they were all tiny, I couldn't see which was ours, and anyway I thought "I don't know what I'll do if I see a thief because I'll just be stuck up here, I can't get down." Jemima started crying, she said "I don't like it, its too high" but mum said "don't be a silly, Lamikin" and then she did a funny thing, she took Jemimas hands and sort of danced her round and round until she stopped crying and laughed. I didn't like this dancing, actually, because it made everything swing, so I thought "what if it just breaks off?" but mum noticed I was worried and then she danced me round too, and though I was still scared it was funny too, I laughed a bit, and nothing broke off in the end, we went down.

After that we went on the merry-go-round. Jemima said she wanted to go on her own horse, so I thought "oh good, I can go with mum" but then she changed her mind like she always does, that was annoying. We did the Coconut Shy and Jemimas balls didn't go anywhere near the coconut, so I said to mum "you shouldn't give her any, its just a big waste of money." But the good thing about the fairground was Mum talking in italian. First she talked it to the ticket man at the big wheel, then she did it to the merry-go-round woman and to the coconut man, and they all talked right back so it was just like mum always talked in italian every day. Jemima was so amazed she put on her silly surprised look, and I was amazed too. It was really funny to think mum had that italian in her all this time like some special secret.

When we went back to the car Hermann was fine just like Mum said, nobody stole him after all, so I gave him some fresh water and more nuts. When we started driving again me and Jemima made a hole between the bags on top of Hermann's cage and we invented a funny game. I pulled her hands and she pulled mine and then we let go suddenly and shouted "help help I'm falling." Jemima is annoying, she is such a silly baby, but sometimes she is all right. After lunch mum said "its still quite early, what d'you say we keep on going till we get to Tuscuny." I never heard of Tuscuny actually but now everything seemed exciting, I don't know why, so me and Jemima shouted "oh yes, hurrah hurrah, lets go to Tuscuny." But actually it took ages, it took hours and hours, so it was getting dark when Mum said "oh look, there's the sign, we are in Tuscuny" and by then Jemima was off away in dreamland and I was really bored of driving, so mum and me only shouted "hurrah we are in Tuscuny" a little bit.

After that mum said "we've all done so well today, let's spend a little money and have a treat" which was funny actually, because usually when mum talks about money she says we mustn't spend any. So we went off the motorway, we paid our tole and we followed a sign for an agro tourismo, which mum said means stay-

22

ing on a farm. It was a big house with a husband and a wife who helped us take things out of the car and laughed when they saw Hermann in his cage. Hugh Prowse at school says everyone is like an animal and if you want to know what animal it is you just have to think of the tail, so I decided the Wife was a giraffe, because she was tall and thin and watching everything, her tail would be like a little string. The Husband was slow and fat, he was a bear and had a round fluffy tail. Our room had pictures of mountains, mum gave us our baths and she said we must be good at dinner or we wouldn't get any food.

Of course Jemima wasn't good at all. She kept on getting off her chair again and again though mum said she mustn't, it was because she wanted to find the taby cat, though it ran away as soon as it saw her, I thought "I don't blame you taby cat." But luckily nobody minded, the giraffe Wife just smiled and said "kaybeller" which mum said means "how pretty." I was so tired that I could hardly eat my dinner even though it was really delicious, but later it was funny, because when I went to bed, even though I was really really tired, I just couldn't sleep. I think it was because I was too exited, because the day had been so amazing, the crussons for breakfast and alps and going to the amusement park. So I decided that this adventure of going to Rome to get away from dad was the best thing I ever had done.

ONE DAY SCIENTISTS got very excited because they found a moon, it is called Europa and it goes round the planet Jupiter. Europa is blue, it is covered with ice and it has lots of lines on it like vains.

But what made the Scientists so excited was that there is water under that ice, it is a whole ocean and it is lovely and warm like a bath because there are volcanoes. Scientists said "I bet theres life in that water, I bet there are animals."

Nobody knows what the animals might be. They might be tiny and boring like germs or they might be monsters, they might be huge like sharks or dinosaurs. Sientists want to send a space craft to see but its hard because Europa is so far away, and they will need a huge drill to get through the ice, because it is miles and miles thick.

Of course it might be a stupid mistake to send a space craft. When they drill through the ice the monsters might all escape and get onto the space craft and then come back to earth so there will be a disaster. Everyone will think they are safe, they will have their lunch and watch telly like usual and suddenly the monsters will rush out, they will destroy all the houses and shops and every-thing. But then sometimes I think "but what if the monsters are nice?" I think "then they must send a space craft really soon, ac-tually" I think "or all the poor monsters will die."

The next morning something bad happened. I woke up and the sun was shining on a bit of wall really bright like summer, and I thought "hurrah today we will get to Rome." I thought "mum hasn't said I must get up yet so I will just lie here for a bit, its nice here in my bed." Then I heard a big thump which was Jemima of course, and she said "mummy mummy, look what I've got." I don't know what she'd got, I never found out, the night before she was playing with tiny shampoo bottles from the bath-room and mum took them away after she spilt one, perhaps it was one of those. But what was strange was that mum didn't answer, she didn't say anything at all. I thought "perhaps she is in the bathroom" but then I saw her shape under her doovay, so I thought "that's strange." Jemimas voice went all sort of squeeky and she said "mummy, whats wrong" so I got out of bed to see. That was funny, that was terrible, because I was standing right in front of mum, I was looking right at her and saying "what's wrong mum" but it was like she couldn't see me, it was like her eyes just weren't switched on properly, it was like they weren't looking at anything.

I had seen mum when she got worreid but I never saw her like this, this was worse. I said "mum, its time to get up, don't you want your breakfast" but she just talked really quietly so I could hardly hear, it was like she was yawning, she said "I think I'll just stay here, Lawrence, I'm a bit tired." I said "but you can't mum, we've got to go to Rome, remember" but she didn't say anything, she just lay in her bed looking up at the cieling with her eyes. I could feel my breathing going fast and Jemimas lips were going all wobbly like she would cry, she said "whats gone wrong with mummy" and I didn't know what to do, I thought "what about our breakfast?" I thought "I don't know where we get it, we can't go without mum" and suddenly I wanted to cry too. But then I thought of something, it was like I just notised it, I thought "I cant get upset too actually or there will be nobody left." I thought "I will have another go and this time I will make it into a game" so I said to Jemima "come on Jems we've got to make her get up" and I started tickling mums feet. That made Jemima laugh a bit so she tickelled her shoulders and even pulled her hair just a bit, we said "come on mum, come on, what about our breakfast?" But it still didn't work, that was a shame, she just pushed us away a bit and then rolled over, she was holding her face like she had a head ache.

After that Jemima looked desperate again, so I had a different idea. I gave her a serius look and said "Jemima what d'you think we should do now?" I wanted to stop her crying but actually I wanted to know too, I was intrested, because though she is still almost a baby Jemima does know things sometimes. It worked, she looked serious back, she didn't cry after all, and she said "I think we should leave her in bed like she wants and then she'll get better later."

I was really hungry now so I got dressed and went downstairs, and luckily the giraffe Wife spoke English when mum wasn't talking italian, and she said of course we could have breakfast in our room. She brought it on a tray, she did a long look at mum like she was worried, and it was really delicious, though mum hardly ate anything, just a biscuit, she didn't even finish it, and Jemima got blackcurrent jam on the sheet which means it is stained forever. After we finished I tried one more time, I said "ok mum, we've had our breakfast, lets go to Rome now" but she didn't say anything, she just closed her eyes. The wife came up and took away the tray, I think she didn't notice Jemimas blackcurrent stain, that was lucky, she looked at mum and said "you want a doctor" but mum said something to her in italian which made her go away.

Later she brought us soup for lunch, it was really delicious. In the afternoon I was nice, I let Jemima help me clean out Hermanns cage which I never do usually, I let her change his straw and clean his water bowl. Afterwards I read my Space book and I drew a picture of mum lying in bed, Mrs Pierce says I am very good at art and Mr Simmons says my writing is really excellent though I must buck up on my spelling.

Jemima played with her dolls house, I got it out of the car for her, but then she was really loud, it was like she did it on purpose to say "look, I've got my dolls house and you had to leave your hot wheels track and your computer consel behind, ha." That was annoying, I thought "how dare you after I let you clean Hermanns cage." She made her dolls have a tea party and she gave the dolls the glasses from the bathroom so I had to take them away, I said "you can't have those, Jemima, because glasses are dangerous." When she tried to hit me and she bit my arm I told mum, I said "you must put Jemima out in the corridor until she says sorry" but mum didn't do it, she didn't do anything, she just looked at the floor and said "please Lawrence love, I just can't do this today" and it was funny, I was sad like I wanted to cry and I was really cross, it was like I didn't know which to be.

The next morning when I woke up I thought "right mum, you have to be better now, you just have to" but when I went to look at her she was the same, she sort of put her arm over her eyes like she was hideing. This was worse actually, because now it was two days. I thought "what if she just stays like this forever, we'll be stuck here spending all our money." Suddenly I felt really serious, I thought "all right then." So I got up and I helped Jemima get dressed, we both went to the girafe Wife and made her bring our breakfest, and when we finished our crussons I started trying, I said "mum, we've got to go now so we can get to Rome and then go home, I've got my tests remember." When that didn't work I said "all right we will just stay here forever and spend all our money till theres none left." But that didn't work either, so I packed my boxes and Jemimas, I got the car keys and put everything in the car, and then I had another idea. I said "mum, we've got to go. What if dad finds us here." And d'you know this worked.

Though Mum still didn't look at me, she sort of blinked and then she sat up really slowly and picked up a tiny piece of crosson. It was funny, she hardly did anything, she didn't even talk but I knew, I thought "hurrah, everything will be fine now" and I was right. Though she was really slow and still talked in her yawn, she went into the bathroom and had a shower, then she got dressed, she packed her bag, Jemima and me helped, and we went downstairs where she paid the Giraffe Wife, who still looked worried even though I told her that everything was fine now, so that was silly of her. Then we got into the car and drove away, we did it.

The thing that finally got mum's smile back again was a sign beside the motorway, it said Roma 286. I saw it first and I said "look, Roma 286, that's not very far." I had watched all the signs in France you see, so I knew 286 didn't take so long. I looked at mum in the mirror when I said this and I noticed she smiled, and even though it was just a tiny tiny smile I thought "hurrah, mum is really getting better now."

After that I kept a careful look out and every time there was a sine I shouted "oh look Roma 253" or "look Roma 223" and each time I did it Mum's smile got just a little bigger, until d'you know she was watching for the signs too, so we would both say together "Roma 184" or "roma 139" and Jemima said it too but she was always after us because she still can't read, she was laughing and squeeking because mum was all better now. Then the car made a funny banging noise so Mum frowned and said "oh god, d'you think he's done something to the engine" but even then her smile didn't go away completely, actually she did a little laugh, she said "well he can't dam well stop us now, we're almost there" and then we realized it wasn't the engine at all, it was just Jemima playing with a pen, I don't know how she got it, she's not allowed pens because she will draw on anything, she is a wrecker, she was hitting it against her door.

The number on the signs got down to 56 when Jemima said "mummy mummy I have to pee." I told mum we should just go on because we were almost there, I said "tell her she can just pee in her pants, you can put her towel in a plastic bag" but mum said no, we must stop, so we went to the next Service Station, which was called Auto Grill and went over the motor way like a bridge. After Jemima finished her pee we were hungry so we all had pizza with ham and cheese, it was really delicious, and then mum said "I'd better ring Franseen" who was her friend from when she lived in Rome years ago before I was born.

So we went to buy a phone card, you had to break the corner off to make it work, and we went to the telephone. We had to wait for a man to stop using it and mum said "god, it's so long since I spoke to her, she's probably moved" but she hadn't after all, that was lucky. Mum started talking on the phone, sometimes it was in english and sometimes it was in Italian, and then she started crying, but I thought "its not sad this time its happy, her eyes look different." And I was right, actually, because after she finished she crouched down and gave me and Jemima a big hug, she said "I'm really sorry I was so down like that at the agro turismo, lesonfons, I really don't know what came over me, but everythings going to be all right now, I promise you, everythings going to be just fine."

Then something bad happened. We all went down and got in the car but when mum turned the car key there was nothing, there was no noise at all. She tried and tried but it was just the same untill she started getting all worried, I thought "oh no not again, just when everything was all right" she was scraching her arm and rubbing her face, she said "oh god this is a disaster, I told Franseen we'd be there by seven and we're still miles away."

Suddenly I didn't feel worried any more, I just felt really cross. After all I'd done, packing the car and getting us here and making mum get out of bed at the aggrotourismo I thought "how dare everything go wrong now when we're almost there" it just wasn't fair, I thought "dam dam, I'm not going to let it." So I undid my seat belt and opened my door and though mum tried to grab me, she said "where d'you think your going" I was too fast for her, I said "I'll do this mum don't worry." I ran to some cars getting petrol, mum was shouting but she couldn't come after me because she is always scared of leaving Jemima behind in case someone steals her, though I don't think anybody ever would actually, she is such a stupid cry baby.

I didn't know any italian of course so I did it in english, I said "excuse me but can you help us please, our car won't start." The first man gave me a smile but then he just went away, so did the second, who was a woman, and the third gave me a little tiny coin, it was brown, that was a suprise, I put it in my pocket. The fourth had a mustash and was climbing into a truck with a big picture of cheese, so I thought he would go away too, but then he stopped and climbed down after all, he said something in italian which I didn't undestand so I just pointed at the car, mum was waving and waving. He was called Ugo and he was a hipopotomus because he was quite fat with really fat arms but he was quiet, he hardly said anything, he had a little thin tail. Mum wasn't angry with me any more when Ugo talked to her in italian and he tried the car key, she said "how clever of you Lawrence." But then her smile went away again because Ugo frowned, he looked under the hood but his frown got worse, he shut it again and shook his head, he said "non low sow" which mum said meant he didn't know why it didn't work, he said "kapoot" which meant it was broken.

This was bad. Mum looked desparate, she said "what on earth are we going to do, and we've got all this dam luggage too." I tried to think how I could help but I couldn't think of anything actually, all I could think of was "we need something really big to pull the car, like an elephant" which was just stupid really. But then mum and Ugo started talking in italian and all of a sudden mum was smiling again, so I thought "this is good, whats happened?" and she said "Ugos a complete angel, he says he'll drive us all into Rome, isn't that wonderful." I said "what about all our things, what about Hermann" but Mum said "Ugo says he'll take it all."

31

Even then I was a bit worreid. When Ugo went to get his truck I said "we can't just leave the car here, what if someone steals it?" but mum laughed like this was the funniest joke she ever heard and she said "Lawrence love, whose going to steal a car that doesn't work, tell me that" and though Jemima got upset too because we were leaving our car behind, Ugo was already putting our things in his truck. So we all helped, even Jemima carried small things, I took Hermann of course, and though Ugo rolled his eyes sometimes like he was saying "you've got an aw-full lot of things" he kept on putting it in till finally our car was completely empty. Mum locked it, all the sticks in the doors went down, I checked, we all climbed into the front of the truck, mum said it was all right just this once even though I didn't have a seat belt, and we went off.

When we were driving before it was like the numbers on the signs just wizzed down, but now that we were leaving our poor car behind us at Auto Grill they were really slow, it was like it took forever. Finally we were in a long road with lots of shops and buses so I thought "this is Rome, it isn't very nice" but later on I suddenly saw a big brown wall and mum got really exited, she said "there's the wall, Lawrence thats thousands of years old." I had never been to a town with a wall round it, especially a wall that was thousands of years old, so I thought "that's intresting." We drove through a big doorway, I noticed all the bricks were really thin like sandwiches and after that we went past big build-ings with lots of flags on them, we went past a big fountain, and mum was pointing at everything and saying "you see that res-taraunt I ate in there once, it was wonderful" or "I knew someone who lived just down that street." Then she pointed at a big building with lots of windows and she was about to say something but then she stopped, so I thought "that's funny." I said "what's that mum?" and she gave a little laugh, she said "that's where I worked teaching english, actually thats where I first met your father" and it was funny thinking of mum and dad being here years ago.

The sun was almost gone down and everything was really orange, so I thought "I like this Rome actually." We went over a bridge over a river which mum said is called the Tiber, it is in a big trentch in the ground, and then Mum had to hurry up and look up the number of Franseens flat because Ugo said we were almost there. We stopped beneath a big building, mum went up and rang the bell and a moment later Franseen came out and she laughed when she saw we were in Ugo's truck with pictures of cheese. Franseen was from France, she had frizzy gray hair like cotton candy and she was a cat I decided, a nice cat, her tail was long and thin and white. She kissed all our cheeks and then when Ugo carried almost everything inside all by himself and when mum offered him money, an orange yuro note, and he waved his hand like he was hitting away a little fly and he said "no no" Franseen kissed him too.

The lift was really small, so we had to go up and down lots of times before we got everything there, and Franseens flat was really small too, we piled everything against the wall by the door so it was hard to walk past without making something fall off. But the first thing I thought was "look at all those pots" because there were tons, some were tiny and others were taller than Jemima, they were painted with patterns and Franseen said she got them in africa. Mum said she was so sorry about all our lug-gage, we shouldn't have brought so much, she said "don't worry we'll find a hotel right away." But Franseen said no no she was sorry actually because her flat was so small, so it was like a whose more sorry argument, she said she wished it was bigger so we could stay for ages but we must stay tonight at least, she insisted, and besides she had asked all mums old friends over for dinner. I was pleased mum lost the whose more sorry argument, I thought "thank goodness" because I was really tired now, I didn't want to move all our things back down in the lift again, and I could smell the supper cooking and it smelt really delicious.

Mum was excited when she heard all her old friends were com-ing and she said "you shouldn't, Franseen, really you shouldn't, how lovely" she said "whose coming, I don't suppose you've asked Beppo." I never heard of Beppo before, I thought "thats a funny name" so I asked "whose Beppo" and mum said "just an old friend" and I noticed Franseen made a face like she just ate some-thing nasty by mistake like a beetle, so I thought "I don't think Franseen cat likes this Bepo." She said "no I didn't I'm afraid, ac-tually I havent seen him for years" and Jemima said "Beppo Beppo, someone did a Beppo in his pants" so we all laughed, es-pecially Franseen, she laughed so much that a bit of spit came out of her mouth and she had to make it go away with her fingers.

After that Franseen said she wanted to hear all mums news, every little bit, and she got out lots of snacks to eat. I thought "those look nice" there was salami and pizzas that were tiny like coins, but unfortunately I hardly ate any because we kept having to get up again and again to stop Jemima from playing with the pots, because she wanted to put them on top of each other or make them in to patterns. I thought "uhoh this will be a disaster, she will break them all and then Franseen will make us go to a hotel after all." Mum told her "lamikin please, I told you not to do that" but Jemima didn't listen, she never does, she just got cross and said "leave me alone" and though we tried putting them high up, it was impossible because the shelves already had lots of pots on them. Franseen said "don't worry, if she breaks them she breaks them" but then I had a good idea, I said "why don't we take the pots out of the bathroom, because there are just a few in there, and then we can just lock her in, that will stop her." But Mum didn't like it, she said "Lawrence, please" so I thought "you'll wish you lisened to me, mum, you just wait" and the doorbell rang.

This was the first of mums old friends who was called Gus, he was tall and thin and had funny hair like a big string which is called a pig tail, though he wasn't like a pig at all, I decided he was a dog with a ropey tail. Mum was really surprised to see him, she said "my god Gus, I never thought you'd still be here" but he just laughed and said "oh you know, the dolchay veeter" which mum said means having a lovely time. I think Gus was really hungry because when mum asked what he thought went wrong with our car he just said "I don't know cars" and he started eating all the tiny pizzas really fast till there were hardly any left, which mum always says we mustn't do because its bad mannars, so I thought "you are greedy, Gus dog."

Then there was a big crash, it was Jemima of course, I thought "I told you we should have just locked her in the bathroom" but

35

none of the pots broke, that was a surprise. We were still trying to catch her when the doorbell rang again and this time it was Cloudio, Chintsier, and Gabrielley. Cloudio had a big woolly beard so he was a bear, he said "kara Hannah" to mum and then he kissed everyones cheek except Jemimas because she was still hiding under the bed. Chintsier was a nice squirrell, she was small with black hair that was really flat on her head like a cloth, she kissed everyone too. Mum said "Cloudio how wonderful to see you, you look really well, and Chintsier your prettier than ever" and she kissed Gabrielly so I thought "they really do a lot of kissing here." Gabrielly had eyes that looked sleepy like someone forgot to switch them on and though I tried I couldn't think what animal he was. He was just a bit bigger than Jemima, so I thought "that's the end of the pots then" but actually it wasn't, because mum did a clever thing. She got out Jemimas dolls house, which made Jemima come out from under the bed, and then they both played with it in the hall for ages, Gabrielley didn't mind that it was girley, that was lucky.

Suddenly I thought "what about poor Hermann, I forgot all about him, he must be really hungry" so I took the last tiny tiny pizza, I got it just before Gus did. I put the cage in the hall, which was the only space, and Hermann was in his nest, I think he was still frightened after getting carried by Ugo. I changed his water and put the pizza in his bowl in little bits and said "come on Hermann, dinners ready" but then I had to move the cage again because the doorbell rang and he was in the way, that was annoying. It was Crissy, who was the last freind, she had yellow hair that was short and went straight up from the top of her head so she was a chick. When she finished kissing everybody she said "you must be Lawrence and Jemima" and she gave me a hug so I thought "actually you are nice, I don't mind that I had to move Hermanns cage."

Franseen said dinner was ready, I could hardly wait I was so hungry. There weren't enough chairs, so Franseen sat on one that went round and round for computers, which was funny. I picked all the mushrooms out of my pasta because I don't like them, and then suddenly I had a funny thought, I thought "on Saturday I was just at home watching robot wars just like usual and I never thought that on Wednsday I would be thousands of miles away in Rome eating pasta." Mum looked so exited, her eyes went all sort of soft, so I thought "this is nice, I like sitting here with all mums friends from years ago." My favorites were Franseen and Cloudio bear, but I liked Crissy chick too, and Chintsier, and even Gus greedy dog, I thought "I like them all."

After the pasta Franseen brought chicken and potatos and more wine, I had fanta, which mum doesn't usually let me have, and suddenly they were all asking mum lots of questions one after the other. So mum told them about driving down to Rome and how our car was kapoot, she told them how we left dad's house in Scotland years ago when Jemima was still a baby when mum and dad got divorced, and about our cottage with its lovely view of the hill. I put Hermann on the floor in the corner, he was out of his nest now, so I gave him a piece of mushroom from my pasta but he didn't like it either. When I got back on my chair Crissy the chick said "so tell me, Lawrence, how long are you going to be with us in Rome?" and I didn't really think about it, I was thinking "what else can I give Hermann for his dinner" so I said "just a few days, until dad's gone away so its safe again, I've got my tests at the end of term." But it was a mistake of course, I got it wrong again, that was stupid, because when I looked up Franseen was giving me a funny look and she said "what d'you mean until its safe again?"

I thought "what will I say now?" and Jemima was looking at me with her mouth open full of chewed pasta, so I thought "I hope mum will say something clever like she did with the alps" but d'you know she forgot too, that was strange. She never forgets anything usually, but now she looked sad and she said "that's why we came here. Mikie came down from Scotland to the village, he was spying on us and he got in the house, he was turning our neighbors against us, it was just awful, I was scared to death he was going to do something to the children." Now they looked really shocked, they all started talking at the same time, Franseen said "but that's just dreadfull, I can hardly believe it, Mikie of all people" and Cloudio said "you told the police?" But I was looking at Jemima, I thought "hasn't anyone noticed?" because her mouth was opening wider and wider, you see, it was like someone hit her really hard but she wasn't crying straight away, she was getting ready. Mum said "I suppose I should have, but I just couldn't stay another moment, I just had to . . ." but she didn't finish of course because that was when Jemima went off, she was like an airaid siren, you couldn't hear a thing. I thought "uhoh" I thought "it wasn't just me this time, mum did it worse actually."

Mum looked like a bee stung her, she turned to Jemima, who

was sitting beside her, and she said "lamikin, love" and she put her hands over her ears, though it was much too late, she should have done that ages ago. Jemima sort of choked a bit, she spat out her pasta and a bit went in Cloudios wine, I saw it, then she said "what d'you mean about dad, what dyou mean he was in the house" and mum gave her more fanta, she said "I was just being silly, I'm so sorry lamikin, I was just telling a stupid joke." Then all of the others started doing it too, they said "yes it was just a stupid joke" because though they didn't really know what was happening, they all just guessed I think, that was clever. Jemima looked round at them all, she drank some fanta, and she had a funny look like she wasn't sure, but she didn't say anything, I think it was because there were so many and they all said the same thing.

After that everything went quiet, I could hear everyones forks go "chink chink," and they all looked like they wanted to ask mum lots more questions but they didn't dare. Suddenly mum laughed and she looked strange so I couldn't tell what she would do now, if she would go happy or sad, I thought "I wonder which it will be" but it was happy, that was good. She said "its just so wonderful to be here with my friends again, my best friends in the whole world" and then she turned her head sort of sideways, so I wondered if she might cry a bit and didn't want everyone to see, and she said "I feel like I should never have left."

Now they all started talking at once again. Franseen said "its just so nice to have you here" and Crissy the chick said "why don't you come and stay at my place for a few days, Hannah, it'll be easy actually, because Hans has gone away to see some friends in

Sisily, he won't mind if you use his room." Mum laughed like Crissy was joking, but I could tell she was intrested, I could see it in her eyes. She said "that's really kind Crissy but I know we'd drive you mad in five minutes" but Crissy said "no, no, I just love children, and it would be so wonderful to really get to know Lawrence and Jemima."

After they all went home, Franseen and mum did the washing up, Jemima and me helped dry, we didn't break anything. We did the beds, Franseen said she would sleep on cushions from the sofa and mum said "no no we couldn't possibly take your bed" but actually there wasn't anywhere else, so we did. Mum and Jemima fell asleep really fast, I could hear them breatheing, but I couldn't sleep at all, I don't know why. I heard cars going past, sometimes there were bells ringing, and my thoughts went wirr wirr, they would not stop. I thought about our driving in the car and the Giraffe Wife and mum in the bed and breakfast with her yawn voice. Eventually I got bored of just lying there, so I got up and I went to the window. I could see people in another flat across the road, there was a party and they were all drinking wine. So I watched them for a bit and I thought "isn't this strange, isn't it funny" I thought "I wonder what Tommy Clarke and Ritchie Matthews and Mr Simmons at school would think if they knew I wasn't at home with the flu after all, but I was standing here looking out of the window at a party here in Rome."

CHAPTER TWO

Emperor Caligula was bald, he had hardly any hair on his head though his body was very hairy. He was worried people would laugh at him so one day he made a new law that said nobody could ever talk about goats, because goats were hairy like he was, and nobody could go up to a high place and look down on to his head, if anybody did they would get executed. Caligula could execute anyone, he didn't need to give them a trial or anything, when he walked down the street he could just point at somebody and say "I don't like them" and they would be executed, so everybody was frightened of him.

One day someone told emperor Caligula that he should fight a war, though he never had fought one before. Caligula said "all right." So he marched his army all the way to Germany and he had some fights there, but none of them were real, actually, they were just pretend, because Caligula was frightened he might get killed, so he made his own solders dress up like enemies and fought them so he knew he would be safe.

After that he marched his army to the English chanell opposite England. England was invaded by Julius Caeser years before but not properly, so Caligula could invade it all over again if he liked. He made his army go down to the beach, he got his arrow throwing machines and his rock throwing machines and he put them in a long line with their arrows and rocks all ready, and his solders wondered "what will he do now?" they thought "will he invade England?" Then suddenly Caligula shouted in a loud voice "I order you all to pick up seashells."

The solders thought "this is strange" they thought "why does he want us to do that?" but nobody said anything, because they were scared of him, they thought "we must be careful or he will get angry, he will do something really terrible, we don't know what he will do." So they obeyed, they picked up sea shells and put them in their helmets until they were full. When they finished Caligula said "well done soldiers, that is plunder from the ocean, it is ours, its a great victory." Then he gave them pieces of gold, and they all took it, they didn't say anything, they just kept quiet like everything was normal. So Caligula and his army marched all the way back to Rome to have a big party to celebrate.

In the morning I woke up and mum was gone, there was just Jemima, who was upsidown like usual, she is terrible when she sleeps because she goes round and round like a fire work, she is a kicker. I could hear mum's voice, she was talking in a funny way, I could not tell if she was laughing or crying, and I couldn't hear anybody else, just her, so I thought "uhoh, what now?" I jumped out of bed fast like a hurricane and I went into the sitting room but actually it was all right, everything was fine, she was talking on the telephone, that's why it was just her, she was smiling. When she finished she said "that was Crissy, we're going to go and stay with her tonight."

Franseen was already gone, she went to work, but she had got us breakfast from a cafe downstairs, it was crussons and mine had chocolate in it, it was really delicious. Mum said Franseen left a book for me so I would know more about Rome, it was called Calamitous Caesaers and it was from a series called Hideous Histories. I already had one actually, it was about Henry The Eighth and it was really interesting, especially when Henry's cook tried to poisson him so Henry boiled him in his own pot. Then there was a thump because Jemima woke up, her crusson was called cremer and she got yellow cream all over her face, and when mum gave her her bath to clean it off I read some of Calamitous Cesears, I read about Emporer Caligula.

Then mum said "all right lesonfon, lets go and see Rome." Rome was different from anywhere I had ever seen before. Its streets are really narrow like alleys and they go round and round so its impossible to know where you are going, its like a maize and mum says even real romans get lost sometimes, though we only got lost two times. You have to be careful of the traffic, especially the motorbikes because they come round the corners really suddenly, they shouldn't be allowed, actually, they should be prohibited. When you hear one you must stop at once and stand still by the wall, so we had to catch Jemima lots of times. The houses are painted, most of them are orange and the paint is all stained, so I thought "they are old and dirty" but actually they are supposed to be like that, they are really beautiful and they are much nicer than houses in rainy old england which all look the same mum said.

First we went to see a square that is called the Piazer Navoner, it is long and thin because it was a stadium for races when it was ancient rome, but now there are just fountains. They are really famous, so we stopped by the biggest one for a bit to watch it dripping. Mum said "isnt it just wonderful here" she smiled so much it was like she might go "pop" so I thought "that's good, probably she won't go sad again now for ages." It had four statues of fat men sitting down, mum said they were rivers, I didn't really understand, one had his arm over his eyes like someone was going to throw an egg at him and mum said "theres an interesting story about that Lawrence" but she never told it in the end because then Jemima climbed over the railing which was so low it couldn't stop anyone, it couldn't stop a cat, they should have made it really high like a proper fence, so we had to catch her and stop her going into the fountain. I think she wanted to put her hand down the fish where all the fountain water goes down, it goes right down the fishes mouth which is like a big plug hole, so I thought "its lucky we got you Jemima or you might have fallen right down it and disappeared forever."

After that we went to another place called the Pantheon which has a huge hole in the roof, but it isn't broken at all, the ancient Romans made it like that on purpose and when it rains it all just falls right down and then it goes away through tiny holes in the floor, it's one of the most famous buildings in the world. We sat on a bench and when I looked up through the hole I could see birds flying, mum said they were seaguls because Rome is near the sea. I asked mum if Emporer Caligula ever came here and she said "he might have." I thought he would like it, actually, because nobody could go high up, there were just walls, so nobody could look down and see his bald head, he wouldn't have to execute anybody.

After lunch we went to the Forum where the ancient Romans used to go. Its all ruins, there are just a few colums and walls so I thought "this is boring" but actually that was wrong, you must close your eyes and use your imagination you see, you must think " thousands of years ago it was all brand new" because then it was full of temples and famous Romans, mum said "arent the trees wonderful, they are called umbrella pines because they look like umbrellas, you cant find those in rainy old england."

Mum said we would go to the Coliseum next, so I thought "oh yes hurrah" because that was where they had lots of gladiator fights, but then Jemima got annoying, she said "I don't like this road with its old stones, they're slippery" she said "I'm staying here." I tried to help, I said "come on Jemima, stop being such a big fat lazy" but it didn't work, she made her biting face and shook her fist at me. Mum looked tired, she said "all right lamikin, I'll carry you" so I thought "oh good, that's all right then." But then the queue was really long and when mum asked how much tickets cost she said it was better from the outside, she said "lets have an ice cream instead." I was annoyed, I said "I don't want an ice cream, I want to go in the Coliseum," but she got them anyway, mine was strawberry, so we all sat on a wall, and when I ate it I felt a bit better, actually, I didn't mind so much about the Coliseum after all.

After that something funny happened. Mum cleaned the ice cream off Jemimas face and she said "isn't it just amazing here, it's almost like summer, you'd never think it was still just march." Then she looked at us in a special way, so I thought "I bet shes going to say something serious" and I was right, she said "what would you say, lesonfon, if we stay on for a bit here? Perhaps until the summer?" Jemima laughed, she said "yes yes, lets stay" but I don't think she understood really, she just thought "if we stay then I can have more ice cream."

Mum looked at me. She was waiting. I was surprised actually, I didn't know, I thought "yes its nice here, the lovely weather and the delicious food and all the buildings and mums' friends." I said "but what about school, what about my tests?" Mum looked like she was thinking and she said, "I can give them a ring. I'm sure they wont mind if you take a bit of time off, after all you'll be learning lots here, you will be learning about Rome. For that matter you could even go to school here." That made me laugh, I said "but how can I mum, don't be silly, I don't speak italian" but mum said "you can learn some, I can teach you." I wasn't sure, I thought "I bet it will be hard, it will take ages" but then I thought "if mum says they wont mind about the tests she must know." I thought "she's not sad here, thats good" I thought "dad won't ever find us in Rome, and we won't have to worry about Hermanns pets passport yet, that's good too" so I said "all right then mum, lets stay."

Mum was so pleased she gave me a big hug and then she gave Jemima one too when Jemima pushed in. After that mum looked serious again and she said "not that it'll be easy. I'll need to earn some money, Rome's dreadfull for that sort of thing, and of course we'll need somewhere to live" but then she laughed, she said "who knows maybe I'll meet that film director again and he'll put me in some film, but no, he'll be in Holywood by now, or he'll be working as a waiter in some restaurant, that's more likely" and I thought "that would be nice, if mum was in a film, we could all go to the cinema and see her."

On the bus going back mum started teaching us italian, she pointed at things out of the window and I learned "keyazer" which means "church" and "makiner" which means "car" and "pizza" which means "pizza" so I thought "this is quite easy, actually, perhaps I can learn italian after all." When we got back mum told Franseen we were going to stay till the summer and Franseen gave a look like she was surprised, she said "but that's wonderful news."

We couldn't go to Crissy chicks yet because she was still at work, so Franseen said "just sit down and relax, have a glass of wine" and mum said "oh thank you, what would you like, Lawrence, red wine or white?" which made me laugh because I don't like wine of course, I just drink juice. Then Franseen started asking mum all about dad, so I thought "uhoh, be carefull, don't forget Jemima." She wasn't doing the pots this time, that was lucky, she was watching telly in italian instead, there was a man with a tiny beard asking questions and some ladies standing in a line just wearing their underpants, but she was listening to us, I could tell, her eyes looked round at us sometimes, so I thought "don't make her go off like an airaid siren again."

But it was all right, mum just said things she already said lots of times, how she and dad didn't see eyetoeye, he was always going away on his work trips, she was lonely in Scotland and dad always wanted her to visit his reletives. Franseen said "you were from different worlds" which was funny, I thought "what d'you mean Franseen cat, dad is from space?" Mum said it was all right when she and dad were in Rome, she said she really tried to be friends with his reletives but they never liked her, they thought she was stuckup, though actually I really like uncle Kevin and auntie Susie and my cousins Robbie Charlie and Alice. It was always nice seeing them when we went up to stay with dad for his weekends, even though they laughed at how I had an english accent now. They live in a big house in Glasgow, uncle Kevin is a plummer and he has his own company, uncle Harry in London says plumming is not a profession its just a job, but they are nice, cousin Robbie has a really good computer, we played Flying Ace, Asasins and Nortilus Ned.

Then Franseen went and checked on Jemima because she wasn't watching the telly any more, she was lying flat on the sofer now and her eyes were closed, I thought "I bet shes just pretending" but then she snored a bit too. Franseen came back and now she talked to mum in a wisper, so I thought "she's being careful, that's good" she said "and then he comes down and frightens you at your home, that's so terrible" and mum said "it really was" she said "you can't imagine, Franseen, he just wouldn't leave us alone, he got into the house and he told things to the niegbors to turn them against us, I was so scared for the children, it was just awful."

Franseen did blinks with her eyes, it was in a funny way like she wasn't sure, and she said "but Mikie of all people, I can hardly believe it, has this been going on for a long time?" Mum went a bit quiet, she said "I've felt it was coming for ages." Then Franseen looked like she still didn't understand, actually, she said "he always seemed so gentel" and I notised mum was frowning, she was getting annoyed, so I thought "I will help" and I said "he was all right before, when we went up to Scotland for our weekends, he bought us treats and took us to the zoo, but that wasn't real actually you see, because he was just pretending to be nice."

Franseen shook her head, she said "what did he do, did he hurt any of you?" Mum was giving her a look now, she was holding her arm with her hand like she wanted to really scrach it, I saw it, so I thought "that's enough asking lots of questions, Franseen, don't make mum get upset now when she's all cheerful again." Mum said "I didn't let him." I thought "I know, I will stop this, I will interupt" so I said "actually I'm really thirsty, Franseen, can I have a glass of water please?" but it didn't work. Franseen got up and got me the glass of water but then she just went on, that was stupid, she said "did the police come?" Now Mums voice started going different, I heard it, it was like a sort of growel, she said "there would have been no point, he'd have just turned them against us, he could fool anyone" and she gave Franseen a funny look, she said "we just had to get away."

I thought "uhoh, something will happen now" but it didn't, actually. They both just sat there, Franseen was frowning and

49

sqinting her eyes like it was too sunny, which was silly because we were all inside, and mum was just looking down at the table so it was like she was reading a newspaper but there wasn't one of course, it was the table cloth. Then the telephone rang and it was Crissy saying she was back from work now so we could come over, that was good, and Mum said "we'd better go, can I ring for a taxi?"

So we woke up Jemima and started getting ready, and suddenly Franseen was really friendly, she was smiling and saying "I'm just so glad your all here" and I thought "I know what you are doing, you are trying to make us like you again after you made mum cross" I thought "but it wont work, I am still annoyed actually." She helped us take all the bags down in the lift, it took lots of goes. The taxi was big like a van, mum asked for it specially, and we had to move everything round to make it fit, but it all went in the end. I had Hermanns cage beside me on the seat and we were all ready to go at last when Franseen said "wait wait, just one second" and she ran back into the building. But she was much longer than one second, it was ages before she came back, which was stupid because you have to pay for a taxi even if its not driving, so I thought "I am really cross with you now Franseen cat, first you make poor mum anoyed and then you make us sit in this taxi so it costs more."

Finally she came back, she was breatheing fast from running, she leaned in through the window and said "I forgot to give you these." Jemima got a blue and purple furry monkey and I got another Hidious History, this one was called "Petrifying Popes." I thought "that's nice actually" so I wasn't cross with Franseen after all, I thought "I suppose you are quite a nice cat actually."

Mum kept on getting annoyed on the way to Crissys. First it was because we got stuck. We were in a road that was really narrow like an alley and a car just stopped right in front of us while a very old man walked to it from his house, and though he had a stick and a tiny lady to help him it took for ages, so each step seemed to take forever, untill mum said "oh for goodness sake, we haven't got all day, you know." After that she got annoyed when the taxi driver went the wrong way, she talked to him crossly in italian and made him go back, and she said he was trying to cheet us so we would have to pay more. Finally she got annoyed again when we were almost at Crissys, she lived in a place called Montyverdy and mum didn't like it, she said "I really don't know how she can live out here, its so boring." I thought it was nice, actually, because the buildings were all tall and new like Spiderman might jump off their rooves, but I didn't say anything, I kept quiet. When we got there I was worried mum would get annoyed with Crissy the chick too, but fortunatly she didn't. In fact when Crissy came down to the taxi they had a nice hug.

Crissy had a big lift so we got it all up in four goes. Her flat was white with pictures of ladies in old dresses and there were no pots this time, that was good, just some glass fishes in pretty colors which we put on a high up shelf right away. Crissy showed us Hanses room where we were staying, we stacked all our things up against the wall and then Crissy said "now come into the kichen and keep me company." She was banging pots and cutting up vegtables and she said "tonight I'm going to make you a real Roman dinner." Mum told her our news, she said "but don't worry Crissy we'll find our own place, you wont be stuck with us until the summer" and Crissy laughed, she said "I'd love to be stuck with you if Hans wasn't coming back. Oh Hannah that's really wonderful, it'll be so nice having you here again."

Then she looked nervous and she said "actually I've got news too, but don't think I should even tell you Hannah because you'll just laugh at me, I know you will. You see I've joined a church. There, your thinking oh how ridiculous. I knew I shouldn't have said anything, but its really wonderfull, its changed my whole life." Mum doesn't like going to church, we all went once for the School Birthday and she said the vicker was like a frog, she said he looked like he wanted to be on the telly, but she didn't say anything like that now, that was good, she just said "that's marvelous Crissy, I'm so glad your happy."

Then Crissy said "oh dam I forgot the onions" and mum said "don't worry we'll get some for you." So we all went down and we were almost at the shop when mum made a funny little noise, it was like she laughed or sneezed, I couldn't tell which, so I said "what's that"? and she said "I just can't believe shes gone all religious like that." I was suprised, I said "but you said you were glad she's happy" but mum said "shes not happy, Lawrence, she's a very unhappy person, that's why she's started this whole church thing."

I thought "that's a shame" I thought "I really like that chick" and then I thought "I wonder what will make her cheerful?" In the shop I saw a nice tin of biscuits with an airoplane on it so I said "why don't we get that as a present for Crissy?" but mum said "no, lets get her a nice bottle of wine" though it didn't seem nearly so good to me, actually. So when we got back and had the real Roman dinner I tried to remember to do all the things mum says I always forget. I did all my table mannars, I didn't just reach across the table and grab things, I said "could you pass the salt, please" and when Crissy drank all her water I noticed it and I said "would you like some more water?" Then I had another idea and I told her all about the amusement park we went to, I said "its near the alps and you can drive through a really long tunnel, you should go Crissy, theres a big wheel and a merry-go-round and a coconut shy, you'd have a really nice time, we could all go together" and Crissy said "what a nice thought" so I thought "that's good, that will help."

Then mum started getting excited, I could see it in her face, she said "I'm so out of touch with rome, tell me all the latest, whats it like finding a flat, are there any jobs out there?" I wasn't sure about that actually. In England mum read books and wrote her reports which she does at home, I thought "what if she gets a job here like dad, what if she has to go on worktrips, she can't just leave us behind." But then I noticed Crissy didn't look exited back, she just looked serious, I thought "mum won't like this" and I was right. Crissy said "everythings really hard here these days, Hannah" she said there weren't many jobs, especially for foriegners, so I thought "oh good" and she said flats were really expensive, anything cheap was a really long way from the center. That made mum get cross, she said "but we have to be in the center, that's the whole point, thats Rome." I thought "if we can't find a flat then I suppose we'll just have to go home" I thought "then I can do my tests after all" but then I thought "but mum might go sad again, at least she's cheerful here" so I didn't know what I thought any more.

THE NEXT MORNING when we ate our breakfast Crissy was really cheerful so I thought "thats good" I thought "I bet it helped that I remembered my table mannars and told her about the amusement park." She said "I don't want to go on and on about my church" but then she talked about it for ages actually, it was like she couldn't stop, it just bubbeled right out of her. She said that when she got lost she asked Jesus, it was like she could ring him on a special telephone and he told her which way to go. I thought "that's intresting" so I told her how we got lost twice yesterday because the streets went round and round, and then I told her how we looked in mums guide book which had maps at the back, so we always found our way in the end, I said "you should get one like that."

Crissy smiled, she gave me her special eyes wide open look, she does that sometimes, and then she said to mum "will you be here for dinner tonight? Your probably too tired, you've only just got here, but you see I was thinking of asking some of my new friends over, they'd so like to meet you." Mum said "Of course Crissy that would be really lovely" but afterwards when we went down in the lift she said "god I hope she's not trying to convert us" which she said meant making us go to her church.

Mum said we must try and find a flat now, so she bought a magazine called porter portaisy and then we went to a café. We all sat on stools, even Jemima, though her feet were miles off the ground, so I thought "I bet you fall off" it was because mum said it cost more if you sit down at a table. Jemima got a glass pot of sugar and she started pouring the sugar in a little mountain, so I thought "now there will be trouble" but actually Mum didn't see because she was too busy reading her porter portaisey, she said "god Crissies right, I just can't believe these prices" and though I knew I should tell her about the sugar it was really funny watching and I wanted to see how big the mountain would get, so I just kept quiet.

Soon Jemima finished the whole pot, her mountain was so big now that some was spilling on to the floor, she reached for another pot but it was too far, and mum said "wait a minute, that looks nice. It's still a lot more than I was thinking of but its not that bad, its better than all the others, and it would be so amazing to be in Trasteveray, I bet its already gone." Then suddenley she was in a real hurry, she got up from her stool and said "come on lesonfon, lets give them a ring" and I thought "watch out now Jemima, you just wait" but d'you know mum never even noticed the mountain. I think she was too excited about her flat, you see, she lifted Jemima off her stool and Jemima didn't say anything of course, she just smiled like she was thinking "ha ha." So we went out into the road, we left the mountain behind, and I couldn't tell mum about it now because it was too late, she would say "why didn't you tell me before" and I would get blamed. So she never ever knew about that mountain at all, that is strange. I think about it sometimes, actually, and it makes me a bit sad. I think "now its too late."

We went to a telephone in the street, mum talked in italian and she got a big smile, she said "we've got an appointment, isnt that fantastic" and I thought "oh yes that's good, if we live in a flat then we wont have to take all our things up and down in lifts again and again every time." We took a tram, I never went on one before and it is like a train that goes down the road, I learned "gato" which is "cat" and "carnay " which is "dog" and "pigiony" which is "pigion." Then mum got up from her seat really quickly and she said "actually lets get out here, we've got ages." I thought "I wonder what it is, is there some treat, is there a zoo?" but it wasn't that at all. Mum took us down a couple of streets and then she pointed up at a high building, her eyes went sort of dreamy, and she said "you see those windows, I used to live up there with Crissy and another girl, that was such a nice time."

I thought "when mum lived there I wasn't here, I wasn't any-where actually, she didn't even know about me." That was strange, it was like I couldn't think it, I just couldn't. Actually I felt a bit cross with mum for being here having such a nice time without me, so I didn't want to look at the window, I thought "there are too many so I can't see which it is." I said "what about the flat, we'll be late, we'll miss it mum" but she said "there's still lots of time. I know, lesonfon, lets go to the bar, that's where I always went for my morning coffee."

So we went to the bar, mum squinted her eyes at the lady like it was really sunny and she said "Clarer say too?" which means "Clarer is it you?" and the lady squinted up her eyes as well, but she said no, she wasn't Clarer, actually, she was Jeener, she didn't know about Clarer, so I said "then lets go and see the flat then mum" but mum said "no, lets stay here anyway and have a drink" she said "lets sit outside" though it was stupid actually because it meant we had to pay more, and of course that was what made everything go all wrong.

Mum sat in her chair, it was a lovely sunny day, we were all sitting side by side in a line looking at the square, there was a market and people were buying vegtables, and she said "I just loved living round here, it's a real neyberhood" and I said "I don't like this apple juice, its nasty" I said "can I try some of yours Jemima?" She had blackcurrent you see, I never had that one before, and actually mum shouldn't have given it to her, because she would stain everything forever. Jemima didn't say anything, so I said "Jemima you have to share remember" but she just made a sucking noise with her straw, so I thought "that's rude, that's not good mannars." I looked at mum but she was just leaning back on her chair with her eyes closed, so I thought "all right then."

I was quick, I leaned over and got Jemimas bottle from her, it was just to make her share, because mum says we always must. But Jemima was bad, she did a shriek and she tried to grab it back though I hadn't even got any yet, I was still just getting it to my mouth. Then mum said "Lawrence for goodness sake," which wasn't fair so I said "I just want to try a bit" and I didn't let go, we were both holding it, you see. I said "she has to share" and then when mum said "let go Lawrence" there was an accident, it wasn't my fault, it just sort of jumped, it happened by itself, and it went all over Jemimas shirt with rabbits, so I thought "uhoh, thats stained forever then."

Mum gave me a really cross look, which wasn't fair either because I hadn't done anything wrong, it was Jemimas fault, I asked her nicely, and then mum reached down under her chair. I think she wanted to get a paper hankercheif to wipe Jemima's shirt with rabbits but I don't know actually, because she never got it of course, she just stood up really fast like she got stung by a big bee and she shouted "my bag, wheres my bag?"

It was her hand bag, she took it everywhere, so I thought "oh no, this is a disaster." Mum said "I put it under my chair, oh god, I can't believe I was so stupid, someone must have gone behind us and taken it." I helped, I got up and looked under all our chairs but it wasn't there at all, so I thought "I told you we shouldn't come here" but I didn't say anything, I thought "I won't upset mum." I said "was all your money in it?" and she said "no thank goodness, that's in my purse in my pocket" so I thought "that's lucky" but then she looked like she got stung all over again by another big bee and she said "my passport, oh god, I put it in there in case I had to show the flat people, oh god, I really can't believe this."

This was bad, mum was scraching her arm now, so I thought "I must help her or she will fall down into a big hole." Suddenly I really hated that theif, I wished we hadn't sat in a row because then I would have seen him, I would have shouted out really loudly and frightened him away, I would have run after him and got the police to put him in a jail forever, I would blow him up, I would do a Caligulla. I said "wait here mum, I will go and ask Jeener" so I ran into the bar really fast, but it didn't do any good, she didn't understand me because she could only speak italian, she just put up her hands like she was surendering and said "banyo?" which means loo.

Probably it was a mistake to leave mum alone, because when I went back Jemima looked scared, it was because mum was speaking faster and faster, she said "we're supposed to be at this flat in half an hour and now I haven't got any documents to show them" then she said "oh god and its Friday too, the embassy will be shut all weekend, I just don't believe this." She was squeezing her hair with her fingers and then she looked under the chairs again, though of course the bag still wasn't there, I thought "it won't just come back by its self mum." She said "I had all my makeup things in there, they cost a fortune, and there was Jemimas cup too, I just don't know what I'm going to do."

I didn't know either. I thought "what if she goes really sad again and stops talking like she went at the bed and breakfast" I thought "I don't know how to get back to Crissys, I don't even know which road goes back to the tram stop, and mums much too big and heavy for me to pull her up from her chair, we'll be stuck here all day." I thought "what will I do, I must do something" so I got some paper napkins from another table and I said "mum shall we wipe Jemima's shirt now?" but it didn't work, it was like mum didn't hear at all, she said, "I've had that bag for years, it was such a nice bag." So I said "I tell you what, I'll start wiping mum, and then you can come and help" but that didn't work either, Jemima pushed me away and her eyes were all funny like she was going to cry now, she said "I don't want you, I want mummy."

Then a funny thing happened. Suddenly I remembered a really bad day that happened ages ago. We had just got back to the cottage when mum remembered she left her bag somewhere, she didn't know where, and it had all her work in it writing reports about books, so she got really worried, she wanted to go back and look right away, but then another bad thing happened too, because she couldn't find her car keys. This was before she started getting all sad so she just looked serious and she said something really intresting, she said "one step at a time." So that's what we did. The first step was looking for the car keys, and eventually we found them, they were in the dolls box, which was because Jemima had got them, you see, she put them in that really stupid place. And then we did the second step, which was driving round and finding mum's bag, it was at the post office, actually, Mr Miller had got it safe, so mum said "there we are, everythings all right after all."

So now I said to mum "lets do it one step at a time. What is the first step, is it going to see the flat or the passport?" Mum looked at me, she was blinking in a funny way but at least she stopped squeezing her hair, she said "the passport I suppose. You have to have your documents or you can't do anything here, actually its against the law, they can put you in jail." So I said "all right then, lets go to the embassy, is it really far?" Mum shook her head and she said "we can get a taxi" but then all at once her voice went sort of wavy and she said "but we have to go to the police first and get a riport, it'll take ages, that sort of thing always does, and even if we get to the embassy on time, we're bound to miss the flat, someone else will get it, I know they will, oh god, we might never see another one as good as this."

I knew I had to think of something else now so I said "why don't we just ring them up again and ask if we can come later?" I wasn't sure if this would help actually, because someone else might come soon and get it, but d'you know it worked, that was good, mum stopped scratching and she said "I suppose we could try." She still had her phone card, she had it in her purse which was in her special inside pocket, I thought "I wish you put your passport in there too" so we rang the flat people and they said "oh yes of course, just come this afternoon." Then we went as fast as we could, we were almost running, mum carried Jemima on her sholders. We went to the police station and mum was right, it did take ages, a policeman with a really big hat did it all on a typewriter. But it wasn't too late, we got a taxi, we stopped at a machine so mum could get passport photos of herself, and then we went to the british embassy but it was still open, mum said "god, we just got here in time" so I thought "hurrah."

A VERY PETRIFYING POPE was called Stephen VI which meant he was the sixth Stephen. Stephen was really angry with another pope called Formosus. He came before Stephen, which meant he was already dead, but Stephen still really hated him, it was because their families were deadly enemies. One day Stephen said "Formosus shouldn't ever have been pope actually, he broke the law, so he has to have a trial." So Formosus had a trial which was famous, it was famously hidious, it was called the Synodus Horrenda.

They dug Formosus up. He had been buried for months so he was really horrible and smelly but Stephen didn't mind, he got his servants to dress him up in all his old pope clothes and put him in his big popes chair and then he said "now the trial will start." Lots of Romans came, they put on their Sunday best, it was because they were frightened I think, they were scared that Stephen would send them all to hell because he was friends with god.

Stephen shouted really loud, he shouted rude insults at Formosus, he said "you are so bad, you are so stupid, you shouldn't ever have been pope should you?" Then he said "come on, Formosus, say something, make God do a miracal" but Formosus didn't say anything because he was just a dead body. Stephen was really pleased, he said "look he lost" and all the Romans shouted "oh yes, he's gilty." So the trial was all finished and they took off all Formosuses popes clothes, they took him off his big popes chair and they put him in a big sack, they took him to the river Tibber, they did a big heave and they threw him in, then they all cheered. So the Romens never did say that it was strange to do a trial for a dead body, in fact they didn't say anything at all. But after, when they all went home to their houses, when they sat down and ate their dinner and it was really quiet, so they could hear their knives and forks go "clink clink" and the clock go "tick tock" then I think they all knew.

At the British Embassy we went to a room with lots of people sitting in chairs waiting and though mum wasn't scratching her arm any more she was still upset, she said "there aren't any numbers or anything, this is so stupid, how do we know when its our turn." But I had an idea, I thought "I will go and ask whose just arrived because they will be before us." So I asked several different people and they all said "no, its not me, I've been here for ages" and some of them were a bit cross, I think they thought I was trying to queue jump, until a lady heard me, she said "I think its us" and that was how we met the Vanhootens. She was Janiss Vanhooten who was the mother, she was quite fat with black hair and a nice smile, so she was a pretty pig, she would have a little pretty tail. She said to mum "so what happened to you?" and mum was still upset, she was blinking and looking at the floor so I thought "I wonder if she will answewer" but she did. She said "someone took my bag at a café" and then Janiss pretty pig said "oh that's awful, your whole bag, poor you, I don't even know what happened to my passport, isn't that awful, one moment it was in my pockit and then it was gone." She said "Its not a very good start, is it? You see we want to stay here for a year, we've just moved into a flat in Trasteveray."

That made mum intrested, she looked up from the floor and she said "thats where we want to live, in fact we're seeing a flat there this afternoon." So they looked at Janisses map, which was really big and noisy, people looked round and frowned, and Janiss said "its really close, we'd almost be nieghbors, you must come and see us." Then she wrote down her address and her telephone number on a piece of paper and she showed us all the other Vanhootens.

First there was Bill, who was the father, he wasn't english like Janiss, he was American, he was thin and old and he had a thin white beard so he was a goat, he said "nice to meet yer." The little daughter was called Leonora and she was three like Jemima but she hardly said anything, when Jemima said "mummy got her bag taken by a theif under the chair" she didn't answer at all, she just looked nervous, so she was a mouse. But the big daughter who was six and was called Tina was completely different, it was like she had got all Leonoras talking because she never stopped, she told us about Janisses passport getting stolen and her favorite food which was raviolies and how many dolls she had, so she was a bossy rabbit. I thought "I like these Vanhootins because they've made mum cheerful again." When Janiss finished talking to the passport lady and they were all going away because it was our turn now, Bill made his hand open and shut like a mouth and he said "see you round kids" which was funny too, I thought "mummy isn't a kid , she is old."

The passport lady said mum couldn't have a new passport till next week, but she gave us a peice of paper so we wouldn't get put in jail, and mum wasn't cross even though it cost lots of money, she said "god I hope I've got enough" but she did, she gave some blue yuro notes and a red one. Then we got a bus back to Trasteveray and after lunch we went to see the flat. When we got quite near mum started getting excited, I could see it, she pointed at cafes and shops and said "that looks nice" or "that would be handy" so I thought "I hope we can get this flat, I hope nobody else got it already because we went to the Embassy." We were late, that was Jemimas fault because she kept escaping on the stairs, there were lots as it was on the fourth floor, she giggeled and ran back down again and again until mum got fed up, she said "all right, that's enough" and she just picked her up even though she screamed really loudly and said "I want to do it by myself." So I thought "uhoh, even if the flat hasn't been taken by somebody else, I bet they won't let us have it now because Jemima is so noisy" but actually it didn't matter of course, because the flat was so horreble.

The man who opened the door had hardly any hair, he was bald just like emporer Caligula, he was a sneaky dolphin, and he showed us round but it didn't take long because there was hardly any flat, the rooms were all tiny, they were much smaller than Hanses room. They were dirty too so Jemima, who had stopped shrieking now, said "I don't like it here, it has a nasty smell" and though sneaky dolphin kept pointing at things like a cuboard or a radiater, I think he was telling mum in italian how nice they were, mum was just blinking and not saying anything, so I knew "she doesn't like it either." I thought "uhoh, this will be bad."

I was right. When we went back downstairs she looked down at the ground and it was like the breathe went out of her. She closed her eyes and said "we should never have come here, this was so stupid, all I've done is waste money and wreck the car." Jemima was looking worried and I was thinking "oh no you don't mum" so I said "but its good we came here, mum, I really like it, it was nice seeing the Panthion and Piazzer Navoner and the lovely fountains." I said "I'm sure well find a nice flat, mum, we'll just have to look in porter portaisy again" but it was like she didn't hear, she just said "I'm such a fool."

Then I had an idea, I said "I know lets go and see the Van-hootins." Mum said "whats the point" but I said "they might know about a flat, you never know" and though mum said "they've only just got here" I told her "give me that peice of paper with their address, give me the guide book" and she did, she just did what I said, I think it was because she was sad. I tried to find their street on the map but it was hard, I don't really know maps and the streets all just went round and round like a big jumble. So I thought "uhoh what will I do?" then I thought "I know I will ask somebody." Mum was just standing there not looking at anything, it was like she was asleep or something, so I went in a bar and I asked the man, I showed the piece of paper, and he was nice, he pointed and talked in italian. So I said "come on" I took Jemimas hand and started pulling her, and though mum didn't say anything, she came too, and it was really near.

I thought "I hope those vanhootins are in, otherwise I don't know what I'll do" but fortunatly they were. Janniss pretty pig didn't look suprised to see us actually, it was almost like she expected us to come, she just said "hello again, how was the flat?" Mum started saying something but then she stopped, she put her hands over her eyes and she just started crying. She said "oh god, I'm so sorry Janiss, I'm not normally like this, its just been a really awful day" so I thought "uhoh, this is bad, what will that pretty pig do now, will she say go away?" but she didn't seem surprised by this either, that was funny, she just said "there there, Hannah, why don't you come in."

The vanhootins flat was really really huge, I thought "sneeky dolphins would fit into this tons and tons of times" and even mum stopped crying, she said "wow this is amazing." Janiss laughed and she said "It ought to be, its costing us enough." She took us into the kitchen where a lady called Manuela gave mum some wine and Jemima and me both got apple juice, they didn't have blackcurrent which I decided was my favorite now, that was a shame.

After that everything was better. Mum drank her wine and she told Janiss how sneaky dolphins flat was so horrible, and she got a bit more cheerful and even laughed a bit, she said "and it said in porter portaisey it was a charming pent house." Janniss showed us round, she showed us the bathrooms, there were three and one had a lady called Lara in it who was cleaning the sink. We saw Bill nice goat, who was in his studio, he didn't say hello because he was too busy painting, but he smiled and waved his hand sideways like he was wiping a tiny window, that was funny. I looked at the painting he was doing and I thought "I know that" because he was doing the Pantheon you see, but he colored in all the squares in the cieling blue like they were little windows, which was strange. Then we went to Tinas room where Leonora mouse and Tina bossy rabbit were playing dolls, and Tina told Jemima she could stay and play but she could only have one doll, it had a leg missing.

I didn't stay, it was too girley. I went down with mum and I found a book about animals which had a picture of a lizard sticking out his tounge, which was really long like a rope, and eating a fly. Manuella gave mum and Janiss more wine and I noticed mum was really cheerful now, she said "that's so kind of you Janiss, it really is, but I don't think we can afford that sort of thing just now" so I wondered "what's she talking about, what can't we afford?" Janiss said "oh don't worry about that, we'll be doing it anyway, and actually it'd be nice for the girls to have someone else, they might take it more seriously" then she put her hand on mums arm and she said "really I'd like us to do this, Hannah, and anyway its no big thing, its only till easter."

I thought "is she saying we can live here?" I thought "theres lots of rooms so it would be easy, that would be good because I like these vanhootins apart from Tina bossy rabbit." Mum said "are you sure?" but Janiss pretty pig didn't answear, instead she looked at me and said "Lawrence, how would you like to come here and have some italian lessons with Tina and Leonora." I thought "so we won't be living here after all, that's a shame" but then I thought "but I suppose its about time I learned Italian" so I said "oh yes."

After that Tina and Leonora came down with Jemima, who had got two dolls now though she was only supposed to have the one with a leg missing, and then Bill goat came down as well, Manueller gave him and mum and Janiss more wine and they were all laughing. I finished the book on animals and then Janniss said "I do hope you'll stay for dinner" and mum started answering, I thought "she will say yes" but then suddenly she stopped and she hit her head with her hand a bit, she said "oh god, I completely forgot, the person we're staying with said she'd give us dinner." I thought, "oh dear" I thought "we forgot about poor Crissy."

So we went away in a big hurry, and as we went Janiss pretty pig said "just bring them over on Monday, siniora Morrows coming at eleven." Mum carried Jemima on her shoulders and we went almost running to the tram stop, but then we had to wait for ages for a tram, that was really bad. I thought "that poor chick, this won't make her more cheerful at all" and when we finally got one and we got out mum said "oh god its after eight now, I said we'd be back by seven" so I thought "I hope she won't be really annoyed with us" though actually it was hard to imagine Crissy ever getting really annoyed.

We went up in the lift, mum opened the door with her key and they were already all having their supper, they were eating olives and salami. Crissy got up, she was frowning but I notised it wasn't a cross frown, it was like she was sad so I thought "thats strange." She said "Hannah, theres been a bit of a surprise I'm afraid" and she pointed at a man sitting at the table, he was big with very short pail hair, he was a seal, and then he got up, he said "I'm Hans, so nice to meet you. Yes, I'm really sorry but my trip to Sisily got canceled, I didn't know you were all here, but don't worry, I can sleep on the sofa tonight" and Crissy said "I'm so sorry Hannah."

So I thought "that's why shes sad" I thought "uhoh, that means we'll have to take everything down in the lift again, I wonder where we'll go now?" I thought "mum will get upset now." But d'you know she didn't at all, that was a surprise, that was good. Actually she laughed, she just said "don't you worry, Crissie, we'll be fine." So I thought "perhaps everything is getting better, perhaps being here in Rome will make everything all right."

CHAPTER THREE

Scientists are very clever, just by looking through their telescopes they can tell how much a planet wieghs though its millions of miles away. Planet earth seems so big, it took days driving from england to Rome though we went really fast on the motorway, and places like Africa and Australia are much farther, they would take weeks. But earth is quite small, actually, thousands of earths would fit into planet Jupiter and millions would go into the sun.

But though scientists are clever, there is one thing they do not know at all. If you wiegh all the planets and stars and comets etc of the universe together they are just a small bit of the universes wieght, they are less than a twentieth. All the rest is a mystery, nobody knows what it is, its called dark matter. Some scientists think dark matter is just really tiny things that are much smaller than atoms, so they would make atoms look like mountains. They are called neutrinos or wimps and they are so small that they can go right through a wall or a car, they can go through people, in fact scientists say millions of them go through everybody everyday but nobody ever notices, it doesn't hurt at all.

Nobody has ever seen these Wimps yet because they are too small, so nobody is quite sure they even are there. I hope its them actually. Sometimes I think "what if the scientists are wrong, what if all that dark matter is really a huge black hole that nobody has notised?" It could be somewhere right at the other end of the universe or hidden behind a big galaxy. It would be like the Great Attracter but trillions and trillions of times bigger, so eventually all the stars and planets and comets will get pulled into it, it will take ages but nobody will be able to stop it, they will disappear forever.

When I woke up everybody was already in the kitchen, they were trying to find new people we could stay with now we had to leave Crissies, but they were not succesfull. Mum said "I wonder if Beppos still here, he might know of a place" she said "dyou have a phone book?" Crissy made a funny face, so I thought "you don't like this Beppo either" I thought "I don't like him too actually" but she gave mum the phone book. Mum found his telephone number but when she rang it he wasn't there after all, I thought "oh good" she just left a message on his answer phone, she said "everybodies probably gone away because its such a lovely weekend."

I thought "uhoh, I bet mum will go sad again now because we don't have anywhere to go" but she didn't at all, that was a surprise, she smiled and said "we can always stay in a hotel for a night or two." Actually Crissy chick looked sadder than mum, she said "there must be somebody, if only I could think" and Hans looked sad too, he was standing in a corner with a funny smile like he hoped nobody was cross with him, he said "convents are cheaper than hotels and they are very clean."

Then a funny thing happened. I thought "I will be pleased because mum hasn't gone sad after all" I thought "I will be really happy now" but then I wasn't at all, that was strange. In fact it was the opposite, because suddenly I felt crosser than I had for ages, since before I got the flu and dad came down from Scotland secritly, it was like I was cross just because mum was fine now, I wanted to hit her really hard or I wanted to cry, it was like I didn't know which. In the end I didn't do either, I just said "I don't want to go to a stupid convent, I don't want to go and stay with other people, I just want to stay here" and Jemima was a copy cat, she said "I want to stay here too" so I thought "uhoh now they will think we are just a lot of cry babies." But I was wrong, actually, everybody was really nice. Crissy said "oh you poor things, this is just awful" and Hans seal said "I'll try my friends in Parioley, I'm sure they said someone was leaving soon" and even mum didn't get cross, she said "don't worry lesonfon, it'll only be for a day or two." So I felt a bit better, I thought "all right then" and I ate a piece of toast.

Mum rang a convent and they said yes, they had a room. Then Crissy said "why don't you leave some of your stuff here, that'll make things easier." So we divided all our lugguge all into things we would take and things we would leave behind, which was most of it. Mum said the convent didn't allow pets so we couldn't take Hermann, he was prohibited, we would have to leave him at Crissys, she said "I'm really sorry Lawrence love." I didn't like that at all, I thought "I don't want to leave him all by himself" but then Crissy said "don't worry Lawrence, I'll look after him, I'll take him in my bedroom each night so he's always got company" and that made me feel better. In the end I just took five tintins, a few hot wheels, my Space Book and my hideous histories that Franseen gave me. Then Jemima got upset, she said "I want my dolls house" and she started crying, so I almost said "you shouldn't have got it in the first place, Jemima, you should have just left it behind instead of making me take my box out of the trunk." But I didn't in the end, I thought "she will only cry more" so I said "we'll come back and get it soon."

At least it was easier getting it in the lift because we just had two bags now, it all went in one go. I ran up to the taxi really fast because mum said they just drive off if you don't get them quickly, I opened the door so it couldn't get away, and as we drove across Rome I thought "now I am all right, I am all better now."

The convent was like a hotel but with nuns. There was one standing at the desk and she had a nuns hat and big brown sunglasses which were seethrough so I could see her eyes. She gave us a long look like she was deciding what was dreadfull about us, something was really dreadfull, and when mum showed her the piece of paper from the British embassy she asked lots of suspicious questions, so she was a nasty panda. Finally she gave us our key and the floor was funny, it made all our shoes make noises, mine went "squeak squeak" mum's went "tap tap" and Jemimas just went "thump thump thump." Our room was all white, there was nothing in it except beds and a Jesus on the wall on a cross, he looked like he was rolling his eyes, so I thought "what are we going to do here, this will be boring, I havent even got most of my toys because I left them at Crissy chicks."

Mum put down her bag and she looked around the room and she said "but this is awful." I thought "yes it is" and I felt cross, I thought "you made us come here mum" so I said "its really awful." Then Jemima looked like she might cry again and she said "its really really awful." But now mum made a funny face and she said "no, lamikin, actually its really really really awful" which was funny so I laughed a bit even though I didn't mean to, because I still meant to be cross, I wasn't finished, but instead I said "no its not, mum, its really really really really awful" and then Jemima laughed a lot, she couldn't stop actually, it was like she would go "pop" and she said "no its, no its not, its really really really really really really really really really really awful." After that mum did a funny thing, she did a little clap with her hands and she said "you know what, lesonfon, lets escape." So we just went straight out again, mum said we mustn't run but we walked really fast, I made my shoes go "squeak" as loud as I could, and when we went past the nasty pander nun we all giggeled.

Mum said we must do something fun now because the convent was so awful, so we took a bus to a big park which was called viller borgasey. We went on a machine that looked like a kind of car but it was a bicicle, it had four wheels and a floppy roof and me and mum did the peddling because Jemimas feet wouldn't reach, but it was hard so we went really slowly. After that we walked for miles and miles, mum said she was amazed how far we walked, and we ended up at the Piazzer navoner again with the lovely fountains and the fish plug hole. There was a toy shop there, in fact there were two, and mum said "you know lesonfon, you've been so good that I think you both deserve a treat." Jemima got a little green furry thing, I don't know if it was a dog or a cat, it was hard to tell, and I got an ancient roman. I wanted emporer Caligula but they didn't have one, the man looked quite surprised actually, and he said they just had Julius Caesear so I got him instead, but he was still really good, he had leaves on his head and was waving a sword.

By now it was dark, we were really hungry and mum said "lets go to a proper restaraunt this time, I know we shouldn't really, but to hell with it." I had spaggetty with bacon and eggs, it was called cabonarer, mum said it was like spaggetty breakfast and it was really delicious but it was a bit bad because when mum tried to pay her card didn't work, so the waiter gave her a funny look, I saw him. But then she did the other one which is blue, and that worked so it was all right. Afterwards when we left she saw a telephone beside the road and she said "I'd better ring Crissy, I promised I would" and then something really good happened. Mum started talking and suddenly she got a big smile and she said "but that's marvelous." When she finished I said "what is it, mum, is there a place we can stay, is it Hanses friends in Parioley" but she said "no, no, its much better than that, its Cloudio and Chintsier. Actually, Gus said we could come and stay with him too, but I think Cloudios will be nicer." So I thought "oh yes, that's really good, hurrah for Cloudio bear and Chintsier pretty squirrel and little Gabrielley no animal, hurrah hurrah."

Mum said we must stay at the convent tonight because we already gave the nuns her piece of paper from the embassy, but then we changed our minds. We went past the nun, it was a new one but she was just the same, she was a horrible panda too, and when we went into our room with its white walls and its Jesuz, mum made a funny face and she said "you know lesonfon lets just run away." So she rang Cloudio and Crissy and they said "oh yes come right now" and we took our bags, it was easy because we never unpacked them at all, and we went straight out. Mum had an argument with the nasty nun, mum said we must pay less because we weren't staying all night and she won in the end.

We got a taxi. Mum made it stop at Crissys and we went up and got Hermann and Jemimas dolls house, then mum quickly put some of my tintins and some of Jemimas dolls in a box so we had them too. After that the taxi went past all the old Roman buildings and they were lit up now so they looked really beutiful, mum said "isn't it just amazing" and we went to Cloudios. He lived in the suburbs so it took ages, I looked out of the window at the lamposts wizzing by and suddenly I felt really sleepy, I felt like nothing was real, that was funny. I looked up at the sky, I could see a big star and I thought "I'm not scared of you Black Holes, I'm not scared of you Boots Void and Great Attractor" I thought "here I am with mum and Jemima in a taxi going across Rome in the night" I thought "isnt it lovely."

EMPORER NERO WAS QUITE FAT, he had a beard and a really thick neck, so it was like his head was just stuck into his body like a tube. When he became emperor he decided "I know what I want to do now, this is what I always really wanted, I will become a famous singer."

He started right away. He got the best singers in ancient Rome to come to his palace and sing every night so he could copy them, and he practiced singing all the time, he never ate apples anymore because people said they were bad for singing, and every day he went to bed with a big piece of metal on his chest to make his breatheing stronger.

One day he decided "right, I am ready now" and he went to Naples to a big theater. There were thousands of people inside, they were all waiting, and Nero was really nervous, he thought "what if they don't like my singing, what if they all shout boo." He went up onto the stage and he started, he sang and sang for hours, and they didn't shout boo at all, every time he finished a song they all clapped and cheered. Nero was so pleased, he thought "hurrah, I really am a good singer" but actually it wasn't true, he was an awfull singer you see, his voice was horrible and rasping so nobody liked it at all, they only clapped because Neros servants secretly told them "you must clap really loudly or you will all be executed."

But Nero didn't know about that. He thought "now I will go and sing everywhere" so instead of going off and fighting a war like emporers usually did, he went to Greece instead, because Greece had lots of singing contests. Nero asked if he could have a try too and all the Greekes said "oh yes of course" and though he was really nervous, he won them all, every single one. He was so pleased, he thought "I really am the best singer in the world" but it was all a cheat really, his servants gave money to the other singers so they would sing really badly and they gave money to the judges too, they said "you have to make Nero win or you will be executed."

Nero was so happy, when he went back to Rome he had a triumph, which was funny because that was what generals did when they conqered a new country and Nero didn't conquer anything of course, all he did was sing. He had a huge procession, he went in a special carriage with big signs saying the singing prizes he won, and all the Romans came and stood beside the road and cheered and cheered, so Nero thought "they think I am wonderful." But that wasn't real either, because they were just pretending, they thought "he is a terreble singer" they thought "he is a really silly emporer."

After that Nero sang more and more, he just couldn't stop. When he started singing in a theater, people wanted to get away because he was so terrible but they couldn't, it was prohibited. Neros servants made solders lock all the doors so even if ladies started having a baby they couldn't leave, they had to stay and have the baby there and they had to do it really quietly so it wouldn't spoil Neros singing. Some people got so desperete to escape that they pretended to be dead so they would be taken out and buried.

A few times Neros friends and generals didn't clap and cheer him very much, they just forgot I think, and that made Nero really angry, he thought "whats wrong with you, don't you know I am the best singer in the world?" so he had them executed. But mostly when Nero asked people if he was a good singer everybody said "oh yes, you are really wonderfull, Nero, you are the best singer ever." It was only much later when there was a rebellion aganst Nero and everything was a disaster that people started saying "he's a terrible singer actually" and even then they were careful I think, they only said it quietly when he was in another room. So he never really knew, he always thought "I am just wonderful."

Cloudio was nice, he said "how would you like to go to a lake today Lawrence" and Chintsier pretty squirrell was nice too, she said "would you like some choclate serial for your breakfest?" so I thought Gabrielley would be nice too, but he wasn't at all, that was a surprise. Their flat was really small, it was full of books, they were everywhere like Franseens pots but Jemima didn't like them, that was lucky, she never tried to make them into patterns. We slept on a sofa bed in the sitting room which made my sholder ache, mum said sofa beds often do that, and there was only just space for Hermanns cage in the corner, so we had to put our bags and Jemimas dolls house in the hall and my box of tintins in the kitchen, and mum said "I wish I'd left it all at Crissys." The kitchen was small too, there was hardly enough room for us all to sit round the table and have our breakfast, and then when Gabrielley came in he started shouting crossly in italian and pointing at mum.

I thought "whats this?" I thought "thats not nice mannars, he's very rude." Cloudio and Chintsier both said "Gabrielley, no" which is the same in italian, but mum got up from her chair, which was what Gabrielley wanted you see, and she said "is that your chair Gabrielley, oh I'm sorry." I didn't say anything but I thought "don't give in, mum, that's your chair" but she did, she and Cloudio had a kind of argument, it was a whose being nicer argument and mum won, that was a shame, she drank her coffee standing up by the sink and she said "I've already finished my breakfast." So Gabrielly sat in her chair eating his serial like he was thinking "ha." I gave him a look when nobody was watching, I thought "that's why you haven't got an animal, Gabrielley, because you are a horrible cry baby."

Then something happened. There was a ring at the doorbell, Cloudio got up to answer it and he did a big smile and said "I wonder who that is?" so I thought "I think you know about this person whose coming, they are your secret surprise" and I was right, because it was Franseen. She came in smiling like it was a big joke and she said "I've come to eat your breakfast." I thought "this is nice, this is good" but then I noticed mum. She said "how lovely" but it wasn't real actually, I could see it, because her eyes were really cross. Franseen noticed too I think, because suddenly she went quiet.

After that it got worse. Soon everybody was ready, we were all standing outside, and Franseen gave mum a little smiley look and she said "so who wants to come in my car? I warn you, you will have to listen to my music, today its motsart and motown, it will be loud." I looked at her car, which was new and blue, it was much better than Cloudios which was small and brown and had lots of scrapes on it, so I gave mum a look, it said "come on mum, lets go in her car." But it didn't work, mum put on her quick voice, it's the one she does when she gets cross, and she said "I think I'll go with Cloudio and Chintsier so I can catch up on all their news." I thought "that's silly mum" I thought "yes Franseen made you annoyed but shes nice now, and she gave me my hideous histories and Jemima her blue and purple monkey."

Suddenly I felt sad for that poor cat, so I thought "I know what I'll do" and I said "I'll come in your car Franseen" but it didn't work at all. Mum gave me a look, it was a really bad one too, that was a surprise, and she said "I think we'd better stay together Lawrence, in case someone gets lost." Suddenly everything went all quiet, that was bad. Franseen gave mum a funny look like she was saying "whats this then?" Cloudio was frowning at the ground like he was pretending he wasn't there and Chintsier was looking at everybody, her eyes were going side to side flicky flicky flick. But she was the one who stopped it being quiet, that was good, she said "I'll come with you Franseen, I really like motown" so I thought "thank you Chintsier."

Then it was all right except for Gabrielly. Chintsier wanted him to come with her, she started getting his car seat out of Cloudios car, but then he said no in his winey voice and nobody stopped him so he won, he came with us. He was in the back with mum and Jemima, who was on mum'slap, mum said it was all right just this once, and I was in the front with Cloudio. But mum never did catch up on all his news in the end, because every time she started talking Gabrielly just interupted, he was dreadfull, and then Jemima started interrupting too because she thought it was funny, she just shrieked, because she really liked Gabrielly even though he was just a stupid cry baby, which was silly of her. So Mum and Cloudio just talked a tiny bit in the end, first it was in Italian and then mum said in english "really, everythings fine. Its just so lovely to see you and Chintsier again" and he liked that, he did a big smile.

Lunch was pizzas, it was by the lake, you could see it over the fence if you stood on your chair. We had a long table and mum and Franseen were at different ends, so it didn't matter that they didn't talk to each other, because they couldn't anyway. Gabrielly didn't get cross either, but he looked round with cross eyes so I thought "I know what your doing Gabrielley no animal, your cross now just because you can't find anything to get cross about."

After lunch we went to see some ruins at a place called Chervettery, they were made by the Etruscans who mum said are really really old, they are even older than the Romans. The ruins are tombs, which are where you put dead bodies, and Cloudio said the Etruscans were really clever because they invented lots of things, they invented pesto which is a sauce you can put on your spaggetties, it is green, mum gave it to us once and I don't like it. The tombs were made of stone, they were huge and round so they looked like a whole lot of flying saucers. You could go into them down metal stairs but they were really steep so you had to be careful you didn't fall and smash your head open, mum picked up Jemima, she just grabbed her even though she screamed "but I want to go down by myself."

When we got to the bottom of one toomb Gabrielley ran round a corner and Jemima ran right after him. I thought "I bet theres trouble now" I thought "I will go and see" so I followed, and I was right too. You see, when I went round the corner Gabrielly was looking at something on the floor, it was a beetle I think, and Jemima ran up because she always has to do everything too, and she pushed Gabrielley a bit. It was just an accident, she is very clumsy, but it really annoyed Gabrielly so he pushed her back. Jemima just laughed, she thought "this is a funny game" but I thought "uhoh" I thought "watch it, Gabrielley no animal, don't you hurt my sister, she's mine."

He hadn't seen me yet because he was looking the other way, and I was getting near them when Jemima pushed him back again, I knew she would. Of course now Gabrielley got really cross, I knew that too, he didn't think it was a game, so he did something bad, he got her arm and he pinched it, and I think he did it really hard because Jemima jumped up really quick like she would cry now. I thought "right Gabrielley" I thought "I told you" and I did a funny thing. When he finally notised me it was too late, because I already got the bottom of his ear, you see, and then I just turned it round and round like it was clock work, I said "that serves you right, Gabrielly."

Even when I was still winding his ear I thought "uhoh, I bet something will happen now" I thought "perhaps I shouldn't have done his ear so much" but it was too late, and I was right, something did happen. First Gabrielly screamed and screamed like he was blown up, it was like someone broke all his arms and legs, which was really stupid because I only did his ear a bit, I thought "you silly cry baby" and then he ran back to his mummy and daddy shouting in italian. Next mum came round the corner, she was the first, she was sort of stamping her feet and she had her slit eyes so I thought "uhoh" so I said really quickly "it was Gabrielley mum, he started it, he hurt poor Jemima, he pinched her really hard."

But Jemima wasn't crying after all, that was stupid, that was bad, she was just sitting on the ground looking at that beetle so I thought "come on Jemima" I thought "you big stupid silly." But I didn't say that, I said in a nice voice "Jemima, Gabrielly pinched your arm just now didn't he?" She looked up but her eyes were all swiched off, so I thought "how dare you Jemima, I only did his ear for you" but then it was all right, she looked at mum and said "yes and it really hurt" and suddenly because she remembered her mouth started wobbling like she might cry after all.

Another good thing was that Cloudio and Chintsier and Franseen and Gabrielley came round the corner just then, so they heard her say it too. Now Cloudio started telling off Gabrielley in italian and mum told me off, it was a bit like the whose-being-nicer agument at breakfast. Mum said to me "how dare you hurt Gabrielly, he's only a little boy" but Cloudio shouted at Gabrielly in italian and he said to mum "Hannah, Gabrielley shouldn't have hurt Jemima either." Mum said "it still doesn't mean Lawrence was right to hurt Gabrielley" and Cloudio said "I know, but he was only looking after his little sister" so I thought "thank you Cloudio." Then they made us both say sorry and I was better, I did my sorry really quick but Gabrielley didn't want to say it at all, Cloudio had to wave his finger. I thought "that's all finished then, that wasn't too bad" but it wasn't finished, actually, because then I notised Chintsier gave me a really nasty look, so I thought "uhoh that squirrel really hates me now."

Then a funny thing happened. Franseen came up to me, she hadn't said anything until then so I suppose it was her turn now. She wasn't horrible, she said "better you don't hit the little ones, eh?" and then she gave me a little smile. But mum was standing right there and she looked really cross, she said "I've already talked to Lawrence, Franseen." After that it got worse, Franseen gave mum a slitty eye look and she said "what have I done, Hannah, why aren't you talking to me, why do you treat me like this?" I thought "uhoh, what will happen now, what will she say?" but it didn't go like I thought, actually, because mum did a big smile like it was so funny, and she said in a loud voice "I really don't know what your talking about." But that didn't work at all, because Franseen said "for goodness sake" and then they just looked at each other like their looks were ray guns. Suddenly I got annoyed, I said "stop it, this is just horrible" and d'you know it worked, they both looked at me like they were sorry.

Afterwards we all walked back through the tombs and mum walked really slowly so Cloudio and Chintsier and Gabrielly and Franseen got far ahead. I thought "uhoh, she will tell me off now, she has been waiting" but she didn't, she just did a quiet voice like she was tired. She said I must understand that it was hard for Gabrielley because we were staying in his tiny flat, she said I wouldn't find it easy if we had lots of people coming to stay in the cottage, how would I like it if they were sleeping in our sitting room so I couldn't watch the telly when I wanted. So I said "yes mum, I'm sorry" but secretly I was still pleased I did his ear. When we got to the cars he gave me a look, it was an "I'll get you, you just wait" look, but I didn't care. I gave him a look back and mine was better, it said "you can't do anything to me Gabrielley no animal, because you are too small, watch out or I will Calligula you."

POPE BONIFACE VIII WAS THE EIGHTH Boniface, he was tall, he had a loud voice, and when he became pope he decided "I am going to be the most petrifying pope ever." If anybody annoyed him he said "you'd better do what I say or I'll tell god and you'll go to hell" and it worked. Everybody was scared of him, he ordered around all the kings of England and France etc etc, he was like an emporer.

One day lots of his brothers and sisters and aunts and uncles came to visit him and said "Boniface, please help us, we don't have anywhere nice to live, we are desperate." Boniface thought "oh dear, I must help my poor relatives." So he got lots of land and cities, he bought them with his popes money or he sent his army to get them, and his relatives became princes and princesses, they had lovely palaces. But it wasn't enough, because there were more relatives who were still poor, they didn't have anywhere. Boniface thought "uhoh, theres hardly any land and cities left, what will I do?"

Then he had an idea. There was a very famous family called the Colonnas who were really rich because they had been pope lots of times, they had lots of land and cities, so Boniface thought "they will do." But when he started taking their places the Colonnas got angry, they said "you shouldn't be a pope, actually, Boniface, you cheated" so it was like when Pope Stephen dug up Formosus. Boniface got really angry too, he thought "I really hate these Colonnas, they have so many places and my poor relatives don't have anywhere, they have to carry all their things round in a big cart." He said "I will fight a war with you Colonnas and it won't be an ordinary war, actually, it will be a Crusade." This was funny because crusades were only supposed to be for invading Jeruselem, not for fighting Collonnas, but Boniface did it anyway, he told his soldiers "you can do anything now because you are crusaders, I promise you will go straight to heaven." So the solders fought lots of battles, they destroyed the Colonnas cities and they burnt their food and vegtables, they killed lots of enemies even if they werent Collonas but were just there by accident, until Boniface got all of the Collonnas places except one.

This was called Palestrina and it was really hard to get, it was impregnible because it was on a high mountain and it had huge walls, it was old and beautiful. Boniface got worried, he thought "how will I ever get Palestrina, this is impossible, it is a disaster" but then he had a good idea. He sent a messenger who told the Collonnas "if you give up, then Boniface will stop this war and give back all your cities and land." The Collonnas weren't sure, they thought "what if he is just playing a trick?" but then they thought "no he can't, he's pope, remember, Popes can't tell lies" so they opened the door and they all came out.

But this was a big mistake, actually, because Boniface thought "oh good, that worked" and he just laughed, he didn't give them anything back after all, he told his solders "put them in the dungeon." Suddenly a few Colonnas escaped, but Boniface didn't mind, he said "that's all right, I got most of them." Then he thought "now I will do something really petrifying" so he told his soldiers "I order you to destroy Palestrina, I don't care if its old and beautiful." The soldiers thought "all right, we will go to heaven anyway" so they knocked down all the impregnible walls and all the lovely buildings and it took ages, it was really hard work. When they finished Boniface thought "hurrah, now I have won."

But he forgot about something. It was the Colonnas who escaped. They went to see the king of France you see, because he didn't like Boniface either and they all made a clever plan. They got an army but it was special, it was tiny and secret, it went all across italy and nobody ever noticed, they thought "who are they, I don't know, they are probably just turists" so Boniface never knew.

One day Boniface was on holiday, he was in a lovely palace in the countryside, when suddenly there was a big crash, the door opened, and the secret army rushed in with their swords. Boniface thought "oh no, they have got me." But then a funny thing happened, because the secret army couldn't decide what to do. The Colonnas said "lets just kill him" but the others were scared, they said "but then we will get sent to hell." So they just stayed there for days shouting rude insults at Boniface until there was another crash, and this time it was Bonifaces solders, they came and rescued him.

Boniface went back to Rome, but he wasn't pettrifying any more, in fact now he was scared of everything. He sat in his palace and he thought "what if those Collonas come and get me again, what if there is another secret army?" and he was frightened of everybody, even the waiters who came to bring his breakfast, until he just died. After that the Collonas got all their land and cities back, so that whole Crusade was just a big waste of time. All

Bonifaces brothers and sisters and aunts and uncles and nephews and nieces etc etc lost their lovely palaces, they didn't have anywhere to live, they had to put all their things back in the cart. That was quite sad, actually, though Boniface was so terrible I think the Colonnas should have given them something like just a little house. So even though Boniface was so petrifying, though he was one of the most petrifying popes there ever was, he didn't get anything in the end, it was like he never was pope at all.

In the morning there was a big surprise. Chintsier already took Gabrielly away to his day care, I thought "thats good with him gone" there was just Cloudio, and then the telephone rang, it was for mum and I noticed she got a big smile, she said "but that's just wonderfull Crissy." I thought "what's this, has that nice chick found us a flat to live in?" but it wasn't that actually, Crissy said some of her cristian friends told her they might have a job for mum, it was going round showing houses to people who wanted somewhere to live. Mum said "isn't that great, and it'd be a really good way for me to find a flat for us" she said "I don't even mind if they want to convirt me, I'll go to church ten times a day if that's what it takes."

I wasn't sure, actually. I said "but what about us, if your away all day what will we do?" and Jemima was a copycat, that was good, she looked like she might cry and said "yes what about us?" That made mum go quieter again, she said "Crissy said it can be part time, I won't have to be away that long." Then Cloudio said "they could go to Gabrielley's day care, it has a school too, its very nice" but I thought "oh no, not Gabriellies" so I said "I don't want to go there" which made Cloudio go a bit cross. Mum

89

thought a bit, she said "what about the vanhootins, they wanted you to come and learn italian with them, perhaps they won't mind if you stay a little bit later, just for now?" I thought "I suppose that wouldn't be so bad" so I said "will you take us there and collect us afterwards?" and mum said "of course, Lawrence love" she said "it probably won't even be for long, its just something to get us started." I thought "if she gets us a flat then we can get away from Gabrielley, and I can get all my things that we left at Crissys, thats good I suppose" so I said "all right then mum" and when Jemima looked like she might cry anyway I told her "it'll be good Jemima, mum will find us a flat where you can put all your dolls and animals" and it worked, she didn't cry after all, she had her toast instead.

Then Crissy rang again because she forgot something, because her friends wanted to know did mum have a car, because some of the houses were outside rome so you had to drive. That made mum worried, she said "dam I should have got someone to look at the renno, that was so stupid, I bet its been toed away by now." But Cloudio said "its probably still there, I've got a friend who fixes cars, he won't charge much, I can give him a ring if you like" and mum said "oh yes, that would be wonderfull." Then she rang Janiss pretty pig vanhootin and said could we come tomorrow, could we stay a bit later, and Janiss said "certainly" and after that she rang somebody else, she said "I just told you, can you post it straight to the bank."

Cloudios car fixer was called Loochio, he was very thin and his head sort of stuck forwards on his neck so he was a bird, I saw one like him on television once and it dived out of the air right under the water and caught a fish. He drove us in his van, we all sat in the front, I didn't have a seat belt but mum said "just this once." Soon we went out of rome and into the countryside, Loochio and mum talked and talked in italian, and I thought "I hope Cloudio's right and the car hasn't got toed away" but he was right actually, when we went into autogrill there it was in the car park. It hadn't even been robed by thieves, everything was just the same, and when I looked through the window there were some bits of old pizza beside Jemimas car seat. That was strange, because we had only got to Rome a few days ago but already it seemed like ages since we were stuck here and I got Ugo the cheese truck man to come and help.

Loochio tried the car key but the car didn't go, it didn't do anything, it didn't make a noise. Then he opened the hood, I went round to watch, and he looked at the engine, he frowned a lot so I thought "uhoh" but then suddenly he noticed something, he laughed and pulled up a wire, he showed us the end and he said "la batteriyer" so I thought "thats good, whats that?" He leaned over and screwed the wire in, then he got into the drivers seat and tried the car key and d'you know it just worked, the engine started at once. Mum laughed, she said "so it was just a wire from the battery, oh god, even I could have seen that, I feel such a fool" and I was a bit cross with Ugo hipopotomus, I thought "why didn't you notice?" but it didn't really matter, I thought "hurrah hurrah, our car works again."

We drove back, mum followed Loochio so we wouldn't get lost, and we parked in front of Cloudios house, we didn't need a ticket because it was the suburbs. Mum paid Loochio his money, she gave him four blue yuro notes but he gave one back because fixing our car was so easy, and after that when we went to a bar and had pizzas mum said "you know I'd really like to do something for Cloudio and chintsier, they've been so kind having us to stay, lets give them a nice suprise, lets cook them dinner tonight." She said she would make a curry, she likes doing them, but then when we went round the supermarket looking for ingriedients she shook her head, she said "its amazing they don't even have fresh jinger" and so eventually she got some little glass pots, she said "it won't be as nice but it'll have to do".

After that we went back to Cloudios, mum had her key, and we cooked and cooked for ages. We made chicken curry and potato curry and some other things, I helped chop the onions and Jemima broke a cup. After a bit Chintsier came back with Gabrielly and she looked at the chicken curry in its pot and said "how lovely" but her face was funny like she just ate a beetle by mistake so I thought "you are still cross because I turned Gabriellies ear like clock work, which isn't fair actually because he started it" I thought "you arent a nice squirrel any more, you are a nasty squirrel."

But Cloudio was friendly when he came back. He said we must celibrate that mum might get a job now so he had got a bottle of fizzy wine which was called proseco, the cork shot out like a bullet and hit the cieling but it didn't break anything. Cloudio said mums food was delicious, he had thirds, which was right because it was really nice. But of course Gabrielly cry baby didn't like it at all, he didn't even try it actually, he just made Chintsier cook him some spaggetties, and she didn't like it either, she just ate just a tiny bit and said "how intresting" but then she made a little face like she thought "yuck yuck" and she put down her knife and fork and pushed her plate away.

After that it was time to go to bed. I went into the bathroom and brushed my teeth four times like mum said, and I was going to get into my pijamers when I thought "I will just change Hermanns water" and that was when I notised. You see when I went over to Hermanns cage, it was in the corner just like usual, suddenley I saw something, because the cage door wasn't shut at all, it was wide open. I felt sick, I felt like I could not breath, I reached into his nest but of course he wasn't there, there was nothing, just empty straw. So I shouted out as loud as I could "Mum, mum, Hermanns gone." I knew what happened, there was only one thing it could be, so when she came in looking worried I said "the cage was just open, Gabrielley did it." Mum closed her eyes, she said "we don't know that, Lawrence love. Are you sure you didn't leave it open by mistake" but I never do that. I was thinking "oh no, where is poor Hermann, what if Gabriellies squashed him and thrown him in the garbage, what if he's thrown him out of the window so hes all alone in the road and a car will run him over?"

Now Cloudio and Chintsier came in too, they heard me shouting. Cloudio looked really worried, he said "we'll search the house, he must be somewhere here" and Chintsier said "don't worry Lawrence we'll find him" and she gave me a smile but I didn't believe her, I thought "you are still a nasty squirrel." I thought "where's that Gabrielly, he hasn't come has he" and then I had an idea, I thought "I will go and have a little talk with that cry baby right now." So I didn't follow the others, they were all going into the kichen, instead I went straight into Gabrielleys room, I just pushed open the door, I could hear the others all turning round and following, I didn't care what they did.

Gabrielly was sitting on his bed, I almost just grabed him by his neck and bashed him, I wanted to, I thought "I will caligula you" but mum was already coming in behind me now so I just said "what have you done with Hermann?" Mum gave me a look and then she asked him in italian, but I bet she changed it actually, because it took much longer and Gabrielley didn't get cross, he just shrugged his arms and said "non lowso" which means "I don't know." I thought "oh yes you do, you nasty lying horrible no animal Gabrielley" I thought "I will get you for this."

We looked all round the house, we looked in the sitting room and in the kitchen, in the bathroom and Cloudio and Chintsiers bedroom and in Gabrielleys room too, but we didn't find him, I didn't think we would, I thought "lets look in the garbage." But then there was a surprise, because suddenly Jemima came running up, she said "I just heard a funny noise, it was in our bed" and d'you know when we looked there was Hermann. He had sort of sneaked between the side and the matrass, I could just see a bit of his fur, so he was all right, he hadn't been squashed after all. I said "hurrah hurrah" and Jemima said "hurrah" too and mum looked really pleased, so did Cloudio, he said "I'm so glad" and even Gabrielley made a smile but that wasn't real of course, that was just pretending.

Cloudio took out the matrass and though Hermann tried to run away I got him, he tried to squeeze out of my hands so I thought "you really like being in this sofer bed" I said "no you don't." Afterwards I put his cage right next to my side so I could watch him when I woke up in the night and make sure he was still there. Then when we were all ready to go to bed, I put a chair up against the door handle, just like we used to in the cottage to stop dad. Mum gave me a look, she said "Lawrence love, I really don't think that's necessery" but I said "I'm not letting that Gabrielley sneek in here and get Hermann so hes lost forever" and mum didn't say anything, she just went to bed.

EMPEROR DOMITIAN WAS FAT but he had thin legs and his toes stuck out sideways a bit so they were like ducks feet, nobody liked him because he kept executing them. One day a prophet made a prophecy about him and it was really terrible, he said "you will get assasinated and it will be quite soon actually." Then he told Domitian what day it would happen, he said "it will be before six o'clock."

Domitian got really worrid, he thought "uhoh, this is awful, what can I do?" he thought "I must make a plan." First he exicuted lots of people, he executed them if they made a rude joke about him years ago, or if they carried a map of the world around them, because that was the sort of thing only emperors did, it was just in case they were going to assassinate him. After that he looked all round his palace for places where he might get assassinated, he thought "I bet its in the colonaide where I go for a walk" so he had the walls polished until they were like mirrors, so he could see if anyone came sneaking up with a dager to stab him.

Then he had a different idea, he thought "I know, I will proove that all prophets are wrong." So he went to a very famous prophet and he asked him "tell me then, how will you die?" and the prophet said "I will get eaten by dogs, actually." Domitian clapped his hands, he was so pleased, and he said "then I order you to be executed straight away by being burnt on a big fire with logs." His soldiers got lots of logs and they put the prophit on top, they lit it and Domitian thought "that's good, now everybody will see how stupid those prophits are, I will go home." But that was a mistake in fact, because after he went there was a huge wind, it was like a hurricain and all the logs on the fire got blown over, the prophets body fell down and suddenly a whole lot of dogs rushed up and ate it, so the prophet was right. When Domitian heard he said "oh no, that's bad, it didn't work after all."

Finally the day came when Domitian would get assasinated. He thought "I will just have to be really careful." First he scratched a big boil on his head and made it bleed because he hoped that would be enough to stop the prophecy, he thought "perhaps that will do." After that he walked round and round his palace, it was huge, it was so quiet he could hear his shoes go "tap tap tap." He walked along the corridors and round the garden with its pretty flowers, he carried a big dager just in case, because he didn't trust anyone, he didn't trust the cooks or the cleaners or his gardners or his best freinds or his body guards, he gave everybody suspicious looks, and when he got to the colonaide he looked behind him in the polished wall to see if anybody was sneaking up on him, but nobody was.

It seemed like that day went on for ages, Domitian thought "its like it will never stop." But finally it got later so he asked one of his servants "what time is it?" and the servant said "oh, its just after six o'clock." Domitian said "six o'clock, really?" and he was so pleased, he shouted "hurrah hurrah, I am still all right, and the prophecy said I would get killed before six, which means it was wrong after all." He thought "perhaps scratching that boil was enough" so he put down his dager and said "I know, I will go and have a lovely bath."

But actually this was a big mistake because it was all a trick, you see. Because the servant told him the wrong time, it was still only five o'clock really. Domitian went to the bathroom, he ran a nice big bath and then suddenly another servant came in. He had his arm in bandeges for days, he said it was because he broke it, but that was a trick too, because he had a dager hidden secretly in the bandages. Now he got it out and Domitian thought "oh no, this is terrible, I wish I'd brought my dager." which was right, because the servant stabed him and stabed him, Domitian could not stop him because he just had a little towel. So he was assassinated, even though he was so careful, even though he was emporer he couldn't do anything, that prophet was right after all.

The next morning mum woke us up early, she said "time to go to the vanhootins" but I didn't want to go, I said "I'm not leaving Hermann, what if Gabrielley gets him?" Mum said "don't be silly Lawrence, I'm sure it was just an accident, and anyway Gabrielly won't even be here, he'll be at his day care, remember" but I said "what if he comes home early, what if he pretends he is ill?" I said "I'll only go if you put him somewhere really high up where Gabrielly can't get him." So we put him on a high cubord in the kitchen, and mum got annoyed because she couldn't reach so she had to ask Cloudio, she said "Lawrence is worried a cat might come in" which was a lie of course. I thought Hermann might be scared of being so high but then I thought "its better than getting squashed and thrown in the garbage."

We went to the Vanhootins in our car. Mum had never driven in Rome before, she always walked or went by bus when she lived here years ago, and we got lost three times, she kept shouting "for gods sake" or "I just don't believe what he just did." But eventually we got there, Manuella opened the door, and mum had to hurry because there were some cars behind her honking, I said "be careful driving back mum, don't crash."

Our teacher was called siniora Morrow and she was nice, she was really funny, when you got it wrong she made big cross eyes and pinched your nose but it didn't really hurt, it was just a joke, she talked so fast it was like she couldn't keep still, she was a jumping puma. She taught us "commistiy" which means "how are you" and "me keyamo Lawrence" which means "I'm called Lawrence." Little Leonora mouse was better at italian than big Tina bossy rabbit, that was a surprise and it made Tina cross. Another surprise happened when we were having lunch, which was Manueller's lovely sandwiches, because Tina and Leonora kept saying "mum, can we go to the dvd shop later" or "can we go out and have pizza" but Janiss pretty pig didn't answewer them because she was always too busy, she was reading a magazeen or talking on the telephone, she said "not now girls" so I thought "that's strange" because mum always answers us straight away, even if she just says "don't be silly."

Another strange thing was that Tina and Leonora hardly had

any toys, they just had a few dolls and games and things which were quite boring, we had tons more at the cottage, actually we had brought more to Rome in our car. So I felt a bit sorry for those little Vanhootins, even bossy rabbit, and I told them "when we get a flat you can come over and play with our toys, we've got lots."

When mum came to collect us she was cheerful, she said she met Crissies cristian friends and they said yes, you can have this job and they didn't ask her to go to church ten times a day after all, that was good, mum said she went to the British embassy too and got her new passport. When we walked back to where she parked the car she said "the only bad news is that I don't think they've got a flat for us" she said "they had a look in their books but everything was so expensive, I couldn't believe it. They said our best chance was asking everyone we know in case someone has something cheaper." Jemima was silly, she tried to help, she said "lets ask everyone right now mummy, lets ask him" and she pointed at a man, he looked at us like he was very surprised, he was cleaning the road with a brush. I thought "if only we knew someone like pope Bonniface, he would get us a nice place" I said "you must know some other Romans mum" and she said "I suppose there are my old students, I'm sure they've all moved ten times since then but I could try and look them up, I remember one was a countess." I didn't know countess, but mum said it was a bit like being the queen but smaller, so I said "oh yes, I bet she has thousands of flats" but mum said "there are lots of countesses in Rome, Lawrence, and some don't have any flats at all" she said "but we can always try."

Another thing she said was that we must babysit Gabrielley tonight, which was because Cloudio and Chintsier were both going out, Cloudio had a meeting and Chintsier had to eat supper in a restaurant for her work. I thought "that's good actually, because I'll be able to watch that sneaky no animal and make sure he doesn't do anything horrible to Hermann."

Then when we got near Cloudio's house and mum parked the car a funny thing happened, I remember it. Mum walked down the road a little bit and then she said "look at that car parked over there, its just the same color as your fathers" it was yellow. I said "his is a bit paler" but mum said "no, its just the same, I'm sure of it" so I said "but his is different, its bigger" and mum said "oh yes" but she still went up and had a really good look in the windshield.

After that we went back to Cloudio's house. I got a bit worried, I thought "what if Gabrielly went home early, what if he pretended he was ill, what if he got a ladder" but fortunatley he hadn't, Hermann was still on the cuboard. Mum got him down, she climbed on the table, and I gave him new water and seeds, and actually the babysitting was really easy. Gabrielly didn't do anything awful, I gave him some Calligula looks when mum wasn't watching and I think that helped, because he hardly said anything and he ate the spagetties mum made. When I was brushing my teeth Cloudio bear came home because his meeting finished early, and he put Gabrielly to bed, so mum didn't have to do that, which was good too.

Then suddenly I woke up, it was because there was a noise, and though I was asleep when the noise happened I could still remember it, that was funny, it was like it was on a Cd in my head and I could play it again if I wanted. It was a scrapeing noise, I thought "I bet that's a chair." I looked around and though it was dark I could see because there was a bit of light beside the curtains. Hermann was there in his cage, he was awake, he usually is in the night, he is nocturnel, and he was sticking his nose through the bars and looking at a wall, I thought "hes all right, that's good." Mum wasn't there, she often goes away again once we are sleeping, so I thought "she probably made that scraping noise" so that was all right too.

But then I had another thought, I thought "what if it wasn't mum at all, what if its Gabrielly?" Then I thought "what could he do when everybodies sleeping?" and I thought "well, he might go in the kitchen where my box is and he might start wrecking all my tintins" I thought "he might put my hotwheels in the garbage." After that I thought "no, he's probably not doing that, he's probably just asleep" but then I thought "but he might be" and d'you know that thought just wouldn't go away, it wouldn't budge, it kept coming back until it made me go all awake, it made me get really cross. So I thought "he'd better dam well not be doing that, that little sneaky, nasty no animal." Now I thought "perhaps I'd better just go and see" and I got up from the sofa bed, but then I stopped, because I thought "what if it's a trick, what if I go out and then he sneaks in behind me and does something terrible to Hermann?" But then I thought "no he can't, not if I'm really quick."

So I went out of the sitting room, I walked across to the kitchen, and the door was open just a tiny slit so I looked in. And

it wasn't Gabrielley at all, actually, it was Cloudio and mum instead, they were sitting at the kitchen table and they had glasses
of wine so I thought "thats all right then, I'll go back now before
Gabrielly sneaks in behind me." But then I notised something,
because Cloudio had his hand on mums back, so I thought "that's
strange." I heard mum through the door, she said "don't be silly,
bear, really we can't" and I thought "thats strange too, how does
she know Cloudios a bear?" Then Cloudio said "her dinner won't
finish till eleven and its a long way." Mum said "really bear, no"
and then Cloudio made a kind of little moan like he was going to
cry and he did a really funny thing, because suddenley he put his
head down, it was like he was divving into a swimming pool but
he put it down between mums arms, and I felt funny like I
couldn't breath, it was like when I noticed that Hermanns door
was wide open.

Cloudio said something, it was a bit hard to hear because he
said it into mum's boddy but I heard it any way, he said "I don't
care about Chintsier all I care about is you Hannah" and I thought
"hes definitely going to cry now" I thought "I don't like you any
more" I thought "I wish we never came here to these Cloudios
because they are all awful, Chintsier nasty squirrel and Gabrielly
sneaky no animal and Cloudio horrible bear, I wish we'd stayed
with those nuns." Now Cloudio popped his head up again, he
said "I just feel so lost." Mum said "no bear no" like she wanted
him to go away, so I thought "that's right" I thought "make him
go away mum, just come back to bed right now" but then something happened, that was a real surprise. Because suddenly mum

reached forward with her head and she gave Cloudio a big kiss, it went on for ages and she put her fingers round his ears.

That was when I sort of went into the room. It was strange, I just found I was going in, it was like I hadn't decided at all, it was like my feet just went by themselves. I thought "uhoh" I thought "what will I do now?" then I thought "oh yes I will get a tintin." So I walked past, I didn't look, it was like I hadn't noticed they were there. I heard a chair scrapeing noise, it was just like the one I heard when I was asleep, and suddenly mum shouted out "what are you doing here, why aren't you in bed" and she said it loud like she was really cross with me.

I didn't say anything, I didn't answer, I just kept quiet and went very carefully across the room to my box and got my Tintin, it was "the crab with the golden claws" It was funny, I felt like nothing was happening, I felt like I wasn't there at all, it was like I was in space or something, but then suddenly everything just changed complitly, suddenly I got really really angry, I thought "why is mum shouting at me, thats not fair, I haven't done anything wrong, I'm just getting my Tintin, how dare she" and I really hated her for shouting at me. So I threw the crab with golden claws right across the room, I didn't even look where it went, I think it landed on the micro waive.

I ran right out of the kitchen and I slammed the door behind me as hard as I could, I didn't care if someone was behind me and they got their hand caught but nobody did. I ran straight into the sitting room, I slammed that door too, so Jemima woke up, she said "whats happening" but I didn't say anything, I could hear Gabrielley shouting, he woke up as well, and I got into bed. Mum came in, she came over to me and she said "Lawrence love I'm so so sorry" but I didn't care, I said "you shouted at me and that wasn't fair, I'm not talking to you" but she kept on talking anyway, she said "please lawrence listen, I didn't mean to shout at you, I'm so sorry, this is all a big mistake, Lawrence love, please, please." I could tell she was getting upset but dyou know I just didn't care, actually I was pleased, I thought "you go and be upset mum, you squeaze your hair and scrach your arm and say dam dam, you go sad, I don't mind." I didn't take any notice of her, I thought "I will just talk to Herman now" I said "I wish mum would just shut up and go away forever, don't you?"

CHAPTER FOUR

A long time ago when we just moved to the cottege mum said "let's have a treat today Lawrence love, let's go to Wipsinaide zoo." It was sunday, there wasn't anything to do, actually, but I felt cross, I remember it, I thought "I want to go back to Scotland, I want to see my cousins and play on Robbies computer" and I said "I don't want to go to Wipsinaide zoo I want to stay here."

So we just stayed at home, I watched telly and it was quite boring in fact. I sat in the kitchen playing with my cars and it was very quiet, I could hear the fridge going wirr wirr. After that we went to London zoo once and dad took me to Edinburuh zoo when I went to see him for his weekends but I never did go to Wipsnaide. Its strange, I think about that day sometimes. I wonder what animals there were that we never saw, and what food we didn't eat for lunch, I bet there was a cafeteria, there were ice creams, and it makes me feel funny. I think oh I wish I'd just said "yes mum lets go to Wipsnaide Zoo" but of course its too late, that day is gone away now.

I wasn't speaking to anybody in the morning at Cloudios, I only talked to Hermann, I told him "we are moving to Guses now, thats good because it will be much nicer there, you will be safe from Gabrielley." I just ate my toast, Cloudio made it but he didn't look at me, he looked at the table or the walls, so I gave him my Caligula glaire, I think he knew but he didn't look back, it was like he was scared. I thought "I don't like you Cloudio" and then I read my Calamitous Cesaers.

Emporer Nero's mother was called Agrippina and she was always shouting at Nero and ordering him around so he got really cross, he thought "how dare she say that to me." He thought "how can I stop her from shouting at me?" He was so annoyed he took away all her soldiers, he made her move out of his palace, and then he got his freinds to ride past her house on their horses and say really rude insults at her, he thought "that will stop her" but he was wrong. None of it worked, actually she shouted at him more than before, she was terrible. So he thought "all right, I will just get her killed then, I will get her assasinated, that will stop her."

First he tried to poisson her but she was too clever and she always drank the antidoate first so the poison didn't work. Then he got someone to break her bedroom ceiling really carefully so it would suddenly fall on her when she was sleeping, but she found out about this plan too, and she went to sleep in another room, so that didn't work either.

Then one day Nero had a new idea, he thought "I know I will

make a special collapsible boat." He got his servants to make the boat, it took ages and then he invited his mother round for supper at his palace by the seaside, he said "lets not have any more of these stupid arguments mum, lets be friends again." Agrippinna said "all right Nero, lets" and she came to dinner, it was very nice, it was really delicous and when they finished she said "thank you for a lovely time" and he said "not at all" so it was like they really were freinds again now.

But then they went down to the sea, it was almost dark now, and Agripina notised that her boat had sunk. Nero said "oh dear, look at your boat, it must have had an accident" which was a lie of course, because he made his servants crash it. He said "don't worry mum, you can use mine." Agrippina said "oh thank you Nero" she never guessed, and so she sailed off in the special collapsible boat. There wasn't a storm, the sea was calm, it was a lovley night, but then suddenly the boat began to collapse, pieces broke off and the masts dropped out until everything fell apart completly so there was nothing left, just little bits of wood. But Agripinna was a very good swimmer, so she and her servant swam all the way to the seashore, though it was a long way away, they were saved.

Agripina still didn't guess what happened, she thought "oh dear, that wasn't a good boat" so she sent her servant to tell Nero what happened. Nero sat on his emporers chair listening to her servant tell him that they were saved and he thought "oh no this is bad, my plan didn't work after all" but he didn't say anything, he pretended he was pleased, he smiled and said "poor mum, thank goodness shes all right." But then he got someone to sneek up behind the servant and suddenly they dropped a dager on the floor beside him, it made a loud clang and Nero shouted "oh look there, its a dager, he was trying to assasasinate me, mum must have sent him." So the servant and Aggripina were both arrested, they were executed, and he finally got her killed, he thought "hurrah."

After that Nero was worried everybody would hate him for executing his mother, he thought "I don't want to go back to Rome, because they will all shout really rude insults" but he was wrong. When he went back all the Romans were waiting along the road in their Sunday best, it was like Nero had just won a big war, they all cheered and shouted "well done Nero, thank goodness you weren't assasiniated" but it wasn't real of course, they really thought "how dreadful, he killed his own mummy" it was just so they wouldn't get executed. So Nero thought "hurrah, I'm all right after all."

But then a strange thing happened. Suddenly Nero knew his mother was watching him. It was her goast actually, he couldn't see her but he knew she was there, he could feel it, she followed him everywhere and now she shouted at him even more crossly than before because he executed her. Nero thought "this is terrible" he thought "I wonder how I can make her go away?" He got special wizers from Persher to do spells to make her appear, so he could say "I'm really sorry mum for executing you, now please just leave me alone" but the spells didn't work, they never suceeded, and she never did appear. So he never got rid of her actually, her goast followed him for years and years, it never left him alone until he was dead too.

It wasn't just me who wasn't speaking in the morning, because hardly anybody was. Chintsier wasn't speaking, she just stood by the sink with cross arms and slit eyes, so I thought "she really really hates us now." Cloudio wasn't speaking either, his eyes were funny like he swiched them off, it was like he was hiding behind them so he wouldn't cry, I thought "go on Cloudio cry, cry a lot." And Gabrielly wasn't speaking, but that wasn't because he was cross, actually he was really cheerful now we were going away. As soon as mum finished packing our bags he got lots of his toys and put them all in the sitting room instead of us, then he switched on the telly really loud and he sat there watching it. In fact the only one who was speaking that morning was Jemima and she wouldn't stop, she kept saying "I want some more choclate serial" or "why are we going away again?" or "I don't want to go to Guses, I want to go back to Crissies, I want all my animals and my dolls." Mum answered in a funny voice, it was sort of squeeking, and her smile was too big like it might just go "pop" she said "lamikin we can't crowd out poor Cloudio and Chintsier any longer."

I didn't help pack the car, I let Cloudio and mum carry everything, I thought "you do it." I just took Hermann, I put his cage on the seat beside me and I told him "we don't ever have to come back here again, Hermann, thats good isn't it" and I don't know if Cloudio heard, he was quite near, he might have. Then we drove off and I didn't wave goodbye.

Mum got lost twice, she almost hit a red car and she said "it says we're not supposed to go down here, oh god" then finally we got to Guses. A car behind us couldn't go past because the road was too narrow and it started honking, so Mum ran out really fast and rang the doorbell. Then lots of people came out, one was Gus, and they got all our things. Gus took Hermanns cage, I said "bye bye Hermann, don't worry I'll come back soon" and though they all smiled and waved at me I didn't smile and wave back, I just didn't feel like it. I thought "I don't like any of you new Gus dog people, I'm not going to think what animals you have, that means you don't have any."

There were two cars honking now and mum had one leg in the car and one leg out, she said "where can I park?" Gus lifted his hands in the air like this was the funniest thing, he said "Hannah, your in the middle of rome, you'll be lucky if you find anything. The free parking spaces have white lines." So we drove round and round looking for white lines but there were hardly any, they were all blue or yellow, and they all had cars in them anyway. We drove round for hours, Jemima fell asleep, till finally we were going up a hill, the road went round and round like a big snake, and I could see Rome out of the window with all its doames and rooves, then suddenly mum braked really hard so we swerved a bit, the car made a noise like in a film, and we went right in a parking place with white lines, mum said "oh thank god."

I watched mum as she woke up Jemima and got her out of her seat, she was all slow and floppy from being asleep so mum had to carry her. Then Mum opened my door, she said "come on Lawrence" and it was funny, I didn't feel cross until then, I just sat in the car as we drove round and round, I watched all the cars and the motorcycles and buildings out of the window, I wasn't thinking anything at all, I was just thinking "that's a funny looking car" or "theres a really big doame" but now when mum opened my door suddenly I got really really cross, I thought "you shouted at me in Cloudios kitchen, you put your fingers on his ears." So I didn't move, I just sat there and looked out of the windshield, there was a bird fighting another bird so it could get some crums. Mum gave me a look, she said "Lawrence, please" and her voice started getting annoyed, so I thought "don't you get cross with me, don't you start shouting again" and I said "I want to go back to england, I don't like Rome, its horreble."

Mum gave me a funny look, it was like she was cross and she was scared, she didn't know which, and she said "for goodness sake Lawrence, you know we can't do that." Then I looked at Jemima, she was rubbing her eyes, and I said "I want to go home to the cottage so I can play with all my toys there, and Jemima can play with all her other dolls and her marbles game and her spirograff." Those were some of her favorite things that she left behind actually, so she sort of woke up more and she said "I want to go home too."

Now Mum got really cross, she said "I haven't time for this" she put Jemima down on the ground and she reached into the car to get me. But I was ready, I thought "no you don't" and when her arm went past to undo my seat belt I got it with my hands and then I bit it really hard with my teeth. That was a big surprise for mum, she shreeked and she pulled her arm out so fast, and Jemima laughed, she thought "this is a funny game" but then she saw our faces and she started crying instead. Mum said "Lawrence" and she stood there staring at me. I thought "go on mum, cry" but she didn't, so I thought "she isn't going sad anymore" I thought "that's a shame, I want her to get sad." I thought "if she isn't going to cry then she'll go really cross" but she didn't do that either. She looked at me like she was just really tired and she said "what is it you want from me Lawrence?"

I thought for a bit, I thought "what can I have?" and I said "I want a treat, a really good treat." Mum frowned like I was horrible and she said "all right all right, you can have your dam treat." I thought "I must check" so I said "anything I want, anything at all?" and mums eyes went really big because she was annoyed, she said "yes, anything you want."

So we had pizzas, and then we got a bus that went almost to Piazza Nevoner where the toy shops were. Because I could have anything I wanted, which never happened usually, I thought "I must be really careful, I mustn't get it wrong" so I took a long time. I went to both the toy shops three times, I looked at all the shelves to make sure I didn't miss anything, and then finally I chose my treat, it was a radio controlled car, it was really big and its head lights lit up. I said "I want that, and I want its batteries too." Mum got cross, she closed her eyes and she said "Lawrence, for goodness sake, that's more than a hundred yuros, why not have this one, it's a third of the price and its almost the same" but I shook my head, I thought "your not going to cheete me out of my treat" and I said "no I want this one, you said I could have anything I want, you promised, remember."

Mum told the shop lady and she got it down, and Jemima got a doll that was floppy like clothes because Jemima always has to have something too, but when we went to pay mum's card didn't work. Mum said "oh god" she said "look Lawrence, I bet it will work if we get that other car" but I thought "no you don't" and I said "what about your blue card because that worked when we went to that restaurant." So we went to a cashpoint machine, it was quite far, it was by the panthion, mum got out the money, she said "that'll be the last of it" and I said "come on mum, hurry up."

We got the car and we put in the batteries, we got the man in the shop to do it because you needed a screw driver, and then I made it go in the Piazza Nevona. The lights didn't light up after all, that was just in the picture on the box, that was annoying. Mum and Jemima sat on a stone bench and watched, mum said "are you happy now" which meant she was cross, but I didn't say anything. It was a bit borring once I got used to the controls, I made it go round and round a fountain until the batteries began to run out so it went more and more slowly, it sort of creped. I thought "I don't much like this treat actually" I thought "maybe I will let us stay in Rome, maybe I won't."

WHEN WE WENT BACK TO GUSES they were all in the sitting room which was the kitchen too, they were drinking wine, and I thought "this is old and dirty" I thought "I don't like it here." They all said "welcome to our house" and mum said "this is so kind of you" and then she said "come on Lawrence, say hello, don't be unfreindly" but I didn't say hello, I just didn't feel like it, so mum said "he's a bit tired today" which just was a lie of course. But then I changed my mind. I thought "even if its old and dirty here its still better than being at Cloudios." So I looked at all the people, there were five of them, and I thought "and you are not Cloudio and Chintsier and Gabrielly" I thought "all right then, I suppose I will give you your animals after all."

Gus didn't need one of course, he was already a dog, he asked mum "so how was Cloudios" and mum said "it was lovely, but I just didn't want to croud them out in that little flat" which was another lie, I thought "what a lot of lies your saying today mum." Gus said he was writing a play for doing in a theater, Mum said "but you were doing that last time" and Gus said "this is completely different, this is much angrier" so I thought "that's silly, how can a play get angry?"

Next to Gus there was Marther who had funny eyes, she looked right at you with a special smile, it was like she was saying "I am Martha and I am looking at you" so she was Marther the special monkey, I thought "do I like you marther?" I thought "I'm not sure." She asked me what I liked best at school and when I said "stories" she was pleased, she said I would like this house because everybody here was an artist, they were all writing or singing or something. I said "but an artist doesn't sing, an artist does paintings" but Marther said "no, Lawrence, a singer can be an artist too, like Oska here" and she pointed at Oska, who was sitting in the corner with his giutar, she said "Osker is our song writer" and Oska laughed, he said "no he is your busker" which I knew, because mum told me once, it is somebody who sings outside restaraunts so people give him money. Marther said "Oska will be the next Bob Dillin you just wait" but I didn't know Bob

Dillin, I wanted to ask mum but I didn't because I was still cross with her.

Oska was very thin with black hair and he only played his guitar a bit sometimes, so it was like he was talking with it actually, it said "oh yes" or "no I don't think so" he was a smiley guitar ferrit. Marther said "your all staying in Oskas' room actually, he's sleeping down here on the sofa, we so wanted to help you" and mum said "that's so kind, Oska, I really don't know how to thank you" and he didn't say anything, he just smiled and made his guitar go "pling pling pling" like it was saying "that's ok" which was funny.

So I thought "actually you new people are quite nice after all I suppose, even greedy Gus and Marther special monkey" I thought "I'm glad I'm giving you your animals." My favorite was Hilary, she was chopping vegtables and putting them in pots, she had brown hair that was round like a ball and she was fat, whenever she looked at me she gave me a nice smile, so she was a nice cow. Martha said Hillary was brilliant at cooking, one day she would have lots of restaraunts all over the world, and Hilery made a funny smile, she said "I don't know about that."

The last one was really easy to get an animal for. He was called Freddy and he had a white beard which was so big it was bigger than his head, and it was frizzy like stuff that comes out of cushions if theres a hole, so he was Freddy the Father Chrismas Bear. Freddy talked like Bill Vanhootin, Marther said he was from Canada, which is near America, she said "Freddies our brilliant poet, he had his poems published in a book, and now hes helping me write poems too, poor fool" and Freddy said "Marther's really good." Then Marther gave him her special smile and she said "Freddy, maybe you should show Hannah Lawrence and Jemima round the house."

So we saw all the rooms. Hilary nice cow had a blue bottle on the table with a flower in it, Freddy said "Hilleries our angel, she looks after us all." There was a computer room, mum had a computer like that ages ago when I was small, so I thought "thats really old" but Freddy liked it, he said "feel free to use it any time, just put a yuro in the trust box" and mum said "that's kind." Guses room was almost empty, there were just some books and a bed that was flat on the floor like a carpit. Next door was Martha special monkeys room but it was locked, Jemima tried the handle, Freddy said "Marthers the boss, this is her house" and mum said "just leave it alone, Jemima." Our room was upstairs and it had a bed like a carpet like Guses, Hermann and all our bags were there. So I went to say hello to Hermann, I said "I told you I'd come back" and then I looked out of the window at the road, two ladies were looking at a shop, and I thought "its not very nice but its much better than horrible Cloudios house" I thought "all right I will let us stay here."

Freddy chrismas bear said "I'm next door, if you ever need anything just shout." So we went to see his room which had funny pens, they were very long and thin and mum said they weren't pens actually, they were quils. But the really intresting thing was the pieces of paper which were stuck all over the walls, there were hundreds, so you could hardly see the walls at all. Freddy said "those are my poems, I like to have them up so I can look at them and write them better." Then Jemima blew like she was blowing out a candel and some of them moved, it was like they wanted to go off flying, so of course she blew at them again and I thought "uhoh, watch out, poemes" but they were saved, because then Hilary nice cow shouted up the stairs, she said "dinners ready."

Usually mum says I must eat some vegetables but this time she forgot so I just ate pasta with cheese. The reason she forgot was because she was talking and talking with Gus, he was telling her about how his play was so angry and she was telling him how lovely it was being in Rome again, it was just so wonderfull. At first I didn't mind but then I got annoyed, I thought "I'm watching you mum" I thought "you'd better not be like you were in Cloudios kitchen" I thought "you'd better not put your fingers on Guses ears."

Then something happened, because the telephone rang, Hillery got it, she said "it's for you Hannah" and she gave mum a funny look, she made her eyebrows go up and she said "its someone called Beppo." I thought "oh yes, Beppo who I don't know and who Franseen and Crissy chick and me don't like at all." Mum started talking and talking on the telephone, she said "how amazing, how clever of you to track us down." Now Gus looked cross, so I thought "that's good, ha ha Gus" but only for a bit, because mum went on and on, she wouldn't stop and she was smiling and smiling so I thought "you really like this Beppo." Everyone was quiet, I thought "they are all listening" mostly it was in Italian but some bits were in english, she said "really, oh god that would be so good, actually we are getting a bit desperate." Finally she stopped, she said "till tomorrow then" and Gus said "Beppo, wasn't he the one who used to drive round in that open top" which I didn't know, mum said it was a car without a roof. Mum said "that's right, and he said he might have a flat for us, isn't that wonderful" but I thought "I don't know about that" I thought "I don't like your flat Beppo."

After that it got worse, because mum started talking and talking to Gus all over again. I thought "this is really enough now, its like it just goes on forever" I thought "there are so many of them, these Guses and Cloudios and Beppos, I cant stop them all." Then I noticed an intresting thing, because Marther looked cross too. She said "can you get us some more wine Gus" so I thought "I know, you are trying to interupt them" I thought "go on, Marther" but it didn't work, Gus got the wine but then he just started talking to mum all over again. I tried too, I said "mum, I want a tintin, the red sea sharks, can you go up stairs and get it out of the bag" but that didn't work either, she said "not now Lawrence, can't you see I'm still having my dinner." I thought "how long are you going to be, are you going to be ages?" so I looked at her plate, and d'you know it was like she told a big lie, because there was just a tiny bit left, it was sitting on her fork, it would all go in one bite easily. I thought "you are being on slow on purpose" I thought "you are keeping that bit so you don't have to get my tintin, its so you can say you are still eating so you can go on talking and talking with Gus, its so you can do his ears" and suddenly something happened. I felt so cross, I could feel it in my stomack and arms, it was in my teeth, it was like it might lift me right up, and I thought "I wonder what will happen now" I thought "I wonder what I will do?"

I looked at Jemima, her eyes were going funny like she would go to sleep in her chair, and I thought "I think I will wake you up" so I said "Jemima, d'you want to come and play with Hermann?" which worked of course, her eyes went wide open straight away. When I got up from the table mum gave us a little smile so I thought "oh yes, your pleased we're going away." We went upstairs to our room, I got Hermann out, I let her hold him just for a bit, I let her change his water and put more food in his bowl, and when we finished I said "I'm going into Freddies room now to look at his poems and his funny pens but you can't come, all right Jemima, because you will break them. You have to go back downstairs right now." I thought "you'd better not follow me, Jemima, or it will be your fault." But d'you know that's just what she did, she ran straight after me, that was silly, so I warned her, I said "Jemima, I just told you that you couldn't come in."

It was funny standing in Freddies room without mum or Freddy, it was all quiet. I said to Jemima "you mustn't touch any of Freddies funny pens, all right?" and d'you know what she did, she made her bad face and then she ran over and grabed one though I just said she mustn't, that was stupid. I could see her hand was all inky now, so I said "Jemima, I just told you you mustn't do that, now give that to me right now or I will hit you on the head with a pillow." But she didn't lisen at all, she just did her squeaking laugh and ran into the corner with her back to me so I couldn't get the pen off her. I thought "I warned you Jemima" so I got a pillow from Freddies bed and I went up and hit her on the head, but she just gigelled, and I noticed all of Freddies poemes on the walls were going "flap flap" because the pillow made a little breeze, I thought "look at those."

After that I hit Jemima with the pillow again, which was because she wasn't listening, and I said "don't hit me with a pillow, Jemima, you really mustn't all right" and d'you know that's just what she did, she just dropped her quil and then ran over to Freddies bed and got one. I thought "uhoh you've made it all inky with your hand Jemima, now that will be staned forever." I thought "uhoh, what bad thing will she do next?" I thought "I must stop her" so I said "whatever you do you mustn't do this" and I hit the wall a bit with my pillow. It was just to make her see what she mustn't do, but some of the poemes fell down, it was an accident, I thought "that silly Chrismas Bear didn't stick them on properly, he should have used more selotape."

Now Jemima did something really bad, she hit another wall and it wasn't an accident at all, it was on purpose, so suddenly lots of poems came off. I said "look what you've done" I thought "I will stop her now" and I tried to get her pillow off her by hitting it with my pillow, I think I hit a few poemes by mistake, but it didn't work anyway, because she was holding her pillow too tight. I thought "you are so bad, Jemima" because now there were poems everywhere, they were flying in the air and they were all over the floor, it was like it was raining poems, but it was Jemima who jumped up and down on them, I didn't do that, I only trod on a few because I was trying to stop her, they were all slippy and scrunchey under my feet.

I thought "I know, I will stop her in a different way" so I ran out of Freddys room. I had to take my pillow because she took hers but I didn't want to fight any more, I said "stop it Jemima" but she wouldn't, she followed me right into Guses room, so it was her fault his books got knocked off the shelf. I said "Jemima no" and I ran down the stairs, I just threw away my pillow, I said "don't hit me Jemima" but she didn't listen. She was squeeking like she thought "I can really get him now" she was gigelling like she would go "pop" and when we ran into the dining room she hit me on my arm but then she saw them all staring at us and her mouth went open like a fish.

Mum looked like a big bee just stung her, she stopped talking to Gus dog, and d'you know what she said, that wasn't fair, she said "Lawrence what are you doing." I thought "how dare you mum" I said "it wasn't me, it was Jemima" I said "look I haven't even got a pillow." But Jemima is a big cheet, she is a liar, her lips wobbled and she started crying, so I thought "you are trying to win just by crying" I thought "no you don't" and I said "she was the one who knocked down Freddies poemes." Now Freddy got stung by a bee, he jumped up from his chair and mum said "Lawrence what have you done" which was stupid, because didn't I just tell her it was Jemima? Everything went quiet, Freddy ran upstairs and then there was a kind of moan, he found his poems, so I thought "now you will know you must use more selotape."

Marther gave mum a look, it was like she was a bit pleased actually, that was funny, and she said "Hannah if you want to stay in our house then you must keep your children under controll" and mum looked like she would go double triple "pop" she would just burst, she said "Lawrence and Jemima, you will both say your sorry right now" and d'you know I knew just what to say, it just came into my head, I said it before Jemima could say anything,

I thought "this is the right thing" I said "I don't like you mum, I really hate you" and then I ran up to the bath room before she could get me and I locked the door.

Mum came up lots of times, she banged on the door with her hand "thump thump thump" and she shouted that I must let her in right this moment, Lawrence, I must say I'm sorry and help clear up this dam mess, but I didn't say anything, I just sat on the floor next to the key hole so I could hear. First they went into Guses room and mum said "I'm so sorry about all this Marther, really I am, he's never like this usually" but Marther was still cross, she said "we really can't have this sort of behavior, we are artists here, we need our peace and quiet." Jemima tried to clean up a bit, I could hear her saying "where does this go?" so I thought "you won't be much use." Then I heard Gus but he wasn't angry actually, he was joking, he said "my rooms pre-recked, I can't see much difference" so I thought "why aren't you cross now, go on, be cross, I don't like you Gus."

After that they all went up to Freddies room, they were quieter because it was upstairs but I could still hear them, mum did a kind of shreek, she said "oh god, I can't believe this." I couldn't hear what Freddy said but his voice wasn't cross actually, it sounded like he was telling mum "don't get too angry with him" so I thought "thank you Chrismas bear."

Then a strange thing happened. It was like my crossness started going away. It was like when you have a bath and you let all the water go down the plug hole but you don't get out, you are still sitting there and suddenly you just feel cold. I thought "someone will want to go to the loo soon but I don't want to see any of them, I don't want to open the door, so I will get stuck in here" I thought "uhoh, what will I do?" But they were still talking upstairs, they weren't coming down yet, so then I thought "I will just go right now." I opened the door and I ran upstairs carefully, I didn't make any noise. I could see Guses foot and the bottom of his leg sticking out of Freddies door but it didn't move, he didn't look round, so I just ran into our room, I shut the door really quietly, I got into my pijamers and I got into the bed, then I shut my eyes so it was like I had been asleep for hours.

Eventually the door opened, I heard Jemima say "look mum theres Lawrence" and I thought "uhoh, mum will shout at me now, this will be bad" but she didn't, she didn't say anything, I thought "that's funny." I didn't move at all, I could hear mum getting Jemima in her pijamas, she said "there you are lamikin" I felt the bed go down when they got in, and then mum switched the light off. Jemima went to sleep really quick like she always does, but then just when I thought "hurrah hurrah, I am all right after all" mum said in a wisper "Lawrence, I know your awake" so I thought "oh no, here it comes." I thought "her voice will be like a stick" but it wasn't at all, that was strange. It wasn't cross or sad or nice or anything, it was just nothing, it was like she was saying "oh yes we need to get some more milk" or "what dyou want for your breakfast?" But it was funny, because it was even worse because she wasnt cross after all, I thought "I wish you were just shouting actually" I thought "you really hate me now."

Mum said "I'm sorry about what happened at Cloudios Lawrence" but she didn't sound sorry, she sounded like I was her enimy now. I thought "now I will be cross again, its my turn" but it didn't work, I just thought "this is dreadfull, everybody hates me, I bet even Jemima hates me except she is asleep." Mum was quiet for a long time so I thought "has she gone to sleep too?" but then she said "theres something you should know, Lawrence. When I lived here years ago Cloudio and me were very close, I hadn't met your father then and he hadn't met Chintsier. In fact he wanted us to get married, but I didn't want to marry him, and that made him very sad." I thought "I'm glad" I thought "you leave my mum alone, Cloudio from ages ago before I was born, you just go away and be sad." Mum said "but I never thought he still liked me like that now. When you saw us I was just trying to tell him no, Cloudio, this is imposible." I thought "no you werent, mum that's a big lie" and it was like I wanted to cry, I said "but you put your fingers on his ears, I saw it." But mum just went on in her nothing voice, she said "I was just trying to stop him from getting more upsit."

I thought "its good if he gets upset" and I said "what about Gus, does he want to get married too?" I thought "mum will just say poor Gus is sad as well" but she didn't at all, suddenly she sounded really cross, she said "for goodness sake, is that what all this is about then Lawrence" she said "Gus isn't intrested in getting married to anyone." I said "but he was talking and talking to you" and mum said "this is so stupid. Gus just likes talking, but he's only intrested in himself. In fact if Gus married anyone he'd marry himself."

I didn't want to laugh, I wanted to be really serious, but it was so hard, because it was just so funny thinking Gus will get married to himself, he will be mr and mrs Gus dog. I tried to sort of put my laughing in a box, but then it all just came out in a big kind of snort and after that I couldn't stop. That was bad, because mum didn't laugh at all, she was just quiet like she was thinking "you are so stupid" she said "stop it Lawrence, you'll wake Jemima" so I thought "you really really hate me now." I thought "why did I think Gus dog was horrible, that was silly" and suddenly I just wanted to hide under the bed, though this was impossible of course because it was just a matrass on the floor, nobody could go under it, not even a beetle. I thought "I wish I hadn't done that pillow fight. I wish I hadn't done Guses books and Freddies quils and poems."

Then mum started again in her serious voice. She said "Lawrence this is a very difficult time for us" she said "we don't have anywhere to live, we need peoples help, cant you see that?" so I said "yes mum." She said "I want you to promise you'll behave really well to everybody from now on, will you do that?" After that she stopped, she was waiting. I didn't really want to promise actually, I don't know why, but I knew I had to. I thought "mum hates me now, and if I don't promise then I bet she will really really hate me, she will probably hate me forever" so I just did it, I made myself. I said "I promise mum" and she gave a hug, it wasn't a really big one but I didn't care, I wanted it.

THE SUN IS MADE OF GAS, it is soft, it is like a big hot jelly. The middle of the sun is like a bomb, it is always blowing up and this makes waves go out, they make the edges vibrate in and out every few minutes so its almost like the sun is breatheing.

Scientists looked at it a lot, they had to use special telescopes because it is so bright, you must never look at it just with your eyes or they will get burnt out, you will go blind. Scientists noticed the sun is always changing, sometimes its just normal, it is quiet, but then slowly it gets busier, its like it gets angry, it takes years and years. First it gets sun spots, they are colder than the rest but they are still really hot of course, they are boilling, and they are really huge, they are as big as a planet. Then when the sun gets really angry it spits out flares, they are made of electric gas which is called plasma, and they shoot out like huge arms, they explode like bombs.

One day the Sientists looked up and saw that a flare was coming right at earth, and though we are millions of miles away, it was coming really fast, they thought "uhoh its going to hit us" but it was all right, everybody was safe because it was stopped by something called the magnetic field, so it didn't blow us up after all, actually nobody even notised.

But then scientists thought "those flares could be really dangerous." Because they might hit satelites that are up in space, because they are not protected by the magnetic field at all, they will get broken, and then suddenly peoples sellphones and televisions won't work any more, it will be a disaster. Scientists got so worried that one day they built a special satellite, it is called soho and it is far away in space, it watches the sun all the time really carefully and says if its making a terrible flair that will come right for earth. Then the scientists will say "switch off all the satelites right now." But I think they must be really quick or it will be too late, the satelites will get broken after all. Then nobodies television will work so they will miss their favorite programs, and their sell phones won't work either, which will be really bad, because they won't get any warnings.

The next morning I thought "I don't want to meet any of those animals, Freddy chrismas bear or Gus dog or Marther, I just don't." Mum said "up you get you two, your going to the van-hootins, I've got to get to work" but when we went out of our room I notised all their doors were closed so I thought "oh thank goodness they're still sleeping." I said "lets be really quiet Jemima, its a new game."

Mum took us to the Vanhootins on a bus, and it was really nice being in their house, where we hadn't had a pillow fight or done anybodies poems, it was like I was good again. Jemima started telling Janiss pretty pig about what we did, she said "last night we did a big fight with . . ." but I stopped her, I said "Jemima come and look at this picture of a wale jumping out of the water."

When we finished our lessons and mum came to collect us she hardly looked at me, I just got a little kiss, so I thought "you are still cross." She said "we're just going to the house for a moment and then we're going to see Beppo because he's asked us over for dinner, isn't that nice?" Jemima said "oh yes, Beppo Beppo Beppo" but I thought "no it isn't nice, I don't want to go at all" but I couldn't do anything because I promised I'd be good, that was bad, that was awful.

Another awful thing happened when we were almost at Marther's house. Mum stopped and she said "Lawrence, Jemima, I want you to do me a favor, I want you to say your sorry about last night" and though she said both of us she only looked at me, I noticed it, so I thought "its like you are saying you are the really bad one Lawrence." Jemima didn't care, she said "oh yes" but I didn't want to at all, I just didn't, I looked at the house and I thought "I don't want to go in" but then I thought "but I promised."

They were all in the kitchen, Oska wasn't there, he was still busking, they were drinking wine, and mum sort of pushed us towards them, she said "Lawrence and Jemima have got something to tell you." Jemima said "sorry" she shouted it so loudly that Hilary laughed, and then they all looked at me, they were waiting. I thought "I wish we could just go back to those Vanhootins" but I made myself, I just did it, I said "I'm sorry about the pillow fight." I said it to Freddy Chrismas Bear because they were his poems, and he gave me a little smile, he said "that's okay Lawrence." Then Gus said "forget it kid" so I thought "you are nice after all, I'm sorry I made you a nasty dog." Hillery cow smiled too and even Martha gave me a look like she was saying "all right I suppose."

After that we went to Beppos. Mum said it wasn't that far so we walked. It was getting dark, I saw a shop selling postcards and I thought "I want to see those actually" so I went in, I just did it, mum and Jemima had to come after me, and then there was another shop with lots of glass bottles in different colors, so I went in there too, but then mum got annoyed, she said "stop daudeling Lawrence." After that we got to a square, there was a statue of a man in a big coat looking cross, and mum was looking at the map in her guidebook, she said "its somewhere round here" when suddenly I had a really good idea, because there was a stone bentch, I thought "I know, I'll go right to the end and then I'll jump off onto one leg, that will be good." But then d'you know what happened, I sort of fell down with a big crash so I thought "uhoh my leg really hurts now" and I sat down on the bench and I said "mum, I can't walk at all, I think its broken." Jemima got worried, she poked at my knee with her finger and said "will it come right off?" but mum wasn't nice at all, she said "I just haven't got time for this" and then she pulled my arm so I sort of had to walk, that was awfull, I thought "now everyone in this square will think I'm just stupid" I really hated that.

Then we went to Beppos. Beppo opened the door, he had funny hair, it was black with gray bits so it looked like someone on a ladder dropped paint on him, and he was very thin, he was a weasil. He and mum kissed their cheeks and I thought "I didn't like you even before when I never met you, and I really don't like you now" I thought "you made me look silly in the square." We sat down on sofas and I noticed there were some pictures on the walls, I thought "I know that one, its the colisseum" but it was the wrong color, it was red, and on the other wall there was the panthion but it was blue, so I thought "you have stupid pictures Beppo." But there was a lady there too, that was a surprise, Beppo said "this is Mariser who is from brazil, Mariser can you get us some olives?" and Mariser was very thin, she was pretty but cross, she was a cross otter. I thought "you don't want to get those olivs, you don't like us" I thought "but I'm glad you're here, Mariser, because then perhaps mum won't do Beppos ears after all."

I thought "I hope she won't, anyway" because mum was sitting next to him on the sofa and looking right at him like he was really interesting, it was like he was her favorite program on telly. She said "hows your wine collection going?" and he looked sad, he said "times are hard, Hannah, I had to sell it all" and mum frowned like this was terrible, she said "poor Beppo." Then I notised something, it was a big silver car on a shelf, so I thought "I bet that's heavy" I thought " I bet if you threw it it would really break something."

That was when Marisa said it was time for supper. I had an idea, I said "I have to go to the loo" but I didn't actually, I went back to the sitting room. I picked up the car and I was right, it was really heavy, but it had no floor with pipes and things underneath, it was just hollow, so I thought "this is a stupid car you've got Beppo, everyones feet will get scraped on the ground till theyre just bones." I looked round the room, there was a lamp shade and a funny animal on the floor, I think it was a lion, and a big table made out of glass. I made the car point at them all with its head lights, I went "vroom vroom" that was funny, but then I thought "all right mum" and I put it back on the shelf.

Dinner was lasanya, it was burnt, there were black bits, so I thought "I bet you did that on purpose, cross otter." Mum asked Beppo about the flat, she said "we'd just need it till the summer. So where is it?" and he said "its in Trastaveray" which mum really liked of course. He said "its my brothers flat actually" and mum said "how is Marco?" but Beppo looked cross like he ate a big piece of burnt lasanya, he said "he's doing pretty well, actually, he's in New York now, he's got his own gallery" which I knew, it's where you put pictures, I thought "why are you cross because Marcos got his gallery, don't you like pictures?" Then Beppo made a smily face like he was saying "I am such a nice kind weasil" and he said "I'm not really supposed to rent it out but I thought as your so desperete." Mum said "that's really nice of you, I'd love to see it" so when we finished our burnt supper we went to see the flat, we took a taxi. Mariser came too and I thought "thats good" I thought "you watch them, Mariser."

The flat was at the top of a big building so there were lots of stairs and as we went up I thought "actually it will be all right because I bet its horrible just like sneaky dolphins was, it will all just be a big waste of time." When we went in it was dark so Beppo had to switch on a light, but then he started opening the shutters, all the noise got in from the road, and suddenly I thought "actually this is a nice flat." It was really big you see, and it wasn't dirty or horreble, there were paintings on the walls of people in old clothes and when I looked out of a window I could just see a green tram going down the road with its lights, it went "ding ding ding" I thought "that's nice."

Mum was blinking and blinking, she said "oh and there's a little balconey, how lovely, and a washing machine too, that's so useful" she said "and it would be wonderful being here in Trasteveray" so I thought "she likes this flat" and Jemima was running up and down singing "itsey bitsy spider" so I thought "she likes it too." Then suddenly I thought "I don't like you Beppo but actually it would be really nice to have our own place, then we wouldn't have to stay with any more Cloudios or Marthers" I thought "the paintings are all high up, so Jemima won't be able to reck them" I thought "and I could get all my cars and Tintins back from Chrissy chicks" and I thought "I can always put a chair against the door to keep Beppo out."

Mum said "how long could we have it for?" and Beppo said "Marco probably won't come back before the summer, but if he does you'd have to move out straight away, you'd have to leave everything just like it was, then you could come back again when he's gone." Mum just nodded, she said "so how much d'you want?" and a funny thing happened, you see suddenly she wasn't looking like Beppo was her favorite program on the telly and he wasn't looking like he was the nicest, kindest weasil. So I thought "its like they were just pretending" I thought "you were just being nice to him because you wanted to get this flat, mum" I thought "I don't think you're going to do his ears after all" I thought "hurrah hurrah."

Beppo said it was such a lovely flat he could get lots for it if he put an advertisment in porter portaisey, he could get three thousand yuros. Then mum got annoyed, she said "but you can't put it in porta portaisey, Beppo, because your not supposed to be renting it out, remember." Beppo gave her a look like he thought "you are rude" he said "so how much d'you want to pay?" and mum said "five hundred." Now Beppo looked like this was a really silly joke, he said "all right you can have it for a thousand" and Mariser was watching them from the sofa, she was laughing like they were a really funny cartoon. I thought "uhoh, I bet that's too much for mum" I thought "but I really want to live here now, I don't want to go back to special monkeys." Mum shook her head, she said "five hundred is all I can pay, not a penny more, if its not enough then we'll just go right now."

Beppo didn't say anything, he didn't answewer at all, and then something bad happened. Mum got all our jackets and she put them on us really quick. Jemima giggeled, she didn't understand, and I gave mum a look, I was saying "no no, don't do this, I like it here" but she didn't take any notise. I thought "why didn't you ask us if we like this flat" I thought "you always ask us usually" but it was too late, because she was already pushing us through the door. Then there was a really strange thing. We were outside on the landing you see, we just started going down the stairs and I was thinking "oh no this is a pity" when suddenly Beppo came out after us and shouted "all right all right, you can have it."

I thought "oh yes, how amazing, hurrah" I thought "clever mum." We went down to the cash machine, mum got out her blue card and I thought "uhoh, I hope theres still some left" I thought "I wish I hadn't got that stupid radio controlled car" but there was enough actually, I thought "thank goodness." Beppo gave her the key and then he and Mariser went home, he said we mustn't break anything, especially the paintings.

So we went back up all the stairs, mum unlocked the door with her key and it felt really different now that Beppo and Mariser weren't there, because it was just ours now, it was so nice. I thought "hurrah hurrah, now we are real Romans" I thought "now we will really be safe."

CHAPTER FIVE

One day before I got the flu and dad came down from Scotland secretly, we were walking by the river near the cottege. It was really cold, there was a puddle with ice but it was holow, it was like glass with nothing underneath, so I jumped on it and broke it into little bits, that was fun. I said "mum, how come this puddles all frozen but the river is just water?" but she didn't answer, I don't think she heard me, actually, because she was looking at something up ahead, it was two bigger boys. I thought "what are they doing?" because they were throwing something and then suddenly mum shouted really loudly, it was like a scream, she said "stop that."

Then I saw what they were doing, because they were throwing little stones at a swan. When they saw mum they ran away but she ran after them, she was screeming so loud, I thought "you are really angry" she said "leave that poor thing alone." I looked at the swan but it was all right, actually, it was swimming along, it wasn't bleeding or dead or anything, it just looked cross. Then a funny thing happened because mum started crying, her face went red and I could see tears dribling down her face. Jemima looked all worried, so I said "what is it mum, the swans all right" but she said "I really just hate that. And the poor things all alone." Then she did a little smile, that was better, she crouched down and gave us a hug, she said "I'm so lucky, I've got you two, I don't need anybody else" and I laughed, I said "that's good, because we hardly know anybody else."

I think about that day sometimes, I don't really know why. I went right down to the edge of the water to be nice to the swan, I thought "mum will like that" but it just gave me a great big hiss and swam away.

I thought of my brilliant new plan just after we moved all our things into our new flat. Mum said we could have a treat to celebraite, just a little one, so we went to the toy shops in piatsa Navona. I got a Roman soldier, it wasn't an emperor because they didn't have any new ones and I didn't want two Julius Casaers, it was a gladiater, and Jemima got one too because she always wants what I have. Afterwards we went to a market so mum could look at all the vegetables, because she wanted to have a dinner party to say thank you to all her friends for helping us, she said "look at these oranges, aren't they amazing, you never see them big like this in rainy old England" and that was when I suddenly had my brilliant idea, I thought "I know, I will get lots and lots of roman solders so I have a whole army, I will get a fort and enemies so I can make real battles."

I told mum my idea but she just made a face, that was annoying, she said "Lawrence love, their eight yuros each, maybe you can have another one for easter." I said "but then I'll just have three, that's not an army at all." I thought "even if I can get Jemimas off her, if I can swop it for something, and even if she gets another one for easter and I swop that too, I'll still just have five, which isn't enough for a battle at all" but mum said "you've just had a big car, Lawrence, remember." After that we went to the supermarket and I went into a toy shop near it, I just ran in so mum and Jemima had to follow, but they only had three solders and they were just the same, they were eight yuros too, and Mum got a bit cross, she said "I told you, Lawrence, you can have one at easter."

When we got back there was a surprise. I saw her first, sitting at the café by our buildings door, I said "look mum, its Franseen." Franseen stood up, she smiled like she was a bit annoyed actually and she said "you never even told me you found a flat. Gus told me."

I thought "uhoh, please don't have a big argument you two, don't do your ray gun looks" and Jemima was watching too, but actually it was all right, mum said "we've only just moved in, Franseen." Then Franseen said "are you going to ask me up?" and mum said "of course." Franseen really liked it, she said "look at this, well done Beppo, I must ask if he has somewhere for me." I wanted her to stay, I wanted to show her my Julius Ceasaer and my new gladiator, but she said no, really she must go. Then she said "I brought you something" so I thought "oh good" and Jemima squealed and ran up to see. Mine was another hideous history, it was called Fanatical Fascists, I thought "I bet that's

136

good" and Jemimas was a furry frog, when you pressed its tummy it did a croke. Then Franseen said a silly thing, she said "I wrote my telephone number in back of the book Lawrence, you know, just in case something goes wrong or someone gets lost" she said "its my sellphone so you can ring me anytime." I thought "that's nice but its silly" so I said "but we never get lost, mum has her guide book with maps" and I looked at mum, but she didn't say anything, she just sort of blinked.

ONE DAY THERE WAS a big fire in Rome, it went on for days, some people said Nero did it because he was emporer but nobody was sure. Thousands of famous temples and houses got burnt down and Nero went up a tower to watch, he said "doesn't it look beautifull" and then he sang a long song.

When the fire finished rome was all burnt, there were just little black pieces of stone and wood, even Nero's palace was burnt down, so he was really sad, he said "oh no, this is dreadfull, where will I live now." Then he decided "I know, I will build myself a new palace and it'll be much better this time, it will be huge" and that's what he did. It was the biggest palace in the world, it took years and it was called Neros golden House, theres still a bit left but you have to ring up and book and we never remembered. It was so big that there were arcades you could walk along for miles, there was a lake that was like the sea, there were huge gardens and forests. There were bathrooms with special different taps so you got seawater, or water with sulfer in it, that is yellow and smells horreble, and there were dining rooms with cielings that went round and round so flowers fell on your head. When you went in there was a huge room with a statue a hundred and twenty feet high, it was of Nero.

When everything was finished and the builders went home Nero took all his things to his new palace, he arranged them nicely and then he asked all his freinds round for supper. He walked all round his new palace and he felt so happy, he smiled and smiled, he said "thank goodness, at last now I have my own place again, isn't it lovely" he said "now everything will be all right."

The next day was Sunday and we went to Ikeyer which was miles away, so we went in the car, it was because mum said it was very cheap. I said "will they have roman solders there?" and mum said "we'll just have to wait and see." Ikeyer was huge, it was like an air port, but they didn't have anything, they just had lots of tables and cuboards etc and some balls and big green snakes and plastic tents, they didn't have any roman solders at all. A man tried to rob mum again, he started unziping her hand bag when she was looking at forks but he ran away when mum screemed and after that we got Jemimas bed, which was why we went to Ikeyer actually, because she didn't have one in our flat you see, she was still just in mums bed. The bed came in big card board boxes that were really heavy, mum said you had to put it together yourself, it cost sixty yuros and mum said it was a real bargin, so I said "mum when we get back home can I have roman solders that cost sixty yuros, that will be fair" but mum got really annoyed, she said "Jemima needs a bed, you've already got one, now stop it Lawrence."

When we drove back I thought "I wonder what I can do?" I thought "Peter Norris does a paper round, he gets up really early in the morning and goes on his bicycle but mum says he is much too young and anyway Rome is all just flats and I don't have a bicicle." When we got back and stopped the car mum said she couldn't carry Jemimas bed because it was too heavy, she said "I don't know how I'm going to do this" but fortunately just then a man with a tiny beerd like a triangle parked his motor bike and he helped us, he carried the really heavy box up the stairs. I helped with the other one, I held the end, and as we were going up I had another really good idea, I thought "oh yes hurrah, that's the answer."

I told it to mum when we went back down, we had to hurry because mum blocked another car, we could hear it honking, I said "I want to swop my new radio controled car for lots of Roman solders." But mum didn't like my new idea, she said "this really isn't the time Lawrence, and anyway they won't take it back now, we threw away the box remember, they'd only take it back if it didn't work." I thought about that, and then as we drove round and round looking for a parking place I had another idea. When we got back to the flat I gave Hermann his new water and nuts and then I looked everywhere until I found a screw driver, it was in a drawer in the kitchen, and I unscrewed the radio controlled car really carefully, I opened it up like it was a big mouth. Then I got some scissors and cut a little red wire and it worked, when I screwed it all together again it didn't work at all, I moved the control stick but it didn't do anything. Mum said "that was a really stupid thing to do" but I thought "you just wait mum."

Then a funny thing happened. I thought "what will I do now, I know, I will read my new Hidious History, Fanatical Fashists" but I couldn't find it. It wasn't in the sitting room or my bedroom or anywhere. I asked mum and she helped look, but we still couldn't find it, and then she said "unless it dropped in the trash can by mistake." I thought "uhoh, of course" because I often worry about that actually, because once the garbagemen take it away its lost forever, because they will put it in a huge field full of millions and millions of bags of rubbish, they will never remember where they put yours. So I went really quickly into the kitchen to look in the garbage bag but there was hardly anything, it was just egg shells and things. Mum frowned and said "actually I took out a bag last night" so we all went down stairs, Jemima came too so she wouldn't be left behind, but there weren't any garbage bags at all, they were gone.

That was sad. I said "my lovely new hideous history, and I never read any of it." Mum was nice, we started going back up the stairs and she said "don't worry Lawrence, I'll get you another one." Jemima was silly, she said "and can I have another frog" which wasn't fair at all, because she still had her frog, it didn't get thrown away, but I didn't take any notice, I said "we can ask Franseen where the shop is where she got it when she comes to our dinner" because that was all arranged now, it was going to happen the day after tomorrow, mum already asked her friends and they all said they were coming. But then mum was just unlocking our door with her key when she said a funny thing, she sort of said it into the door, she said "Franseen isn't coming."

That was strange. I said "why not, mum, is she ill?" but mum said "no, there just aren't enough chairs." I said "but we have to ask Franseen, mum, because she's really nice, she let us stay in her flat and gave me and Jemima all those things" and Jemima said "yes yes, Franseens nice" but it didn't work. Suddenly Mum looked really cross, she goes like that sometimes, her voice went really loud and she said "didn't you hear what I said, there aren't enough chairs? We'll just have to ask her another time" and I almost said "no you have to ask her now, mum, you must" but I didn't in the end, I just didn't feel like it.

THE NEXT MORNING MUM WOKE us up early so we could go to the market and get food for the dinner. She said "tell me, lesonfon, is there anything special you want me to make? You have to tell me right now." Jemima jumped up and down, she said "I want a pink cake" which was stupid actually, so I told her "don't be silly Jemima, because that is for babies, this is a grown up dinner" but mum said "no, we can have that" and I got a bit annoyed, I thought "mum always does what Jemima says, its not fair" so I said "I want chicken with black sauce" but mum just laughed, she said "I'll see what I can do."

We went to the market, we bought all the things, and mum said "the vegtable lady wasn't very friendly today" and I said "perhaps she was just really busy" and Jemima said "she was nice, she gave me my apple" but mum said "the cheese man wasn't friendly either" though I thought he was all right, I said "he said chow bella."

After that we took everything back home and then Jemima

and me went to the Vanhootins. That was annoying actually, because I wanted to do my new plan, but then it was all right after all, because mum wasn't late from work this time, she said "I need to get a few things from a shop just across the river" so I thought "oh good, hurrah" and I said "is it near the piazzer Navona, because then I can take my radio controlled car back." Mum just looked at me, she said "you are a real pest sometimes Lawrence" but we went anyway. We had to go home first to get the car, mum said "this is just ridiculous" and d'you know it worked. I cleaned the wheels so it didn't look like I drove it round and round the fountain, I said it just broke down, and though the man was really suspicious, he looked at the car and tried to make it go, he changed the batteries and then he looked at mums riseet again and again, in the end he said "all right" quite crossly.

So I got twelve new solders and a catapult, I already had two of course, which meant if I got Jemimas off her I would have fifteen. I thought "hurrah, this is a really good army" I thought "if I get another one at easter and I get Jemimas easter one too I will have seventeen." Only one solder was an enemy. Mum said the romans worst enimy was the Germans but they didn't have any left so I got a Swiss Guard instead. He had a helmet and clothes with lots of colors, mum said they guard the pope, she said he would be fine because the Swiss are right next to Germany, they are almost the same, he was holding a spear with an ax on the end.

After that we went home, and when we were walking down our street mum said "oh look, that yellow car, I notised it there before" so I said "that's not like dads either, its too small" and mum said "I know Lawrence love" but she looked in the windshield and then up at the building above it, which was flats just like ours. Then Jemima did a kind of jumping dance, she sang "yellow car, yellow car" like it was a song, she is so silly, I got so annoyed, I said "shhhh Jemima, just shut up."

When we got home I showed Hermann all my new roman soldiers and I think he liked them too, he poked his nose through the bars. Then we did lots of cooking for the meal. Mum made red sauce for the spaggeties, it was tomato, she made lots in a big pot, it smelt really nice, and we helped, I peeled all the onions even though they made me cry, I said "what about the black sauce?" and mum said "we'll do that tomorrow." After that we made Jemimas pink cake, Jemima and me poured lots of things in the mixture and mum let us lick the spoons, then she did the pink iceing, she said "we'll put in the strawberries and cream tommorow."

That night I couldn't sleep. There was a big thunder storm with lots of rain so it sounded like there was something really heavy like a steam roller on the roof, there was thunder and lightning. Hermann was going round and round in his wheel, I think he was a bit frightened, actually, so I went up to his cage and wispered "its all right Hermann, its just thunder" and actually I didn't need to wisper I think, because Jemima didn't wake up even when the thunder was so loud it made me jump, mum says she would sleep through an earth quake. I kept thinking about my soldiers, I had them all in a neet line on the shelf and I kept looking at them, even though it was hard to see them in the dark, they were just like sort of black lines. I thought "they are really

143

really good" I thought "tomorrow I will build the fort, I will tell mum I need some gray paint, I will make it out of cardbord from serial packets, it will have towers and a flag and it will be just like a real fort, I will show all mums friends when they come." I could imagine every bit of it, there were doors and a draw bridge, it was amazing. I decided "I will put the enemy in the fort and then Julius Caesaer will shout 'now' and all the romans will attack, they will fire stones with the catapult and some will sneak up from the side so the enemy won't see."

I was still thinking about my fort when I heard footsteps going past outside the bedroom door. I thought "the thunderstorm has woken mum up and now shes going to the loo" which she does in the night sometimes, but then a strange thing happened. Eventually the thunderstorm stopped you see, it just went drip instead, but I then heard mum walking past again so I thought "she just went to the loo, wheres she going now?" After that she came back again so I thought "she is going to bed now, thats all right" but then she was walking again, actually it was almost like she was running, her feet were going so fast, they went "tap tap tap," that was funny. I thought "what are you doing mum?" I thought "I will lisen really carfully to see what you do next" but I don't remember anything after that, so I think I just fell asleep.

When I woke up the sun was shining on the floor in a thin line, it was warm and something was strange, something was wrong, I didn't know what. Jemima was still sleeping, I thought "you big lazy bones" and I got out of bed. Mum was in the sitting room, she was in her dressing gown, she had a chair but she wasn't sitting in it, she was standing and looking out of the window like there was something really intresting out there. I said "what are you looking at, mum?" and she jumped a bit, she gave me a cross look and said "Lawrence, you scared me" and that was when I realized what was funny. Everything was quiet you see, there weren't lots of cars, and the sun was really warm, so I looked at the clock and I was right, it said "ten oh five." I said "mum, why didn't you wake us up, its really late, what about the Vanhootins and your job?" Mum gave me a funny look, she sort of blinked, and she said "lets just stay here today, Lawrence love, I think its going to rain."

The window was open and I could hear a man shouting "percay" which means "why." I thought "theres a little cloud over there but mostly it is nice, its a lovely sunny day, I don't think it will rain and usually mum doesn't mind getting wet anyway." I said "but you have to go to work, mum, the cristians will be cross." Mum frowned like she had a headake, she didn't say anything, I thought "she's not going to answer me, shes not going to talk at all," and then I thought of something else, I said "and what about your diner." But mum just shook her head like I hadn't listened to her, she said "I think perhaps we should do that another time."

Now I thought "what will I do?" I thought "probably it is too late for the cristians and the Vanhootins because Jemima is still in dreamland, we aren't dressed and we haven't even had our breakfast" but I thought "but we have to do the diner party, if we don't then everything will go bad, I just know it." So I said "but you've asked them all, you promised, and I was really looking forward to it" which was true actually, I wanted to show them all my new solders. Mum made her headache face but I thought "oh no you don't" and I was really quick, I said something I don't say to mum, even if she has gone funny I don't say it, I just don't like to, I thought "I will just try" so I said "mum, are you all right?" She gave me a look so I thought "uhoh it's not working" but then she said "I'm fine Lawrence, don't be silly" so I said "then lets do the diner party" and d'you know it worked, mum closed her eyes like I was a really big pest but she said "all right all right we'll have the dam thing" so I thought "that's good."

After that everything was a bit better. Mum rang the Vanhootins and her cristians to say we werent coming today, she said Jemima had a bad nose bleed which was a lie of course, and the Vanhootins didn't mind but the cristians were annoyed just like I thought, they told mum "all right just this once." Jemima woke up, we had breakfast and we went out to go shopping, but on the stairs mum kept stopping and sort of looking round the corner, that was funny, it was like she was scared, so I thought "who are you frightened of mum, is it Chintsier and Gabrielley, is it Beppo, does his brother want his flat back?" Eventually we got all the rest of the food for the diner, so I said "mum, can we go and get some gray paint now, I need it for my fort" but she got cross, she said "no we have to hurry up and get all the food ready" that was a shame.

So we did the strawberries and cream in Jemimas pink cake, and then mum did another cake which was choclate. After that we did the chicken too, mum did a sauce with mushrooms, and I said "but that's not black that's brown" but mum said "its near enough." When we finished the potatoes I thought "there's a bit of time left, I can still do a little bit on my fort, I can make a start" but then mum said "Lawrence, can you help me clear up the sitting room." So we moved all the chairs, mum put lots of plates and glasses on the table, she said "they'll just have to help themselves and eat it on their laps" and I thought "doesn't it look beautifull."

After that mum put on new clothes and they all started arriving. The doorbell rang again and again, Jemima tried to get it but I was quicker, so I never did do my fort in the end, but I didn't mind, actually, I just thought "hurrah, it's a party." First it was the Vanhootins, and they really liked our flat, everybody did actually, Bill vanhootin said "these paintings are quite something." After that it was mum's cristians, and they weren't cross any more that mum didn't go to work today, they said "what a wonderful cooking smell" so I thought "I really must give you your animals now, you cristians" but there wasn't time, because more people kept coming.

It was Crissy, she gave mum a big hug and then she said "is Franseen here yet?" and mum gave her a look, she said "she's not coming actually" so I thought "uhoh" but it was all right, because then the door bell went again and it was Marther special monkey's house, all five of them. They really liked our flat too, Gus said "you jamy beggars" and Freddy chrismas bear said "a penthouse of wonders." Then suddenly I looked all round and I thought "what a lot of people there are in our flat, isn't it amazing, its like we are in a train."

Though I hadn't done my fort I showed Crissy chick my roman solders, I told them I was going to make a fort later, and she said "how lovely." Then I showed Hermann to Tina mouse and Leonora bossy rabbit, I let them hold him for a bit and they really liked him, they said "hes so cute" and then I showed them all our toys to cheer them up and they said "wow you've got lots of leggo." After that I showed them how we could make lots of things like cars and airoplanes, not just walls, and I showed them my tintins but they could only look at them a bit because mum came in and said dinner was ready.

Everybody said mums pasta with tomato sauce was really delicious, I had seconds, then I had chicken too, I scraped off all the mushroom sauce because I don't like that, and though it was on my lap so I had to be really careful I only spiled a tiny bit, it didn't go on the carpet. Janniss pretty pig made everyone say "cheers" she said "heres to the cook, heres to Hannah" and mum was smiling like she might go "pop" she wasn't sad at all any more, so I thought "that's good, shes all right now."

After that we had the cakes, everybody liked them too, but then Crissy and mums cristians said they had to go home now, so I thought "no don't go yet, please don't go because this is all so nice, why can't you stay." Jemima fell asleep on the sofa so mum put her to bed, and then the Vanhootins all went too, that was a shame, which just left Marthers ones. They stayed a bit, Gus opened some more wine, which was nice even though they weren't my favorites, I thought "my favorites are Crissy chick and the Vanhootins I think." But then they all got up too, Hillary nice cow said "I brought you some jinger biscuits I made" I tried one and it was nice, you had to chew it really hard. Freddy Crismas bear gave mum a poem on a piece of paper, it was about the moon going up into the sky above rome and watching all the people eating dinner and drinking wine and driving on their motor bikes, mum said "oh freddy, how lovely." Marther special monkey said "you must all come over to dinner really soon, come next week" and Gus was funny, he said "no come tommorow, actually come right now" and Oska did his funny face like he was going "pling pling" because he didn't have his giutar of course, he left it at home, but everyone laughed anyway.

So we shut the front door and suddenly the flat was really quiet and empty, it felt all sad. Mum started clearing up all the plates and things and she looked tired so I said "I'll help you mum" but she said "no Lawrence love, you go to bed, its really late" so I did. I got into my pijamas, I brushed my teeth and I said good night. Then I lay in bed, I could hear mum doing washing up in the kitchen, and I thought "mum should let me help, actually, because I cant go to sleep at all because I am so excited" I thought "I bet I'll be awake all night, I bet I'll be awake till dawn" I thought "I must remember to tell mum we must have another dinner party like that really soon."

SUDDENLY IT WAS DARK and someone was shaking my arm so I thought "whats happening?" She was wispering "Lawrence wake up, please wake up" and it was mum, I could see her face from the light that came round the curtin and her eyes looked funny, it was like she was scared but she was all excited. I thought "uhoh, whats this?" She said "we mustn't wake Jemima, something's happened" so I got out of bed quietly, I followed her out, and I was thinking "I wonder what it is, is it a burgler or did something get broken, was it one of the pictures of people in old cloths? Or did somebody ring up from england, did the cottage get burnt down?" But it wasn't any of these things at all actually. We went to the kitchen, the light was really bright so my eyes went blink, then mum opened the fridge and took out one of the cakes that we had for pudding, it was Jemimas pink one, there was just a big slice left, and mum said "look."

I looked but I couldn't see anything, it just looked like cake, so I said "what is it, I don't understand." Mum pointed at it again and this time I notised that there were some tiny red spots, I didn't see them before, so I said "what are they mum, are they juice from the strawberries?" but mum shook her head, she looked sort of sad now, she was holding the cake and she was looking at the floor. She said "smell it, Lawrence love, its poisson."

I didn't understand. I smelt it and I thought "actually it does smell a bit funny I suppose." I said "what d'you mean?" and then mum started crying a bit, she said "Lawrence love, I'm so sorry, the last thing I wanted is to scare you with all of this but I'm so worried, I found out yesterday but I didn't want to tell you, actually I didn't want to believe it myself. But you have to know, for your own safety. Your fathers here in Rome. He's followed us. Its so awful. Just when we've finally got everything sorted out this happens."

I could hear a car go beep somewhere, it was quiet so I thought "that cars a long way away" and then I thought "here I am with mum by the fridge in the middle of the night" I don't know why I thought that. I looked at the red spots and I thought "if I eat those will I die?" and suddenley I wanted to touch them, that was stupid, I knew I couldn't really. I thought "so that was why she kept stopping and looking round the corner when we went down the stairs, she was watching for dad." I felt like my arms went all heavy, I thought "this is dreadfull, we came all the way here to be safe and now we aren't after all" and suddenley I got angry, I thought "why does he have to follow us everywhere like this, why does he have to put poison on the cake and spoil everything every time." I thought "I really hate him" I thought of his face with his hair that went up like smoke and I wanted to hit it hard so it was just gone, it was all smashed away to nothing. But then a funny thing happened, I thought "wait a minute" and I said "but he cant be, mum, he doesn't even know we're here."

Now mum was exited again, she wasn't crying any more, she wiped her nose with a paper hankercheef, her eyes were all quick and looking and she said "just come over here." We went into the sitting room to a window, I thought "is he down there in the road?" but when I started looking out of the window she stopped me, she said "be careful Lawrence love" and she just let me look round the edge. She said "over there, d'you see?" It was another big building down the road a bit, it was just like ours, I didn't understand. Mum said "you see those windows at the top, the shutters were all closed before, now they're open, he's in there, he's watching us. I saw him, I'm sure of it. That was last night, but it was just the same. The shutters were shut during the day but open in the evening."

I said "are you sure it was him?" and mum gave me a look

like I was being so stupid but she didn't want to get cross, she said "don't you remember the car, the yellow car, it was parked just below there." I thought "but mum . . ." I said "that wasn't his car, it was different" but she said "of course it wasn't his, but he always likes that color, don't you see, so he hired that one when he flew here. I bet he came with rianair, they come from scotland now, I saw it on a poster." I said "but you still haven't told me, mum, how would he know we're here in Rome?"

Now mum got annoyed, her arms went in the air like she was throwing up little balls and she said "Franseen of course. She told him. Haven't you noticed how strange she's been to us. She really hates me, I know it." Then she wispered. "I never told you this, Lawrence, because I didn't want to upset you, but all those years ago when I lived here, Franseen really liked your father." I said "you mean she wanted to get married to him?" and mum said "that's right. So that's why she wants to hurt us, d'you see, she hates me because I got away from him, because I got us all away, they both do."

I didn't know, actually. I thought "mum is clever" I thought about Franseen cat liking dad years ago, I thought "go away cat, leave him alone" but then I thought "but Franseens nice, she gave me my hideous histeries." And then suddenly I thought of something else, I thought "oh yes, hurrah" I thought "why didn't I think of that before, thats silly" I thought "we're safe after all" so I said "but mum, he can't have poissoned the cake, because the front doors locked, remember, he can't get in." But Mum didn't look pleased like I thought, that was a pity, she just shook her head and said "it was Beppo, Lawrence love, can't you see. Beppo gave him the key. Beppo would do anything for money." She said "your father must have been here for days. That's how he's already been turning people against us, like the woman in the market."

Suddenly I felt all sort of tired, like all the breathe went out of me. I thought "it was all so nice, and now its broken." I think mum saw, because she looked sad again, she closed her eyes and said "I'm so sorry about all of this, Lawrence. I really shouldn't have told you, I tried not to, but I was so worried, I thought you just had to know." Then everything went quiet, mum was looking at me, so I thought "now she is waiting" and d'you know I couldn't think what to say. It was like all my thoughts went somewhere else and there was just an empty space.

I didn't want to make mum worse, I didn't mean to, I thought "I must help her" but it was like it didn't work. I thought "I want to go back to bed" and then suddenly I just said it, I didn't mean to, it was like an acident, I said "but Franseens always really nice." That was wrong, mum looked surprised like I hit her. She said "he could come back at any moment, for goodness sake Lawrence, I really need your help." I tried to get scared, I really did, but somehow it all went wrong again, so I said "its really late mum, hes probably gone to bed" and she turned away, she frowned like she had her headacke, she said "what d'you think, should we put a chair against the door?"

She was waiting again. I thought "why are you asking me, mum, you usually do the chair against the door, you don't ask me" so I said "I don't know, I suppose so" and d'you know that was what got her really angry, it was funny, I only said "I don't know I suppose so." She gave me a look like I was horreble, like

I was a really bad boy, and she said "all right then I'll just do it myself." So she went off with a kind of thumping walk and got a chair from the dining room and I tried to help her, I tried to carry one of its legs, but it was too late, she wouldn't let me now, she lifted it high up so I had to let go, actually it hurt my hand a bit but I didn't say anything. Then she put it against the front door and walked off, she didn't look at me at all.

I thought "all right then, mum, I'll just go to bed then, it's the middle of the night isnt it." But it was hard to sleep, I could hear Jemima breathing and then I heard mum walking about, she went past again and again so I thought "shes not tired" her feet went "tap tap tap tap" really fast so it was like she was in a race.

WHEN EMPORERS DIED they got made into Gods but only if they were good and everybody liked them. Caligula was bad and no-body liked him so one day he thought "I know, I won't wait until I'm dead, I will make myself into a god right now."

So he told everybody "I am a god actually" and he made his servants build a new temple. They made a statue out of gold and put it inside, it looked like Caligula, it was just the same size and every morning his servants dressed it up in the same cloths he was wearing that day. After that Caligula said "everybody can come and wership me now" and lots of people did, it was so he wouldn't execute them. Caligula was really pleased, he thought "I like being a god" and he started talking to all the other gods because he was just the same as them now, he talked to their statues in their temples. Sometimes he was cross with them, he shouted "I will get you for that" and sometimes they were his friends. His best freind was a god called Jupiter and Caligula liked him so much that he built a little house right next to Jupiters temple so he could go and stay with him sometimes.

After that Caligula decided that now he was a god everything had to be really special, it had to be just what a god would do. He had his bath in oil that was really expensive and for his supper he had pearls that were melted down in viniger, or special meat and vegtables that were all colored gold. I don't know what they tasted like, probably they were a bit funny but Caligula didn't mind as long as it was real gold gods food. Then he thought "wait a minute, what about my holidays, what does a god do for that?" so he got his servants to build him a boat which was enormous like a palace, it had thousands of slaves to push the oars, it had jewels stuck on the outside, it had a huge bath, it even had a collonnade where you could go for a nice walk. Calligula sat down on a special sofa on the boat, he listened to singers singing him lovely music and he watched the land go past far away, and he thought "oh yes, this is good, this is right, now I really am a proper god."

But there was a strange thing. Even though Caligula was like a proper god and did all his gods things, he still got really scared. When there was a big storm with thunder and lightning he hid under his blanket because it made him jump. Sometimes he got worried that Germans would invade Rome, he thought "oh no, they will come and get me" though of course this was impossible because there were no Germans for hundreds of miles and the Roman army was really strong, it would defeat them. Most of all he was scared that someone would sneak up and assasinate him, which was possible, actually, because everybody hated him. So he had thousands of people executed so they couldn't assassinate him, it was just in case.

Often he couldn't sleep at all, he lay awake for hours, he thought "its boring lying here." He got headaches which were really bad, he said "I feel all confused" he thought "I don't know whats happening." So he decided "I know, I will go to the seaside, that will help clear my head." But it didn't work. So poor god Caligula executed more and more people, he went to the seaside again and again, but it didn't help at all, his head just got worse and worse.

When I woke up I could hear the cars were quiet and the sun was hot which meant we hadn't gone to the Vanhootins again, mum hadn't gone to her job, so I thought "uhoh, those cristians will be really cross now." I could hear mum and Jemima outside, Jemima said "I don't want that one, I want my red dress" but I just stayed in bed, I didn't want to get up, I thought "I just don't feel like it." The shutters were open a bit so I could look out and see some sky and a roof, I thought "I wonder if dads in his building, I wonder if hes watching us" I thought "he might be." I thought "what will I tell Hermann?" but I couldn't think of anything, so I just said "hello Hermann."

A bit later the door opened and mum looked in, she was still cross, I could see it. She said "hurry up Lawrence, we're going out to get some breakfast at a café." I thought "that's strange, why does she want to go outside to a café when shes worried dads out there?" But then when I got up I saw there were two garbage bags by the door and I understood, I thought "oh yes of course, mum has thrown away all our food in case its poissoned, so we have to go out." I thought "I hope it really is poissoned or thats a big waste of food" but I didn't say anything, I didn't want to make mum crosser. I decided "I will just stay really quiet today, I will be like a mouse, it will be like I'm hardly here at all, then everything will be all right."

Mum rang up someone, I think it was her bank again, she said "no I can't come in and see you, I already told you that" so I thought "uhoh mum" I thought "you shouldn't have annoyed your cristians like that, they won't pay you now I bet." Then we went out, mum took both the garbage bags, she didn't even ask me, and on the stairs she kept stopping and looking round the corner. I thought "I know why you are doing that now, mum" and then a funny thing happened, because Jemima noticed too, she said "what are you looking for mum?" so I thought "what will you say now, what will you tell her?" and mum said "I'm just checking everything's all right, lamikin, I'm just checking there isn't a big dog or something." That was a big lie of course, and it was a mistake, actually, because Jemima is really frightened of dogs, even silly little ones like chiwawas, so she said "I want you to carry me mum" which mum couldn't do because of the garbage bags, so she made me stay with Jemima while she took them down, but then Jemima was a cry baby, she shouted "mummy mummy, what about the big dog, it will bite you." I told her "stop it Jemima, there isn't any dog, you silly" but it didn't help, she kept shouting until mum ran back up again.

Outside in the road I could see mum looking up at dads building, actually she was watching everywhere, her eyes were pointing like arrows. I looked for the yellow car but it was gone, so I thought "perhaps he has hidden it now." I thought "is dad suddenly going to come out of his buildings door right now?" I thought "is he going to jump out of that green tram, is he going to run out of that choclate shop" I thought "that will be really really bad" but he didn't, and then somehow I couldn't quite think it any more, I just kept forgetting, I thought "I wonder what crusson will I have, will I have jam or cremer?" We had to eat our breakfast really fast because mum got annoyed, she said "hurry up you two, we've got so much to do" and then in the end she got fed up and just pushed us out of the door, she said "you can finish your crussons on the way" but Jemima dropped hers on the pavment so we had to go back and get another one.

Then a funny thing happened. Mum went to the bank machine, I thought "that won't work I bet" but then she opened her purse and she undid a zip, I think it was a secret part, because she took out a new card, I never saw it before, it was brown. I said "that's new mum" but she just frowned, she pressed all the buttons really carefully and it worked, I think she got quite a lot of money actually, I only saw it for a moment because she put it into her purse but they were orange which are bigger than red or blue ones, they are fifties. Jemima tried to see too, she jumped up and down, but then mum gave us a look, she said "don't get any ideas, this really has to last. And then I have to think of some way to pay it all back."

After that we went to the supermarket, Jemima sat in the cart like she always has to, and we were both saying "I want strawber-

ries" or "I want that serial because I never had that one before."
Usually mum gets things we ask for, some of them anyway, but
this time she just got cross, she said "lisen you two, what did I
just say, I told you we have to make this money last." So we just
got lots of really borring things, it was spaggetties and tins of
tomatos and vegetables like onions, because mum said she was
going to make a really big sauce, and she got some funny milk in
blue boxes which she said you don't have to put in the fridge, she
got lots of oranges and tangerines but she wouldn't get any cherries, she said "they cost a fortune."

I thought "I wonder if there were cherries in that garbage bag
you threw away" I thought "if our food wasn't poissoned after all
then we could have spent this money on roman solders, I would
have a really huge army now, and roman solders are much better
than food, actually, because they last forever" but I didn't say anything, I was still keeping quiet, I just said "don't forget to get
more nuts for Hermann." I carried two bags and mum carried
two and she kept shouting "Jemima hold on to my fingers, I said
hold on to my fingers" which was because she was worried
Jemima would run off the pavement and get squoshed by a car,
or dad would jump out and get her, but he didn't actually.

After that we went to the lock shop, mum showed the man
her key and they talked in Italian, mum said "god, I didn't think
it would cost that much." Then she and the man went and looked
at bolts, which are big metal things which you pull out across
the door, and the man said "pomedridgeo" which I knew actually,
because siniora Morrow did that, it means "afternoon." Mum
opened her purse and she got out her blue card, she looked at it

for a bit, but then she put it back and she paid with her new yuro notes, there were still quite a lot left I think.

When we were going I thought "I will ask now" so I said "can we go to a paint shop now, mum, because I need some gray paint for my fort that I'm going to make" but mum said "not now Lawrence, we have to get all this food in the fridge." I thought "I don't care actually" I thought "I will make my fort anyway, the writing on the serial packet will just be grafeety, because my calamitous casears book said the romans had lots of grafeety." So I started, I did it in the sitting room, I brought Hermann over in his cage so he could watch, but he was asleep. I took the serial in its bag out of the packit, I thought "oh yes, this is really big, it will make a really good fort" but then when I started cutting it up it sort of went all smaller, I thought "I hope I've got enough selotape."

That was when the telephone rang. Mum said "hello, hello?" like there was nobody there, but she did a strange thing, I noticed it, Jemima didn't because she was busy trying to take her dolls dress off, which she couldn't because it was the cloth doll she got when I got my electric car and the cloths were all sewn on, that was silly. What mum did was she pulled the telephone plug right out of the wall. She did it quickly but I saw because roman phone plugs are really big you see, they are gray and round like half a tomato. I thought "why are you saying 'hello hello' mum, because you know you can't hear anything because you just pulled out the plug." I thought "nobody will be able to ring us now" but I didn't say anything, I just didn't feel like it, I did my fort.

I finished the tower, it was a bit wobbly but I thought "its not so bad". Then I went and looked for more boxes. One was biscuits, I put them all in a bowl, and another was for pasta, it was smaller but I thought "its still a box" so I put the pasta in another bowl, I thought "I wish we hadn't thrown away all the boxes for Jemimas bed, because they were really huge." Then I made the other tower, Jemima fell asleep, I ran out of selotape but I found a stapler with lots of staples, I joined the towers together with a wall, but the new one was wobbly too, and the writing didn't really look like grafeety even though it was upside down, it just looked like biscuit and pasta box writing. I tried to put the swiss guard on the tower but he kept falling over, it was because the roof wasn't straight, and I was still trying to fix it when mum came in. I said "this forts really difficult, mum" and she said "Lawrence, come with me, theres something you need to see."

I thought "what is it now, I hope we don't have to throw away all our new food again." I thought "I hope shes not cross because I took the boxes and put the pasta and biscuits in bowls." But she didn't take me to the kitchen, instead she took me into my and Jemimas bedroom, so I thought "I hope my roman solders are all right" but they were all still there in their line on the shelf. Mum took me over to my bed and she said "I was just making it and . . ." Then she lifted up the doovay and d'you know what was under it, that was a big surprise, I could hardly believe it, I thought "how did they get there?" Because you see there in my bed were two nives from the kitchen, I recognized them, they were the little sharp ones that mum used for chopping onions and carrots and things.

I said "I don't understand." Mum gave me a look like I said

something stupid or got a math sum wrong but she didn't mind, she said "he must have come in this morning when we were out at the shops." I looked at them and then I reached out and touched one, I don't know why I did that, I knew it was real of course, the metel bit was cold. I thought "I didn't put them here, Jemima didn't, because she was always with me" I thought "mum wouldn't put them here."

Then a funny thing happened, it was like a big door opened and suddenly I could see right in. I thought "so mum's right." And d'you know I could feel it now, it was like it was in my stomach, I thought "he really is in his building watching us" I thought "he did get in last night and poisson the cake" I thought "he was out there this morning, he might have jumped out of that green tram." Suddenly I felt all shivery, I thought "he was here in our flat when we were having our breakfast at the café" I thought "what if mum hadn't noticed, then we would have eaten that cake, we would have got poisoned, I would have just got into bed and got stabed."

I felt so angry. I thought "how dare you dad." I looked at mum but she wasn't sad, that was good, she wasn't squeezing her hair or scratching her hands, she was just watching me with her serious look, she was waiting, so I said "I really hate him." Then a funny thing happened, she sort of closed her eyes and she gave me a hug, she said "Lawrence love, we're going to be all right. All that matters is that we're together." That was good, that was nice, I thought "yes we can do this, actually its just like before" so I said "we mustn't tell Jemima because she is too young to understand" and mum said "your right, Lawrence." I said "we'd better put them away before she wakes up" so we got all the nives and put them back in the kitchen in the drawers.

I thought "what will we do now? We must make a plan." I said "let's check our food" and I counted it all, I said "this will last for ages but we'll still have to be carefull, we mustn't eat too much for our supper" and mum said "okay Lawrence" then she said "perhaps we should have a good look round the flat, so we know just what's here." So we did that, we looked in all the rooms, but we didn't find any more food except a few tins of tomatoes. But then mum said "how about up there?" and she pointed at the cieling, because there was a little door in it, mum said it was a hatch. She said "I think I'll have a look" so she put the table under it and then she put a chair on the table and climbed up.

I said "be careful mum" but she didn't fall down, she pushed the hatch so it opened and then she pulled herself up so she disappeared, even her feet. That was funny, I climbed on the table and I said "what is it mum, is there more food?" because I could hear her scraping lots of things around, and she said "nothing like that" so I thought "thats a shame" but then there was a surprise. Suddenly there was a bang and a big empty cardbord box fell right down on the table beside me, and then two more as well. Mum was looking down out of the hatch and she was holding a tin, she said "look what I found." I didn't understand, I said "what is it mum" and she laughed, she said "paint you silly, we can make a new fort." It wasn't grey, it was cream, mum said it was for the walls, but that was all right, I thought "oh yes, hurrah."

So we started the new fort. Hermann woke up now so he

watched through the bars. Mum said this time we must do a plan first, she found some paper and a pencil and she did a picture, shes really good at drawing actually, it had four towers and four walls holding them together, there was a flag. I thought "these boxes are much bigger than the serial box, and the card board is much thicker too" I thought "this fort will be amazing like the one I thought about in the night" and that was when I heard the doorbell ring. At first I didn't think anything, I just thought "I wonder who that is" but then I suddenly remembered.

I looked at mum and the smile she had from drawing the fort all went away, it was like someone just switched it off, her eyes went blink blink and she started touching the back of her hand with her finger nails. I looked out of the window at dads building and the shutters were still open, but then I thought "that doesn't mean he's still in there." I said "what if its not him mum, it might be someone nice like the vanhootins or your cristians?" But mum didn't say anything, she just shook her head. I stood up, the buzzer for the door was on the wall just there, I said "shouldn't we find out who it is, because if its someone nice then we can ask them to bring us some more food" but mum put her hand over the buzer, she said "if its him and we answer then he'll know we're up here."

I thought "all right" so I sat down again, I thought "we won't do anything then." I looked at mum's drawing of the fort and I said "so where will the enemy go?" Mum sat down too, and that was when we heard it. The front door was behind us, you see, so you could hear right through it, and suddenly there was a noise, it was quite small, it went "tap tap tap" and it was footsteps. I looked at mum and her eyes went wide, I said "its probably just someone going to another flat" because there were lots in the building you see, but then the footsteps kept getting louder and louder. Then mum got up, she ran into the kitchen and she came back with a nife, it wasn't like the tiny ones in my bed it was a big one, you would cut up something big like a chicken with it, and she whispered, and though her voice was quiet it was like she was shouting, that was funny, it was like she was spitting it, she said "I'm not going to let him hurt you." I thought "what will I do?" I looked at the door and the lock was locked, the key was in it, the bolt was shut too, so I thought "that's all right" but then I turned round and picked up a chair anyway, I picked it up so I could hit him on his head.

I was all ready when the footsteps stopped, I thought "he is just outside" that was strange, I thought "hes just inches away" I thought "if it wasn't for this door I could just reach out and touch him, I could hit him with my chair." Then suddenly there was the knock on the door, it sounded so loud, it was like it was a gun, and a voice said "Hannah, are you there?" and I thought "wait a minute" I thought "its not dad after all" and just for a moment I thought "its all right, its Franseen" and I wanted to just open the door. But then I looked at mum and she was frowning and holding her nife so I thought "oh no you don't Franseen you traiter cat" and I gave mum a special angry look, I held my chair a bit higher and mum gave me a little serious nod, so it was nice actually, it was like we were solders in a battile.

Then something funny happened, there was another voice and it said "Hannah, Lawrence, Jemima, are you there, we tried your doorbell but I'm not sure its working." I could hardly believe it actually, but this time I was readier, I didn't think "oh hurrah" I thought "Crissy chick, you too" I thought "how dare you after all I did, trying to cheer you up passing the salt and telling you about our amusement park." I was so angry, I thought "he has turned them all against us" I thought "she was our freind, I really hate you, dad."

Then I got worried, I thought "what if Jemima wakes up because they are shouting, she won't understand, she will run out and shout hello and they'll know we're in here." So I gave mum a look to say "I have to do something" I put my chair down really carefully so it didn't make any scrapeing noise, and I went back to our bedroom, I closed the door with just a tiny click, and it worked, she didn't wake up at all. When I got back mum was pointing at the floor and I saw a piece of paper got pushed under the door, I could see writing on it and it said "we came over but you were out, think your phone isn't working, give us a ring, love Franseen and Crissy."

Then I heard their footsteps again and this time they were going away down the stairs, so I thought "oh good, hurrah" and that was when I noticed. I listened really carefully and suddenly I thought "why didn't I notice that before" and I felt all shiviry. Even though they were quite far away now I was careful, I told mum in a wisper "listen to the footsteps, dyou hear?" She gave me a look like she was saying "what d'you mean" so I said "there aren't two lots, there are three. He's down there." Mum gave me a look like she was really surprised, but then she listened really carefully and then she whispered back "oh god, Lawrence, your right."

WE ARE IN A GALAXY called the Milky Way, you can see it if it isn't cloudy, it looks like a big blur in the sky. The Milky Way is huge, it is shaped like a flying soucer with arms going round and round, and we are half way to the edge.

One day scientists decided they really wanted to know whats right in the middle of the Milky way, they thought "I bet theres something really intresting." They looked through their telescopes and they saw there was a big bulge which was really crowded, there were so many stars that if earth was there there wouldn't ever be night, it would be day all the time because lots of suns would wizz around the sky in different directions, I think it would be really hard to sleep. Scientists noticed the bulge is like a real battlefield, there are huge huge stars which don't last long, suddenly they just blow up, so the bulge is full of broken bits of them.

Then scientists said "wait a minute, we still don't know whats right in the middle of the Milky way. Whats in the middle of that bulge?" It was hard to see because all the blown up bits of stars got in the way, but the scientists kept trying, they used all their teliscopes, and eventually they noticed a little tiny star that was really near the middle, it was going round and round it very fast. The scientists thought "thats intresting." So they watched the star really carefully, they knew it was going round something, and though they couldn't see this something because it was all dark, they could find out lots about it anyway, just from the way the star wizzed round it. They said "lets see, this something is quite small but it is really really heavy, it is millions of times heavier than the sun, and its dark so we can't see it at all." Then suddenley they said "wait a minute, actually we know just what this is, oh no, this is a disaster, how horrible, its a big black hole."

Now the scientists got really worried, they thought "what if that black hole just gets bigger and bigger, what if it swallows up everything, eventually it will swallow up the whole galaxy, it will swallow up earth and everyone will get killed." But then they looked at it more carefully and they weren't sure. They said "perhaps its not so bad actually, it doesnt look like it is swallowing up much right now, everything just keeps going round and round." So they decided "actually perhaps its useful, perhaps it keeps the galaxy from just flying apart, otherwise the stars would wizz off all over the place." So they changed their mind, they said "dyou know perhaps this black hole is really our friend."

I thought "this flat is much better than the cottage was, its so high up that dad can't ever get in through the windows, he would have to have special sticky feet like spiderman." Those days were good actually. Mum wasn't cross or sad or scraching any more, and I did lots of things to help her, I had really good ideas. I closed all the shutters opposite dads building, I thought "now you can't see us after all, dad, so you will feel really silly." I told Jemima "we have to keep them closed or it will get too hot."

Jemima was the worst trouble, because she was too young to undestand. She kept saying "I want to go out, I want to have an ice cream, I want to go on the swings" she said "I'm bored of eating spaggetties with red sauce, I want to go out and have pizza" and when we said "no you can't Jemima, not today" she just shreeked. Even telling her she would get bitten by dogs only worked for a little while, then she said "I don't care, I'll hit the dogs with a stick." I tried to help, I read to her from my tintins and I even let her play with my hot wheels. Mum had a good idea too, she said "I know its borring, lamikin, but if your good then when the dogs have gone away and we can go out again you can have your own hamster." Jemima was really pleased, she said "oh yes, I'll be good" but even that didn't last very long, soon she started saying "when can I go out and get my hamster?" But I thought "actually it doesn't really matter" because even though it was anoying when she screemed she couldn't do anything really, because mum hid the key to the door on a high shelf she couldn't reach, so she couldn't get out.

Once a funny thing happened. It was the afternoon and I looked through the shutters at dads building and there was a big surprise, because there in the window was an old lady, she was watering a plant. I thought "wait a minute, who are you?" so I went to find mum, I had to be careful because Jemima was with her so I said "mum, I'm spelling a word, can you come and help me" I thought "that will work" because Jemima can't write anything yet, and it did, she didn't follow mum, she just sat there watching telly in Italian. I whispered "look mum, theres a funny old lady in dads building." Mum looked but then she just shook her head, she wispered "it must just be the cleener." I saw her again once actually, it was in the night and she was walking past a window, so I thought "you are lazy dad, why don't you clean your flat like we do?"

We did my new fort, and it was really good this time. Mum cut the walls and battelments with one of the little sharp nives that dad put in our beds, and I did lots of the staples, we painted it with the creem paint, it had a draw bridge with real string and the floors of the towers weren't wobbly now so I put the enemy up there, he didn't fall over, and I did lots of battles, I let Jemima fire the catupult. Sometimes the doorbell rang, it wasn't very often and nobody ever came up the stairs again, that was good, but it was annoying, actually, because we couldn't see who was down there, because if we looked out of the window then they would see us of course, they would know we were there.

Then I had a clever idea, and when it was really late again I did it with mum. First I got the screw driver and I unscrewed a mirror from the bathroom, it was quite small and round and it had a long strechy arm like a trelis, mum said it was a shaving mirror. Then we fixed one of the shutters with wire so it was just open a little bit, and we fixed the mirror to it with more wire, we did it so you could see who was standing by the door downstairs, and after that I always ran and looked to see who it was. Every day really early in the morning it rang but I was never quick enough and they were already gone, mum said it was just garbagemen. Later when we were getting up and having breakfast it rang again, that was the postman, I saw him. Once it was Franseen, that was a bit scary, but she didnt come up the stairs this time, I thought "oh good, its locked" I think she put something in the post box but that didn't matter. And once mums cristians came, they rang the bell four times really loudly like they were cross, so we told Jemima it wasn't for us, somebody was just playing a stupid joke.

The best time was in the night when Jemima was asleep and me and mum stayed up, so it was just like the old days. We guarded the flat, we watched television, which was so we could improove our italian, and sometimes we made pop corn, mum found two bags in a cubord. Once it was funny, it was really really late, I think it was almost dawn, when mum suddenly said "let's have some choclate" which was bad actually because there wasn't that much left, we were supposed to share it with Jemima, but instead we just ate a whole bar. Then mum did a really funny thing, she did a kind of dance in front of the windows, our shutters were shut of course, she pointed towards dads building and she shouted "ha ha ha ha" it was like she was saying "you can't get us" and then I did it too, that was really good, we ran up and down and we gigelled.

The next night something bad happened. Mum went out of the sitting room for a bit, I hardly notised actually, I was watching the telly, it was about a train, when suddenly she came back and I knew something went wrong because her face was all worried. All she said was "Lawrence" but it was funny, we hardly needed to say anything any more, it was like I knew anyway. So I followed her into the kitchen, she showed me a soucepan on the cooker and I could see what was strange right away, I thought "I am getting clever like mum now, I just know everything." So I just pointed and said "that?" and I was right, mum noded. You see in the water there was some white stuff, it was really thin and sort of floating, it was like wisps. Mum said "I just boiled it ear-lier, I was going to make some tea but then I changed my mind, thank god." She said "smell it" and it didn't smell of anything much, actually, it was like metal. I said "so it came from the taps" I thought "uhoh that's bad" and mum said "Beppo must have shown him where the pipe is." I thought "I never liked that Beppo with his stupid car with no floor" I thought "thank good-ness mum didn't drink that tea."

Mum started getting upset, I knew she would, she said "I don't know what we'll do now, we've got nothing to drink, we can't have baths, we can't even wash our hands, because the pois-son will go straight through our skin." Then she gave me a look and she said "I just don't see how we can stay here any longer, Lawrence love." But I thought "there must be some way" so I said "we can't just let him chase us out" I said "don't worry mum, we'll think of something." Jemima really likes her baths, so we found the pipe where all the water came in, we had to look for it all over the place but we found it in the end, it was in the bath-room, and we switched it off. When Jemima woke up mum said "I'm afraid the water doesn't work any more, lamikin, so you can't have your bath today" and then she switched on a tap to show it didn't work, it just made a funny noise like it was breatheing, and though Jemima still shouted "but I want my bath, I want it" there was nothing she could do.

I checked everywhere and there were only two bottles of wa-ter and one was fizzy which me and Jemima don't like, it goes up your nose. I thought "they won't last long." I tried to read a Tintin, red sea sharks, but it was hard because I kept stopping and thinking "there must be something we can do" so I forgot which picture I was on, I thought "I must think of a plan." First I thought "what if we get water from someone elses pipe instead?" but then we would have to make a big hole in the wall, and I knew we would never manage that, actually, it would be impossible. Then I thought "what about the rain" I thought "we can get it from the guter" but when I looked out of the window I saw the guter was really high so we couldn't reach, and anyway there wasn't any rain, it was a lovely sunny day. After that I thought "what if we got someone to send us some bottles of minerel water" but then I thought "but who?" and that was impossible too, because dad had probably turned them all against us now, so even if they sent us minerel water it would just be poissoned. So in the end all I did was pour the fizzy water into a big bowl and stir it a bit to make the bubbles go away.

Suddenly mum was shaking my arm to make me wake up, so I thought "uhoh I fell asleep again" I thought "what has he done now" but I was wrong, because then I noticed mum was smiling like I hadn't seen for days, that was a surprise, that was good, that was wonderful, I thought "whats happened now?" Jemima was awake, she was playing with her animals, so we had to be careful, mum took me to the window, she pointed with her finger towards dads building and she whispered "he's gone away." So I looked quickly and all of dads shutters were shut again now. I whispered back "are you sure mum? He's not just pretending?" and she said "I'm quite sure, he's gone back to Scotland again on rionair, can't you feel it? Look, the yellow cars gone too." And d'you know I could feel it, that was wonderfull, it was like the air was different now, it was all sort of empty and nice now that dad was gone away. I wispered "hurrah" and d'you know Jemima was smiling, I thought "she can feel it too, even though she doesn't know anything."

So we did something amazing. We undid the bolt and unlocked the lock and then we just walked right out of the flat. I looked up at dads building with its shut shutters and I stuck out my tongue, I thought "ha." It felt funny walking down a road after being inside for so long, it was so good, I watched a tram go past and I thought "look at that, isnt it noisy" and when Jemima got worried and said "what about the dogs" mum and me both laughed, I said "don't worry Jemima, they all went home." First we went to the roasticheria and had riceballs, it was a snack just for fun, they were really delicious and hot. Then we went to the supermarket, we got some more food, mostly it was biscuits and things, actually, and we got some more mineral water, mum got Jemima some sweets and she got me a bit of parmer ham, which I really like but she said I couldn't have last time because it was too expensive, she said it was my treat because I was such a good boy.

When we got back I wispered to mum "what about the taps, dyou think he's stopped doing the water now?" and mum said "we'll have to see." So she got Jemima to play with her dolls and we went secretly and switched on the main tap from the pipe. Mum ran the water for a long time, then she filled up a glass and looked at it really carefully, she smelt it too, and suddenly she smiled, she said "its fine." I thought "oh hurrah" I went and told Jemima "you can have your bath now, the waters working again" and Jemima said "oh yes" so it was like we were having a party. We had our lunch, mum said we must or it would already be suppertime, and I had my parma ham, it was really delicious.

After I thought "everything is so good, it is like we are all back to normal, perhaps mum can go back to her job with her cristians, perhaps we can go back to the vanhootins, that would be nice" but then I thought "but we must still be careful just in case" so I made a new plan. I went all round the flat but there weren't many bottles actually, there were five empty minerel water bottles and two big glass bottles with little handles. I thought "this isn't enough, we need hundreds" but I filled them up anyway, then I put them in a neat line by the beeday in the bathroom, I had to roll the glass ones along the floor because they were so heavy, I thought "its a start."

I wanted to go and get some more at once, just in case dad came back really suddenly, so I thought "I will go and ask mum where we can get them." But then a strange thing happened, because I couldn't find her anywhere. I looked in the kitchen and the sitting room and in her bedroom but it was like she had just vanished. I thought "thats funny" I thought "she's always here, she can't have just gone off." I didn't like it actually, I thought "I hope she didn't just go away when I was doing the bottles" and I felt all shivery, I could feel my breatheing going fast. Everything was so quiet, Jemima was sleeping again, so I went to wake her up, because suddenly I wanted her to come and look with me, but then I didn't after all because I had a new idea, I thought "what if shes on the balcony?" We hardly went there, you see, because mum said we mustn't, she said she didn't like the look of the railing, though there was a nice view, you could see a doame. I went towards the kitchen where the doors to the balcony were, and it was funny, it was like I didn't want to look just in case she wasn't there after all, I thought "what will I do then?"

But she was there, she had taken a chair out and she was sitting in the sun. I thought "oh good" but it didn't last, because then I notised she looked all sad. Mum changed so quickly, one moment she was all fine and then it was like a big ray just shon on her and made her go wrong. I thought "not again" and I was annoyed, actually, I thought "you were all right just now, why can't you just stay chearful?" I said "hello mum" but she didn't even look at me, she didn't say hello, she just said in her yawn voice, it was like a weeze "I can't fight him any more, Lawrence. He'll be back again soon, I know it, he'll just get another rionair."

I thought "I will tell her my plan, that will make her better" so I did, I said "even if he comes back he won't be able to get us this time because we'll have all our water, so it won't matter if he does the pipe, I've already done seven bottles." But it didn't work at all, she waved her hand like she was angry, it was like I made her get a headacke, she said "for gods sake, Lawrence, wake up. Can't you see, we'll never be safe, he'll get us if he wants to. We can't stop him with any plan, he'll poison the air or break down the door, he'll find a way."

I sat down on the balcony and suddenly I felt really tired. I looked at the doame and I noticed it had scaffolding on it so I thought "that's all broken." I said "what should we do then?" but mum didn't ansewer, it was like her batteries all got used up when she was cross at me just now, there wasn't anything left. I looked at her but she wasn't moving at all, she just sat really still on her chair with her arms squashing her sides like she wanted to be a bird, it was like she was cold. I thought "what will I do now" and I didn't know, there wasn't anything. So I just sat there, it went on for ages, I listened to cars going in the road, sometimes there was a tram, and I felt a bit cold too, there was a breeze. I thought "my plans never work, I cannot help mum at all, I cannot make us safe." I thought "mum thinks my bottles of water are just a stupid waste of time." I thought "its funny, its like we were walking on a lovely hill and then suddenly we are right on the cliff and theres no way back, we are stuck forever." I thought "I can't even do more bottles without mum, because I can't just go out and do it by myself, I don't know where you get hundreds of empty bottles, I can't speak italian."

Suddenly I got so cross, I thought "everythings spoiled now." And that's when I said that thing. It wasn't serius actually, I didn't really mean it. I said "maybe we should just . . ." and it was like a joke, you see, my "maybe we should just . . ." It was a joke about how we could stop dad from coming and getting us after all.

Mum didn't say anything. I thought "she doesn't like anything I say anymore, she doesn't even like my jokes" but then I notised something. You see, though she was still just sitting still in her chair with her arms like a bird, her eyes weren't just switched off anymore, it was like they were going awake now, they were thinking. Then she turned her head round really slowly and she looked at me, she said "you know, Lawrence, perhaps your right, perhaps we should."

177

CHAPTER SIX

One day Emporer Nero had some really bad news, because there was a rebellion against him in France, which was called gaul then. Nero thought "oh no this is terrible, what will I do?" Sometimes there was good news so it looked like everything might be all right after all, so Nero had a big dinner with lots of delicious food, he asked his friends. When it was bad news again he made up rude songs about all his enimies.

After a while he thought "I really must make a plan." First he thought "I know, I will execute all my generels so they can't become enemies too." But then he thought "no, I will execute all the gauls instead, that will serve them right." Then he changed his mind again, he was always doing it, actually, and he thought "I know, I will tell my solders that if they defeat all my enemies they can steal everything in Gaul, that will work. No no, wait a minute, I will execute all the senaters, that is a better plan, I will invite them to a big dinner and poisson them all at once." Finally he thought "I know, I will burn rome down again, but I will do it much better this time, I will get thousands of wild animals and let them all go so when people run out into the road because their houses are on fire they will get eaten."

But after that he changed his mind all over again, he decided to get a big army and go and fight. It took ages, he needed hundreds of carts to carry all his theater scenery in case he wanted to sing, and he needed lots of money so he could pay his soldiers, but nobody gave him any because they didn't like him. So he made a new plan, he said "I know, when the battle is going to start I will walk up to the enemy army all by myself, I won't take my sword or anything, and suddenly I will just weep and weep. When the enemy solders see me they will be so surprised that they will stop fighting, they will all start weeping too, they will shout 'oh Nero we are so sorry we attacked you' and then they will execute all their generels, so I will win."

But in the end he didn't do that plan either, he just stayed at home and waited. When he was sleeping he had terreble dreams about all the people he executed and the worst ones were about his mother Agripina, she shouted "how dare you Nero, I really hate you for putting me in the collapsible boat, I really hate you for executing me like that." He bought a big box of poisson to drink when his enimies came.

Then one day he woke up in the night, I think he wanted a glass of water or something, so he called out for his servants, but nothing happened. He thought "that's strange." So he got up and walked round his palace which was huge, it was his golden house, he shouted "hello, where are you" but nobody answered, because there was nobody there you see, it was empty and all the rooms were locked. Suddenly Nero noticed that everything was stolen, all the tables and chairs and the sheets on the beds were gone, and so was his box of poisson, so he thought "uhoh, what will I do, I can't kill myself after all." He rushed out of the palace to try and find a gladiator to stab him but the gladiators had run away too. Then he thought "all right, I will just jump in the river Tibber" but then he changed his mind again, he saw three of his servants and they said "lets go to our house in the country, Nero, its really near."

They went on horses, Nero didn't have any shoes or socks because he got up so quickly that he hadn't got dressed properly. He hid his face in his hat so nobody would recognize him, because everybody was going round saying "I wonder where Nero is, the enemy army is coming." When he got to the servants house he was really hungary and thirsty because he hadn't had his breakfast, but there was nothing there, so even though he was emporer he had to eat old bread and drink water out of a nasty pond.

Nero thought "this is terreble, I don't want to die, I am such a wonderful singer, I want to sing lots more songs." But then he saw some enemy solders riding on their horses and his servants said "watch out they will put you in a wooden fork and hit you with metal sticks until you are dead." So Nero said "oh no, that sounds horreble" and he quickly stabed himself with his sword and died. That was the end of Emporer nero.

But there was a strange thing. Nero was dreadful, nobody liked him because he executed thousands of Romans and took all their money, he spent it all on his delicious dinners and his golden House, he was a terrible singer and he cheated in all the compitions. But after he was dead some people weren't sure after all, they said "poor old Nero." It was like they forgot everything and they didn't know any more, they got confused, so they thought "yes he was strange but he was our emporer. Its a shame hes gone now, we miss him, actually, we feel really sad." They put flowers on his graive and they cried. They even made little statues of him and put them in special places. So it was almost like he was a god after all.

Mum said I didn't need to pack much because we would be back soon, she said I could only have one bag, so it should have been really easy, but I kept on changing my mind. I thought "I will take all my tintins" but then I thought "reading tintins makes me get car sick, I will take my lego so I can play that in the car." Mum wasn't sad at all any more, she was serious, she was talking and talking about our new plan, she was whispering so Jemima wouldn't wake up, because it was the middle of the night again, you see. It was like my idea about "how to stop dad from getting us after all" was a big empty room and she was filling it up with chairs and tables and things, because as she talked and talked it got full of little plans, so it was more real.

Sometimes I wasn't sure actually, I thought "it was just a joke really" I thought "I wonder if she will change her mind, she might" but then I got angry again, it was like a big engine started wirring. I thought "but he is horrible though, spying on us like that from his building and putting nives in my bed and poisson in the water and the strawberry cake and turning all mums freinds against us." I thought "mum says it will just take a few days and then we can come back and live in our flat again, and we will be safe, that will be lovely."

Then I was in my bed again and mum was leaning over me and saying "Lawrence love, wake up" so I must have fallen asleep. It was just getting light, when I looked out of the gap in the shutter the sky was half blue and half orange and I felt so tired I could hardly keep my eyes open, it was like they were glude. Mum had black lines under her eyes, I thought "she is like a leemer" and she said "I'm really sorry, I know its early, but its better if we get a good start." Jemima was so cross getting woken up that she shrieked, but she was better when we told her we were going back to the cottage to get more toys, which was a lie of course, she said "oh yes, I want all my animals, and all my dolls too, I want everything."

When we had our breakfast I felt a bit better, and I was just going to pee when I noticed something. When I looked out of the window, I saw that the shutters on dads bulding were all open again. That was a surprise, I thought "does that mean he didn't go after all, did he come straight back again on rionair?" I thought "uhoh, what will we do now?" So I went back to the kitchen and I said "mum can you help me with my bag" which was so Jemima wouldn't realize, and it worked, because Jemima was so busy eating her toast that she didn't even look up. When I showed dads shutters to mum she sort of blinked, but then she just shook her head and she said "its nothing, Lawrence. It'll just be the cleaner" so I thought "all right then, mum" I thought "that's good I think."

Mums bags were already packed, she just had two, and she packed Jemimas for her, so we were all ready to go when something dreadfull happened. Mum put all the bags by the door but then she turned round and she said "I almost forgot, we'd better leave lots of water and food for Hermann." I didn't undestand, I said "what d'you mean mum" I thought "does she want everything to be ready for him when we come back?" So I said "we don't need to do that now, mum, it'll just get old if we leave it out." But mum made a face like she was thinking "don't be silly, Lawrence," and she said "he'll be fine if we leave lots" she said "we can't take him with us, Lawrence, you must see that, he hasn't got a pets passport remember, what if they stop us?" I couldn't believe it, I thought "how can you mum, this is Hermann remember" I said "but we can't just leave him all by himself, he'll die." Mum didn't even say sorry, she just looked like she was really tired and she said "I suppose we could ask somebody in the building to look after him" but that was just as bad of course, because dad had turned them all against us too, they would put poisson wisps in his water.

Suddenley I was so cross, it was like I really hated mum, it was like I wanted to shout so loud she would break into little bits, she would just go away. I gave her my worst look, and I said "I'm not coming without Hermann, you'll just have to go by yourself" and Jemima started too, because she really likes Hermann of course, she said "we can't leave him behind." So mum gave up, she put her hands in the air like she was really annoyed and she said "this is so stupid." I didn't say anything, I just took Hermann in his cage down the stairs myself, I put him beside me in the car and I said "its all right now Hermann, your coming." Even then I was still cross with mum for ages, I thought "I cant believe she said that."

It was strange being in the car on the motor way again, Mum and me and Hermann and Jemima, so it was just like when we came, which seemed like years ago now. I looked at Hermann, he was sleeping in his nest but I could see the end of his nose sticking out of the straw, and I looked out of the window at the country side, there were tiny little towns right on top of mountains, I thought "I am just fine now, actually, I am quite all right." I thought "we are like a secret army now, nobody in these cars knows what we are doing" I thought "we are like the Colonnas when they went across Italy to get pope Bonniface" I thought "we are like Secret Eagles going on our way."

But I did get annoyed because we were going so slowly. I watched all the signs you see, they were for Bologna or Milano, which is Milan, or Firenze, which means Florence, but they were so slow it was like they hardly changed at all. I thought "we've been going for hours but it still says Firenze 119 and Florence is really near Rome, we will never get to Scotland like this, it will take months." I thought "what if he goes away again before we get there, what if he comes back with rionair." Suddenly it was like I was all ichy, I wanted to go really fast so everything would just be done, it would be all finished. I said "hurry up mum, can't you go faster?" but she said "Lawrence I told you I'm going as fast as I can, we don't want to get stopped for speeding." Then Jemima made it worse like she always does, it was like she wanted to stop us ever getting there, she said "mummy I have to pee" or "mummy I want some pizza" so we went to service stations twice, which was really annoying. When she said "I want to pee" again I said "you can't, Jemima, all right, you'll just have to do a pee in your pants" and that made mum cross, she said "Lawrence for goodness sake" but I didn't care, I thought "I won't let us stop again, I will shout and shout and make us go faster."

Then all at once we were at a service station, mum was driving into a parking place so I thought "oh no not again." I said "mum we have to keep going, we have to get to Florence" but mum just laughed, she said "you've been asleep for hours, Lawrence love, we're miles past Florence now, in fact we're past Bologna." That made me feel a bit better, so I didn't mind when we stopped. And actually we didn't take long, because we just got more petrol, mum said "god that's a lot, I'm sure its gone up since we drove down here" and Jemima got cross, she said "I want pizza" but mum said we had lots of biscuits to eat in the car, and I helped her, I said "that's much better, Jemima, because then we'll get your toys even sooner."

After that it was the boring bit, its just flat and nothing to see except motorway and cars and buildings, sometimes we got stuck in traffic jams, so I started playing a new game. I told Jemima "d'you know we're not really on the motorway at all. That view out of the window isn't real you see, its like a computer screene, really we are parked on that hill with a lovely view of rome." Jemima thought this was really funny, she said "actually we are outside Crissies house" and I said "no, we are in the car park at Ikeyer." Then I thought "I know I will make this more intresting" so I said "actually we are in space, we are going towards a big black hole" and Jemima said "oh yes, look there is a shooting star." After that I said "no no, we are in the sea" and I really liked that one, I said "uhoh, we are sinking, we are going deeper and deeper, the water is really cold, watch out Jemima that giant squid is going to break all the windows with his tentecles, then the car will start filling up with water and it will get higher and higher till we can't breath." But Jemima didn't like the game any more, she started crying so mum said "stop it Lawrence. Can't you see your upsetting her."

Then a strange thing happened. Everything was quiet, we were just driving across more flat italy, a sign said "milano 72" and suddenly I felt really sad that I made Jemima cry, it was like this was the worst thing I ever did, which was silly, actually, because usually I don't mind, because its her fault anyway. I thought "I wish I had something to give her, I wish I had a little sweet" I thought "I would let her play with my lego but I forgot to put it in the car, its in the boot" and it was almost like I wanted to cry because I couldn't let her play with my lego, that was funny. I thought "I will tell her we won't ever go to the bottom of the sea again, that will be something" but then when I looked she was in dreemland again, her head was falling over the edge of her car seat, so I didn't say anything.

Later I looked out of the window and we were going past the fair ground where we went before. I saw the big wheel and I thought "it was nice going there" and I wondered if mum would stop again, though I knew we mustn't because we were in a big hurry, I thought "perhaps she will" but she just went right past. Then I decided "I've got an idea, I will remember everything we

did there, all the machines we went on and mum speaking italian and what we all said" mum always says I have an amazing
memory. I thought "if I remember it all then it will take just as
long as when we were there, it will be like we are doing it all
again" and I really tried, I thought and thought, but it was hard,
I kept thinking of other things instead, they just pushed in, so I
had to start all over again, I couldn't help it.

When Jemima woke up she said "I'm bored of these biscuits,
I want pizza, I want chicken, I want sweets" but mum said "we
can't stop driving now, lamikin" that was good. We drove and
drove until it got dark, I could see all the other cars head lights,
and I thought "it feels like I've been in this car forever, I can't believe we just started this morning." Then I must have fallen asleep
again because I woke up and we weren't driving any more, we
were parked in a little road by some trees, it was in the country
side. It was a bit cold in the car, but mum had put my jacket on
me like a blankit, I thought "that's nice" and though I had some
ackes from sitting in the car for so long I didn't mind actually, I
thought "if we went to a hotel it would have taken ages and
wasted all of mums money, so this is better." I couldn't sleep, I
could hear mum and Jemima breathing. I was hungry so I ate
some more biscuits though I was really fed up with them now, I
drank some fanta but it was warm and there were hardly any bubbles. I thought "these biscuits are really loud when I crunch
them" I thought "I wonder if mum and Jemima will wake up?"
but they didn't, Jemima just started snoring. So I looked up out
of the window at the sky and I thought "where are you black hole
in the bulge in the middle of the Milky way?" I thought "where

are you Great Attractor?" but it was a bit cloudy, I could just see a few stars, they looked really small.

When I woke up it was morning, we were driving on the motor way and Jemima was saying "I want a crusson and some apple juice" but mum said "we haven't got time just now lamikin, maybe we'll stop and have some later." So we drove and drove, until I notised a sign that said "Paris 82" and then mum turned round and wispered to me, because Jemima was in dreamland again, she said "we're doing so well, d'you know we might even get to Scotland tonight." I thought "oh this is new" I thought "wow, it didn't take months at all" and it was funny, suddenly I felt really strange, it was like I wanted to go faster and slower all at the same time, I didn't know which, it was like I wanted to get there right now this second, it was like we were late, but it was like I never wanted to get there at all. Then I must have fallen asleep again, because when I woke up there was a sign for England, mum said that's what it was, it said Angletaire and suddenly I felt so exited, even though we were only going back for a day or two to stop dad getting us after all I thought "hurrah hurrah, we are going home."

The numbers on the signs for the channell tunnell got smaller and smaller, and though it was silly because I knew we couldn't, I kept thinking "wouldn't it be nice to see all my friends, Tommy and Ritchie and Peter Norris, I wonder what kittens Tania Hodgsons cat had, were they all tabies, I wonder what Mr Simmons taught everyone at school?" Suddenly we were really near the tunnell, I saw the sea behind a wall, Jemima was shouting "on a train, on a train" and that was when I remembered. I thought "oh no, this is a disaster, how did I forget, thats so stupid" and I said "wait mum, what about Hermann?" because he was in his cage right beside me, anybody could just look in and see.

Mum said "oh god" and she made the car swerve a bit so we stopped by the side of the road so the other cars could go past. I said "should I hide him in my pockit?" though I wasn't sure actually, Phil Greene brought his mouse to school in his pocket once and it escaped and got lost, they never found it. Mum said "let's put his cage in the boot." So that's what we did, I folded up a piece of paper and stuck it in the side of the wheel so it wouldn't go round and make a squeak, poor Hermann tried to make it work and he gave me a sad look, I said "sorry Hermann." Then we covered his cage with a blankit and Jemima said "what will they do if they find him, will they put him in jail" so I got annoyed, I said "shut up Jemima, its none of your busness." When we got back into the car and drove off again mum said "I didn't even look to see if there was a camera, oh god" she told us that when we showed our passports to the passport man we must smile but not too much, we must just look really normal.

I tried to practice looking normal, I looked at my face in the window but it was hard to see, actually, with all the cars and road and sky behind, I looked seethrough like a goast, so I couldn't tell if I was normal or not, and then mum parked at the place where we got our tickets. She said "I hope we don't have to wait too long for a train, sometimes they're full" so I thought "what about poor Hermann, if it takes ages he might sufocaite under that blanket" I wanted to get him out again but mum said "Lawrence, just leave him."

Then she locked us in and we just sat there, Jemima hummed itsy bitsy spider and kicked the chair in front like she does, and I tried not to think about Hermann, I thought "oh look theres a plane really high up, its like a piece of chalk thats drawing a line all by itself." I thought "mums being a really long time getting our tickets." Finally she came back out but her face looked all worrid so I knew something went wrong, and I was right, actually, when she got in the car she said "I just don't believe this, none of my credit cards worked, I could have swarn there was just enough."

This was new, this was bad. I said "what will we do?" and Jemima said "but I want to go now, I want my animals and my dolls" then mum said "quiet you two, I'm trying to think." She was scraching herself, the back of her hand was all red, and she said "we'll just have to sell something I suppose, but what, all I can think of is the car" but me and Jemima both shouted "no no." I said "you can't mum, its ours, its like our house, and then we'll just be stuck here." Mum said "we could always take a train" but I said "what about all our things, they're really heavy, how will we carry them" and mum said "I suppose I could sell my rings."

So we turned round and drove into a town, mum said "god we're almost out of petrol too and I've only got ten yuros left." We went to some shops and mum talked in French but it wasn't as good as her italian, she kept starting and stopping like it needed new batteries. Mum got cross, she said "they're worth twice that, I suppose they can see I'm desperate." That made me sad actually, I thought "poor mums rings" I thought "I really like them, especially the one with the pretty red bit" so I said "are you really sure you have to sell them" but mum said "I'm afraid so, Lawrence." So we went back to the first shop and the man gave her some yuros, mum said "that'll do for now."

Everything was taking longer and longer, I was so annoyed I just wanted to kick something. Jemima said "I'm hungary, I want a sandwich" and when I said "you can't Jemima" mum said "I think we all need some lunch." It took ages, Jemima is such a slow eater, its like she does it on purpose, and then she screamed so everybody looked round until mum got her rasberry ice cream. I thought "now, at last" but then we found we couldn't go on the next train after all because it was full, we had to wait for the third. I wispered to mum "does that mean we can't go to Scotland to-day after all?" and she said "I'm afraid not Lawrence" so I got even crosser, I thought "its all Jemimas fault, we should have just left her in rome in the flat with lots of water and bread."

But then something good happened, that was a surprise. We drove off the train in England and I thought "now we will go on the motorway again" but we didn't actually, instead mum went onto a little road and stopped in a car park by a supermarket. She turned round in her seat to look at me and she said "haven't you forgotten something?" I didn't know, I said "what d'you mean?" and she laughed, she said "Hermann of course." I said "oh yes, hurrah hurrah," that was wonderfull, because you see nobody noticed him after all, so they wouldn't put him in jail. We got him out of the boot and he was fine, he wasn't suffocated, so I took out the piece of paper and he went round and round in his wheel, I gave him new water and nuts and he gave me a look like he was saying "thank you Lawrence."

THE BLACK HOLE IN THE MIDDLE of the Milky way is quite small but its still terrible, its greedy like a big mouth and once anything goes in it never comes back out again, it is gone forever. There is a secrit line all round it, nobody can see it but it is there, its called the Event Horizon, and you must be really careful, you mustn't ever go across it by accident or you will get sucked into the black hole right away, nothing can stop you and you will never come out again.

There is lots of dust by the event horizon, its like a big disk, it goes round faster and faster until it falls in, so it is like water going down the plug hole. And d'you know just because its about to fall down the dust does a funny thing, it spits out lots of rays, they are X rays and radio waves, scientists can see them through their teliscopes, and they are awful actually. It is like the poor dust is screeming, its saying "oh no I'm getting sucked into this black hole, I will never come back, nobody will ever see me again, I will get squoshed flat, this is terrible" its like it is saying "help me."

It was getting dark and Jemima was shouting "oh look there's the church and there's the shop, theres mrs Potters house and the trees like funny hair, we're really almost there now" and I was thinking "uhoh, now there will be trouble, because I bet dad has got in and broken everything, what will we tell Jemima, will we say its burglars?" But actually he hadn't after all, that was a surprise, everything was just the same, so it was strange walking into the sitting room and seeing all our things still on the floor from our packing. When we sat down at the table and had our dinner, mum made beans on toast, I had a funny feeling, it was like we never went anywhere at all, we were just here all the time and rome wasn't real, it was like a film. But then I did a clever thing. I pulled out the Julius Cesaer, I had him in my pockit all the time you see, I said "there you are" and that made it real again.

The next morning it was funny waking up in my old bed in the cottage, I thought "this is nice." Jemima didn't want to leave, she said "its nicer here, the water never goes dirty so I can always have my bath." Actually I wanted to stay too, I thought "just a little bit, just till tommorow" but of course I knew we couldn't really. Mum looked really tired, her eyes were funny like head lights, so I helped her, I said "there won't be that dirty water ever again, Jemima, when we go back you will have your bath every day, I promise" and then I said "now what toys do you want to take?" That worked, she wanted them all, I had to get more and more boxes from the skulery to put them in, she wanted all her animals and dolls and even stupid things like her big spinning top that doesn't go round properley because the handle got bent, it doesn't do its tune, and all her pens though lots were dried up because she never puts the lids back on.

So we got ready. I put Jemimas things in the car and when she wasn't looking I took some of her stupid things out, because otherwise there wouldn't be any room left, and I put my things in instead, it was the box she made me leave behind before we went to Rome because she had to have her dolls house, with my hot wheels track and my computer consel, I thought, "that's fair."

Then just when we were getting in the car she cheated, she said "but I don't want to go, I want to stay here, I want to go another time." Mum looked all desperete, she shut her eyes and said "Jemima for gods sake" but I was ready, because I guessed she would do this, you see. I just grabbed her and then I pulled her jacket down really quickly so her arms were stuck, so when she tried to run away she just fell over, that was funny. Then mum and me got her in the car, we just picked her up and put her in, mum buckelled her up and we drove off, she said "I'm sorry about this lamikin, but we just have to go" and I said "I don't care if your screeming, Jemima, I will just put my hands over my ears so I can't hear."

At lunchtime we stopped in a town where mum went to a shop and sold the man all her silver candel stick and cups and other metal things that we almost took to rome but didn't because the car was full. That was a shame too, I thought "we never used that candel stick actually, because mum said it was only for special occasions, and now we are getting rid of it for ever." I think mum noticed I was a bit sad, because she said "its worth it if it gets us back to Rome, Lawrence love."

Then Jemima was trouble, she said "we've been driving for hours and hours, wheres that river with the nice trees we go past, wheres the channell tunnell" so mum said "we're not going there till tomorrow, lamikin, first we're going somewhere else, because I need to do some shopping." That was a lie of course, and a funny thing happened, it was like Jemima sort of guessed, sometimes she is clever like that, she knows things even though nobody tells here, I don't know how. She gave mum a look and she said "what shopping?" Mum said "tea and that sort of thing, lamikin, you can't get nice tea in Rome" and I thought "uhoh, now Jemima will say we can just get that in a supermarket" but she didn't, she said "I don't want to go shopping, I want to go back to the cottege" so it was all right after all, and she fell asleep just after we went past the "welcome to Scotland" sign.

I looked out of the window at some mountains, I thought "now I am in Scotland" and it was funny, I thought "yesterday morning I was in France, and the morning before yesterday I was in Rome" but I could hardly believe it actually, it was like I was looking the wrong way down a teliscope. It was getting dark but we didn't stop for supper, mum got some sandwiches at the last service station so we just ate them, mine was chicken and bacon, and mum held hers with her hand on the steering wheel, she said Jemima could have hers when she woke up. I was thinking "I wish we had more crisps, that was a really small packit" when suddenly I looked up and saw something, it was a sign that said "Edinburugh 17." I could hardly believe it, I thought "thats quick, usually it takes hours and hours" and even though miles are bigger than kilomiters we would still be there really soon, so I thought "wait a minute, not yet, I'm not ready."

Actually, I think mum wasn't ready either because when I looked in the little mirror at her face I could see her eyes were going blink blink and her shoulder sort of twiched like she wanted to scratch herself all over, but of course she couldn't because she was driving. Her voice was going really fast, she said "dam dam, I should have got it earlier, but I didn't want to when Jemima was awake." I said "get what mum?" but she didn't answer, she just said "I'll try here." It was a service station but then she did a strange thing, she drove in quite slowly and then instead of stopping she just drove out again. I said "why did you do that mum?" and she said "didn't you see, Lawrence, there were cameras." So I said "why can't they have cameras?" and mum frowned, she said "its not good if they take our picture, Lawrence love, they won't understand."

It was like I knew all that, actually, but it still was a surprise, it made me feel all shivery. I said "what will they do if they take our picture?" and mum said "they won't, Lawrence" but I wanted to know, I wanted to stop feeling shivery, so I said "tell me mum, what'll they do?" and mum did a little laugh but it sounded strange, I didn't like it. She said "I don't know, they'd probably try and put me in jail or something, but they won't" and she said "don't you worry, Lawrence love, everythings going to be fine." I thought "I wish we could just go home" but I didn't say anything, I just kept quiet, it was like if I kept quiet then nothing would happen. I thought "I will just sit really still and read my tintin" but it was hard because it was dark and the lamposts light kept moving round and round like they were a big torch that was swinging. Suddenly I thought of another question, I really wanted to know actually, and I was just going to ask it when mum slowed down again, she said "this'll do, perfect" because we went past another service station and a big shop which was like a supermarket for cars and bicycles. We went round the corner and parked and mum said "I want you to wait here and look after Jemima, Lawrence, I won't be long. I'm going to lock you in, all right?"

It was funny being all alone locked in the car in the dark in

Scotland all of a sudden. It was a bit cold, the wind made a noise on the window and I tried to read my tintin but I couldn't, because every time I looked at the picture of captain Haddock saying "bashi bazooks" I forgot why he said it again. I looked out of the window and there was a fat man walking down the road with a tiny little dog like a chiwawa, it kept stopping and smelling things so he pulled its leesh to make it go again. I thought "mums been gone for ages, what if there was a camara after all but she didn't see it because it was hidden, what if they already took her picture, what if they already put her in jail." Then I thought "I won't think that any more, I will just make it go away" but I couldn't, actually, it just kept coming back all by itself, I thought "because we are locked in, we will be stuck in here forever."

Then mum came round the corner, that was lovley, she was all lops sided from carrying the petrol can which was red, and in her other hand she had a plastic bag. She came up to my window and gave me a little tiny smile, that was nice, and then she put the petrol can in the boot, she had to move everything round because it was so full of Jemimas dolls and animals and pens that didn't work.

After that she drove off again and I started recognizing everything, all the shops and roads and houses, so I thought "that means we're here." Suddenly we were on dads street and mum parked the car just across from his house, his lights were on so I thought "he's in." I thought "is this it then?" and I felt shivery again, but it wasn't, actually, mum just sat there waiting, so I thought "she is checking." We sat there for ages, I could hear Jemima snoring and there were tiny bits of rain falling on the car,

I could see them on the windshield, they made a tiny noise like "tip tip tip" and then suddenly there he was, he was walking into the front room holding something. I only saw him for a moment and then he sat down, he disappeared, and it was strange, because I tried to get really angry but it didn't work, I just thought "there you are dad" I thought "you've got your dinner and now your eating it as you watch telly."

Mum started the car, so I thought "where are we going now, are we going away? Has she changed her mind after all?" but she hadn't, she just went round the corner and parked there, so I thought "oh of course, she just doesn't want our car to get noticed." I thought "this really is it then" and though we had been driving here for days I thought "theres no time left, where did it all go?" I thought "what will I do?" Mum was turning round to undo her seatbelt, but I stopped her, I thought "but I want to ask my question" it was the one I thought of earlier when mum saw the car supermarket. So I asked it, I said "if they take our picture will they send me and Jemima to jail too?"

Mum gave me a funny look, she said "don't be silly, your both much too young, now stop this, Lawrence love, nobodies going to jail." Then she gave me a little smile like she was saying "are you allright now?" But she didn't understand, actually, because you see I wanted us all to go to jail, because then we would all be together, it would be quite nice actually, it would be like when we stayed at the agro turismo. I thought "if they put her in jail and they won't let us come too, then where will we go?" and suddenly everything was dreadful. I thought "no no, this is a horreble disaster" I thought "I won't let her" so I said "no mum, stop" and I reeched out to grab her, but d'you know I forgot about my seat belt, which was silly, so all I did was touch her elboe with my fingers. Mum undid her seat belt so I thought "she's just going anyway, she's not even going to ansewer me, that's not fair" but I was wrong, actually, instead she turned round and lent through the seats so her face was looking right at my eyes. She didn't look worried any more, it was like she was happy actually, she said "Lawrence, we've just driven all the way across Yurope to do this, remember. If we give up now then dad will come straight down again on rionair and this time we won't be able to stop him from doing something terreble, he'll poisson the water or the air or the food. I'm not going to let him hurt you."

I thought "I don't want her to go" but then I thought "mums clever, shes always right" and then I thought "its nice being in the car like this, why don't we just stay here." And in the end I never really did decide what I thought of course, because then something happened. I should have geussed it would, that was really stupid, but then mum didn't either, we were so busy talking that we just forgot. Someone said "what d'you mean dad'll do something terreble?" and that someone was Jemima, because we woke her up, you see. I thought "uhoh, we forgot to wisper." I thought "this is bad, what'll we do now?" Then I thought "I know, I'll stop her before she starts, that will help mum" so I said "just shut up Jemima, because you are too young to understand" but it didn't work. Jemima shouted "what d'you mean about dad" and mum sort of scraped her fingers down over her face like she was trying to clean something off it, she said "perhaps we'd better just tell her, Lawrence, she has to know eventually."

That was new. I thought "all right then mum, if you say so." So mum did it. She told Jemima how dad tried to get into the cottage and how he turned all our neighbors against us, which was why we went to Rome. I was watching Jemima over Hermanns cage and I noticed her eyes were getting bigger and bigger so it was like they might go "pop" so I thought "uhoh" but Mum didn't stop. She said how Franseen was an enemy who told dad we were in rome, so he followed us, he came on rionair, and then she said how he did the strawberry cake and the nives in our beds and the poisson wisps in the water, which was why she couldn't have her baths. Now Jemima was making a funny little noise like a mouse, I think mum noticed too but she just went quicker, she said "so that's why we came to Scotland, we have to stop him once and for all you see, lamikin, its the only way." And then she said something else too, she made it sound nicer, like she was just making everything all neet and tidy, but she said it. She said what we were going to do now.

Everything was quiet for a moment. Mum was waiting, but I thought "uhoh" because it was like when the sea goes away before a big wave comes and bashes you. I thought "we should have just told her to shut up because she is too young to undestand, we should have said mum is just going off to the shop now to get her tea" but it was too late, because Jemima started, it was like the car was full up with her, first it was just a screem and then it turned into a word, it was "noo" she said "dads nice, he didn't do that."

Mum gave me a look, it was like she was saying "isn't she annoying" so I gave her one back saying "yes she is." I thought

"Jemima always has to reck everything" and it was funny, it was like our plan again now, it was me and mums, and I wasn't going to let Jemima spoil it. I thought "I wonder what we will do?" but it was easy actually. Mum didn't look worried, she said "you'll understand this later, lamikin, I know you will" then she pulled her head back out from between the chairs and suddenly I understood, I thought "oh of course, Jemima can't do anything anyway because she is all buckelled in." I thought "I will help mum" so I undid my seat belt, Jemima was screaming and trying to get out but of course she couldn't. So I got out and I closed my door to make her screeming a bit quieter. I was going to say "I'll get the petrol can mum" but I never did, actually, because that was when I notised a new thing.

You see there was a man standing there looking at mum. He had a jacket that was red and puffy like there were plastic bags in it, and he had a dog on a leesh which wasn't really small or big, it was inbetween, so I thought "wait a minite I know you, you are mister Andrews." He lived on dads street you see, his job was putting parking tickets on everybodies cars when they parked in the wrong place, dad said he was a bit of a drinker but he was all right really. Once when we were in a hurry and dad parked on a yellow line near the cheese shop he didn't give dad a parking ticket, he came into the cheese shop and told dad to move the car instead, which was nice. Now he looked really suprised, he looked at mum and he looked at the car with Jemima screaming and he said "Hannah, what are you doing here, whats going on?"

Mum smiled but it was funny, she looked like she wanted to shreek really, and she said "oh we were just passing, we've been up to the islands" which was a lie of course, we didn't go to any islands, we came from rome. Mister Andrews started saying "so are you not visiting . . ." but then he stopped and frowned, he looked through the window at Jemima because now she was shouting "don't mum don't mum don't" and I thought "mum looks worried, she looks scared, I bet she won't do anything now after all" I thought "that means this whole journey is just a big waste of time."

And that was when I had my brilliant idea. It was funny, because as soon as I thought of it I thought "oh yes, why didn't I think of it before?" because it was much better in every way you see, it meant everything would get done and they wouldn't be able to put mum in jail after all. Mr Andrews said "whats up with her?" his voice was all sort of mushy like it always was, dad said it was because he was a drinker, and I don't think he really noticed I was there, because I was on the other side of the car. So I crouched down a bit and I sneeked round to the back and when I tried the back door, it was open just like I hoped, because mum already opened it with the little handle on the floor by her feet. I thought "that's good"

It was a bit heavy but I pushed it up, it stayed open because it has little arms that hold it, and Mr Andrews was looking the other way, I could see his back, because he was talking to mum, that was good too. He said "she sounds bad, d'you think she should see a doctor?" and I understood that, mum said Jemima was screaming because she hurt herself. I reached in past all Jemimas silly dolls and pens that didn't work, and I got the plastic bag and the petrol can, it was really heavy but I got it, I thought

"I am strong" then I pulled them down and I sort of ran. I could hear them behind me, Mr Andrews said "Lawrence, hey where are you off to" and mum shouted "oh god Lawrence, no" and I looked back just for a moment, I could see her face, it was the one she got when she didn't know which way to go because me and Jemima ran off in different directions. She shouted "Lawrence" but I didn't take any notice, I thought "this will really help you mum, you just wait, you will be so pleased, you will say I'm so proud of you Lawrence."

I went straight across the road, I thought "this petrol can is heavy but Mr Andrews is old so he will be really slow, I will win" and then I had a good idea. I changed direction and went down a little lane that goes behind all the houses, I went down it once before, you see, dad said it is where the garbagemen come to take everyboddies rubbish. I thought "I bet Mr andrews didn't even see where I went" and I was right, because when I got to the other end I couldn't see him anywhere, he was gone. When I went out of the lane I looked all around, I was carefull and there wasn't anybody, I was safe. And suddenly I was there, I was right in front of dads house, so I thought "hurrah hurrah, you are clever Lawrence."

I looked in the bags, there was a packet of cloths which were white, there were matches and a big plastic funnel. I thought "what do I do?" because mum never really said you see, because she was supposed to do it, not me. I thought "uhoh, I am standing here, I'm not doing anything, seconds are going and soon mister Andrews will come or dad will come out, this is dreadful, this is a disaster." Then I thought "I suppose I have to put the fun-

203

nel through the letter box" and I made my hands do it, but it was hard, actually, because the letter box wouldn't stay open, it hurt my finger. I thought "I will jam in the funnel, that will work" but the funnel just stuck out sideways so I thought "that's silly" and when I tried to pour some petrol down it, it didn't go in at all, it just sperted all over my shoes, I thought "oh mum, I don't understand, what was your plan?"

But I didn't give up, I tried again. This time I held the funnel a bit higher with one hand and with the other hand I did the petrol, I thought "I will do it really slowly and carefully" and though it was hard because it was so heavy, some went in, so I thought "oh yes, hurrah" and then I kept pouring it really slowly, I tipped it more and more, it took ages, until there wasn't any left, it all went in. That was wonderfull. So I put the petrol can down, I put the funnel back in the bag, and I got out one of the cloths. I thought "what do I do with this, I suppose I light it with the matches and then I drop it in."

So I tried, but that was hard too. It was because my fingers were funny and shaky, I thought "stop it fingers." The first match the end fell off, the second one lit but then it just went out again, and the third one lit but when I tried to light the cloth it went out, it made a tiny little smoke. Suddenly I got really annoyed, I thought "don't be silly now Lawrence, don't mess this up, you haven't got any time" so I did it really carefully. I lit the next match and I held it really still, I hardly moved it at all, I just put the cloth near and it worked, it started burning. So I thought "hurrah" I thought "that's all done" and I didn't wait at all, I didn't let myself, I just opened the letter box really wide and pushed it in.

And d'you know what happened? Nothing happened at all. I waited. I thought "now there will be a big noise" but there wasn't anything. So I opened the letter box again to see and then I understood, because you see dad had a kind of baskit made out of wires, it was there to catch all the letters and newspapers and stop them from falling on the floor and getting dirty. I thought "oh yes of course, why didn't I think of that, I often noticed it when I came and stayed for my weekends" because the cloth was just sitting in the baskit, you see, it was still burning a bit but it was stuck. I thought "oh no this is bad" I thought "why didn't you think of that mum?" I thought "perhaps it will help if I do another cloth" I couldn't think of anything else actually, so I got out another one and I was just going to try and light a match but then all sorts of things happened.

First there was Mister Andrews, who was running down the street towards me, I thought "how did you get all the way up there, you went the wrong way" he was on the pavement and he was shouting "Lawrence Lawrence." And then there was a car noise which was really loud like it was in a race so I thought "I bet that's mum" and it was. She braked very fast so she stopped just by dads gate and then she shouted through her window "get in Lawrence."

I felt so sad, I thought "sorry mum" because it was a real shame, we came all this way and it didn't work, I wasn't a hero after all, that was dreadfull. Mister Andrews was getting closer, even though he was old he was quite fast, actually, so I picked up the petrol can which wasn't heavy any more, I picked up the plastic bag and then I just ran to the car, mum was sort of leaning back so she could keep my door open. I got in really fast but Mister Andrews was right behind me, he shouted "hey stop" his dog was barking too, and then he grabbed mums door and pulled it open. I thought "what will I do?" I thought "you should have locked your door mum" but it was all right actually, because then mum pushed the door so he went back a bit and then she used it like it was a big stick, she hit him three times, it went "chump chump chump" and mister Andrews fell over, he hit his head a bit on another car so I thought "well done mum" I thought "poor mister Andrews."

But then something amazing happened. Because just as mum was shutting her door there was a funny noise, it went sort of "whuuump" and I knew what it was, I thought "oh yes this is wonderfull." Because, you see, the petrol lit after all, I don't know why, perhaps a bit of cloth dropped on it. When I looked back I could see a big flaime behind the little window in the door, it had colored glass and the flames made it look all flikery and pretty, so I thought "hurrah hurrah I did it."

But that was when everything went wrong. Maybe it was because mum was so tired after driving all the way from Rome, or it was because Jemima was screaming so loud. First mum made the car go forwards much too fast, and she didn't steer it properly either, so it hit the car in front of us and there was a noise of something going "smash" I thought "what was that, a head light?" After that she went backwards too fast as well, it was lucky that mister Andrews and his dog got out of the way, so we hit the car behind us now.

Finally we went forwards again, we went really fast, but now poor mum was steering completley wrong, she was shouting "oh god oh god" and we went sort of sideways right across the road so I thought "uhoh there is a wall" and we hit it I think, but I don't really know because I didn't have my seat belt done up, you see, so it was like I flew a bit and then I hit the seat in front. I thought "oh this feels funny" because I couldn't breath or anything, and I could hear mum shouting "no, no, no." She was trying to make the car go again but it just made a funny noise, it was like something was scrapping in the engine and the car didn't move at all.

I could hear a beeping, I think it was dads smoke alarm. Then we all just sat there. People came out of their houses and looked at us like we were really intresting. I could hear some sirens getting loud. I notised dad walking round his house, he came out from where he puts his garbage cans, his face was all dirty and black so I thought "he's all right then" and mum was screeming and screeming at the people "get him away, he's a murderer, he tried to poisson us, get him away, get him away." And suddenly I had a thought, I thought "oh dear, how on earth will we get back to Rome now?"

CHAPTER SEVEN

Nobody listened to what I said. In the ambulance I said "I have to go back to mum right now" but the lady policewoman didn't take any notice, I got so cross, she said "you've hurt your shoulder, Lawrence, you have to go to the hospital" and Mr Andrews didn't listen either, he was sitting there with his dog, he said "shes right laddie, you have to see the doctor." I said "but dad will get her, he tried to poisson us all" but they didn't take any notise, that was strange, that was dreadful, it was like they just didn't hear.

So we went to the hospital, we had to wait and wait, I couldn't bear it. After a while Mr Andrews went off to get his head done, which was a shame, I thought "he's nice, actually." I thought "what if somethings happened to mum, what if dads got her?" I thought "what if she gets lost so I can't find her?" The lady policewoman said "don't worry Lawrence, shes quite safe" but I thought "how d'you know, your not there, you're here."

Then I saw the doctor, he said my shoulder was all broken but I couldn't have a plaster because it broke in the wrong place, I could just have bandeges, which was annoying, because when Toby Miklaus broke his leg he got a plaster and everyone wrote their names on it.

Then it was time to go. I thought "oh good, hurrah, at last, now I will see mum." We drove for ages until we got to a big building, it was really quiet except I heard a man talking really loudly behind a door, and his voice sounded funny, he said "devels devels devels" so I thought "this is a stupid place, whats mum doing here?"

Then I went into my room and that was awful, that was a terrible thing, because mum wasn't there at all, you see, it was just Jemima. She jumped out of her bed like I was the best thing she ever saw, she grabbed my leg and she wouldn't let go. I said to the man who came with me "wheres mum?" but he just said "you rest now Lawrence, you'll see doctor Muckaye tomorrow morning and he'll explain everything." That made me so angry, I thought "he's not listening either." I said "I have to see her right now" but he just said "I'm really sorry but that's not possible" and then he did a horrible thing, he went out and locked the door.

The room was just white with a picture of horses in a field so it was like the Panda nuns room without any Jesuzes, and I thought "I'm not going to sleep, I will shout and shout" and I did shout for a bit, Jemima did too, we said "we want mum" but then I lay down on the bed, I didn't mean to, suddenly I just got tired. Jemima had her own bed but she didn't go in it, she came in mine instead, she lay there touching my back, and though it hurt my shoulder a bit I let her. I thought "its nice shes here" I said "don't worry Jems, everything's going to be all right."

The next morning a lady brought us breakfast, she said I had to come and see doctor Muckaye, so I thought "about time too" and I told Jemima "I'll be back soon, don't be scared." Doctor Muckaye had tall black hair that came up off his head like a cliff, it was like a big wave on the sea that got stuck, and I thought "you are like your hair actually" because he was leening forward at me with his arms folded like he was really intrested, his eyes were looking right at me. I thought "its like you want to jump forward off that chair" I thought "you are an eager beaver" I thought "I think you are nice, I bet you will help us."

He said "how's your shoulder? You really hurt yourself there" so I said "wheres mum, we have to see her right away." He did a kind of frown like he was sad and he said "you have to understand something, Lawrence, your mothers been very ill." Now I was worried, I said "what d'you mean, in the car?" because there was a sort of balloon that blew up when we crashed, I saw it, it was on the steering wheel, I thought "maybe it bashed her head?" But doctor Muckaye said "no I mean ill in a different way" so I said "it doesn't matter if shes ill, I have to see her right now." And that was when it happened. Doctor Muckaye looked sad again and he said "I don't know how to say this to you, Lawrence, but I'm afraid that's not a good idea right now. I can't let that happen."

I looked at him and suddenly I understood. I felt funny like I went all cold in a fridge, I thought "I know who you are doctor Muckaye, I know why you wont let me see mum, its because you are a deadly enemy" I thought "how could I be so stupid, because

210

we are in Scotland now of course, dad has poissoned everyone against us." I was so cross, I wanted to shout out "you horrible traiter" but something stopped me, I don't know what it was, I think it was that cold fridge feeling. I looked at doctor Muckaye and I thought "you are pretending to be nice to cheat me" I thought "I will change your animal" which I don't usually do, I thought "you aren't an eager beaver any more, now you are a horrible black hairy spider in a big web" I thought "I don't know what nasty thing you want but I won't let you have it, I won't do anything you want."

What he wanted was for me to answer his questions and talk to him, so I thought "right, that's what I wont do." Not that it was easy, because when I didn't say anything he started looking all sad again, he said "Lawrence, I said hows your shoulder feel, why aren't you talking to me?" so I thought "all right I will say something" and I said "its fine." Then he gave me a look, he said "I understand if you feel angry towards me because I cant let you see your mother right now, but theres a reason for that" but I didn't ask about his reason, I didn't want to know, I just said "I'm fine" and when he said "all I want to do is help you. Is there anything you need? You must be feeling lonely" I just said it again, I said "I'm fine." I thought "this is good, because I can say this to everything" when he said "please talk to me Lawrence, you cant just keep saying 'I'm fine'" I looked at him and I gave him a real stare, but I smiled too, that was funny, I said "I'm fine."

After that I had to see Ann but I was ready for her now. She was thin with brown hair which was round like a hat, she had little glasses and she pretended to be nice too, she said "how're you doing, poor old Lawrence?" but then she said "so tell me about your journey to Rome" so I thought "I knew it, dad sent you as well, so you are a spider as well, you are a little brown one" I thought "you are like mr and mrs spider." Ann brown spiders questions were different from doctor Muckayes, they were all about driving on the motor way and not going to school, she said "weren't you sad to be missing all your lessons and your friends?" so I gave her a different ansewer, because "I'm fine" didn't work, I said "I don't remember." I didn't remember about leaving the cottage or going to Rome or anything, until Ann got a bit annoyed, she said "you don't remember very much, do you?"

Then it didn't work once, because she asked "did your mother hurt you, did she ever hit you, or your sister?" so I thought "that's horrible, how dare you, you horrible spider" so I said "no she didn't" and she gave me a look through her little glasses, and she said "so you do remember some things then, Lawrence?" she said "where did you stay when you drove to Rome, was it somewhere nice?" but I just gave her my look, I said "I don't remember." And it was funny, it was like mum was there with me, it was like she was sitting right beside me when I sat there saying "I'm fine" or "I don't remember" and she was saying "well done Lawrence love, I'm so proud of you."

Sometimes they talked to me and Jemima together but usually they did us just by ourselves. I told Jemima not to say anything, I told her they were enemies, but I think she forgot sometimes, because suddenly Ann spider knew lots of things. She said "and then you all slept all night in the car by the side of the road that time" and she said "and you just ate biscuits and drank fanta for two days, is that right, the car was full of rubbish like a trash can?" and though I said "I don't remember" I thought "oh dam dam" I thought "I don't know what you are doing Ann brown spider but I know its bad." Afterwards I told Jemima "what did you tell them?" and Jemima started crying, she said "I didn't tell them anything" which was a lie, I knew it, but I couldn't stay cross, I thought "your only a baby Jemima, you don't know" so I said "don't worry, its fine, your doing really well Jems, mum will be really pleased."

Once there was a surprise. Doctor Muckaye said "Lawrence I've got someone to see you" and it was dad. There he was standing looking at me with his funny smile like he didn't know what to say. Luckily I was all ready, I didn't wait at all, I just screemed really loudly "go away" and I wanted to throw something at him but there wasn't anything, there was just the sofa, that was too big. I said "I hate you dad, you tried to poisson us" and doctor Muckaye wispered something but I heard it, he said "I'm sorry, its too soon" so I shouted "no it isn't too soon, I don't ever want to see you again, not ever ever." I thought "you are pleased with me now mum, I bet." After that when I saw doctor Muckaye again he gave me a sad look and said "so your dad tried to poisson you, thats terrible, was this in Rome?" but I was ready again, I thought "I will change your answer now, black spider" so I said "I don't remember."

But it got harder. One day Docter Macaye was going on and on like usual, he was frowning and shaking his head, he said "why won't you talk to me Lawrence, all I want to do is help you, but I can't do that if you won't talk to me." My sholder was hurting again and I was really tired, I thought "please just shut up doc-ter Macaye" and then I made a plan. I thought "I know, I will just answeer one of his stupid questions and that will make him stop talking, I won't say anything else, he will go away." So I did that, I said "your not trying to help me, you're an enimy." But it didn't work, because docter Muckaye didn't stop after all, he just gave me a look like I was sort of new now, and he said "why d'you say that Lawrence?" And it was funny, now that I told him one an-swer it was really hard to stop, I don't know why. I didn't mean to talk about mum, I didn't want to say anything, but somehow I did a bit, that was dreadfull, he tricked me.

Afterwards I felt so cross, I wanted to cry, I thought "mum wont be proud of me now." I went to our room and a funny thing happened, because though I didn't say anything it was like Jemima knew, because she stopped playing with the lego they gave us, it was big lego which is just for babies, I hadnt played with that for years, it just made walls, and she came and sat be-side me, she leaned against my arm. She said "hello Lawrence."

The next day something new happened. The door opened and in came Mister Simmons. I thought "oh this is good" because Mr Simmons was my favorite teacher at my old school, you see. I thought "he's not from Scotland so perhaps dad hasn't poisoned him against us, he isn't an enimy yet" I thought "I wonder if he's come to rescue us and take us to mum." He said "how are you then Lawrence, and you've hurt your shoulder, poor you" so I said "We have to find mum, we have to get away from here and go home to our cottage right away" but he gave me a funny look, he said "I'm afraid that's not possible just yet, Lawrence."

So I knew. I thought "that's just what doctor Muckaye says" and I felt so cross, I thought "and you were my best teacher." After that I didn't talk to him, I talked to Jemima instead, I said "this is mister Simmons, you remember him, he taught me writing" I said "and Henry Gibson says he smells of old farts, thats funny isnt it?" Jemima looked like she didn't know, but then she laughed a bit, and Mister simmons was blinking like he didn't know what to say, so I did some more, I thought "this is for you, traiter." I said "and Jemal Mustapha says hes the fattest teacher in the whole school, he says he's fatter than a zepplin, and Lidia Fitzroy says his jacket looks like he goes to sleep in it, she says its like his pyjamas, and his shoes are like dead moles." And though Mr Simmons stayed and talked more it was like all the air went out of him, so I thought "oh good you enimy, go away now."

One day after that something amazing happened. Docter Muckaye came to our room, he looked like he had a big secrit, he had something really new, and he said "someones come to see you." I thought "who is it now?" I thought "is it mrs Potter from next door or Franseen or Crissy Chick?" But it wasn't any of them. It was mum.

She looked really thin, she looked all tired, she was sort of leaning on the table. We just ran right at her, I got her waste and Jemima got her leg, and she hugged me so hard I could hardly breath. I thought "hurrah hurrah, everything will be fine now" I thought "hurrah hurrah, we won, we beat them all." Then mum sort of stood back a bit and she said "I've got something to tell you" and her eyes went blink blink blink so I said "what is it, are we going back to Rome now, is the car all fixed?" She said "no, its not that" and she looked funny like she had her headacke really badly, she said "I don't know how to say this. You see I got all mixed up, I'm afraid. I got all confused. Doctor Muckaye helped me to see that." This was bad, I thought "oh no, whats that spider done to you" and I said "what d'you mean mum?" and she said "I was all wrong about dad trying to hurt us. He wasn't even there. He was here in scotland all along."

I thought "this is new." But it was strange, because even though it was so new it was like a bit of me wasn't surprised actually, it was like a little bit of me knew all that already. I thought "what does it matter" I said "can we go home then? Where are we going, is it the cottage or back to Rome?" and Jemima shouted "Rome Rome." But mum gave us a funny look and her lips went sort of wobbley a bit like Jemimas do when shes going to cry, and she said "this is very hard for me to say, lesonfon, please don't make it harder than it already is" she said "I want you to forget everything I ever told you about your father, it was only because I was so confused. He's a good man."

Suddenly I had a nasty feeling, it was horrible, so I said "why do we have to do that mum?" She turned her head sideways like she was trying to hide, she said "because I want you to stay with him for a while." I felt like I couldn't breath, I think Jemima knew too because she was crying, so I said "but we don't want to, we want to stay with you." But mum wouldn't stop, she closed her eyes like she didn't want to hear us, she talked really fast like a shout, she said "I'm not going to discuss this. I've decided. Its better if you don't see me for a while, even a long while. Because I'm just not safe for you, you see. I don't trust myself. I might get confused again." It was just the horrible thing I guessed, and now Jemima and me were both shouting "no mum no" but she just wouldn't stop, she said "Your going to live with your father now. You have to do this. Its what I want."

SIENTISTS HAVE KNOWN FOR AGES that something terreble will happen to the sun. This is sad but there is nothing scientists can do, they can't stop it with any invention, even something really clever from the future, because the sun is too big you see, it will just happen anyway.

First it will run out of its fuel, that is like its petrol, it is hydrogen which is a gas. Then it will turn red and get bigger and bigger like a balloon, until it gets so huge that it will swallow any planets that are near, like mercury, they will just vanish. Earth won't get swallowed but it will get all burnt up, everything will go on fire, which is sad, there won't be anything left. If you could be there without getting burnt, if you built a special house with a special window, then you will be really suprised, because when you look up the sun will be so huge, it will go a third of the way across the whole sky. But then it will get smaller and smaller again until one day it will just go out. After that everything will be dark, so it will be like there's night all the time, it will be really cold.

But then scientists discovered a really good thing which is called gravitational lensing. Its when there is a galaxy quite far away in space, and it doesn't seem special at all actually, when scientists look at it through their telescopes they just think "so what?" But then one day there is a big surprise, because the galaxy moves a bit and the scientists all say "good hevens look at that." Because, you see, there were lots of other galaxies hidden behind it all the time that nobody saw. The other galaxies are right at the other end of the universe so you could never even see them usually, they are too far away, but when the near galaxy moves out of the way it does a funny thing. It sort of bends the light from the far away ones so they look big, its like it is a huge teliscope, so suddenly you can see them really well.

Perhaps the scientists will see another planet with their gravitational lensing, it will be lovely and green, it will be beautiful. Then everybody will be all right after all. They will build a huge space craft and escape there before the sun goes out.

So we went to live with dad in his new house, it was a bit bigger than his old one. Dad said we could each have our own bedroom but I said "no lets share a room, Jemima" and she said "all right Lawrence" because we did everything together now.

When we first went to dads house he was always trying to make us do things, he said "how would you like to go to the zoo today?" or "d'you fancy a ride out to the sea?" Sometimes I let us go but then I always changed my mind, when we got to the zoo I said "actually I don't want to go after all, I want to go home, don't you Jemima?" and she said "yes I want to go home too" because we did everything together. Dad never liked that, he said "but it'll be great, you can see all the animals, we can have lunch at the cafeteria" and he had his sad surprised look, so I thought "sometimes you are like a big dog who wants everyone to like you" and I just waited, I didn't say anything at all, until he gave in and said "all right, if that's what you want."

I had a new school now, they didn't like me at all. First it was because I sat at my desk and tore up pieces of paper so it made a noise and I went on doing it even when Mrs Gerald said I was disturbing the class. Then it was because I threw Kevin Mclusky's books into the loo. And after that it was because I hit Danny Monros head against the wall so it bled like a tiny little fountain, which was because I didn't like his ginger eye brows, they were so stupid and tufty. After that I had to see Mrs Moor the head-mistress, dad came too and he said I must be really good now or I would get expeled and I thought "oh yes, that will be funny" but I wasn't in the end, dad said "its been a very difficult time" and Mrs Moor said "this is your very last chance."

A few days after that when I got home dad was grinning like something was really good now, he said "I've got a surprise for you today Larry" and it was Hermann in his cage, dad said "I collected him from quorontine just this afternoon." I went over and looked and Hermann peered out through the bars so I thought "you re-member me, Hermann, that's good." Jemima was shouting "Her-mann Hermann" and dad was watching, he was waiting, so I thought "you want me to do something happy now, don't you dad" I thought "what will I say?" and then I thought "oh yes, that will be funny" so I said it, I said "Hermann this is dads house where we all live now" I said "I don't like it at all, I really hate it, actually, but there isn't anywhere else so we're stuck here." I wasn't looking at dad but I could sort of see him, actually, it was from the corner of my eyes, and it was like his smile fell right out of his face, that was funny. I thought "will I say something else?" and then I thought "no I won't."

Then one day we went to see my cousins in Glasgow. That was nice, their mum Susie made a lovely lunch, she said "eat up now Larry, we don't want you fading away to nothing" and afterwards we went upstairs to play. Charlie and Alice started doing a big puzzle with Jemima, it was of lots of things under the sea, and then Robbie said "shall we have a game of checkers then, Larry" and I said "okay." He took a white and a red draft and he hid them in his hands, he said "you choose" and I chose his right hand, it was white. Robbie started putting out his red checkers, he said "come on Larry" and I thought "I wanted to be red" I thought "I bet you cheated on that choosing Robbie." Then I thought "you have to teach these cheats a lesson" and I had a really funny idea, I picked up Robbies blue scalectric car which he always has to have because its his scalectric, I think its faster than the others, and I thought "I will make you into an airoplane." So I threw it right across the room and when it hit the floor some of the wheels came off, I thought "they are so stupid those scalectric cars, they just break."

Robbie was staring at me, they all were, he said "why the hell did you do that?" so I said "scalectrics so boring" and I had another really funny idea, I just kicked the track really hard so it jumped into the air, and then when Robbie ran at me I sort of got out of the way and pushed him a bit so he went right into the little table with his big leggo castle on it, that was funny too, because it fell off and broke into tiny bits.

After that dad didn't look like a dog who wanted everyone to like him, he had slit eyes and he said "this just cant go on." So we left Jemima with Nanna Edith and we went to see doctor Muckaye.

He said "so how are you, Lawrence?" and I thought "this will be easy" I said "I'm fine." After that he said "I hear you've been upsetting some people" so I said "I don't remember." We went on for a bit, I thought "this is fun" until then he gave me a look like he was really sad for me and he said "you must miss your mother very much." He said that before, actually, it wasn't new at all, so I wasn't surprised, I thought "what will I say, oh yes I'll say 'I'm fine' again" but then something funny happened. You see, suddenly I couldn't say anything at all because I was crying, I don't know how it got in, I tried to say "I'm fine" but it just didn't work, the words got all stuck.

That was strange, that was stupid. I thought "you tricked me you spider" and I said it, I said "I really hate you doctor Muckay." But he didn't get upset or angry like I wanted, he just gave me a long look and he said "I'm sorry to hear that, Lawrence" he said "why d'you feel like that?" and then something really really strange happened. Because I said something but I don't know where it came from, it was like somebody elses words just got in my mouth, they sneeked in. I said "I hate you mum." But Docter Muckay didn't look surprised even though I called him mum, that was funny, he just said in his usual voice "whys that Lawrence" and I felt so tired, it was like all my breathe was going out now, I said "because you left us. Because you are a traiter. Because you told me all those lies."

Later I went home in the car with dad, and we didn't say anything, I just looked at all the clouds, I thought "that one looks like a dog." He parked outside the house and I didn't move, I didn't undo my seat belt, and when he said "shall we go in then

Larry" I didn't say anything, I thought "I will just stay like this quite still." So we sat there for ages, that was funny, people walked past and sometimes they notised us and looked in, but we didn't say a word. Then eventually dad opened his door a bit, he said "I suppose I'd better start making our tea" and I thought "I'd better say something" so I made myself do it, I just did it, I said "I'm sorry I burned down your house dad" and he stopped, he gave me a little hit on my back but it didn't hurt, it was friendly, and he said "hey that's all right, Larry. I'm sorry about a lot of things too. I'm sorry I was away so much on all those stupid work trips." Then he said something intresting. He said "try not to be angry with her, Larry" he said "I know she and me didn't get on, it all went wrong, but I don't want you to hate her like this. It's not good for you." He said "she's not so bad, she just can't see things how they really are." That was new, that was different. I said, "all right, dad." I think about that sometimes.

A few days after that we went to the zoo, I let us go in this time, and it was nice actually. I thought "I wonder why I didn't let us come here before?"

After that everything became more like usual. In the morning dad knocks on our door and says "hey you lazy kiddies, time to get up" he makes our breakfast, toast and jam, and then he drives us to school in his yellow car, it has a stereo which mums didn't because it was broken, so we can listen to songs. Sometimes Nanna Edith collects us from school or we go to Sarah and Bill and Jimmy and Louisa till dad comes to get us. Sometimes we go to the sea for a few days, and its nice there, if its not raining you can see Mull and Sky. We often go and stay with my cousins in Glasgow, Robbie says he doesn't mind about the scalectric any more, the track was all right and he got a new blue car. Sometimes I think "actually they're nice all of these people" I think "I like having them." Its strange, sometimes its like I feel sort of sad because they're so nice to me. And sometimes I suddenly just feel really calm and still, I think "now I will be all right, yes, I will be all right now."

Hardly anyone ever talks about mum, Dad or my cousins, or my freinds at school. But I still think about her. I still sometimes think "are you going to come round that corner now mum? Are you going to get off that bus?" but she never is. Sometimes I'm really cross, its like I hate her, so I think "go away mum, I don't like you, I don't want you to get off that bus anyway." Sometimes I'm really sad, I think "I wish I could tell you about the funny thing Kevin Clark said at school." But mostly I just notice her. Because its like she suddenly starts talking to me, it can happen at any time. I am walking across the playground and she says "don't step in that puddle, Lawrence love, you'll get your shoes all wet" or I am in the supermarket with dad and Jemima and she says "put those crisps down, I've told you before, its not really bacon, its just chemicals" or I'm watching robot wars on television with Jemima and she says "that's enough telly, you know you two are turning into a real pair of couch potatoes."

I think Jemima hears her too, or she wouldn't play our secrit game. We don't do it often, just sometimes when we are at home and nobody is watching, when dad is downstairs on his computer or talking on the phone. Its like we both know even though we don't say anything, we just give each other a look, and Jemima has a funny smile like she is really pleased but she is worried too, because sometimes she doesn't like it, you see, sometimes she cries.

We go upstairs to our room, we sit on the floor and then I start. I say "d'you know Jemima, that window over there isn't real, it is just like a computer screen." Jemima always likes this bit, she giggels and says "what d'you mean, we're not in Scotland after all" and I say "thats right, Jemima, those houses and garden fences and television ariels aren't there, its really sky and rooves" I say "can't you hear the bells ringing?" Then Jemima laughs, she says "oh yes I can hear them, their really loud" so I say "now theres a tram going past, theres a police car with its funny siren, its like a donkey isn't it, and listen, theres someone talking in italian."

So we sit for a bit and then I do it more, I just like to, I say "d'you hear that little noise, Jemima, d'you know what that is?" Jemima doesn't really like this bit so she goes nervous, she says "no." But I go on anyway, I say "that's mums footsteps, shes right next door" I say "she'll come in here in a moment and she'll say 'come on lesonfon' because we're going out to get some pizza at the roasticheria." Then I say "what kind d'you want, Jemima?" If she answers its always the same, she says "I want tomato and cheese" but sometimes she doesn't say anything, she just sits there really still and her eyes go blink blink.

Then I sit back too. I close my eyes, we are just quiet for a bit, and d'you know its like we really are there. I feel sort of angry but I feel all calm too, that's funny. I think "it's a bit scary here but its nice" I think "its a real adventure" and I think "one day we'll all come back here again, mum and me and Jemima and dad, and we'll live here for ever and ever."

ACKNOWLEDGMENTS

I would like to give special thanks to Professor Raj Persaud, who kindly gave up so much of his busy schedule to read and reread the manuscript of this novel. I am wholly indebted to his shrewd and expert advice.

I would also like to thank Andrew Kidd, Nan Talese, Deborah Rogers, my wife, Shannon, and our children, Alexander and Tatiana.

"A wryly comic, beautifully told seafaring yarn."
—Newsweek

ENGLISH PASSENGERS

In 1857, on the run from prying British Customs men, Captain Illiam Quillian Kewley is forced to put his ship *Sincerity* up for charter. The only takers are two eccentric Englishmen headed for the island of Tasmania: the Reverend Geoffrey Wilson, who believes the Garden of Eden was located there, and Dr. Thomas Potter, who is developing a sinister thesis about the races of men. And these passengers are only slightly odder than the crew, a diverse and lively bunch better equipped to entertain one another than to steer *Sincerity* across the Indian Ocean. Meanwhile, in Tasmania, an Aborigine named Peevay recounts his people's struggles against the invading British, who prove as lethal in their good intentions as in their cruelty. As the English passengers approach Peevay's land, their bizarre notions ever more painfully at odds with reality, we know a mighty collision is looming.

Fiction/978-0-385-65866-9

SMALL CRIMES IN AN AGE OF ABUNDANCE

A well-intentioned English family unwittingly becomes complicit in state violence while traveling through China. A ploddingly respectable London lawyer chances upon a stash of cocaine and realizes it offers the wealth and status he's always hungered for. A salesman in Africa gets caught up in a riot, and a Palestinian suicide bomber has a moment of self-doubt. Kneale transports readers across continents in a nanosecond, reaching to the heart of far-away societies with rare perceptiveness. With wry humor and razor-sharp satire, these twelve thought-provoking stories illuminate the moral uncertainty of our time.

Fiction/978-0-385-66139-3

ANCHOR CANADA
Available at your local bookstore, or visit
www.randomhouse.ca